Fiat 126 Owners Workshop Manual

J H Haynes
Member of the Guild of Motoring Writers

and Peter G Strasman

All Fiat 126 models, including limited and special edition versions
594 cc & 652 cc

ISBN 978 0 85733 650 7

(305-11R6)

Haynes Group Limited
Haynes North America, Inc

www.haynes.com

British Library Cataloguing in Publication Data

Strasman, Peter G.
    Fiat 126 owners workshop manual. –
(Owners Workshop Manuals).
    1. Automobiles–Maintenance and repair
I. Title II. Series
629.28'722   TL152
ISBN 1-85010-164-7

Acknowledgements

Our thanks to FIAT Motor Company (UK) Limited who kindly supplied the technical information and certain of the illustrations reproduced in this manual. Woolf, Laing, Christie and Partners were also very helpful, Duckhams Oils supplied lubrication data, and the Champion Sparking Plug Company supplied the illustrations showing the various spark plug conditions.

We are particularly grateful to Mr. F. Martindale who kindly loan us his car as project vehicle.

Lastly, thanks are due to all of those people at Sparkford who helped in the production of this manual.

About this manual

Its aim

The aim of this book is to help you get the best value from your car. It can do so in two ways. First it can help you decide what work must be done, even should you choose to get it done by a garage, the routine maintenance and the diagnosis and course of action when random faults occur. It is hoped that you will also use the second and fuller purpose by tackling the work yourself. This can give you the satisfaction of doing the job yourself. On the simpler jobs it may even be quicker than booking the car into a garage and going there twice, to leave and collect it. Perhaps most important, much money can be saved by avoiding the costs a garage must charge to cover their labour and overheads.

Haynes Owner's Workshop Manuals are the *only* manuals, available to the public, which are actually written from practical experience. We buy an example of the vehicle to be covered by the manual. Then, in our own workshops, the major components of that vehicle are stripped and rebuilt by the author and a mechanic: at the same time all sequences are photographed. By doing this work ourselves, we encounter the same problems as you will and having overcome these problems, we can provide you with practical solutions.

The book has drawings and descriptions to show the function of the various components so that their layout can be understood. Then the tasks are described and photographed in a step by step sequence so that even a novice can cope with complicated work. Such a person is the very one to buy a car needing repair yet unable to afford garage costs.

The jobs are described assuming only normal tools are available, and not special tools, but a reasonable outfit of tools will be a worthwhile investment. Many special workshop tools produced by the makers merely speed the work, and in these cases guidance is given as to how to do the job without them. On a very few occasions the special tool is essential to prevent damage to components, then its use is describe Though it might be possible to borrow the tool, such work may have to be entrusted to the official agent.

To avoid labour costs a garage will often give a cheaper repair by fitting a reconditioned assembly. The home mechanic can be helped by this book to diagnose the fault and make a repair using only a minor spare part. The classic case is repairing a non-charging dynamo by fitting new brushes.

Using the manual

This manual is divided into twelve Chapters - each covering a logi sub-division of the vehicle. The individual Chapters are divided into Sections, and the Sections into numbered paragraphs.

Procedures, once described in the text, are not normally repeated If it is necessary to refer to another Chapter the reference will be given in Chapter number and Section number.

There are two types of illustration: (1) Figures which are number according to Chapter and sequence of occurrence in that Chapter. (2) Photographs which have a reference number on their caption. All photographs apply to the Chapter in which they occur so that the reference figure pinpoints the pertinent Section and paragraph number.

When the left or right side of the car is mentioned it is as if looki forward from the rear of the car.

Great effort has been made to ensure that this book is complete and up to-date. However, the vehicle manufacturers continually modify their cars, even in retrospect, without giving notice.

Whilst every care is taken to ensure that the information in this manual is correct no liability can be accepted by the authors or publishers for loss, damage or injury caused by any errors in, or omissions from, the information given.

Introduction to the Fiat 126

The Fiat 126 was introduced in July 1973 to be the eventual successor to the Fiat 500 which it has now become.

Major improvements in comparison with the 500 include a gearbox with synchromesh on 2nd, 3rd and 4th gears and more modern styling.

The car provides extremely low-cost transportation and in consequence its power and comfort cannot be expected to match larger and more expensive vehicles.

It is strong and reliable and very simply serviced and is adequate from the points of view of equipment and accessories in what is essentially an 'about town' car.

The Fiat 126 is produced in a single two-door body style but a variation having a sunroof and opening rear side windows can be specified.

In August 1977, a larger 652 cc engine was introduced, and the c was substantially facelifted in May 1985. These, and other, changes a covered in the Supplement at the end of this Manual.

Contents

FIAT 126 (1976 model)

Buying spare parts

Spare parts are available from many sources, for example Fiat garages, other garages and accessory shops, and motor factors. Our advice regarding spare part sources is as follows:

Officially appointed Fiat garages - This is the best source of parts which are peculiar to your car and are otherwise not generally available (eg; complete cylinder heads, internal gearbox components, badges, interior trim etc). It is also the only place at which you should buy parts if your car is still under warranty: non-Fiat components may invalidate the warranty. To be sure of obtaining the correct parts it will always be necessary to give the partsman your car's engine number, chassis number and number for spares, and if possible, to take the old parts along for positive identification. Remember that many parts are available on a factory exchange scheme — any parts returned should always be clean! It obviously makes good sense to go straight to the specialists on your car for this type of part for they are best equipped to supply you.

Other garages and accessory shops - These are often very good places to buy materials and components needed for the maintenance of your car (eg spark plugs, bulbs, fanbelts, oils and greases, touch-up paint, filler paste, etc). They also sell general accessories, usually have convenient opening hours, charge lower prices and can often be found not far from home.

Motor factors - Good factors will stock all of the more important components which wear out relatively quickly (eg: cylinders/pipes/hoses/seals/shoes and pads etc). Motor factors will often provide new or reconditioned components on a part exchange basis - this can save a considerable amount of money.

Vehicle identification numbers

The data plate is located within the luggage boot and contains details of chassis type and number, engine type and number for spares and the body paintwork reference number (photo).

The engine type and number are stamped on the engine casting adjacent to the fuel pump mounting flange (photo).

The chassis type and number are located on the wing valance within the luggage boot (photo).

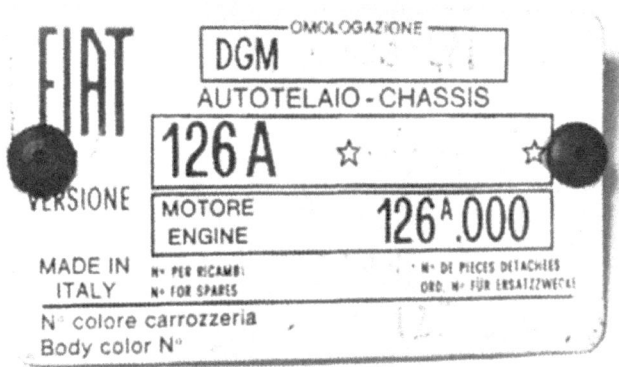

Data plate

Location of engine number

Location of chassis type and number

Tools and working facilities

Introduction

A selection of good tools is a fundamental requirement for anyone contemplating the maintenance and repair of a motor vehicle. For the owner who does not possess any, their purchase will prove a considerable expense, offsetting some of the savings made by doing-it-yourself. However, provided that the tools purchased meet the relevant national safety standards and are of good quality, they will last for many years and prove an extremely worthwhile investment.

To help the average owner to decide which tools are needed to carry out the various tasks detailed in this manual, we have compiled three lists of tools under the following headings: Maintenance and minor repair, Repair and overhaul, and Special. The newcomer to practical mechanics should start off with the 'Maintenance and minor repair' tool kit and confine himself to the simpler jobs around the vehicle. Then, as his confidence and experience grows, he can undertake more difficult tasks, buying extra tools as, and when, they are needed. In this way, a 'Maintenance and minor repair' tool kit can be built-up into a 'Repair and overhaul' tool kit over a considerable period of time without any major cash outlays. The experienced do-it-yourself will have a tool kit good enough for most repair and overhaul procedures and will add tools from the 'Special' category when he feels the expense is justified by the amount of use these tools will be put to.

It is obviously not possible to cover the subject of tools fully here. For those who wish to learn more about tools and their use there is a book entitled 'How to Choose and Use Car Tools' available from the publishers of this manual.

Maintenance and minor repair tool kit

The tools given in this list should be considered as a minimum requirement if routine maintenance, servicing and minor repair operations are to be undertaken. We recommend the purchase of combination spanners (ring one end, open-ended the other); although more expensive than open-ended ones, they do give the advantages of both types of spanner.

Combination spanners - 10, 11, 13, 14, 17 mm
Adjustable spanner - 9 inch
Engine sump/gearbox/rear axle drain plug key (where applicable)
Spark plug gap adjustment tool
Spark plug spanner (with rubber insert)
Set of feeler gauges
Brake adjuster spanner (where applicable)
Brake bleed nipple spanner
Screwdriver - 4 in. long x ¼ in. dia. (plain)
Screwdriver - 4 in. long x ¼ in. dia. (crosshead)
Combination pliers - 6 inch
Hacksaw, junior
Tyre pump
Tyre pressure gauge
Grease gun (where applicable)
Oil can
Fine emery cloth (1 sheet)
Wire brush (small)
Funnel (medium size)

Repair and overhaul tool kit

These tools are virtually essential for anyone undertaking any major repairs to a motor vehicle, and are additional to those given in the Basic list. Included in this list is a comprehensive set of sockets. Although these are expensive they will be found invaluable as they so versatile - particularly if various drives are included in the set. We recommend the ½ inch square drive type, as this can be used with m proprietary torque wrenches. If you cannot afford a socket set, even bought piecemeal, then inexpensive tubular box spanners are a usef alternative.

The tools in this list will occasionally need to be supplemented t tools from the Special list.

Sockets (or box spanners) to cover range 6 to 27 mm
Reversible ratchet drive (for use with sockets)
Extension piece, 10 inch (for use with sockets)
Universal joint (for use with sockets)
Torque wrench (for use with sockets)
'Mole' wrench - 8 inch
Ball pein hammer
Soft-faced hammer, plastic or rubber
Screwdriver - 6 in. long x 5/16 in. dia. (plain)
Screwdriver - 2 in. long x 5/16 in. square (plain)
Screwdriver - 1½ in. long x ¼ in. dia. (crosshead)
Screwdriver - 3 in. long x 1/8 in. dia. (electricians)
Pliers - electricians side cutters
Pliers - needle nosed
Pliers - circlip (internal and external)
Cold chisel - ½ inch
Scriber (this can be made by grinding the end of a broken hacks blade)
Scraper (this can be made by flattening and sharpening one end a piece of copper pipe)
Centre punch
Pin punch
Hacksaw
Valve grinding tool
Steel rule/straight edge
Allen keys
Selection of files
Wire brush (large)
Axle stands
Jack (strong scissor or hydraulic type)

Special tools

The tools in this list are those which are not used regularly, are expensive to buy, or which need to be used in accordance with thei manufacturers instructions. Unless relatively difficult mechanical jo are undertaken frequently, it will not be economic to buy many of these tools. Where this is the case, you could consider clubbing together with friends (or a motorists club) to make a joint purchase borrowing the tools against a deposit from a local garage or tool hir specialist.

The following list contains only those tools and instruments free available to the public, and not those special tools produced by the vehicle manufacturers specifically for its dealer network. You will f occasional references to these manufacturers special tools in the tex this manual. Generally, an alternative method of doing the job with the vehicle manufacturers special tool is given. However, sometimes

Valve spring compressor
Piston ring compressor
Ball joint separator
Universal hub/bearing puller
Impact screwdriver
Micrometer and/or vernier gauge
Carburettor flow balancing device (where applicable)
Dial gauge
Stroboscopic timing light
Dwell angle meter/tachometer
Universal electrical multi-meter
Cylinder compression gauge
Lifting tackle
Trolley jack
Light with extension lead

Buying tools

For practically all tools, a tool factor is the best source since he will have a very comprehensive range compared with the average garage or accessory shop. Having said that, accessory shops often offer excellent quality tools at discount prices, so it pays to shop around.

There are plenty of good tools around at reasonable prices, but always aim to purchase items which meet the relevant national safety standards. If in doubt, ask the proprietor or manager of the shop for advice before making a purchase.

Care and maintenance of tools

Having purchased a reasonable tool kit, it is necessary to keep the tools in a clean and serviceable condition. After use, always wipe off any dirt, grease and metal particles using a clean, dry cloth, before putting the tools away. Never leave them lying around after they have been used. A simple tool rack on the garage or workshop wall, for items such as screwdrivers and pliers is a good idea. Store all normal spanners and sockets in a metal box. Any measuring instruments, gauges, meters,etc., must be carefully stored where they cannot be damaged or become rusty.

Take a little care when the tools are used. Hammer heads inevitably become marked and screwdrivers lose the keen edge on their blades from time-to-time. A little timely attention with emery cloth or a file will soon restore items like this to a good serviceable finish.

Working facilities

Not to be forgotten when discussing tools, is the workshop itself. If anything more than routine maintenance is to be carried out, some form of suitable working area becomes essential.

It is appreciated that many an owner mechanic is forced by circumstances to remove an engine or similar item, without the benefit of a garage or workshop. Having done this, any repairs should always be done under the cover of a roof.

Wherever possible, any dismantling should be done on a clean flat workbench or table at a suitable working height.

Any workbench needs a vice: one with a jaw opening 4 in. (100 mm) is suitable for most jobs. As mentioned previously, some clean dry storage space is also required for tools, as well as the lubricants, cleaning fluids, touch-up paints and so on which soon become necessary.

Another item which may be required, and which has a much more general usage, is an electric drill with a chuck capacity of at least 5/16 in. (8 mm). This, together with a good range of twist drills, is virtually essential for fitting accessories such as wing mirrors and reversing lights.

Last, but not least, always keep a supply of old newspapers and clean lint-free rags available, and try to keep any working area as clean as possible.

Decimal	Spanner size
0.275	7 mm AF
0.312	5/16 in. AF
0.315	8 mm AF
0.340	11/32 in. AF/1/8 in. Whitworth
0.354	9 mm AF
0.375	3/8 in. AF
0.393	10 mm AF
0.433	11 mm AF
0.437	7/16 in. AF
0.445	3/16 in. Whitworth 1/4in. BSF
0.472	12 mm AF
0.500	1/2 in. AF
0.512	13 mm AF
0.525	1/4 in. Whitworth/5/16 in. BSF
0.551	14 mm AF
0.562	9/16 in. AF
0.590	15 mm AF
0.600	5/16 in. Whitworth/3/8 in. BSF
0.625	5/8 in. AF
0.629	16 mm AF
0.669	17 mm AF
0.687	11/16 in. AF
0.708	18 mm AF
0.710	3/8 in. Whitworth/7/16 in. BSF
0.748	19 mm AF
0.750	3/4 in AF
0.812	13/16 in AF
0.820	7/16 in. Whitworth/1/2 in. BSF
0.866	22 mm AF
0.875	7/8 in. AF
0.920	1/2 in Whitworth/9/16 in. BSF
0.937	15/16 in. AF
0.944	24 mm AF
1.000	1 in. AF
1.010	9/16 in. Whitworth/5/8 in. BSF
1.023	26 mm AF
1.062	1 1/16 in. AF/27 mm AF
1.100	5/8 in. Whitworth /11/16 in. BSF
1.125	1 1/8 in AF
1.181	30 mm AF
1.200	11/16 in. Whitworth/3/4 in. BSF
1.250	1 1/4 in. AF
1.259	32 mm AF
1.300	3/4 in. Whitworth/7/8 in. BSF
1.312	1 5/16 in. AF
1.390	13/16 in. Whitworth/15/16 in. BSF
1.417	36 mm AF
1.437	1 7/16 in. AF
1.480	7/8 in. Whitworth/1 in. BSF
1.500	1 1/2 in. AF
1.574	40 mm AF/15/16 in. Whitworth
1.614	41 mm AF
1.625	1 5/8 in. AF
1.670	1 in. Whitworth/1 1/8 in. BSF
1.687	1 11/16 in. AF
1.811	46 mm AF
1.812	1 13/16 in. AF
1.860	1 1/8 in. Whitworth/1 1/4 in. BSF
1.875	1 7/8 in. AF
1.968	50 mm AF
2.000	2 in. AF
2.050	1 1/4 in. Whitworth/1 3/8 in. BSF
2.165	55 mm AF
2.362	60 mm AF

Routine maintenance

Maintenance is essential for ensuring safety and desirable for the purpose of getting the best in terms of performance and economy from the car. Over the years the need for periodic lubrication - oiling, greasing, and so on - has been drastically reduced if not totally eliminated. This has unfortunately tended to lead some owners to think that because no such action is required the items either no longer exist or will last for ever. This is a serious delusion. It follows therefore that the largest initial element of maintenance is visual examination. This may lead to repairs or renewal.

Every 250 miles (400 km) or weekly

Steering
Check the tyre pressures including the spare wheel.
Examine tyres for wear or damage.

Brakes
Check brake fluid reservoir level.
Try an emergency stop. Are automatic adjusters effective or has pedal travel increased?

Electrical
Check all lamp bulbs.
Check battery electrolyte level.
Check operation of wipers and horn.
Top-up windscreen washer reservoir.

Engine
Check oil level and top-up if necessary (photo).

Every 6,000 miles (9,600 km) or six months

Steering
Check steering box oil level and top-up.
Apply grease gun to front suspension (king pin) nipples.
Check steering linkage balljoints for wear.
Check front wheel alignment.

Brakes
Check for lining wear.

Electrical
Check dynamo/fanbelt tension.

Engine
Change engine oil when hot.
Check carburettor adjustment.
Clean and regap spark plugs.
Check distributor contact point gap.
Check ignition timing.
Clean carburettor fuel filter gauze.
Clean fuel pump filter.

Transmission
Check oil level and top-up if necessary.

Body
Lubricate hinges and locks.
Check seat belts.

Clutch
Check clutch free-movement and adjust if necessary.

Every 12,000 miles (19,000 km) or twelve months

Engine
Check and adjust valve clearances.
Renew spark plugs.
Renew air cleaner element.

Brakes
Check and adjust handbrake cable.

Electrical
Check headlight alignment.

Every 18,000 miles (28,000 km) or eighteen months

Steering
Check, repack and adjust front wheel bearings.

Transmission
Check condition of driveshaft flexible boots.
Drain and refill unit with specified oil.

General
Check all nuts and bolts to specified torque wrench settings.

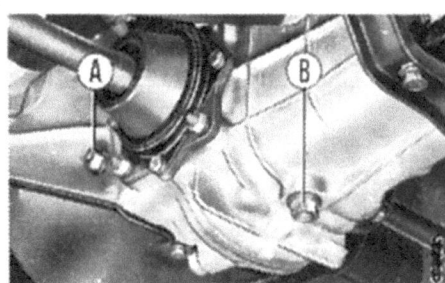

Transmission filler/level plug (A) and drain plug (B)

Every 24,000 miles (38,000 km) or two years

Brakes
Drain hydraulic system, renew all cylinder seals and refill with fresh fluid.

Exhaust system
Check for corrosion and renew if necessary.

Engine
Clean centrifugal oil filter.

Underbody
Clean and take rust preventative measures.

Topping up with engine oil

Topping up brake fluid

Lubricating engine compartment lid lock

General dimensions, weights and capacities

Dimensions and weights

Overall length	...	...	...	...	...	...	...	...	120.2 in (305. 4 cm)
Overall width	...	...	...	...	...	...	...	...	53.8 in (137.7 cm)
Overall height	...	...	...	...	...	...	...	...	52.4 in (133.5 cm)
Wheelbase	...	...	...	...	...	...	...	...	72.4 in (184. 0 cm)
Front track	...	...	...	...	...	...	...	...	44.9 in (114. 2 cm)
Rear track	...	...	...	...	...	...	...	...	47.3 in (120.3 cm)
Kerb weight	...	...	...	...	...	...	...	...	1279 lb (580 kg)

Capacities

Fuel tank	...	...	...	...	...	...	...	...	4.6 Imp. gallons (20.5 litres)
Engine oil	...	...	...	...	...	...	...	...	4.5 Imp. pints (2.6 litres)
Transmission	...	...	...	...	...	...	...	...	2 Imp. pints (1.13 litres)
Steering box	...	...	...	...	...	...	...	...	4.25 fl. oz. (120.3 ml)
Windscreen washer reservoir	...	...	...	...	...	...	...	3.5 Imp. pints (1.99 litres)

Jacking and towing

The jack supplied with the car should only be used for changing a roadwheel. When carrying out repairs or maintenance work, use a hydraulic or screw jack under the jacking points and supplement these with axle stands or blocks.

To jack up the front or rear of the car, place the jack under the front or rear crossmember. When jacking under the rear crossmember use a wooden block as an insulator.

If your car is being towed, thread the tow rope through the two holes in the small bracket located under the crossmember. If you are towing another small vehicle, attach the tow rope to the jacking bracket at the base of the crossmember (photo).

Rear tow rope attachment plate

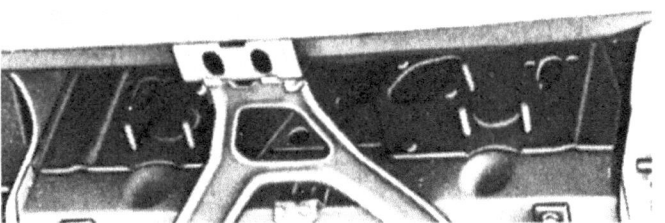

Front tow rope attachment plate

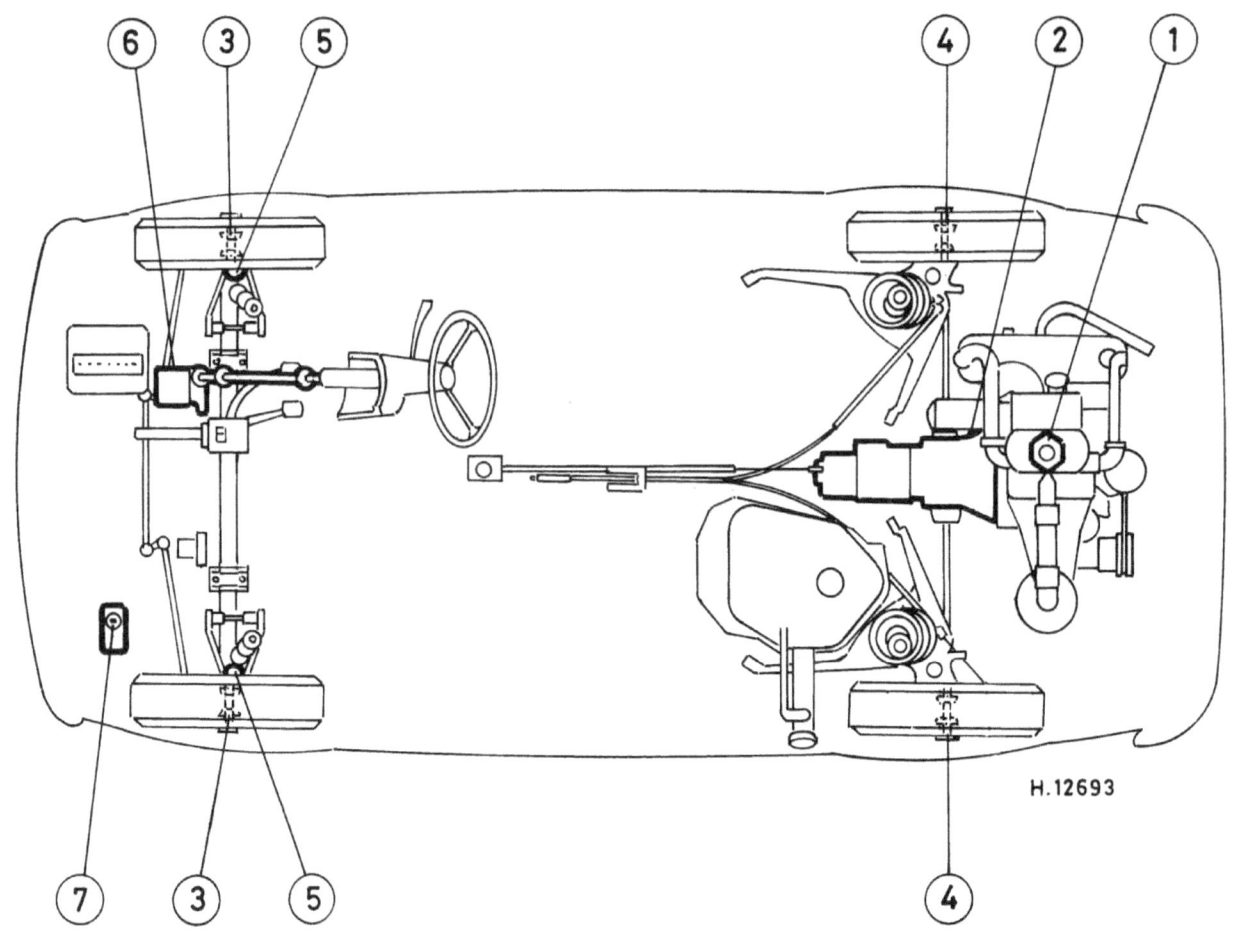

H.12693

Recommended lubricants and fluids

Component or system	Lubricant type/specification	Duckhams recommendation
1 Engine	Multigrade engine oil, viscosity SAE 15W/40	Duckhams Hypergrade
2 Gearbox	Multigrade engine oil, viscosity SAE 15W/40	Duckhams Hypergrade
3 & 4 Wheel bearings	Multi-purpose lithium based grease	Duckhams LB 10
5 Kingpins	Multi-purpose lithium based grease	Duckhams LB 10

6 Steering gear
   Worm and sector
   Rack and pinion
	
	Hypoid gear oil, viscosity SAE 90EP
	Molybdenum disulphide grease
		
		Duckhams Hypoid 90
		Duckhams LBM 10

7 Brake hydraulic reservoir	Hydraulic fluid to FMVSS 116 DOT 3 and SAE J1703	Duckhams Universal Brake and Clutch Fluid

Chapter 1 Engine

For modifications, and information applicable to later models, see Supplement at end of manual

Contents

Specifications

Engine (general)

Engine type	Two cylinder, vertical in-line, air-cooled, overhead valve, rear mounted.
Bore	2.894 in (73.5 mm)
Stroke	2.756 in (70.0 mm)
Displacement	36.23cu in (594 cc)
Compression ratio	7.5 : 1
Maximum HP (DIN rating) @ 4800 rev/min	23
Maximum torque @ 3400 rev/min	29 lb/ft (4 kg/m)

Crankcase and cylinder barrels

Cylinder bore diameter:	
Grading:	
A	2.8937 to 2.8941 in (73.500 to 73.510 mm)
B	2.8941 to 2.8945 in (73.510 to 73.520 mm)
C	2.8945 to 2.8949 in (73.520 to 73.530 mm)
Camshaft bore in crankcase:	
Timing gear end	1.6937 to 1.6946 in (43.020 to 43.045 mm)
Flywheel end	0.8667 to 0.8675 in (22.015 to 22.036 mm)
Camshaft bearing running clearance	0.0006 to 0.0025 in (0.015 to 0.055 mm)
Cam followers bore in crankcase	0.8662 to 0.8669 in (22.003 to 22.021 mm)
Cam followers clearance in crankcase	0.0003 to 0.0017 in (0.007 to 0.043 mm)
Connecting rod big-end bore (diameter)	1.8555 to 1.8560 in (47.130 to 47.142 mm)
Big-end bearing thickness (standard size)	0.0604 to 0.0607 in (1.534 to 1.543 mm)
Big-end bearing undersizes	0.01 - 0.02 - 0.03 - 0.04 in (0.254 - 0.508 - 0.762 - 1.016 mm)
Connecting rod small end bush (diameter) in connecting rod	0.8637 to 0.8650 in (21.939 to 21.972 mm)
Small end bush internal diameter (reamed)	0.7874 to 0.7876 in (20.000 to 20.006 mm)
Small end bush undersizes	0.0076 - 0.0196 in (0.2 - 0.5 mm)
Gudgeon pin clearance in small end bush	0.0002 to 0.0006 in (0.005 to 0.016 mm)

Up to 1974 ... ... 0.0004 to 0,0024 in (0.011 to 0.061 mm)
November 1974 on ... ... 0.0009 to 0,0029 in (0.024 to 0.074 mm)

Pistons

Piston diameter (at right angles to gudgeon pin):	
Grading:	
A (up to 1974)	2.8905 to 2.8909 in (73.420 to 73.430 mm)
A (1974 on)	2.8901 to 2.8905 in (73.410 to 73.420 mm)
B (up to 1974)	2.8909 to 2.8913 in (73.430 to 73.440 mm)
B (1974 on)	2.8905 to 2.8909 in (73.420 to 73.430 mm)
C (up to 1974)	2.8913 to 2.8917 in (73.440 to 73.450 mm)
C (1974 on)	2.8909 to 2.8913 in (73.430 to 73.440 mm)
Piston oversizes	0.0079 - 0.0157 - 0.0236 in (0.2 - 0.4 - 0.6 mm)
Gudgeon pin bore (diameter) in piston	0.7872 to 0.7874 in (19.995 to 20.000 mm)
Piston ring groove width:	
Top	0.0604 to 0.0612 in (1.535 to 1.555 mm)
Centre	0.0800 to 0.0807 in (2.030 to 2.050 mm)
Bottom	0.1562 to 0.1569 in (3.967 to 3.987 mm)
Gudgeon pin diameter	0.7870 to 0.7872 in (19.990 to 19.995 mm)
Gudgeon pin oversize	0.0079 in (0.2 mm)
Piston ring thickness:	
Top compression	0.0582 to 0.0587 in (1.478 to 1.490 mm)
Centre oil control	0.0778 to 0.0783 in (1.978 to 1.990 mm)
Bottom oil control	0.1544 to 0.1549 in (3.925 to 3.937 mm)
Piston ring oversizes	0.0079 - 0.0157 - 0.0236 in (0.2 - 0.4 - 0.6 mm)
Piston clearance in cylinder barrel (measured at right angles to gudgeon pin and 2¼ in down from crown) (57.15 mm):	
Up to 1974	0.0028 to 0.0035 in (0.070 to 0.090 mm)
1974 on	0.0031 to 0.0039 in (0.080 to 0.100 mm)
Piston ring end-gap:	
Top	0.0098 to 0.0157 in (0.25 to 0.40 mm)
Centre at bottom	0.0080 to 0.0136 in (0.20 to 0.35 mm)
Maximum weight differential between pistons	0.902 (0.5 g)

Valves

Valve guide bore (diameter) in cylinder head	0.5492 to 0.5503 in (13.950 to 13.977 mm)
Valve guide outside diameter:	
Standard	0.5527 to 0.5534 in (14.040 to 14.058 mm)
Oversize	0.5535 to 0.5543 in (14.060 to 14.078 mm)
Valve guide internal diameter	0.3158 to 0.3165 in (8.022 to 8.040 mm)
Valve stem diameter	0.3139 to 0.3146 in (7.974 to 7.992 mm)
Valve stem clearance in guide	0.0012 to 0.0026 in (0.030 to 0.066 mm)
Valve seat angle	45° ± 5'
Valve face angle	45° 30' ± 5'
Valve head diameter:	
Inlet	1.26 in (32.0 mm)
Exhaust	1.16 in (28.0 mm)
Valve clearances (COLD):	
Inlet	0.0078 in (0.20 mm)
Exhaust	0.0098 in (0.25 mm)
Valve spring free length:	
Inner spring	1.5748 in (40.0 mm)
Outer spring	1.9685 in (50.0 mm)
Valve timing:	
Inlet opens:	
Up to 1974	26° BTDC
1974 on	26° BTDC
Inlet closes:	
Up to 1974	56° ABDC
1974 on	57° ABDC
Exhaust opens:	
Up to 1974	66° BBDC
1974 on	66° BBDC
Exhaust closes:	
Up to 1974	16° ATDC
1974 on	17° ATDC

Crankshaft

Main bearing journal diameter	2.1248 to 2.1256 in (53.970 to 53.990 mm)
Main bearing shell internal diameter	2.1274 to 2.1279 in (54.035 to 54.050 mm)
Main bearing undersizes	0.0079 - 0.0157 - 0.236 - 0.394 in (0.2 - 0.4 - 0.6 - 0.9 mm)
Main bearing running clearance	0.0081 to 0.0031 in (0.205 to 0.080 mm)
Crankpin diameter	1.7328 to 1.7336 in (44.013 to 44.033 mm)

Clearance between oil pump gears and pump housing	...	...	...	0.0027 and 0.0051 in (0.070 and 0.130 mm)
Oil pump gear endfloat ...	...	...	...	0.0012 to 0.0034 in (0.030 to 0.087 mm)
Oil pressure (HOT)	...	...	...	35 to 43 lb/sq in (2.5 to 3 kg/sq cm)
Oil type/specification	...	...	...	Multigrade engine oil, viscosity SAE 15W/40 (Duckhams Hypergrade)
Oil capacity	...	...	...	4.4 Imp pints (2.5 litres/5.3 US pints)

Torque wrench settings

	lb f ft	Nm
Cylinder head nuts ...	29	40
Connecting rod big-end nut ...	25	35
Flywheel bolt ...	25	35
Camshaft sprocket bolt ...	7	10
Rocker pedestal nut ...	18	25
Main bearing retainer bolts ...	22	30
Rear crossmember to body bolts ...	29	40
Rear mounting bracket to engine ...	18	25
Front mounting bracket to engine ...	30	41
Rear mounting insulator to crossmember ...	11	15
Spark plugs ...	22	30
Filter/pulley hollow bolt to crankshaft ...	108	149

1 General description

1   The engine is rear mounted and is of twin cylinder air-cooled type.
2   The vertical in-line cylinders are of cast-iron construction while the cylinder head and the crankcase are of light-alloy.
3   The crankshaft is supported in two main bearings.
4   Light-alloy pistons are used having an upper chromium plated compression ring and two lower oil control rings.
5   The overhead valve gear comprises valves, rockers, pushrods and tappets operated from the camshaft which is located in the crankcase.
6   Lubrication is by means of a gear type oil pump driven by a dog clutch at the forward end of the camshaft.
7   Cooling is by fan-generated forced draught. Cooling fins are cast into the cylinder block and the system incorporates ducting and a thermostat to control the volume of cooling air being exhausted depending upon the engine temperature level.
8   The engine/transmission unit which comprises the engine, the clutch, the gearbox and the final drive are mounted as one assembly

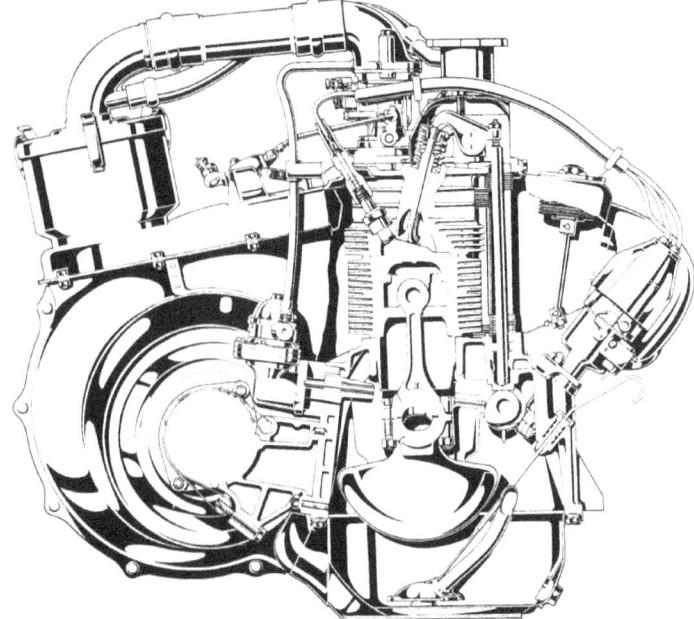

Fig. 1.2. Cut away view of engine (transverse)

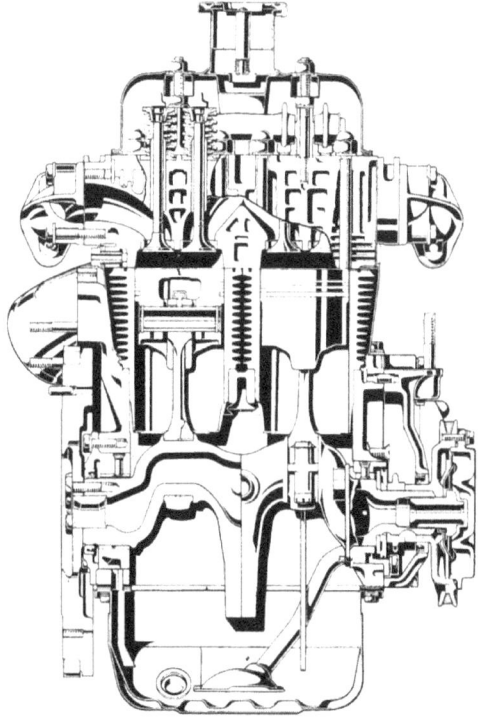

Fig. 1.1. Cut away view of engine (longitudinal)

on two flexible front mountings and one flexible/coil spring rear mounting.

2 Operations possible with engine in car

The following operations are possible without having to remove the engine from the car.

1   Removal and installation of the cylinder head.
2   Decarbonising and attention to valves.
3   Removal and installation of timing gear components.
4   Removal and installation of oil pump and centrifugal oil filter.
5   Removal and installation of the sump.
6   Removal and installation of the big-end bearings.
7   Removal and installation of the connecting rod/piston assemblies.
8   Removal and installation of the cylinder barrels.

If more overhead room to work is required for the last two operations, the rear crossmember can be unbolted and the engine lowered slightly on a jack.

engine from the car.

1 Removal and installation of the camshaft.
2 Removal and installation of the crankshaft.
3 Removal and installation of the main bearings.
4 Renewal of the crankshaft front oil seal.

Removal and installation of the flywheel can be carried out either by removing the engine or alternatively by withdrawing the gearbox and then unbolting the clutch mechanism.

4 Engine - method of removal

1   It is not very often that the engine and gearbox require major overhaul at one and the same time. It is therefore recommended that the engine is withdrawn separately from the rear of the car leaving the gearbox in position.
2   The gearbox can be removed independently towards the front of the car leaving the engine in position.
3   The engine combined with the transmission unit can be removed rearwards, as one unit if required, but all the engine and gearbox controls and the driveshaft must be disconnected, which is wasting time and effort if only one assembly is to be worked upon.

5 Engine - removal

1   Disconnect the battery which is located in the (front) boot.
2   Raise the rear of the car and support it securely on axle stands placed under the body side brackets.
3   Disconnect the engine compartment lid check strap (prise up the tab to release the anchor from the securing clip) and then withdraw the lid by sliding it out of its hinges after the single self-locking nut has been unscrewed (photo).
4   Disconnect the leads from the generator.
5   Disconnect the LT and HT leads from the ignition coil.
6   Disconnect the lead from the oil pressure switch (photo).
7   Disconnect the accelerator and choke controls from the carburettor.
8   Disconnect the fuel inlet pipe from the fuel pump. On some later models, disconnect the fuel return hose from the carburettor.
9   Disconnect the trunking which supplies cooling air to the engine fan unit.
10 Unbolt and remove the shield from above the exhaust silencer.
11 Disconnect the rear licence plate lamp leads at the connector plug (photo).
12 Working under the car, remove the under tray (photo).
13 Unbolt and remove the lower cover from the clutch bellhousing.
14 Unscrew and remove the lower bolts which secure the clutch bellhousing to the engine.
15 Extract the split pin and disconnect the operating cable from the starter motor switch.
16 Disconnect the two leads from the starter motor terminals.
17 Remove the bolts from the starter motor mounting flange which also secure the clutch bellhousing to the engine.
18 Disconnect the car interior heater ducting from the hot air outlet, by extracting the ratchet type plastic hose band.
19 Drain the engine oil.
20 Again working within the engine compartment, reach over the engine and unscrew and remove the upper bolts which secure the clutch bellhousing to the engine.
21 Take the weight of the engine on a trolley jack with a stout piece of timber placed under the unit in a crosswise attitude so that it supports the exhaust silencer on one side and the base of the cooling fan housing on the other. This arrangement will help to steady the engine and prevent it dropping on one side as it is withdrawn (photo).
22 Disconnect the coil spring type engine rear mounting by extracting the centre bolt (photo).
23 Unscrew and remove the two nuts at each end of the rear cross-member - note the earth strap which is located under one of the nuts (photo).

6 Engine ancillaries - removal

With the engine removed from the car, the engine ancillary components can be detached at this stage by reference to the appropriate Chapters listed. Alternatively if complete dismantling of the engine is to be carried out, continue as described in Section 8 onwards.

1 Distributor complete with HT leads (Chapter 4).
2 Exhaust silencer/manifold assembly (Chapter 3).
3 Air cleaner and carburettor (Chapter 3).
4 Fuel pump (Chapter 3).
5 Generator (Chapter 10) (photo).
6 The engine cooling fan assembly (Chapter 2).
7 The engine air temperature regulating unit (Chapter 2).
8 The clutch mechanism (Chapter 5).

Fig. 1.3. Engine compartment (note lid check strap)

Fig. 1.4. Preparing to remove the engine on a trolley jack

5.3 Self-locking nut on engine compartment lid hinge

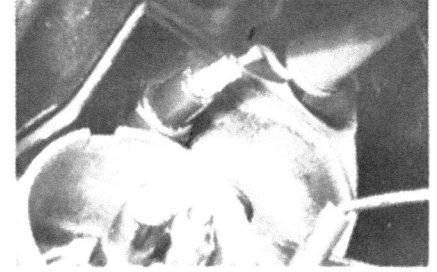

5.6 Location of oil pressure switch

5.11 Rear licence plate lead connector plug

5.12 Engine undertray

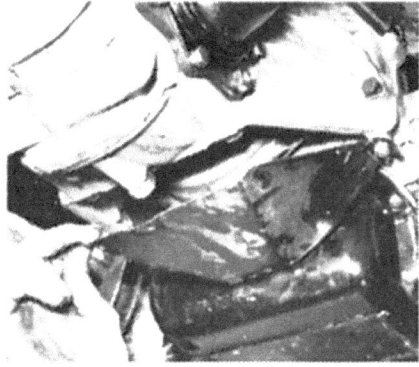

5.13 Removing lower cover from clutch bellhousing

15.21 Engine supported on trolley jack ready for removal

5.22 Engine rear mounting

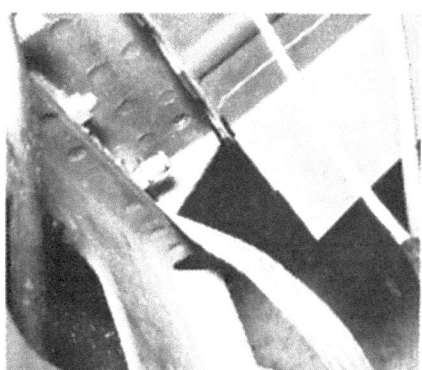

5.23 Earth strap connection to rear crossmember bolt

5.25 Gearbox supported on second jack

6.5 Engine withdrawn showing exhaust, dynamo and right-hand cooling casing and rocker cover removed

7 Engine - dismantling general

1 It is best to mount the engine on a dismantling stand but if one is not available, then stand the engine on a strong bench so as to be at a comfortable working height. Failing this, the engine will have to be stripped down on the floor.

2 During the dismantling process the greatest care should be taken to keep the exposed parts free from dirt. As an aid to achieving this, it is a sound scheme to thoroughly clean down the outside of the engine, removing all traces of oil and congealed dirt.

3 Use paraffin or a good water soluble grease solvent. The latter compound will make the job much easier, as, after the solvent has been applied and allowed to stand for a time, a vigorous jet of water will wash off the solvent and all the grease and filth. If the dirt is thick and deeply embedded, work the solvent into it with a wire brush.

4 Finally wipe down the exterior of the engine with a rag and only then, when it is quite clean should the dismantling process begin. As the engine is stripped, clean each part in a bath of paraffin or petrol.

5 Never immerse parts with oilways in paraffin, ie; the crankshaft,

6 Re-use of old engine gaskets is false economy and can give rise to oil and water leaks, if nothing worse. To avoid the possibility of trouble after the engine has been reassembled **always** use new gaskets throughout.

7 Do not throw the old gaskets away as it sometimes happens that an immediate replacement cannot be found and the old gasket is then very useful as a template. Hang up the old gaskets as they are removed on a suitable hook or nail.

8 To strip the engine it is best to work from the top down. The sump provides a firm base on which the engine can be supported in an upright position. When the stage where the sump must be removed is reached, the engine can be turned on its side and all other work carried out with it in this position.

9 Wherever possible, replace nuts, bolts and washers fingertight from wherever they were removed. This helps avoid later loss and muddle. If they cannot be replaced then lay them out in such a fashion that it is clear where they came from.

---

8 Cylinder head - removal

1 *If the engine is in the car,* disconnect the battery, remove the engine compartment lid and the air cleaner.

2 Remove the rocker cover after unscrewing the two securing nuts and their fibre washers.

3 Pull the waterproof cover from the distributor, release the cap clips and remove the cap complete with HT leads.

4 Turn the engine crankshaft until No 1 piston (the rearmost one when installed in the car) is at TDC. This can be established by checking that the timing marks on the oil filter cover and on the timing cover are in alignment and that Nos 1 and 2 valves are fully closed (slight movement discernible at their rocker arms).

5 Now mark the position of the contact end of the rotor arm in relation to the distributor body and also the distributor body in relation to the engine crankcase. Unbolt the distributor clamp plate and remove the distributor.

6 Disconnect the throttle operating rod from the carburettor.

7 Disconnect the fuel pipe which runs between the fuel pump and the carburettor.

8 Unbolt and remove the carburettor. Withdraw the carburettor drip tray.

9 Unscrew and remove the suppressor cap from the spark plugs.

10 Extract all the bolts which secure the top sections of the engine air cooling assembly and lift these sections away.

11 Unbolt the exhaust pipe flanges from both sides of the cylinder head. Pull the flanges slightly from the cylinder head and extract the joint gaskets.

12 Unscrew and remove the rocker pedestal nuts.

13 Lift off the rocker shaft assembly, noting the location of the rocker oil feed pipe.

14 Withdraw the four pushrods and keep them in sequence for refitting in their original positions.

15 Unscrew the four centrally-located cylinder head domed nuts and the four ordinary nuts on the outer edge of the cylinder head.

16 Lift off the cylinder head directly upwards. If it is stuck, tap it carefully with a plastic or wooden mallet.

---

9 Cam followers (tappets) and cylinder barrels - removal

1 With the cylinder head removed as previously described, extract the pushrod tubes.

2 Extract the circular flexible seals from both ends of the tubes.

3 Extract the cam followers (tappets) keeping them in sequence for refitting in their original positions.

4 Mark which way round each cylinder barrel is fitted and which one is the rearmost and then carefully draw them off the pistons upwards.

---

10 Sump. pistons/connecting rods - removal

1 If the engine is in the car, drain the engine oil and remove the

3 Unbolt the exhaust silencer brackets and remove the silencer assembly.

4 Unbolt and remove the front flange of the generator pulley, extract the shims used for tensioning the drivebelt and remove the belt.

5 Release the generator mounting strap.

6 Unbolt the fan cooling assembly from the engine crankcase and remove the assembly complete with generator. It will be noticed that two of the bolts which secure the fan cooling assembly to the engine are of hollow type. This is a safety feature necessary where the air used for cooling the engine is also used to heat the car interior. Should the cylinder head gasket blow, exhaust gas could leak into the car interior through the heater. A groove is located on the upper surface of the cylinder barrel which connects to these hollow bolts and if exhaust gas is heard or can be felt emerging from these bolts, then the cylinder head gasket must be renewed immediately (photo).

7 Unscrew the connecting rod big-end nuts and remove the big-end cap.

8 Push the connecting rods complete with pistons out of the crank-case through the top face. Note that the connecting rods and their caps are numbered 1 and 2. No 1 is the rearmost, and all numbers face towards the camshaft.

10.6 Engine cooling casing hollow bolt

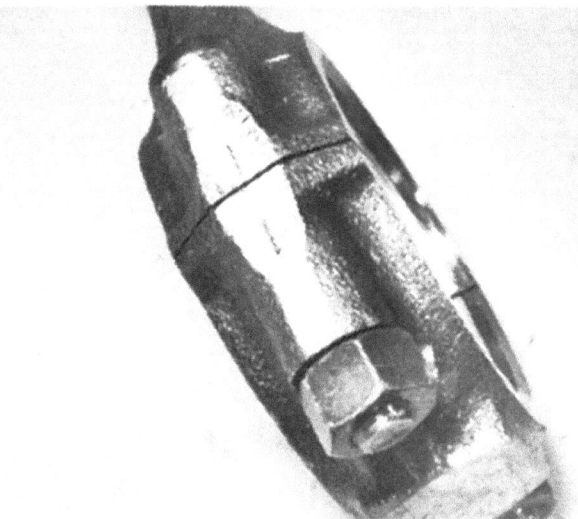

10.7 Connecting rod and cap numbers

them from their connecting rods, they should be marked with a piece of adhesive tape so that there can be no doubt from which rod they were removed and also which way round on the rod they were fitted.

2 Extract the circlip from both ends of the gudgeon pin and push out the pin. Finger pressure only should be required to do this.

3 To remove the piston rings, start with the top compression ring first. Expand it slightly and slide two or three old feeler blades behind it spacing them at equidistant points of a circle. These will extract the ring from its groove and also provide slides to prevent the lower rings dropping into empty upper grooves as these too are removed.

4 Remove the rings using a twisting motion.

12 Flywheel - removal

1 With the clutch removed as described in Chapter 5, mark the position of the flywheel in relation to the crankshaft mounting flange.

2 Unscrew and remove the flywheel bolts and remove the flywheel. In order to remove the flywheel bolts it will be necessary to prevent the crankshaft rotating. To do this, either place a block of wood between the crankshaft web and the inside of the crankcase or jam the starter ring gear with a large screwdriver.

13 Oil pump, filter, timing gear and camshaft - removal

1 If the engine is in the car, support it on a jack and remove the rear crossmember.

2 Remove the drivebelt, as previously described.

3 Unscrew and remove the cover from the centrifugal oil filter (five bolts).

4 Bend back the locking tab from the nut now exposed within the oil filter housing.

5 Unscrew the nut first having jammed the crankshaft with a piece of wood to prevent it rotating.

6 Extract the thrust washer and the oil thrower.

7 Pull the pulley/oil filter housing straight off the rear of the engine.

8 Unscrew the timing cover nuts and remove the cover.

9 The timing gears and chain are now exposed. Note the timing marks on the gears (dot on camshaft gear and scribed line on crankshaft gear).

10 Unbolt the camshaft gearwheel and remove it complete with crankshaft sprocket and the timing chain.

11 Withdraw the camshaft carefully taking care not to damage the camshaft bearings as the lobes pass through them.

14 Crankshaft and main bearings - removal

1 From the oil pump end of the crankshaft, extract the Woodruff key which secures the timing gear (previously removed).

2 Remove the bolts and countersunk screws which secure the bearing retainer at the oil pump end of the crankshaft. An impact screwdriver will almost certainly be required to remove the screws.

3 Unbolt and remove the bearing retainer at the flywheel end of the crankshaft.

4 Unbolt and remove the oil pick-up tube from inside the crankcase. Note the mounting plate used between the tube flange and the crankcase.

5 Withdraw the crankshaft from the crankcase.

15 Lubrication system and filter maintenance

1 The lubrication system comprises a sump and a gear type oil pump which is mounted within the timing cover and is driven by a dog clutch at the rear end of the camshaft (Fig. 1.5).

2 A large coil spring is used to key the pressure relief valve on its seat and excess pressure causes the valve to lift against the spring pressure.

3 A centrifugal type oil filter is used and this is mounted on the rear

5 Oil is drawn from the sump through the pick-up tube, filtered by the centrifugal type filter and then pressurised by the gear type oil pump and distributed to all the bearings and friction surfaces of the engine.

6 At the intervals specified in 'Routine Maintenance,' unbolt the cover from the centrifugal filter and let any oil residue drain into a container.

7 Clean out both the filter housing and the filter cover. The hard grey deposits will probably require the use of a blunt tool to remove them but take care not to damage the metal surfaces.

8 Scrape off the old gasket and fit a new one, then install the filter cover, tightening the bolts evenly.

16 Crankcase ventilation system - description and maintenance

1 The crankcase ventilation system is simply a hose connecting the rocker cover to the air cleaner so that engine oil fumes and blow-by gases can be extracted from the crankcase and rocker box and be drawn into the inlet manifold where they can be burned during the normal combustion cycle.

2 Refinements incorporated in the system include a valve in the oil filler cap and a backfire eliminator in the connecting hose stub of the filler neck.

3 At the intervals specified in the 'Routine Maintenance' section thoroughly clean the backfire eliminator and check the condition and security of the system hoses. The backfire eliminator is removed simply by extracting it with a pair of pliers (photo).

17 Examination and renovation - general

With the engine stripped down and all parts thoroughly cleaned, it is now time to examine everything for wear. The following items should be checked and where necessary renewed or renovated as described in the following Sections.

18 Crankshaft and main bearings - examination and renovation

1 Use a micrometer to check the main bearing journals for out of round. Check at several different points and if the difference in these measurements exceeds 0.0002 in (0.005 mm) then the crankshaft must be reground and new main bearings fitted (Fig. 1.6).

2 This procedure must also be adopted if there is scoring or scratching on the main bearing journal surfaces.

3 If the crankshaft must be reground, this is obviously a job for your Fiat dealer who will decide how much to grind off and supply the

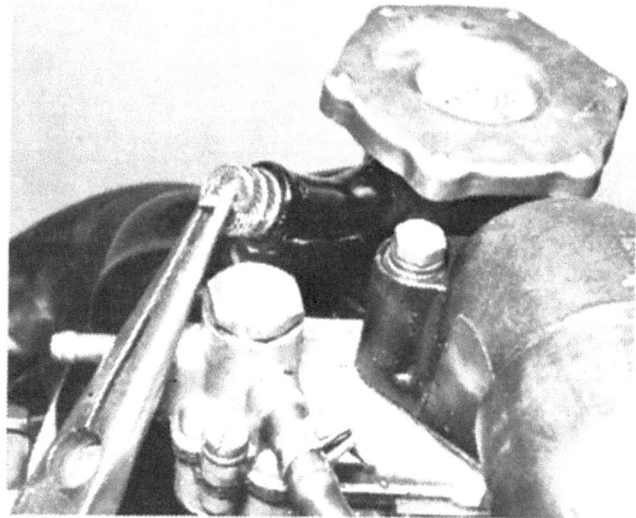

16.3 Extracting anti-backfire device (crankcase vent system)

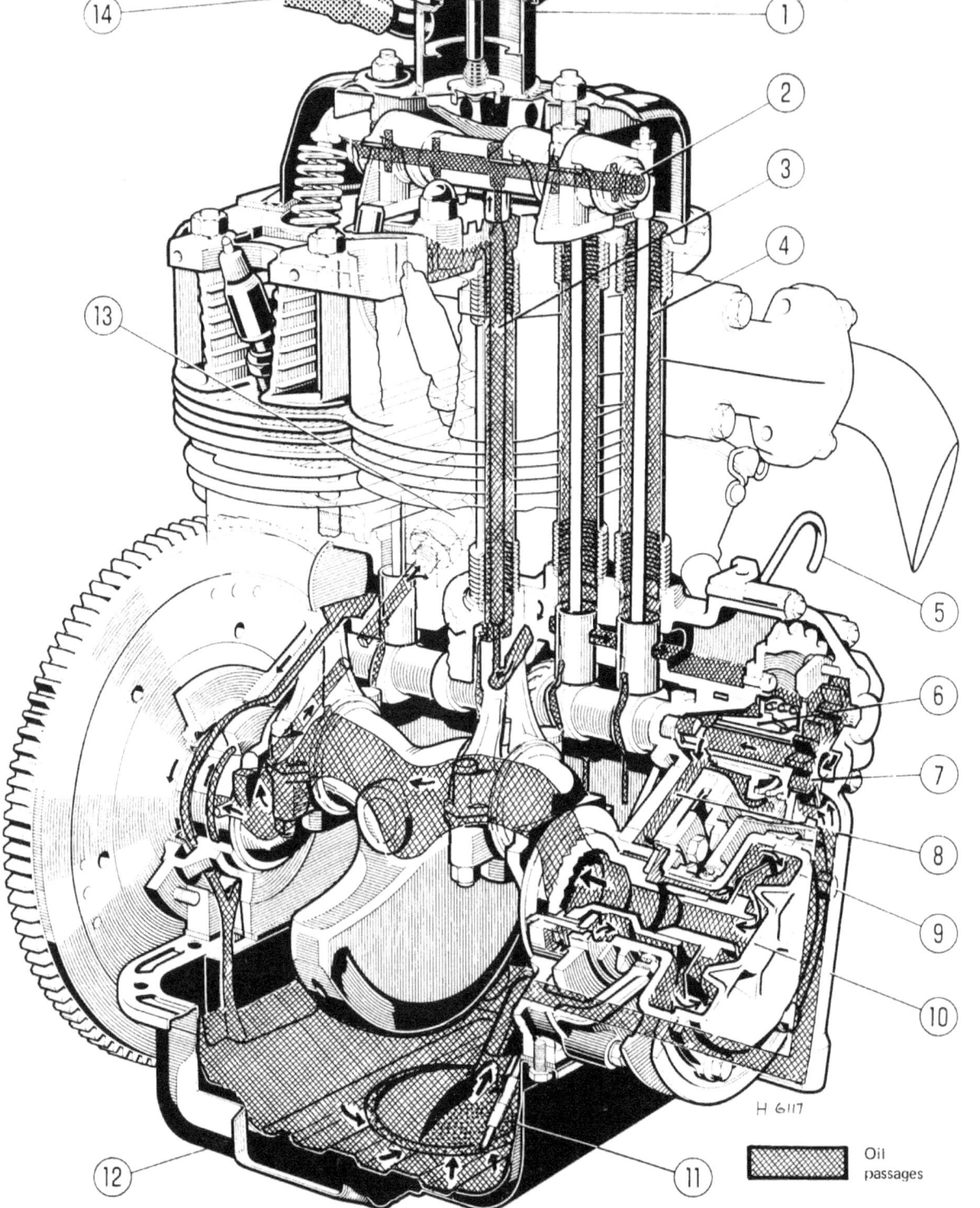

Fig. 1.5. Diagrammatic view of engine lubrication system

1 Oil filler cap	4 Oil return passages from	7 Oil pump gears	11 Oil pick-up tube filter
2 Rocker shaft	cylinder head	8 Oil passage to filter	12 Sump air cooling duct
3 Oil delivery tube to rocker	5 Dipstick	9 Centrifugal type oil filter	13 Oil pressure switch
shaft	6 Oil pressure relief valve	10 Crankshaft oil drilling	14 Fume extraction pipe to
			air cleaner

Oil passages

5 The oil seal in the main bearing assembly at the flywheel end can be renewed if necessary (Section 28).

6 The main bearing assembly at the timing gear end incorporates a piston ring type oil seal and a thrust washer (photo).

7 Whenever the crankshaft has been removed, always check the effectiveness of the oil plug staking (Fig. 1.7).

8 In the centre of the flywheel mounting flange of the crankshaft is located the gearbox input shaft pilot bush. If this is badly worn, extract it by tapping a thread into it, screwing in a bolt and using the bolt to withdraw the bush. Drive in the new bush and apply some grease to its centre.

19 Big-end bearings and connecting rods - examination and renovation

1 Check the crankpins for scoring and out of round as for journals described in the preceding Section.

2 New shell bearings are installed simply by extracting the old ones from cap and rod and fitting the new ones.

3 Any wear in the small end bush can only be overcome by pressing out the old bush and pressing in the new one. As the new bush will then require reaming to the specified size, this is a job that is best left to your Fiat dealer.

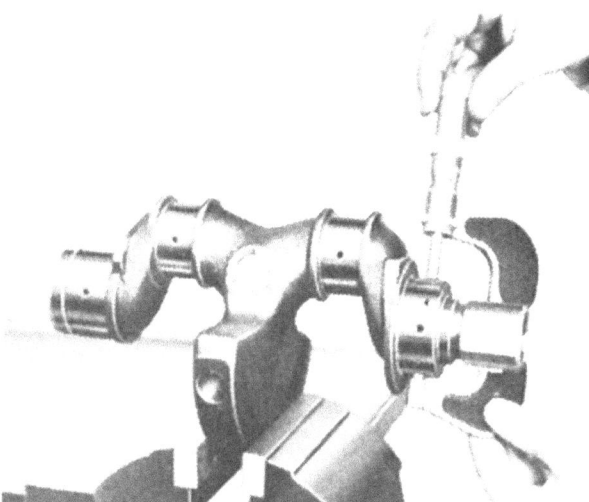

Fig. 1.6. Checking a crankshaft journal

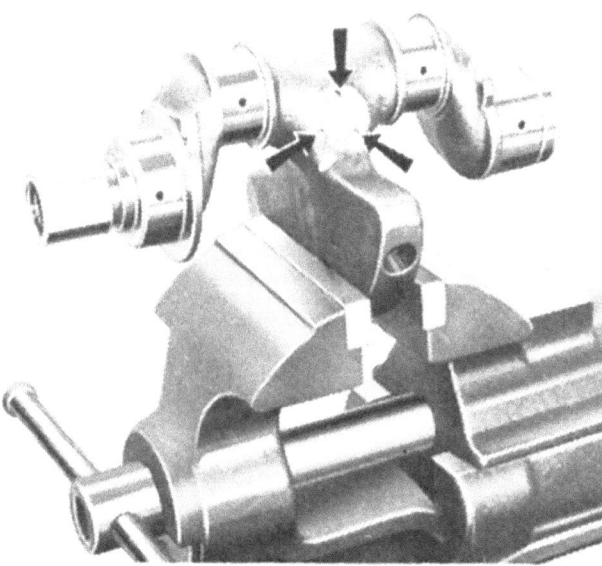

Fig. 1.7. Crankshaft oil plug staking

18.6 Main bearing at timing cover end showing piston ring type oil seal and thrust washer extracted

20 Cylinder bores - examination and renovation

1 The cylinder bores must be examined for taper, ovality, scoring and scratches. Start by carefully examining the top of the cylinder bores. If they are at all worn a very slight ridge will be found on the thrust side. This marks the top of the piston ring travel. The owner will have a good indication of the bore wear prior to dismantling the engine, or removing the cylinder head. Excessive oil consumption accompanied by blue smoke from the exhaust is a sure sign of worn cylinder bores and piston rings.

2 Measure the bore diameter just under the ridge with a micrometer and compare it with the diameter at the bottom of the bore, which is not subject to wear. If the difference between the two measurements is more than 0.0008 in (0.02 mm) then it will be necessary to fit special pistons and rings or to have the cylinders rebored and fit oversize pistons. If no micrometer is available remove the rings from a piston and place the piston in each bore in turn about ¾ in (19.05 mm) below the top of the bore. If an 0.0012 in (0.03 mm) thick feeler gauge slid between the piston and cylinder wall requires less than a pull of between 2.2 and 5.5 lbs (1 and 2.5 kg) to withdraw it, using a spring balance, then remedial action must be taken. Oversize pistons are available as listed in the Specifications.

3 These are accurately machined to just below the indicated measurements so as to provide correct running clearances in bores bored out to the exact oversize dimensions.

4 If the bores are slightly worn but not so badly worn as to justify reboring them, then special oil control rings and pistons can be fitted which will restore compression and stop the engine burning oil. Several different types are available and the manufacturer's instructions concerning their fitting must be followed closely.

5 If new pistons or rings are being fitted and the bores have not been reground, it is essential to slightly roughen the hard glaze on the sides of the bores with fine glass paper so the new piston rings will have a chance to bed in properly.

21 Pistons and piston rings - examination and renovation

1 If the original pistons are to be refitted, carefully remove the piston rings as described in Section 11.

2 Clean the grooves and rings free from carbon, taking care not to scratch the aluminium surfaces of the pistons.

3 If new rings are considered necessary, consult your local engineering firm as to the availability of a set of rings with the top one 'stepped'. This 'step' will avoid the ridge which occurs near the top of the bore after a high mileage and will prevent the new ring being broken. Be guided by the advice of the engineering firm, as the fitting of new rings to an otherwise worn piston and bore can only be a very temporary cure to the inevitable rebore!

piston ring end gap.

5　This gap should be as shown in the Specifications, otherwise carefully grind the end faces of the ring.

6　Each piston ring should now be tested in its respective groove for side clearance. Use a feeler blade to do this and compare the clearances with those listed in the Specifications (Fig. 1.8).

7　Where the side clearance is excessive, renew the piston as it will be the grooves that will have worn.

8　Where necessary a piston ring which is slightly tight in its groove may be rubbed down holding it perfectly squarely on an oilstone or a sheet of fine emery cloth laid on a piece of plate glass. Excessive tightness can only be rectified by having the grooves machined out.

9　The gudgeon pin should be a push fit with the fingers in both the piston and small end bush of the connecting rod. Any slackness must be rectified by renewal of the small end bush or piston or both.

22 Camshaft and cam-followers (tappets) - examination and renovation

1　The camshaft runs directly in the crankcase. Any wear in the bearing surfaces will seriously affect the engine oil pressure.

2　Where any wear is found in the camshaft journals after measuring their diameters with a micrometer and comparing the dimensions with those given in the Specifications, the camshaft must be renewed. This action will also have to be taken if the camshaft journals are found to be out of round.

3　If the camshaft bores in the crankcase are found to be worn, then the crankcase will have to be renewed.

4　It may be possible to have the crankcase and camshaft built up by metal spraying or a similar technique and then refinished to provide the specified running clearances but check the cost of new components against the charge for this type of work first.

5　Wear in the camshaft lobes can only be satisfactorily measured with a dial gauge. Use this to compare the lobe lift figures with those specified which are: inlet and exhaust - 0.244 in (6.2 mm).

6　Any wear in the lobes or skew gear can only be overcome by renewal of the camshaft.

7　If the cam followers are slack in their crankcase bores, oversize cam followers can be fitted if the bores are first reamed out. This is a job best left to your Fiat dealer. Oversizes supplied 0.0019 to 0.0039 in (0.05 to 0.10 mm).

23 Timing components - examination and renovation

1　Examine all the sprocket teeth for wear or 'hooked' appearance and renew if necessary.

2　Wash the timing chain, thoroughly in paraffin and examine for wear or stretch. If the chain is supported at both ends so that the rollers are vertical then a worn chain will take on a deeply bowed appearance while an unworn one will dip slightly at its centre point.

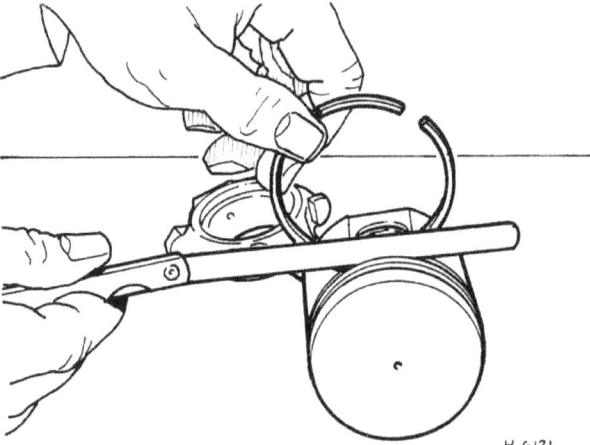

H.G121

Fig. 1.8. Checking piston ring side clearance

24 Valves and valve guides - servicing

1　Each valve should be removed from the cylinder head using the following method.

2　Compress each spring using a valve spring compressor, until the split collets can be removed. Release the compressor slowly, remove and then remove the retainer, valve springs, and the valve spring sea Finally withdraw the valve from its guide (photos).

3　If, when the valve spring compressor is screwed down, the valve spring retaining cap refuses to free to expose the split collet, do not continue to screw down on the compressor as there is a likelihood o bending the valve stem.

4　Gently tap the top of the tool directly over the cap with a light hammer. This will free the cap. To avoid the compressor jumping of the valve spring retaining cap when it is tapped, hold the compresso firmly in position with one hand.

5　Slide the rubber oil control seal off the end of each inlet valve stem and then drop out each valve through the combustion chambe Later engines do not have oil seals on the valve stems.

6　It is essential that the valves are kept in their correct sequences unless they are so badly worn that they are to be renewed. If they a going to be kept and used again, place them in a sheet of card havin holes numbered 1 to 4 corresponding with the relative positions the valves were in when fitted. Also keep the valve springs, washers etc the correct order.

7　Examine the heads of the valves for pitting and burning, especia the heads of the exhaust valves. The valve seatings should be examin at the same time. If the pitting on valve and seat is very slight the marks can be removed by grinding the seats and valves together wit coarse, and then fine, valve grinding paste.

8　Where bad pitting has occured to the valve seats it will be necess to recut them and fit new valves. Cut the valve seat in three stages a indicated, using first a 45° cutter then one of 20° and finally a 75° cutter to give a seat contact width of between 0.71 and 0.83 in (1.8 and 2.1 mm) (Fig. 1.9). In practice it is very seldom that the seats are so badly worn that they require recutting. Normally, it is t valve that is too badly worn to use again and the owner can easily purchase a new set of valves and match them to the seats by grindin

9　Valve grinding is carried out as follows. Smear a trace of coarse carborundum paste on the seat face and apply a suction grinder too the valve head. With a semi-rotary motion, grind the valve head to i seat, lifting the valve occasionally to redistribute the grinding paste When a dull matt, even surface finish is produced on both the valve seat and the valve, wipe off the paste and repeat the process with fi carborundum paste, lifting and turning the valve to distribute the paste as before. A light spring placed under the valve head will grea ease this operation. When a smooth unbroken ring of light grey ma finish is produced, on both valve and valve seat faces, the grinding operation is completed.

10　Scrape away all carbon from the valve head and the valve stem. Carefully clean away every trace of grinding compound, taking grea care to leave none in the ports or in the valve guides. Clean the valv and valve seats with a paraffin soaked rag, then with a dry rag, and finally, if an air line is available, blow the valves, valve guides and valve ports clean.

11　Wear in the valve guides can best be checked by inserting a new valve and testing for rocking movement in all directions. The cleara between the guide and valve stem must not exceed 0.003 in (0.08 r

12　Reassemble the valves, springs and collets in reverse order.

13　Valve guides are an interference fit in the cylinder head and the may be renewed using a suitable mandrel as a drift. New guides are supplied in (outside diameter) oversizes to provide the correct interference fit.

14　Install the valve guide in accordance with the diagram (Fig. 1.1C

25 Cylinder head - decarbonising and examination

1　With the cylinder head removed, use a blunt scraper to remove a trace of carbon and deposits from the combustion spaces and ports

compound. Clean the cylinder head by washing it in paraffin and take particular care to pull a piece of rag through the ports and cylinder head bolt holes. Any dirt remaining in these recesses may well drop onto the gasket or cylinder block mating surface as the cylinder head is lowered into position and could lead to a gasket leak after reassembly is complete.

2 With the cylinder head clean, test for distortion if a history of gas leakage has been apparent. Carry out this test using a straight edge and feeler gauges or a piece of plate glass. If the surface shows any warping in excess of 0.0039 in (0.1 mm) then the cylinder head will have to be resurfaced which is a job for a specialist engineering company.

3 Clean the pistons and top of the cylinder bores. If the pistons are still in the block then it is essential that great care is taken to ensure that no carbon gets into the cylinder bores as this could scratch the cylinder walls or cause damage to the piston and rings. To ensure this does not happen, first turn the crankshaft so that both the pistons are at the top of their bores.

4 Before scraping the carbon from the piston crowns, press grease into the gap between the cylinder wall and the two pistons. With a blunt scraper carefully scrape away the carbon from the piston crown, taking great care not to scratch the aluminium. Also scrape away the carbon from the surrounding lip of the cylinder wall. When all carbon

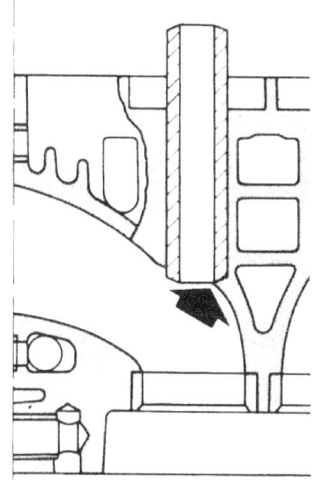

Fig. 1.9. Valve seat cutting diagram
1st · 45⁰   2nd · 20⁰   3rd · 75⁰
Seat width (L) is between 0.071 and 0.083 in (1.8 and 2.1 mm)

24.2a Compressing a valve spring

24.2b Removing valve spring retainer

Fig. 1.10. Valve guide installation diagram (note flush fitting at bottom chamfer (arrowed)

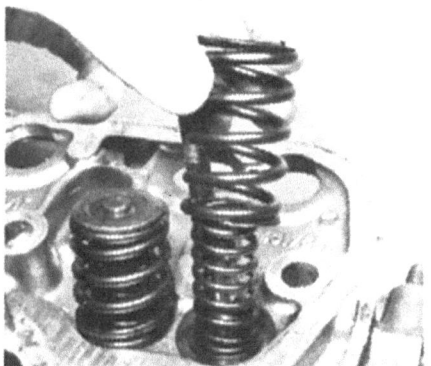

24.2c Removing an outer valve spring

24.2d Removing a valve spring seat

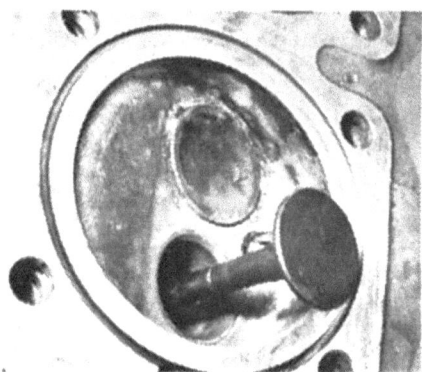

24.2e Removing a valve

has been removed scrape away the grease which will now be contaminated with carbon particles, taking care not to press any into the bores. To assist prevention of carbon build-up the piston crown can be polished with a metal polish.

26 Flywheel - examination and renovation

1 Check the clutch friction lining mating face of the flywheel. If it is grooved or scored, then the flywheel must be renewed.

2 If the starter ring gear is worn or the teeth are chipped, a new ring gear can be fitted using the following method.

3 Either split the ring with a cold chisel after making a cut with a hacksaw blade between two teeth, or use a soft headed hammer (not steel) to knock the ring off, striking it evenly and alternatively at equally spaced points. Take great care not to damage the flywheel during this process.

4 Heat the new ring in either an electric oven to about 230⁰C (446⁰F) or immerse in a pan of boiling oil.

5 Hold the ring at this temperature for five minutes and then quickly fit it to the flywheel.

6 The ring should be tapped gently down onto its register and left to cool naturally when the contraction of the metal on cooling will ensure that it is a secure and permanent fit. Great care must be taken not to overheat the ring (indicated by the ring turning light metallic blue) as if this happens the temper of the ring will be lost.

1 Inspect the crankcase for cracks particularly of the stud and bolt holes.
2 Renew any studs which have stripped or damaged threads.
3 Inspect the security of the Welch plugs. Renew any that are suspect.

28 Oil seals - renewal

1 At time of major overhaul, renew the oil seals as a matter of routine.
2 Drive out the timing cover oil seal using a piece of tubing as a drift and install the new one by the same method. Apply grease to the seal lips after fitting (Fig. 1.11).
3 Renew the oil seal in the crankshaft main bearing retainer (flywheel end) in the same way (Fig. 1.12 and photo).

29 Oil pump - overhaul

1 With the timing cover removed, the oil pump can be dismantled if necessary.
2 A compressor will be needed to compress the pressure relief valve spring so that the retaining circlip can be extracted. A valve spring compressor used with a suitable adaptor might serve the purpose, otherwise bolt a flat bar across the timing cover flanges and use this as a leverage point to depress the relief valve and in turn, the spring (Figs. 1.13, 1.14 and 1.15).
3 The components of the oil pump may now be removed and the cover unbolted.
4 Check the teeth of the gears for wear or chipping and renew them if evident.
5 Measure the length of the spring. This should be between 1.38 and 1.46 in (35.2 - 37.2 mm) in its free state. If it is shorter, renew it.
6 Reassemble the pump by reversing the dismantling operations.

30 Rocker gear and pushrods - examination and renovation

1 Any wear in the rocker shaft or arms can only be rectified by renewal of the components.
2 If the circlips are extracted and the rocker arms are removed from the rocker shaft, keep all components in strict sequence so that they can be installed in their original positions.
3 Check the pushrods for distortion. If any of them appear to be bent, renew them.

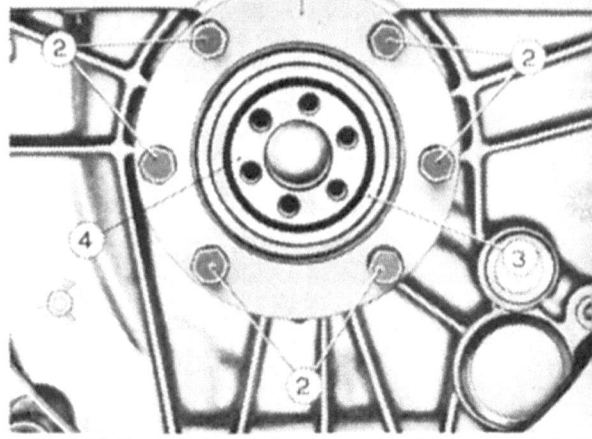

Fig. 1.12. Crankshaft main bearing retainer(1) Securing bolts(2) Oil seal(3) and Crankshaft flywheel mounting flange (4)

Fig. 1.13. Oil pump within timing cover

1 Timing cover	4 Circlip
2 Pump securing bolts	5 Oil pressure relief valve
3 Pump drive shaft	6 Relief valve spring

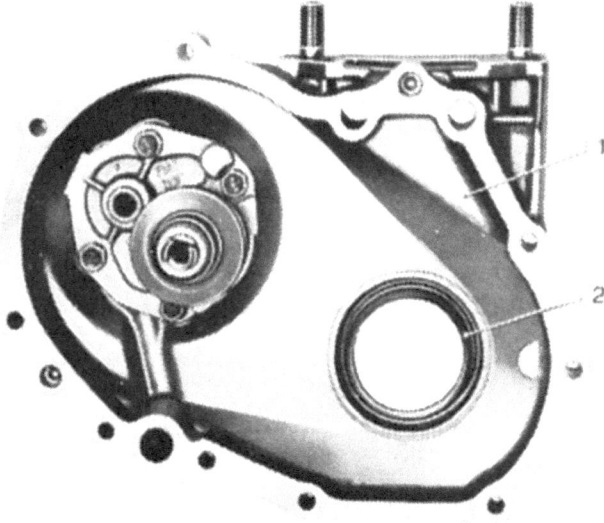

Fig. 1.11. Timing cover (1) and oil seal (2)

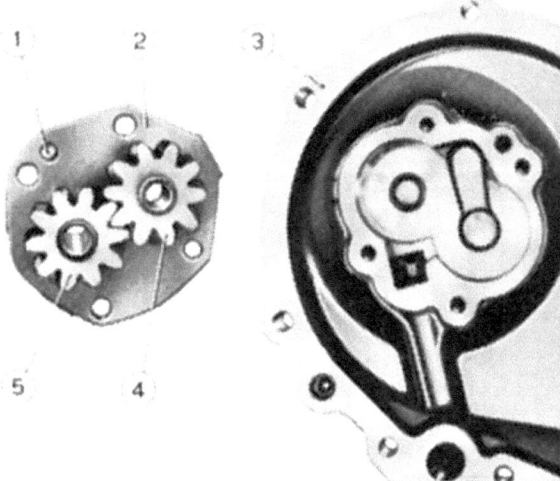

Fig. 1.14. Oil pump cover removed

1 Locating dowel	4 Driven gear
2 Pump cover	5 Drive gear and shaft
3 Timing cover	

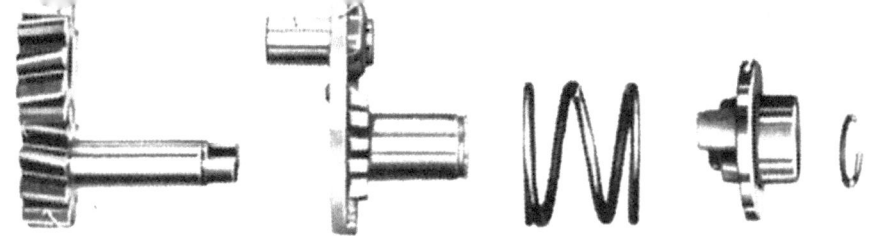

7   6

Fig. 1.15. Exploded view of the oil pump

1 Driven gear	3 Cover	5 Relief valve	7 Drive gear and shaft
2 Shaft	4 Spring	6 Circlip	

31 Engine reassembly - general

1   To ensure maximum life with minimum trouble from a re-built engine, not only must everything be correctly assembled but everything must be spotlessly clean, all the oilways must be clear, locking washers and spring washers must always be fitted where indicated and all bearing and other working surfaces must be thoroughly lubricated during assembly.

2   Before assembly begins renew any bolts or studs the threads of which are in any way damaged and whenever possible use new spring washers.

3   Apart from your normal tools, a supply of clean rag, an oil can filled with engine oil, a new supply of assorted spring washers, a set of new gaskets and a torque wrench, should be collected together.

32 Crankshaft and main bearings - refitting

1   Pass the crankshaft into the crankcase and push it as far as possible through one of the main bearing holes, then bring it back so that it rests in the main bearing holes of the crankcase. The flywheel mounting flange will obviously be towards the bellhousing (photo).

2   Lubricate the main bearing surfaces liberally and install the front and rear main bearings. A gasket is used on the main bearing flange at the flywheel end only (photos).

3   The main bearing retainers will only fit one way as they have a flat on one side which aligns with the sump flange.

4   Install the bearing retaining bolts and screws and tighten to the specified torque.

5   Install the Woodruff key to the end of the crankshaft (photo).

28.3 Main bearing retainer (flywheel end) showing oil seal

32.1 Installing the crankshaft

32.2a Installing the main bearing retainer (timing gear end)

32.2b Installing bolts and screws to main bearing retainer (timing gear end)

32.5 Woodruff key installed to end of crankshaft

1 Lubricate the camshaft bearings liberally and install the camshaft into the crankcase (photo).
2 Temporarily fit the camshaft and crankshaft chain sprockets to the ends of the camshaft and crankshaft. The camshaft sprocket can only be fitted in one position as the bolt holes are offset.
3 Turn the sprockets until the dot on the edge of the camshaft sprocket is in alignment with the scribed line on the crankshaft sprocket and an imaginary line drawn through the sprocket centres (photo).
4 Remove the sprockets and keeping them in this relative position, engage their teeth within the loop of the timing chain. The tensioner plates of the timing chain must be furthest from the crankcase (photo).
5 Install the two sprockets complete with chain without moving the previously set position of the camshaft or crankshaft. Some slight re-adjustment of the sprockets within the chain may be necessary to align the camshaft sprocket bolt holes and yet maintain the alignment of the timing marks.
6 Fit the camshaft sprocket bolts, tighten to the specified torque and bend up the tabs of the lockplates (photo).
7 Install the timing cover using a new gasket. Make sure that the oil pump mates correctly with the drive dog on the end of the camshaft as the timing cover is offered into position (photos).
8 Push the pulley/oil filter assembly into position on the end of the crankshaft, fit the lockplate and hollow bolt and tighten to the specified torque. Jam the crankshaft web with a block of wood to prevent it turning while the bolt is being tightened. Bend up the tab of the lockplate (photos).
9 Fit the oil filter cover using a new 'O' ring oil seal (photo).

34 Flywheel - refitting

1 Install the flywheel to the mounting flange on the crankshaft so that the marks made before removal are in alignment.
2 Install and tighten the securing bolts to the specified torque wrench setting. To prevent the flywheel turning as the bolts are tightened, jam the crankshaft with a block of wood (photo).

35 Pistons, piston rings and gudgeon pins - reassembly

1 If the piston has been removed from the connecting rod, refit it so that the larger offset and the numbers on the connecting rod will be towards the camshaft when installed (Fig. 1.16).
2 Push in the gudgeon pin using finger-pressure only and then fit new securing circlips (photo).
3 Fit the slotted oil control ring to the lowest groove of the piston followed by the plain oil control ring (stepped on its lower edge) and then the chrome-plated compression ring. This is marked 'TOP' on its upper face.
4 When the rings are installed, stagger their end-gaps at equidistant points of a circle to avoid gap alignment which might cause gas blow-by.

36 Pistons/connecting rods and sump - refitting

1 Fit the shell bearings to the connecting rod and to the big-end cap. Make sure that the backs of the shells are quite clean also the recesses into which they fit. Lubricate the shell bearing surfaces (photo).
2 Pass the connecting rod/piston assembly into the crankcase through the hole in the top of the crankcase (photo).
3 Engage the connecting rod with the crankpin of the crankshaft, install the big-end cap and screw on and tighten the securing nuts to the specified torque (photos). The numbers on the rod and cap must face towards the camshaft. Remember No 1 rod and piston are in the rearmost position in the engine.
4 Install the second piston/rod assembly in a similar manner.
5 Install the oil pump pick-up tube within the crankcase (photo).
6 Fit a new sump gasket and install the sump. Make sure that the oil drain slots in the sump gasket are correctly located (photo).

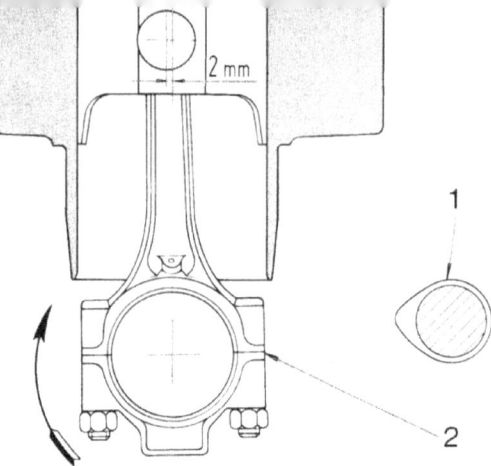

Fig. 1.16. Piston/connecting rod installation diagram

1 Camshaft   2 Rod and cap number

37 Cylinder barrels, cam followers (tappets) and pushrod tubes - refitting

1 Oil the piston rings liberally and fit narrow piston ring compressor. Install the barrel lower gaskets to the crankcase (photos).
2 Make sure that the piston and compressor are sitting quite square on the top of the crankcase and then lower the cylinder barrel onto the piston. Make sure that the correct barrel is installed to its respective piston and it is fitted the correct way round with its bore liberally oiled.
3 Tap the barrel sharply down with the palm of the hand to displace the compressor and engage the lower end of the barrel with the crankcase. If the engine is out of the car, it may be preferred to install the pistons into the barrels and then insert the big-ends of the connecting rods into the crankcase and lower the complete piston/barrel assembly onto the securing studs. This method is not recommended if the engine is still in position in the car.
4 Repeat the operations on the second piston (photo).
5 Insert the cam followers (tappets) in their original positions (photo).
6 Install the pushrod tubes using new seals (photos).
7 Install the rocker oil feed pipe (photo).

38 Cylinder head - installation

1 Make sure that the cylinder head and cylinder barrel mating surfaces are absolutely clean.
2 Position a new gasket on the barrels, making sure that the word 'ALTO' is visible on the top face and then lower the cylinder head position (photos).
3 Screw on the cylinder head nuts (domed ones in the centre) and tighten to the specified torque in the sequence shown in Fig. 1.17 (photo).
4 When installing the cylinder head, make sure that the pushrod tube seals engage correctly at top and bottom ends of the tubes.
5 Release all the rocker arm adjuster screws, install the pushrods in their original fitted sequence and then install the rocker shaft assembly. Make sure that the rocker oil feed pipe engages correctly.
6 Tighten the rocker pedestal bolts to the specified torque.
7 Adjust the valve clearances, as described in Section 39, and then fit the rocker cover using a new gasket. If the carburettor has yet to be installed, do not fit the rocker cover as one of the carburettor flange bolts is difficult to tighten with the cover on.
8 If the operations described in this Section are being carried out with the engine in the car, reverse the work described in paragraphs to 11 of Section 8, but use new flange gaskets at the exhaust pipe connections to the cylinder head.

33.1 Installing the camshaft

33.3 Timing sprocket alignment marks

33.4 Timing chain and sprockets correctly located

33.6 Camshaft timing sprocket bolts and lock plates installed

33.7a Interior of timing cover

33.7b Oil pump driven dog

33.8a Installing oil filter/pulley assembly

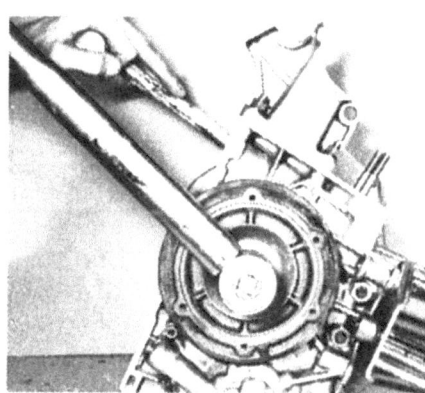

33.8b Tightening oil filter/pulley centre nut

33.9 Installing oil filter cover with 'O' ring seal

34.2 Tightening a flywheel bolt

35.2 Installing a gudgeon pin

36.1 Piston/connecting rod with shell bearings

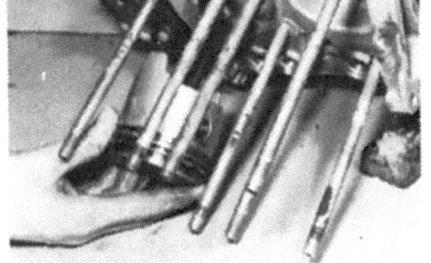

36.2 Installing a piston/connecting rod assembly

36.3a Fitting a big-end bearing cap

36.3b Tightening a big-end bearing cap nut

36.5 Installing oil pump pick-up tube

36.6 Installing the sump

37.1a Piston ring clamp in position

37.1b Cylinder barrel with base sealing gasket

37.4 Installing cylinder barrel to piston

37.5 Inserting a cam follower into crankcase

37.6a Push-rod tube bottom oil seals

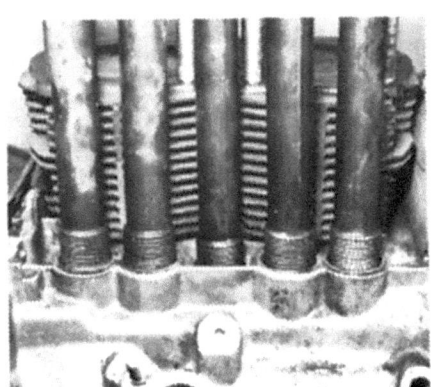

37.6b Push-rod tubes installed

37.7 Rocker oil feed pipe installed

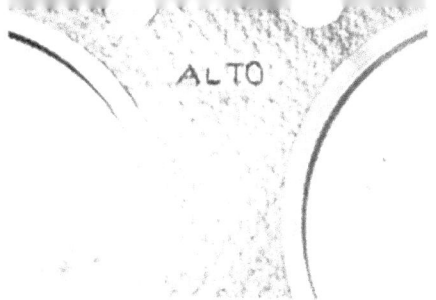
38.2a Cylinder head gasket upper surface

38.2b Installing the cylinder head

38.3 Tightening a cylinder head nut

38.5a Installing a push-rod

38.5b Installing the rocker shaft assembly

39.5 Checking and adjusting a valve clearance

Fig. 1.17. Cylinder head nut tightening sequence diagram

39 Valve clearances - adjustment

1   The valve clearances should be checked and adjusted only when the engine is cold.
2   Turn the crankshaft until one of the valves is fully open (rocker arm depressed. The crankshaft can be turned in several different ways. Always remove the spark plugs to prevent compression making the

crankshaft harder to turn. If the engine is in the car, engage top gear and push the car forward while an assistant watches the position of the rocker arms. If the engine is out of the car, grip the pulley/oil filter housing and turn it with the hands, alternatively, apply a ring spanner to one of the flywheel bolts (if the clutch has been removed) and use this. Whether the engine is in or out of the car, it is not considered advisable to turn the crankshaft by applying a spanner to one of the oil filter cover bolts as it may shear.
3   Check and adjust if necessary the clearance of the appropriate valve according to the table below:

Valve fully open	Check and adjust
No 4	No 1 (EX)
No 3	No 2 (IN)
No 2	No 3 (IN)
No 1	No 4 (EX)

4   The clearance is measured between the end of the valve stem and the rocker arm, using a feeler gauge of the appropriate thickness. The correct clearances are given in the Specifications. Note that the clearances differ between exhaust and inlet valves.
5   Where adjustment is required, slacken the rocker arm adjuster screw locknut and turn the adjuster screw until the feeler blade is a stiff sliding fit (photo). Retighten the locknut without disturbing the adjustment.
6   Rotate the crankshaft and repeat the operations on the remaining valves.

40 Engine - final reassembly before installation

1   Install the fan cooling assemblies to both sides of the engine (Chapter 2).
2   Install the exhaust silencer assembly (Chapter 3).
3   Install the generator (Chapter 10). Adjust the drivebelt (Chapter 2).
4   Install the fuel pump, carburettor and air cleaner (Chapter 3).
5   Install the distributor (Chapter 4).
6   Install the clutch mechanism (Chapter 5).

1 Mount the engine on a timber support placed under the exhaust silencer and the base of the left-hand fan cooling assembly, then position it on a trolley jack.
2 Install the engine by engaging it with the clutch bellhousing. The gearbox input shaft will only pass through the spines of the clutch driven plate hub if the driven plate has been correctly centralised, as described in Chapter 5.
3 Install the rear crossmember, making sure that the earth strap is reconnected under one of the securing nuts.
4 Reconnect the engine rear mounting.
5 Install the bellhousing to engine bolts and then withdraw the trolley jack.
6 *Working under the car* reconnect the car interior heater duct, the starter motor operating cable and electrical leads.
7 Refit the lower cover to the clutch bellhousing.
8 Refit the engine under tray and check that the sump plug is tight.
9 *Working within the engine compartment* reconnect the rear licence plate lamp leads.
10 Install the heat shield above the exhaust silencer.
11 Reconnect the trunking which supplies cooling air to the engine fan unit.
12 Reconnect the fuel pipe which runs between the fuel pump and the carburettor. On later models, reconnect the fuel return pipe.
13 Reconnect the accelerator and choke controls to the carburettor.
14 Reconnect the lead to the oil pressure switch.
15 Reconnect the LT and HT leads to the ignition coil and check that

17 Refill the engine with the correct quantity and grade of engine
18 Reconnect the battery negative lead.

42 Initial start-up after major overhaul

1 Check the engine compartment for tools and rags which have no been removed.
2 If a number of new engine internal components have been instal then the idling speed screw should be turned so that the engine will have a slightly increased slow-running speed to offset the stiffness o the new parts.
3 Start the engine and check for oil or exhaust gas leaks.
4 The car should now be run to normal operating temperature and the carburettor and ignition settings checked as described in Chapte and 4, respectively.
5 Treat the engine as a new unit for the first few hundred miles until the new components have run in.
6 After the first 1,000 miles (1,600 km) check the torque wrench setting of the cylinder head nuts. Do this by slackening the first nut the recommended sequence (Fig. 1.17) through a quarter of a turn, then tightening it to the specified torque. Repeat on the remaining in sequence. Check and adjust the valve clearances while the engine cold. Renew the engine oil at approximately the same mileage while the engine is hot.

43 Fault diagnosis - engine

Symptom	Reason/s
Engine will not turn over when starter switch is operated	Flat battery. Bad battery connections. Bad connections at starter motor. Starter motor jammed. Starter motor defective.
Engine turns over normally but fails to start	No spark at plugs. No fuel reaching engine. Too much fuel reaching the engine (flooding)
Engine starts but runs unevenly and misfires	Ignition and/or fuel system faults. Incorrect valve clearances. Burnt out valves. Worn out piston rings.
Lack of power	Ignition and/or fuel system faults. Incorrect valve clearances. Burnt out valves. Worn out piston rings.
Excessive oil consumption	Oil leaks from crankshaft rear oil seal, timing cover gasket and oil seal, rocker cover gasket, oil filter gasket, sump gasket, sump plug washer. Worn piston rings or cylinder bores resulting in oil being burnt by engine. Worn valve guides and/or defective inlet valve stem seals.
Excessive mechanical noise from engine	Wrong valve to rocker clearances. Worn crankshaft bearings. Worn cylinder (piston slap). Slack or worn timing chain and sprockets.

Note: When investigating starting and uneven running faults do not be tempted into snap diagnosis. Start from the beginning of the check procedure and follow it through. It will take less time in the long run. Poor performance from an engine in terms of power and economy is not normally diagnosed quickly. In any event the ignition and fuel systems must be checked first before assuming any further investigation needs to be made.

Chapter 2 Cooling and heating systems

For modifications, and information applicable to later models, see Supplement at end of manual

Contents

Specifications

System type	Air cooling by belt driven fan and engine outer casings. Interior heating by exhausted air from engine cooling system.
Drivebelt tension	¼ to ½ in (6.35 to 12.7 mm) deflection at centre of top run of belt.

Torque wrench settings	lb f ft	Nm
Fan to dynamo shaft nut	25	35
Dynamo pulley nuts	25	35

1 General description

1 The engine is cooled by ample finning and forced draught generated by a fan driven from the end of the dynamo armature shaft.
2 When the engine is running, air is drawn in through two grilles located one on each side of the engine compartment and pressurised by the fan which is enclosed in a casing which in turn is attached to the engine (Fig. 2.1 and photo).
3 The air having cooled the engine and absorbed some of its heat, then passes out from the casing on the opposite side of the engine.
4 The volume of air expelled is restricted by a flap valve which is connected to a thermostat. This arrangement maintains the engine operating temperature at its most efficient level by continuously adjusting the speed of airflow over the engine.
5 Warm air being discharged from the engine cooling casing is utilised for warming the interior of the car (Fig. 2.2).
6 Warm air for the car interior is fed through a duct which has outlets also at the base of the windscreen for demisting and defrosting purposes. This duct is used to distribute and blend fresh air which is drawn in from a front mounted intake. This fresh air can be used as a fresh air ventilation system independently of the heater.
7 Stale air from the car interior is exhausted through grilles on the body pillars against which the doors close.

2 Heating and ventilation controls - operation

1 The main control for the admission of heated air to the car interior is located on the centre floor tunnel within the rear passenger compartment.
2 Looking down on this lever, moving it fully clockwise opens the warm air inlet valve fully while turning it anticlockwise closes it.
3 Immediately below the centre of the fascia panel is the air distribution and control panel. The operation of these controls is described in the caption to Fig. 2.3.

3 Fan cooling casings - removal, dismantling and installation

1 Release the spring clips on the air cleaner cover and remove the connecting pipes which run between the air cleaner and the intake manifold.
2 Remove the cover from the air cleaner and extract the air cleaner element.
3 Disconnect the accelerator cable swivel from the bracket on the cooling housing upper panel. This is achieved by extracting the circlip from the base of the swivel.

1.2 Engine cooling air intake grille

Fig. 2.1. Diagram of engine cooling air circulation

1	Air inlet grilles	3	Air cleaner element	5	Fan	7	Warm air outlet thermos...
2	Air inlet ducting	4	Fan cooling casing	6	Car interior heater hose connection		and baffle valve

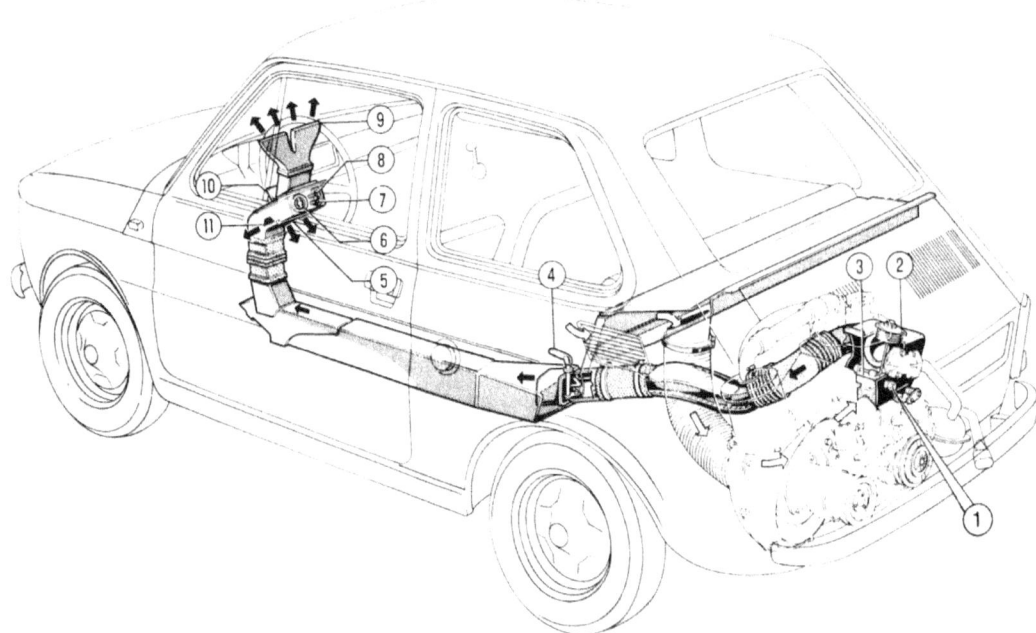

Fig. 2.2. Car interior heating and ventilation system diagram

1	Hollow bolt for gasket blow safety device	4	Main heater warm air inlet valve	9	Demister outlets
2	Warm air outlet thermostat	5	Centre air outlet	10	Fresh air intake (for heater/ventilator)
3	Warm air outlet baffle	6	Upper vents	11	Side air outlet
		7	Air distribution control		
		8	Fresh air control		

it (photo).

6 Unbolt and remove the front flange of the pulley on the dynamo. Retain any shims carefully and detach the drivebelt (photo).

7 Disconnect the leads from the dynamo terminals.

8 Unscrew the mounting strap bolt at the base of the dynamo, pull out the upper strap pin. Note the earth strap located under the strap bolt (photo).

9 Extract the bolts which hold the fan cooling casing to the engine and remove the casing complete with dynamo. Release the air inlet duct from the back of the casing as it is withdrawn (photo), also the outlet duct for the car interior heater (photo).

10 The dynamo can now be removed from the fan cooling casing if required by first unscrewing the nut which secures the fan to the end of the dynamo armature shaft and then unscrewing the two nuts which secure the dynamo mounting flange to the fan cooling casing (photos). Take care as the dynamo is withdrawn, not to lose the small Woodruff key which secures the fan to the dynamo shaft (Fig. 2.4). Withdraw the pulley shield.

11 To extract the fan, split the fan cooling casing by unscrewing the bolts which secure both halves of the casing together (photos).

12 The section of the cooling casing which contains the air temperature regulating thermostat and baffle valve can be removed from the opposite side of the engine simply by unscrewing the securing bolts (photo).

13 An essential part of the air cooling arrangement is the air passage assembly on the base of the sump. Always take great care to spread the load by using a thick piece of wood when jacking up the engine under the sump (Fig. 2.5).

14 If the fan cooling casing was removed complete with dynamo and the dynamo has not been detached, it can be installed in the same way, making sure that the plastic locating dowel peg at the base of the dynamo engages correctly in the hole in the dynamo support cradle of the engine crankcase and that the pulley shield is refitted (photo).

15 If the dynamo has been detached from the fan casing after removal, it is recommended that the casing is refitted first, without the dynamo.

16 In either event, make sure that the hollow bolts which are located at the top of both the left-hand and right-hand cooling casings are correctly positioned for the reason described in Chapter 1, Section 10.

17 Refit and adjust the drivebelt, as described in Section 5.

18 When refitting the air cleaner element, make sure that the open end of the element is uppermost.

Fig. 2.4. Method of holding dynamo pulley while unscrewing fan securing nut

| 1 | Pulley | 3 | Fan to dynamo armature shaft nut (exposed after disconnecting air inlet ducting) |
| 2 | Tool | 4 | Fan |

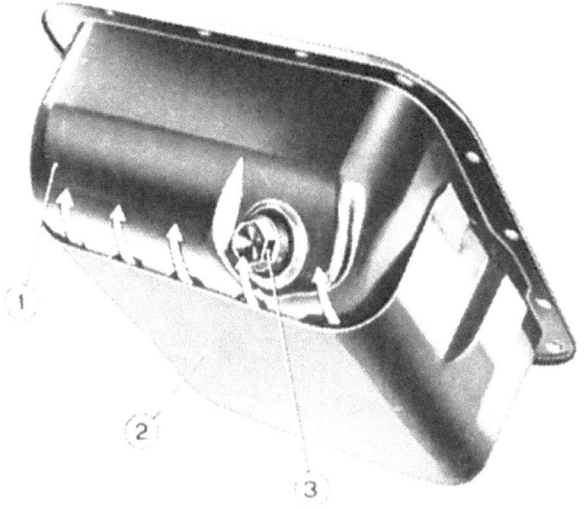

Fig. 2.5. Engine sump cooling air passages

1 Sump   2 Air deflector casing   3 Drain plug

4 Cooling air thermostat - testing and renewal

1 Any fault developing in the thermostat or baffle valve which are located in the cooling casing on the right-hand side of the engine may cause overheating or conversely cool running. Either condition will adversely affect engine performance and fuel economy (photo).

2 Where these symptoms occur, remove the right-hand cooling casing, as described in the preceding Section.

3 To test the operation of the thermostat, immerse it in hot water or hot air at specified temperature levels. If the thermostat is in good condition and the baffle valve and linkage are not seized or broken, operation should be in line with the following temperature ranges:

Valve begins to open   154 to 163°F (68 to 73°C)
Valve fully open   188 to 199°F (87 to 93°C)

4 If the components are found to be faulty as a result of the test, the thermostat can be removed after bending down the tab of the lockplate, and unscrewing the retaining nut and disconnecting the relay linkage.

5 The baffle valve assembly can be removed after extracting the two securing screws.

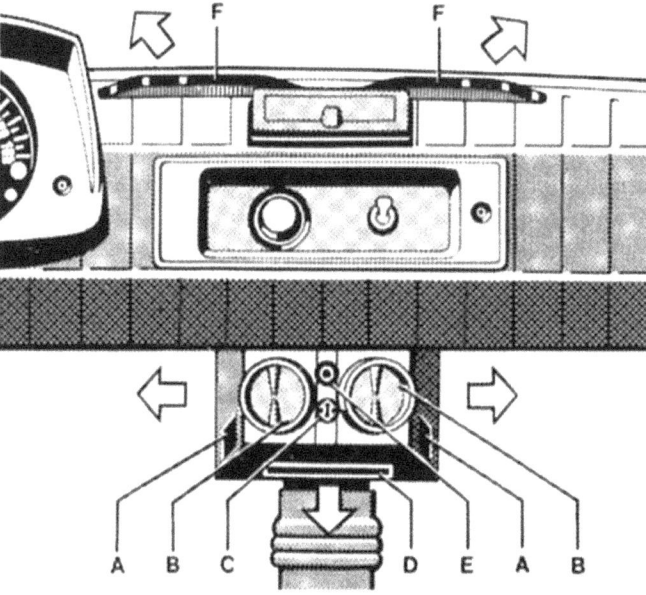

Fig. 2.3. Heating and ventilation controls

A Side outlets
B Upper swivel vents
C Air distribution control (IN to demister outlets F, OUT to all outlets)
D Centre outlet
E Fresh air control (IN closed OUT open)

3.5 Removing top cover from fan cooling casing

3.6 Fan pulley adjustment shims

3.8 Dynamo mounting strap bolt and earth strap

3.9a Engine cooling air inlet duct

3.9b Car interior heater duct from engine cooling casing

3.10a Dynamo flange mounting nuts

3.10b Fan to dynamo shaft securing nut

3.10c Removing dynamo from fan cooling casing

3.11a Fan cooling casing joint bolts

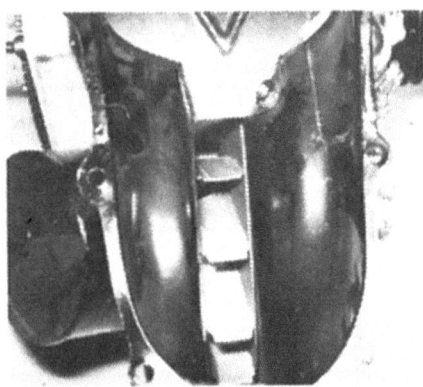

3.11b Fan viewed from above with top cover removed

3.12 Removing the right-hand engine cooling casing

3.14 Dynamo plastic locating dowel peg

4.1 Fan cooling casing thermostat and link rod

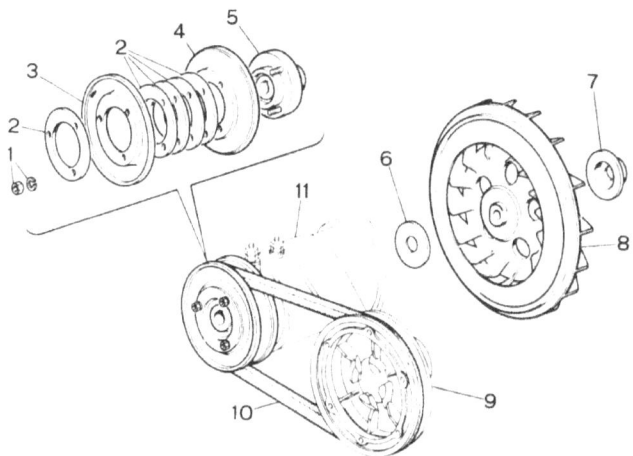

Fig. 2.6. Fan and dynamo pulley components

1	Nut and spring washer	8	Engine cooling fan
2	Adjustment shims	9	Drive pulley (part of
3	Pulley front flange		centrifugal oil filter)
4	Pulley rear flange	10	Drive belt
5	Pulley mounting hub	11	Dynamo
6	Plain washer		
7	Spacer		

5 Fan/dynamo drivebelt - adjustment or renewal

1 Adjustment or renewal of the drivebelt is carried out by altering the effective width of the dynamo pulley groove by the extraction or insertion of shims (Fig. 2.6).

2 The correct tension of the drivebelt is between ¼ and ½ in (6.35 and 12.7 mm) when the centre of the upper run of the belt is depressed with the thumb (Fig. 2.7).

3 To fit a new belt or to adjust the tension, unbolt the front flange of the dynamo pulley.

4 Extract or add shims as necessary and then locate the drivebelt, fit the pulley flange and secure it with the three nuts.

5 If shims have been extracted, keep them for future use by inserting them under the securing nuts on the front flange of the pulley.

6 On cars built after November 1974, the components of the fan assembly have been slightly modified as shown (Fig. 2.7A).

6 Heating and ventilation system - dismantling and reassembly

1 The hot air duct can be removed from the interior of the car after first withdrawing the floor covering.

3 To remove the air blending and distribution unit, which is located under the fascia panel, unscrew the securing nuts and lift it from its location (Fig. 2.10).

4 Once the air blending and distribution unit has been removed, the demister outlets can be extracted from within the rear of the luggage compartment (Fig. 2.11).

5 The main heater control and cover plate can be unbolted from the floor in the rear passenger compartment (Fig. 2.12).

6 Reassembly is a reversal of dismantling but make sure that any foam plastic jointing strips are refitted (or renewed if deformed) and any sealing mastic is renewed where originally found.

7 Periodically inspect the condition and security of the convoluted connecting trunking (Fig. 2.13).

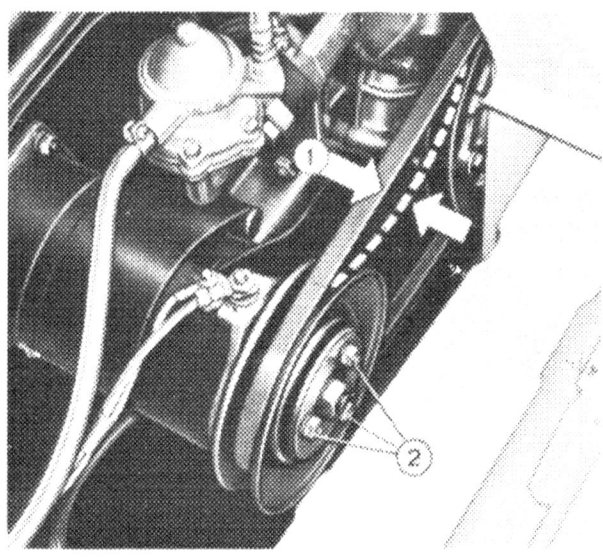

Fig. 2.7. Fan/dynamo drivebelt tension diagram

1 Deflection   2 Pulley flange nuts

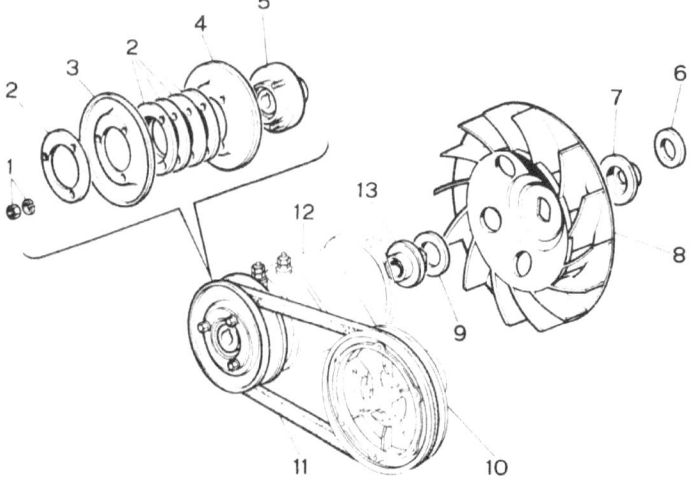

Fig. 2.7A. Fan assembly (Nov. 1974 on)

Keys 1 to 8 as in Fig. 2.6.

9	Washer	12	Dynamo
10	Pulley	13	Hub
11	Belt		

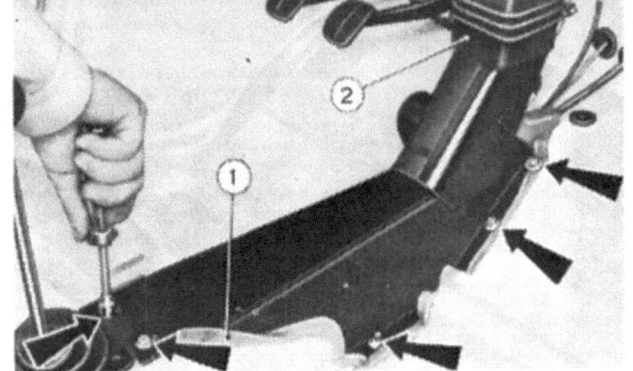

Fig. 2.8. Heater duct attachment nuts (arrowed)

1 Plastic foam jointing   2 Flexible connector

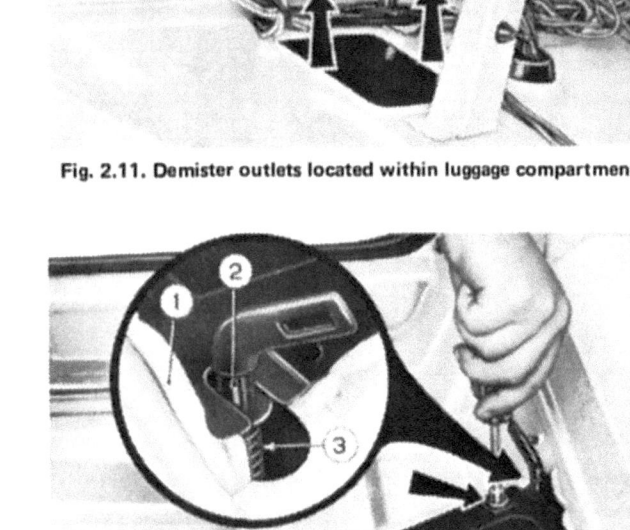

Fig. 2.11. Demister outlets located within luggage compartment

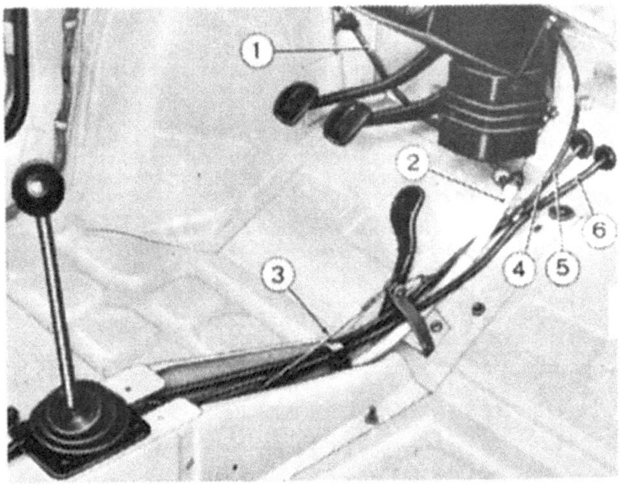

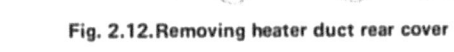

Fig. 2.9. Controls and pipe lines exposed after removal of heater duct

1 Speedometer cable   4 Hand throttle cable
2 Clutch operating cable   5 Rear brake hydraulic line
3 Accelerator cable   6 Positive lead from battery

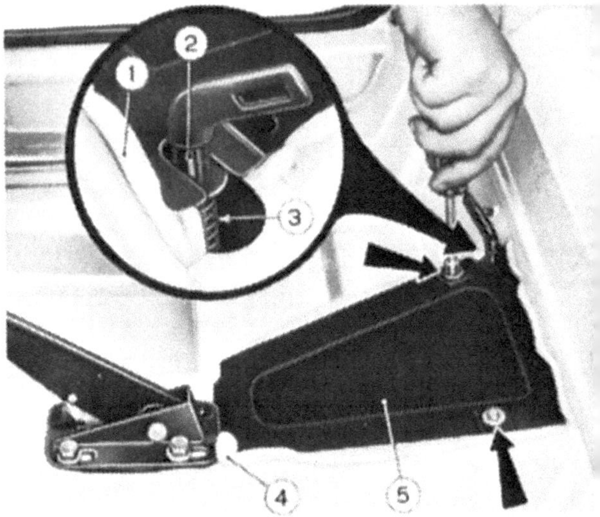

Fig. 2.12. Removing heater duct rear cover

1 Plastic foam gasket   4 Plastic foam gasket
2 Air flow control lever   5 Rear cover
3 Spring

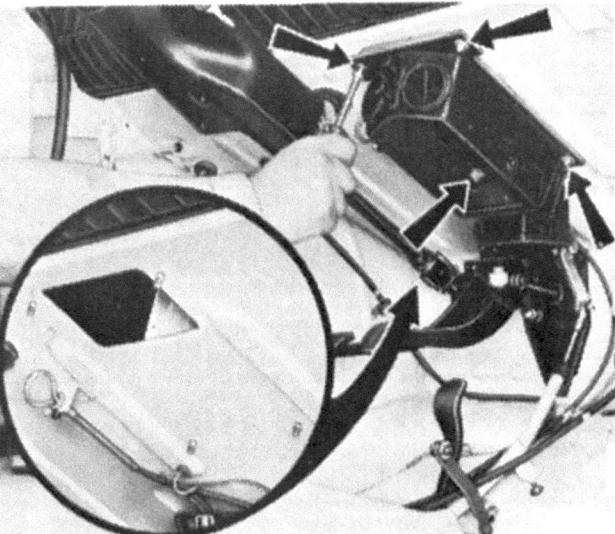

Fig. 2.10. Removing air blending and distribution unit. Inset hand
throttle control

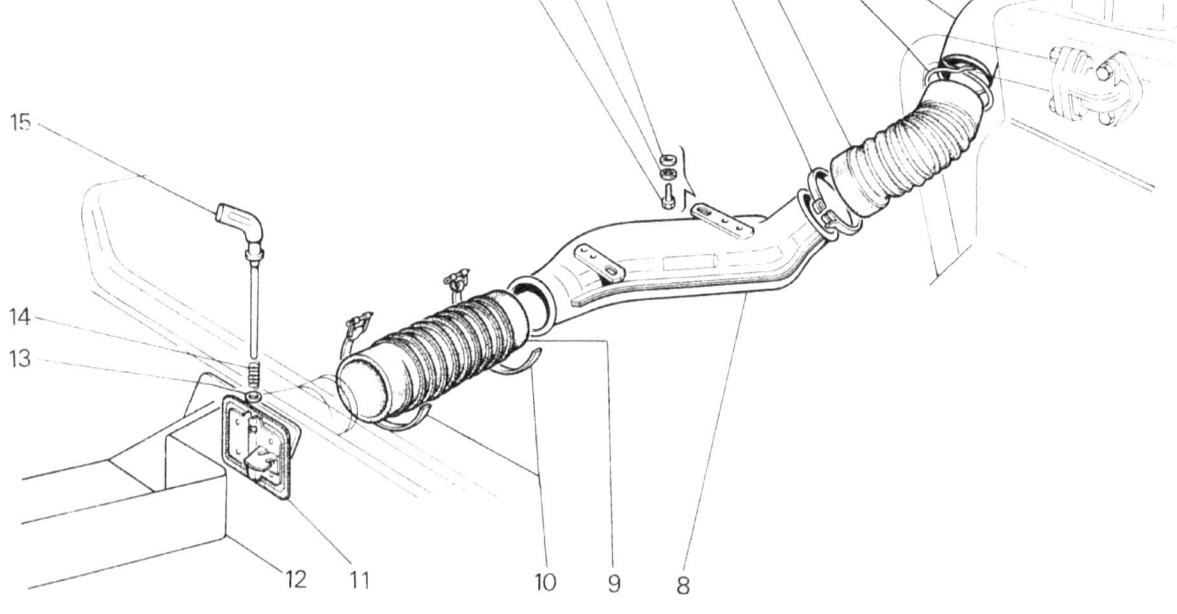

Fig. 2.13. Warm air intake duct components

1	Mounting screw	5	Rear trunking	9	Front trunking	13	Washer
2	Spring washer	6	Clip	10	Plastic hose clip	14	Spring
3	Plain washer	7	Warm air intake nozzle	11	Flap valve	15	Control lever
4	Plastic hose clip	8	Centre duct	12	Floor duct		

7   Fault diagnosis - cooling and heating systems

Symptoms	Reason/s
Engine overheats	Faulty air outlet thermostat. Seized air outlet baffle valve. Lack of engine oil. Broken fan drivebelt. Slipping fan drivebelt. Split or disconnected air inlet trunking to cooling casing.
Engine running cool	Faulty air outlet thermostat. Faulty air outlet baffle valve.
Oil or exhaust fumes evident in car	Blown cylinder head gasket.
Heater ineffective	Disconnected or split connecting trunking. Slipping or broken fan drivebelt. Faulty air outlet thermostat. Seized main heated air inlet valve.

Chapter 3 Carburation, fuel and exhaust systems

For modifications, and information applicable to later models, see Supplement at end of manual

Contents

Specifications

System type	Rear mounted fuel tank, mechanically operated fuel pump, single barrel downdraught carburettor
Fuel pump capacity	5.5 Imp. gal/hr (6.6 US gal/hr/25 litres/hr)

Carburettor

Type:	
Up to November 1974	Weber 28 IMB 3
After November 1974	Weber 28 IMB 1
Throat diameter	1.102 in (28 mm)
Primary venturi diameter	0.905 in (23 mm)
Auxiliary venturi diameter	0.157 in (4 mm)
Main jet	0.049 in (1.25 mm)
Idling jet	0.018 in (0.45 mm)
Starting jet (F5)	0.035 in (0.90 mm)
Air correction jet:	
Up to 1974	0.085 in (2.15 mm)
After 1974	0.088 in (2.25 mm)
Fuel inlet needle valve	0.049 in (1.25 mm)
Emulsion tube	F8
Idling air orifice	0.079 in (2.00 mm)
Fuel octane rating	91 RON (two-star)
Fuel tank capacity	4.6 Imp. gals (5.5 US gals/21 litres)

Torque wrench settings	lb f ft	Nm
Carburettor mounting nuts	20	28
Fuel pump mounting nuts	20	28
Exhaust manifold elbow bolts	25	35

1 General description

1 The fuel system comprises a rear mounted fuel tank, a mechanically-operated fuel pump, a Weber carburettor and a paper element type air cleaner.
2 Devices to reduce emission of fumes are minimal and consist of the crankcase ventilation system (see Chapter 1, Section 16), a return fuel line from the carburettor and the design of the carburettor which it is anticipated will reduce the CO emission level from the exhaust system when the engine is idling.

2 Air cleaner - servicing

1 At the intervals specified in 'Routine Maintenance', open the lid of the engine compartment and unclip the lid of the air cleaner (photo).

2 Move the lid and connecting pipes to one side and extract the paper type filter element and discard it (Fig. 3.1).
3 Wipe out the air cleaner body and check the condition of the connecting hoses.
4 Install a new filter element making sure that its open end is uppermost.
5 Refit the lid and engage the securing clips.

3 Fuel pump - description, maintenance and testing

1 The fuel pump is of flexible diaphragm type and is located on the left-hand side of the engine crankcase (photo).
2 The pump is actuated by a long pushrod from an eccentric on the camshaft which is located on the opposite side of the engine.
3 At the intervals specified in 'Routine Maintenance', unbolt and remove the cover from the fuel pump.

6 Reassemble the components but do not overtighten the cover bolt.

7 If, due to lack of fuel at the carburettor, the fuel pump is believed to be at fault, disconnect the fuel feed pipe from the carburettor and place its' open end in a suitable container.

8 Disconnect the LT lead from the negative terminal of the coil to prevent the engine firing and then spin the engine on the starter. A well defined series of spurts of fuel should be ejected into the container. If this happens, reconnect the fuel line and investigate the fuel inlet valve of the carburettor as the cause of the fuel stoppage. If on the other hand no fuel is ejected from the pipe and some is known to be in the fuel tank, remove the pump for overhaul.

---

4 Fuel pump - removal and overhaul

1 Disconnect the fuel inlet pipe from the fuel pump and plug the pipe.

2 Disconnect the fuel feed pipe which runs to the carburettor from

4 If required, the operating rod can be withdrawn by gripping its end with a pair of pliers (photo).

5 Unbolt and remove the cover.

6 Scribe a line across the edges of the upper and lower body flanges as a guide to reassembly and then unscrew the flange screws and lift the upper body from the lower body.

7 Disconnect the diaphragm/rod assembly from the rocker arm and lift it away.

8 Remove the spacer and springs.

9 Obtain a repair kit which will contain a new flexible diaphragm assembly and the other necessary renewable items.

10 If the inlet and outlet valves are faulty then the complete pump upper body will have to be renewed as the valves cannot be renewed on their own.

11 Reassembly is a reversal of dismantling, but tighten the flange screws evenly in diagonally opposite sequence and only fully tighten them while the rocker arm is held fully depressed towards the pump body.

2.1 Air cleaner components

3.1 Location of fuel pump

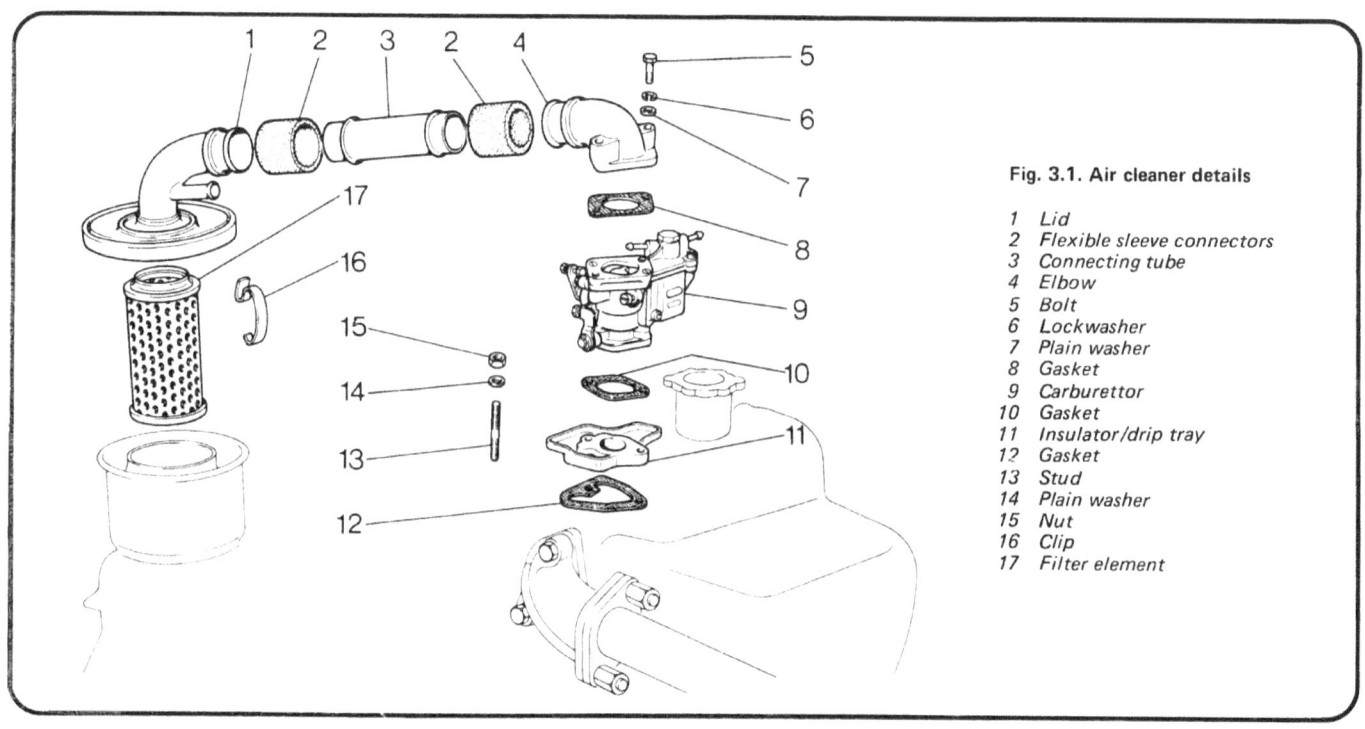

Fig. 3.1. Air cleaner details

1 Lid
2 Flexible sleeve connectors
3 Connecting tube
4 Elbow
5 Bolt
6 Lockwasher
7 Plain washer
8 Gasket
9 Carburettor
10 Gasket
11 Insulator/drip tray
12 Gasket
13 Stud
14 Plain washer
15 Nut
16 Clip
17 Filter element

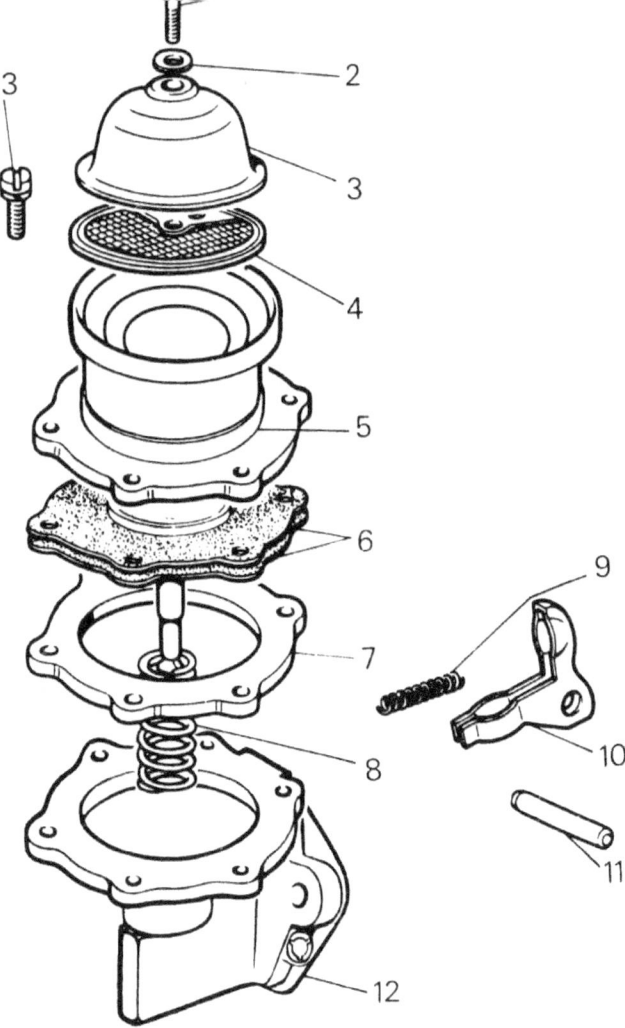

Fig. 3.2. Exploded view of the fuel pump

1	Cover bolt	8	Diaphragm spring
2	Plain washer	9	Rocker arm spring
3	Cover	10	Rocker arm
4	Filter	11	Pivot pin
5	Upper body	12	Lower body
6	Diaphragm	13	Screw
7	Spacer		

5 Fuel pump · refitting

1   To refit the pump, place a gasket (0.027 in /0.7 mm thick) against the crankcase and then install the insulator followed by the second gasket (0.012 in/0.03 mm thick).

2   Insert the pushrod and then turn the crankshaft to the point where the rod is just about to start riding up the eccentric cam of the camshaft. This can be determined by feeling or watching the pushrod just when it starts to move outwards.

3   Now measure the projection of the rod above the outer gasket. This should be between 0.039 and 0.059 in (1 and 1.5 mm) when measured with a feeler blade (Fig. 3.3).

4   If necessary change the inner gasket for one of a different thickness. Gaskets are available in thicknesses of 0.012, 0.027 and 0.047 in (0.3, 0.7 and 1.2 mm).

5   Install the fuel pump, tighten the flange nuts and reconnect the fuel pipes.

mounted into the floor pan and projects below the car.

2   To remove the tank, lift out the rear seat, disconnect the leads from the tank sender unit.

3   Disconnect the fuel filler pipe from the tank, also the vent pipe and the fuel feed and return lines.

4   Jack up and securely support the car. Unbolt the tank and remo[ve] from under the car.

5   The sealing mastic may have to be cut away before the tank can [be] released from its mounting flange.

6   If the tank is contaminated with water or sediment, remove the tank sender unit and shake the tank vigorously using two or three changes of paraffin and a final rinse with clean petrol.

7   If there is a leak in the tank, do not be tempted to solder it: either have it professionally repaired, or obtain a new tank.

8   Installation of the tank is a reversal of removal, but check the security of the seal of the tank sender unit and make good the seali[ng] mastic round the tank flange to prevent entry of water.

7 Carburettor and controls · description

1   The carburettor is a single barrel downdraught Weber 28 IMB u[nit] (Fig. 3.4).

2   A manually operated choke is fitted which gives progressive operation as the engine warms up. The choke control lever is locate[d] on the floor tunnel to the left of the matching starter control lever (photo).

3   A hand throttle is located under the instrument panel.

4   The accelerator linkage is by means of a cable to a lever which i[s] pivotted on the upper surface of the engine cooling casing and from the lever to the carburettor throttle valve through a short link rod (photo).

8 Carburettor · slow-running adjustment

1   Run the car until the engine is at normal operating temperature

2   Make sure that the ignition settings are correct.

3   Adjust the throttle speed screw until the engine is running at an acceptable idling speed without being set too slow so that the engi[ne] hesitates or 'rocks' violently.

4   Now turn the mixture control screw in, or out, until the engine idles at its smoothest. Now re-adjust the throttle speed screw if the[n] idling speed has increased as a result of adjusting the mixture contr[ol] screw.

9 Carburettor · removal and refitting

1   Prise off the clips which secure the lid of the air cleaner body.

2   Move the lid and hose assembly to one side and disconnect the flexible connector from the intake elbow on the top of the carbure[ttor.]

3   Disconnect the fume extraction hose from the top of the rocke[r] box cover.

4   Disconnect the choke inner cable from the lever on the side of [the] carburettor and then detach the outer conduit from its support bracket (photo).

5   Release the spring connecting clip and disconnect the throttle operating link rod from the throttle control lever on the carburetto[r.]

6   Disconnect the fuel feed and return pipes from their nozzles on the carburettor (photo).

7   Unscrew and remove the mounting nuts and washers from the flange mounting studs and lift the carburettor from the insulator/d[rip] tray. One of the mounting nuts is very inaccessible and in the absen[ce] of a special spanner it is recommended that the rocker cover is removed to provide more clearance (photo).

8   With the carburettor removed, detach the gasket, the drip tray a[nd] the second gasket, in that order.

9   Refitting is a reversal of removal but it is recommended that ne[w] flange gaskets are used, between the drip tray/insulator and the manifold and the carburettor mounting flange (photo).

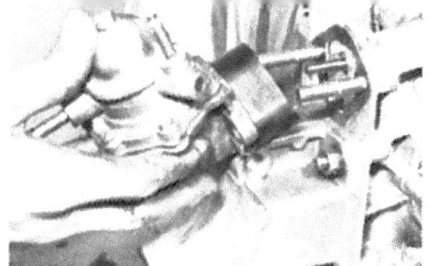
4.3 Removing fuel pump

4.4 Withdrawing fuel pump operating rod

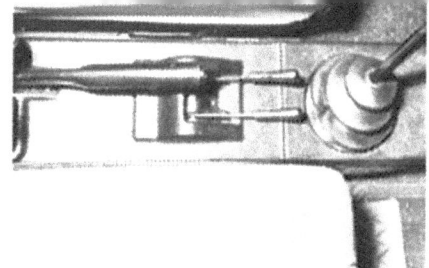
7.2 Choke (left) and starter (right) control levers

7.4a Accelerator control pivot and link

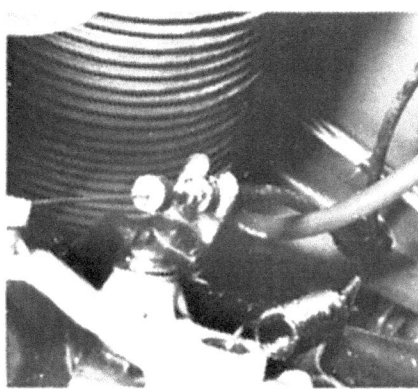
7.4b Accelerator cable conduit bracket

9.4 Choke cable connection to carburettor

9.6 Carburettor showing fuel inlet pipe and return nozzle

9.7 Removing a carburettor flange nut

9.9 Carburettor mounting and insulator/drip tray gaskets

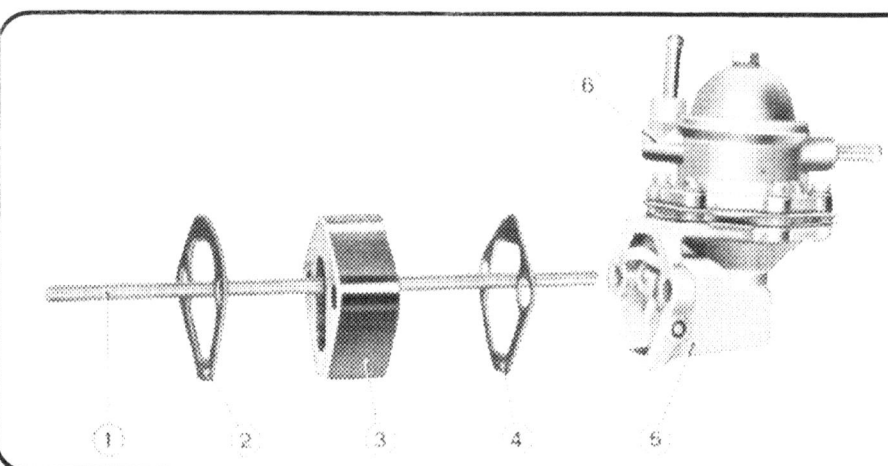

Fig. 3.3. Fuel pump installation details

1 Operating rod
2 Gasket (variable thickness)
3 Insulator
4 Gasket (standard thickness)
5 Fuel pump lower body
6 Fuel pump upper body

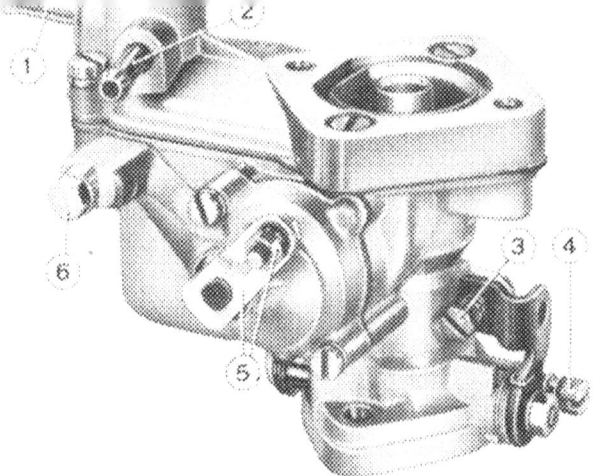

Fig. 3.4. Carburettor details

1 Fuel return line connection
2 Fuel inlet line connection
3 Throttle speed screw
4 Mixture control screw
5 Choke operating lever and inner cable clamp
6 Choke cable conduit clamp

installed to the engine) is to apply a few drops of oil to the choke a throttle control pivots and to clean the filter screen at the specified intervals.

2   To clean the filter screen, unscrew the large bolt on the top cove of the carburettor and lift it out together with the filter. Wash the filter gauze in clean fuel and refit it, making sure that the sealing washer under the bolt is in good condition (photo).

3   More extensive dismantling should be carried out in the followir way if worn components are to be renewed.

4   With the carburettor removed from the engine, as described in th preceding Section, clean away all external dirt.

5   Unbolt and remove the air cleaner connecting elbow and its gask

6   Extract the screws which secure the top cover to the main carburettor body (photo).

7   Lift the top cover complete with float assembly from the carburettor body (photo).

8   The float can be detached from the top cover by extracting the pivot pin. Invert the top cover before removing the float otherwise ` fuel inlet needle valve will drop out of its seat (photos).

9   Extract the needle valve and, if necessary, unscrew the needle va seat using a close-fitting ring spanner.

10 The individual jets can be unscrewed from their seats and are located as shown (Fig. 3.5).

11 The choke cover can be detached after unscrewing the retaining screws (Fig. 3.6).

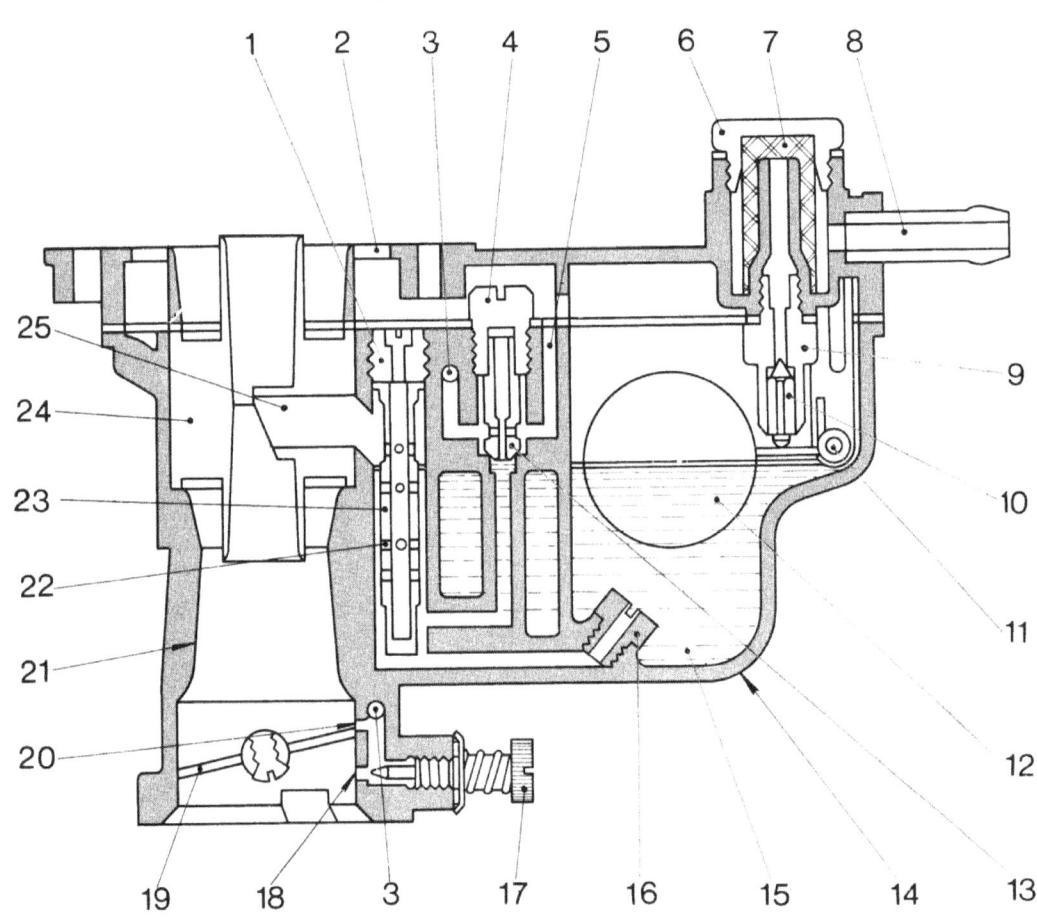

Fig. 3.5. Sectional view of the carburettor

1 Air correction jet
2 Air inlet
3 Idle mixture passage
4 Idle jet holder
5 Idle air orifice
6 Filter bolt
7 Filter gauge
8 Fuel inlet
9 Fuel inlet needle valve seat
10 Needle valve
11 Float pivot pin
12 Float
13 Idle jet
14 Main body
15 Fuel bowl
16 Main jet
17 Idle mixture screw
18 Idle orifice
19 Throttle butterfly valve plate
20 Transfer orifice
21 Primary venturi
22 Emulsion orifices
23 Emulsion tube
24 Axuliary venturi
25 Nozzle

13 With the carburettor dismantled, clean out the float chamber. Clean all the jets by blowing through them with air from a tyre pump. Never probe them with wire or their calibration will be upset. It is worthwhile checking the jet sizes with those given in the Specifications in case a previous owner has substituted any of incorrect size.

14 Obtain a repair kit which will contain all the necessary gaskets and other items which must be renewed.

15 Reassemble by installing the jets. Tighten them securely using close fitting screwdriver blades of correct width and thickness to suit the slots in the jets.

16 Make sure that the washer is included under the fuel inlet seat before tightening it firmly. Do not overtighten it, but make sure that it grips the washer and 'bites' otherwise fuel will bypass the needle valve and cause flooding from the fuel bowl.

17 Once the float and needle valve have been reassembled, check the float level. To do this, place a new gasket on the top cover mating flange and then hold the top cover vertically so that the weight of the float and arm rests on the needle valve. The distance 'A' between the lowest point of the float and the surface of the gasket should be 0.315 in (8 mm) (Fig. 3.7).

18 Now move the float gently outward until it stops and again measure the distance 'B' which should be 0.630 in (16 mm) thus providing a float travel of 0.315 in (8 mm). After November 1974, the distance 'A' has been reduced to 0.275 in (7 mm).

19 Any adjustment required to alter the float setting should be carried out by bending the tongue or lug on the float arm.

20 Before installing the top cover, pour a little fuel into the float chamber. This will make starting easier once the carburettor is refitted to the engine, but remember to keep the carburettor in an upright attitude until it is installed.

21 Refit the remaining components by reversing the dismantling operations.

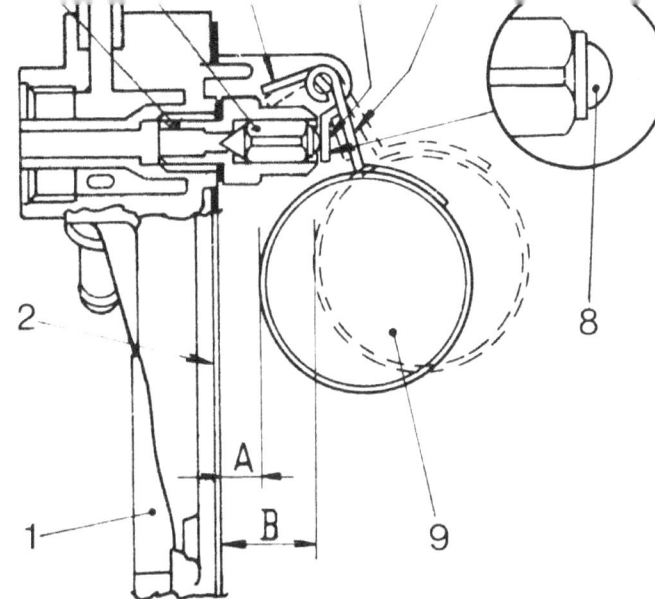

Fig. 3.7. Float adjustment diagram

1 Carburettor top cover   6 Float arm tongue
2 Cover gasket   7 Float arm
3 Needle valve seat   8 Needle valve
4 Needle valve   9 Float
5 Float arm lug
For values of A and B - see text.

11 Manifolds and exhaust system - general

1 The inlet manifold is an integral part of the cylinder head to which the insulator/drip tray and the carburettor are bolted.

2 The exhaust manifolds comprise two cast-iron elbows bolted to the cylinder head (photo).

3 The exhaust system is an integral assembly comprising downpipes, silencer and tailpipe and is renewable as such (photo).

4 When fitting the exhaust flanges to the cylinder head, note the thin washers used to seal the joints.

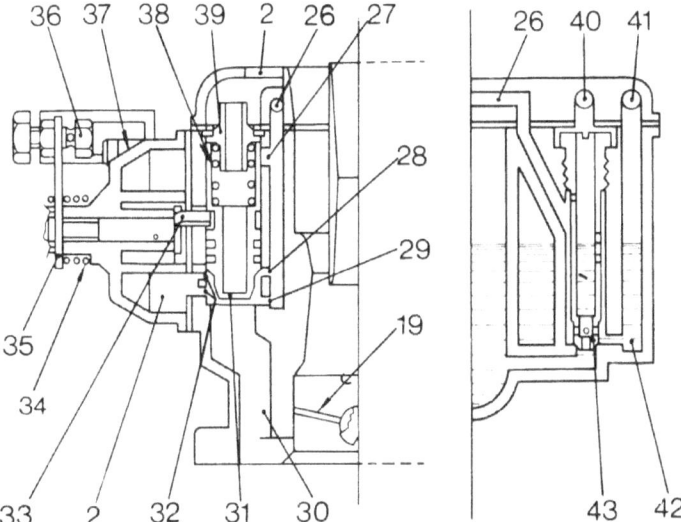

Fig. 3.6. Sectional views of choke mechanism

 2 Air inlet
19 Throttle valve plate
26 Mixture passage
27 Mixture weakening air passage
28 Mixture orifices
29 Mixture orifices
30 Mixture passage
31 Choke valve
32 Air orifices
33 Rocker
34 Lever return spring
35 Choke control lever
36 Cable clamp screw
37 Cable conduit clamp
38 Valve spring
39 Spring retainer and guide
40 Starter jet emulsion air orifice
41 Reserve well emulsion air orifice
42 Reserve well
43 Starter jet

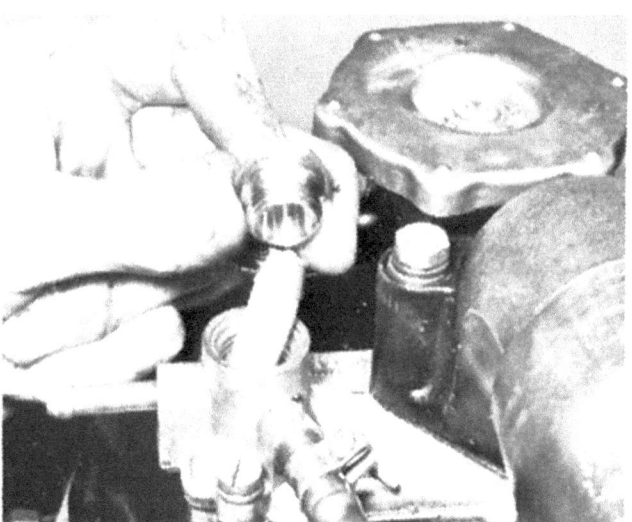

10.2 Extracting carburettor fuel filter

10.6 Removing a top cover screw from carburettor

10.7 Removing carburettor top cover

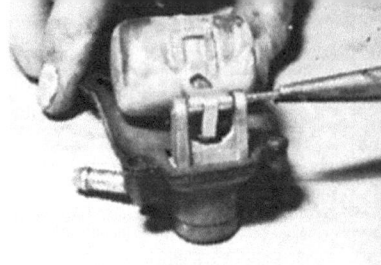

10.8a Extracting float pivot

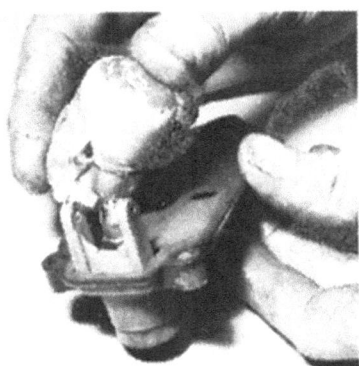

10.8b Removing carburettor float to expose fuel inlet valve

11.2 Exhaust manifold and gasket (one side)

11.3 The exhaust system

12 Fault diagnosis - carburation; fuel and exhaust systems

Symptom	Reason/s
Excessive fuel consumption	Air filter choked.
	Leakage from pump, carburettor or fuel lines or fuel tank.
	Float chamber flooding.
	Distributor capacitor faulty.
	Distributor weights faulty.
	Mixture too rich.
	Contact breaker gap too wide.
	Incorrect valve clearances.
	Incorrect spark plug gaps.
	Tyres under inflated.
	Dragging brakes.
Fuel starvation or mixture weakness	Clogged fuel filter in pump or carburettor.
	Float chamber needle valve clogged.
	Faulty fuel pump valves.
	Fuel pump diaphragm split.
	Fuel pipe unions loose.
	Fuel pump cover leaking.
	Inlet manifold gasket or carburettor flange gasket leaking.
	Incorrect adjustment of carburettor.

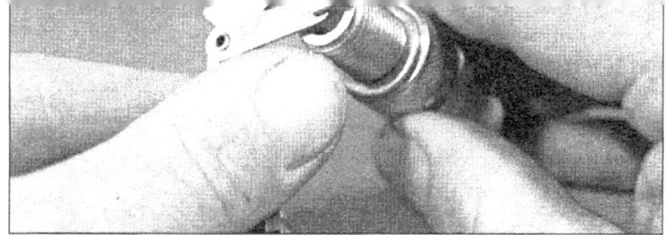

Measuring plug gap. A feeler gauge of the correct size (see ignition system specifications) should have a slight "drag" when slid between the electrodes. Adjust gap if necessary

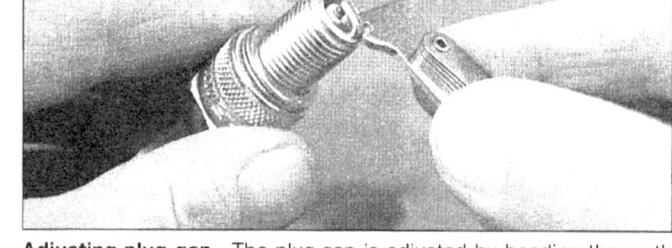

Adjusting plug gap. The plug gap is adjusted by bending the earth electrode inwards, or outwards, as necessary until the correct clearance is obtained. Note the use of the correct tool

Normal. Grey-brown deposits, lightly coated core nose. Gap increasing by around 0.001 in (0.025 mm) per 1000 miles (1600 km). Plugs ideally suited to engine, and engine in good condition

Carbon fouling. Dry, black, sooty deposits. Will cause weak spark and eventually misfire. Fault: over-rich fuel mixture. Check:carburettor mixture settings, float level and jet sizes; choke operation and cleanliness of air filter. Plugs can be re-used after cleaning

Oil fouling. Wet, oily deposits. Will cause weak spark and eventually misfire. Fault: worn bores/piston rings or valve guides; sometimes occurs (temporarily) during running-in period. Plugs can be re-used after thorough cleaning

Overheating. Electrodes have glazed appearance, core nose very white - few deposits. Fault: plug overheating. Check: plug value, ignition timing, fuel octane rating (too low) and fuel mixture (too weak). Discard plugs and cure fault immediately

Electrode damage. Electrodes burned away; core nose has burned, glazed appearance. Fault: pre-ignition. Check: as for "Overheating" but may be more severe. Discard plugs and remedy fault before piston or valve damage occurs

Split core nose (may appear initially as a crack). Damage is self-evident, but cracks will only show after cleaning. Fault: pre-ignition or wrong gap-setting technique. Check: ignition timing, cooling system, fuel octane rating (too low) and fuel mixture (too weak). Discard plugs, rectify fault immediately

Contents

Specifications

System type	12V negative earth, battery, coil and distributor

Distributor

Contact breaker points gap	0.018 to 0.021 in (0.47 to 0.53 mm)
Dwell angle	75 to 81°
Firing order	1 - 2 (No 1 rearmost with engine in car)
Rotation	Clockwise
Static advance	10° BTDC
Maximum centrifugal advance	18° BTDC

Condenser

Capacity at between 50 and 1000 Hz	0.25 microfarad

Coil

	Marelli BE 200 B	Martinetti G 52 S
Type	**Marelli BE 200 B**	**Martinetti G 52 S**
Primary winding resistance (at 68°F - 20°C)	3.1 to 3.4 ohms	3.0 to 3.3 ohms
Secondary winding resistance (at 68°F - 20°C)	6750 to 8250 ohms	6500 to 8000 ohms

Spark plugs

Type	Marelli CW 8 NP	Champion L 81 Y
Size	14 mm	14 mm
Gap	0.023 to 0.027 in (0.6 to 0.7 mm)	

Torque wrench settings

	lb f ft	Nm
Distributor clamp bolt	15	21
Spark plugs	22	30

1 General description

1 The ignition system is conventional, having a battery, coil and distributor with mechanical contact breaker.

2 When the ignition is switched on a current flows from the battery live terminal to the ignition switch through the coil primary winding to the moving contact breaker inside the distributor cap and to earth when the contact breaker points are in the closed position. During this period of points closure, the current flows through the primary windings of the coil and magnetises the laminated iron core which in turn creates a magnetic field through the coil primary and secondary windings.

3 Each time the points open due to the rotation of the distributor cam, the current flow through the primary winding of the coil is interrupted. This causes the induction of a very high voltage (25,000 volts) in the coil secondary winding. This HT (high tension) current is distributed to the spark plugs in correct firing order sequence by the rotor arm and by means of the cap brush and HT leads.

4 A condenser is fitted to the distributor and connected between the moving contact breaker and earth to prevent excessive arcing and pitting of the contact breaker points.

5 The actual point of ignition of the fuel/air mixture which occurs a few degrees before TDC is determined by correct static setting of the ignition timing as described in Section 8. The ignition is advanced to meet varying operating conditions by the centrifugal counterweights

fitted in the base of the distributor.

2 Contact breaker - adjustment

1 Open the lid of the engine compartment and unclip and remove cap from the distributor.

2 Pull off the rotor arm.

3 Turn the crankshaft until the heel of the contact breaker arm is one of the high points of the cam of the distributor shaft.

4 Using a feeler blade, check that the gap is as specified in the Specifications Section. If the gap is incorrect, loosen the screw which secures the fixed contact breaker arm to the baseplate, insert a screwdriver blade in the slot provided in the arm and turn the blade, so moving the contact breaker arm as necessary to adjust the gap. Tighten the securing screw (photo).

5 If the faces of the contact points are severely burned or a 'pip' is built up on one of them, then any checking of the gap with a feeler blade will produce a false reading. The points, if in this condition, must be removed and either renovated or renewed, as described in the next Section.

6 On modern engines, setting the contact breaker gap in the distributor using feeler gauges must be regarded as a basic adjustment only. For optimum engine performance, the dwell angle must be checked. The dwell angle is the number of degrees through which the distributor cam turns during the period between the instance of closing

7 The angle should be checked with a dwell meter connected in accordance with the maker's instructions. Refer to the Specifications for the correct dwell angle. If the dwell angle is too large, increase the points gap, if too small, reduce the points gap.

3 Contact breaker points - removal and refitting

1 Remove the distributor cap and rotor arm, as described in the preceding Section.

2 Release both the locknuts on the LT terminal on the side of the distributor body and unscrew them as far as possible without actually removing them from the terminal stud.

3 Push the terminal stud inwards and release the spring arm of the movable contact arm.

4 Unscrew and remove the screw which secures the fixed contact arm to the distributor baseplate and then withdraw the contact breaker assembly complete.

5 If the points are badly pitted or a 'pip' has built up on one of them, draw a strip of abrasive paper through them until they are clean and square. It is possible to dismantle the contact breaker by extracting the circlip at the top of the pivot post if more extensive dressing of the points is to be carried out on an oilstone, but this is not recommended and if the points are in such a poor condition as this then they should be renewed.

6 Install the new points by reversing the removal operations and set the gap, as described in the preceding Section.

7 Whenever new points are installed as at the intervals specified in 'Routine Maintenance' apply two or three drops of engine oil to the felt pad on the top of the distributor shaft.

4 Condenser (capacitor) - removal, testing and refitting

1 The condenser ensures that with the contact breaker points open, the sparking between them is not excessive, as this would cause severe pitting. The condenser is fitted in parallel and its failure will automatically cause failure of the ignition system as the points will be prevented from interrupting the low tension circuit.

2 Testing for an unserviceable condenser may be effected by switching on the ignition and separating the contact points by hand. If this action is accompanied by a blue flash then condenser failure is indicated. Difficult starting, missing of the engine after several miles running or badly pitted points are other indications of a faulty condenser.

3 The surest test is by substitution of a new unit.

4 To remove the condenser, unscrew its retaining screw and detach its lead from the LT terminal on the distributor body. Refitting is a reversal of removal.

5 Distributor - removal

1 Although the marking of the distributor described in this Section is not essential if the installation procedure, described in Section 7, is carefully followed, it will save time and avoid confusion if the following operations are adhered to.

2 Open the lid of the engine compartment, unclip the lid from the distributor and move it to one side.

3 Unscrew the LT terminal nut and pull off the LT lead. Temporarily refit the terminal nut.

4 Unscrew the spark plug nearest the back of the car and hold the thumb over the plug hole. Turn the crankshaft until compression can be felt being generated in No. 1 cylinder as the piston rises.

5 Continue to turn the crankshaft until the ignition timing mark on the cover of the centrifugal oil filter is opposite the static advance mark on the timing cover (Fig. 4.1). From 1974 the timing mark on the filter cover takes the form of a notch in the pulley flange nearest the engine.

6 Dot punch the rim of the distributor body at a point in alignment

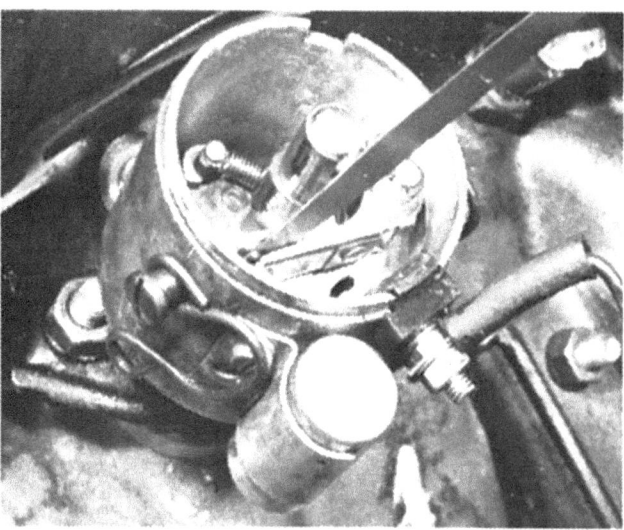

2.4 Checking contact breaker points gap

5.8 Distributor clamp plate and nut

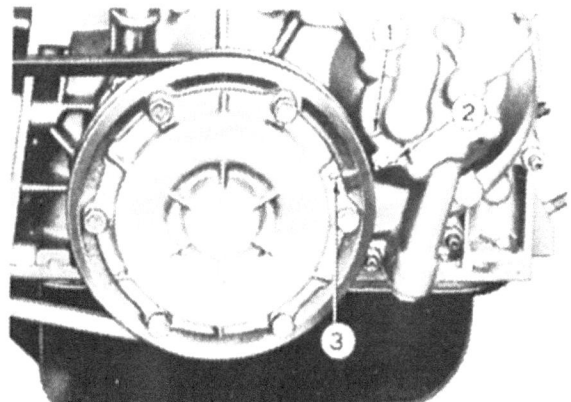

Fig. 4.1. Ignition timing marks

1 Static advance (10⁰) mark   2 TDC mark
3 Filter cover alignment mark

components is rectified by renewal of the unit.

2 Access to the counterweights and springs can be obtained after extracting the baseplate screws and removing the baseplate.

3 The cam assembly can be removed after the felt pad has been extracted from the top of the shaft and the screw withdrawn. Always mark which way round the cam is fitted to the shaft.

4 The driven gear at the base of the shaft is secured by a pin.

5 Examine the carbon brush in the distributor cap. If it has worn away, renew it.

6 If the contact on the end of the rotor arm is severely burned, renew the arm.

7 Distributor - installation

1 If the original distributor is being refitted, make sure that the static advance ignition marks are in alignment by turning the crankshaft, as described in Section 5.

2 The distributor rotates in a clockwise direction and as it is installed, the meshing of the driven gear at the base of the distributor shaft with the drive gear on the camshaft will cause the rotor arm to turn. Therefore set the contact end of the rotor arm about 30° in an anti-clockwise direction from the alignment mark made on the distributor body rim while the distributor is held over its recess in the crankcase in approximately the correct position for installation (photo).

3 Install the distributor and the rotor will turn and take up a positon in correct alignment with the punch mark on the rim (photo).

4 Check that the distributor body to crankcase marks are also in alignment and then that the contact points are just about to open.

5 Secure the distributor by installing the clamp and its securing nut.

6 If the distributor was removed without making alignment marks or a new distributor is being installed, make a mark on the rim of the distributor body which is in line with No 1 (rearmost cylinder) HT lead contact in the distributor cap.

7 Turn the rotor arm about 30° in a clockwise direction from this mark on the rim and then hold the distributor over its recess in the crankcase so that the condenser is almost directly over the hole into which the engine oil dipstick fits (Fig. 4.2).

8 Push the distributor into place when the rotor arm will turn and align with the rim mark.

9 Turn the distributor body in either direction until the contact breaker points are just about to open and then fit the clamp plate and nut.

10 Reconnect the cap and HT leads, reconnect the LT lead.

11 Check the ignition timing, as described in Section 8, using a stroboscope.

8 Ignition timing - adjustment

1 On most cars, two timing marks are located on the timing cover. The arrow indicates TDC while the raised line indicates the advance mark (10° BTDC).

2 A short raised line is located on the cover of the centrifugal oil filter.

3 On some cars, the advance mark on the timing cover is not incorporated but a line can be made by painting or scribing one through the centres of the two raised bosses on the timing cover.

4 Set the initial (static) advance by turning the crankshaft until the mark on the oil filter cover is opposite to the advance mark on the timing cover with No 1 piston on its compression stroke. The crankshaft can be turned by removing the spark plugs and gripping the oil filter/pulley with the hands. Alternatively, place the car in top gear and push it forward.

5 The fact that No 1 piston (nearest rear of car) is on its compression stroke can be ascertained in one of two ways. Either remove a spark plug and with the finger over the hole, feel the compression being generated, or remove the rocker cover and watch the positions of the rocker arms. When the rocker arms of No. 2 cylinder are 'in balance' (any slight movement of the crankshaft in either direction will cause one or other of the rocker arms to move) then the two valves of No 1 cylinder will be closed and the piston near the top of its compression stroke.

8 It is recommended that the ignition timing is now checked with stroboscope after the engine has been run to normal operating temperature.

9 To do this, first paint the mark on the oil filter cover and the 'ADVANCE' mark on the timing cover with quick drying white pai

10 Connect the stroboscope in accordance with the manufacturer's instructions (usually between No 1 spark plug and the end of its HT lead).

11 Start the engine and let it idle at its specified slow-running speec

12 Project the light from the stroboscope onto the timing marks. T pulley mark will appear to be stationary and in alignment with the 'ADVANCE' mark on the timing cover. If it is not in alignment, release the distributor clamp screw and turn the distributor until th marks do coincide. Retighten the clamp screw.

13 A useful check on the operation of the centrifugal advance mechanism can now be made by revving the engine and watching th movement of the timing marks (still under the light from the strobo scope). The mark on the pulley should move out of alignment with timing cover pointer and the amount of misalignment will increase proportion to the increase in engine speed. This proves correct operation of the centrifugal advance mechanism. The timing marks should resume their alignment when the engine speed returns to idl No vacuum advance is fitted to this distributor.

14 Switch off the engine, remove the stroboscope and re-make the original connections.

9 Coil - polarity and testing

1 High tension current should be negative at the spark plug termin If the HT current is positive at the spark plug terminals then the LT leads to the coil primary terminals have been incorrectly connected wrong connection can cause as much as 60% loss of spark efficiency and can cause rough idling and misfiring at speed (photo).

2 With a negative earth electrical system, the LT lead from the distributor connects with the negative (primary) terminal on the co

3 The simplest way to test a coil is by substitution. If an ohmmete available, use it to carry out the following checks, but first apply a volt current to the coil to bring it to normal operating temperature.

4 Check the primary resistance between the coil (+) and (–) termi which should be as shown in the Specifications Section.

5 Check the secondary resistance (secondary to primary terminals this should be as shown in the Specifications Section.

6 Insulation breakdown can only be satisfactorily tested using a megohmmeter between the coil casing and the primary terminals. T resistance should be in excess of 50 megohms.

10 Spark plugs and HT leads - general

1 The correct functioning of the spark plugs is vital for the correc running and efficiency of the engine. The plugs fitted as standard a listed in the Specification page.

2 At the specified intervals, the plugs should be removed, examine cleaned and, if worn excessively, renewed. The condition of the spa plug will also tell much about the overall condition of the engine.

3 If the insulator nose of the spark plug is clean and white, with n deposits, this is indicative of a weak mixture, or too hot a plug.

4 If the top and insulator nose is covered with hard black looking deposits, this is indicative of a weak mixture, or too hot a plug. plug be black and oily, then it is likely that the engine is fairly wor as well as the mixture being too rich.

5 If the insulator nose is covered with light tan to greyish brown deposits, then the mixture is correct and it is likely that the engine in good condition.

6 If there are any traces of long brown tapering stains on the outs of the white portion of the plug, then the plug will have to be renewed, as this shows that there is a faulty joint between the plug body and the insulator, and compression is being allowed to leak a

7 Plugs should be cleaned by a sand blasting machine, which will them from carbon more thoroughly than cleaning by hand. The

7.2 Distributor ready for installation

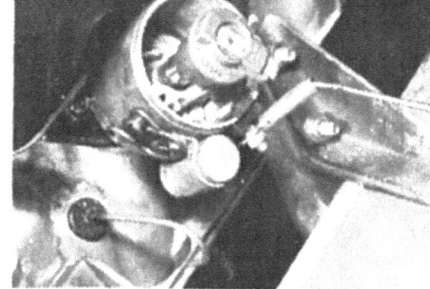

7.3 Distributor installed

9.1 The ignition coil

Fig. 4.2. Distributor installation

1 Spanner
2 Distributor clamp
3 Clamp nut
4 Distributor
5 Moisture protection cover

machine will also test the condition of the plugs under compression. Any plug that fails to spark at the recommended pressure should be renewed.

8 The spark plug gap is of considerable importance, as, if it is too large or too small the size of the spark and its efficiency will be seriously impaired. The spark plug gap should be set to between 0.023 to 0.027 in (0.6 to 0.7 mm) for the best results.

9 To set it, measure the gap with a feeler gauge, and then bend open, or close the outer plug electrode until the correct gap is achieved. The centre electrode should never be bent as this may crack the insulation and cause plug failure.

10 The HT leads are of copper cored cable with separate interference suppressor plug caps which are screwed onto the spark plugs.

11 Occasionally wipe the cables clean with a petrol soaked rag.

12 Always check that the cables are connected between the distributor cap and the spark plugs correctly (see Fig. 4.4).

11 Ignition system - fault diagnosis

Failures of the ignition system will either be due to faults in the HT or LT circuits. Initial checks should be made by observing the security of spark plug terminals, switch terminals, coil and battery connection. More detailed investigation and the explanation and remedial action in respect of symptoms of ignition malfunction are described in the following sub-sections.

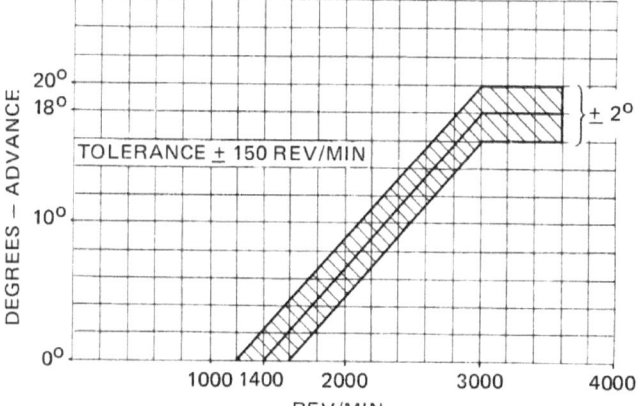

Fig. 4.3. Centrifugal advance diagram

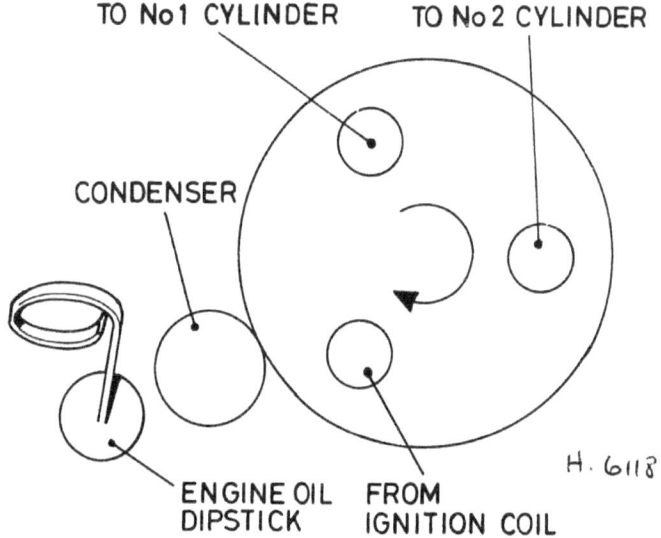

Fig. 4.4. Distributor HT lead connection diagram

charged, then the fault may be in either the high or low tension circuits. First check the HT circuit, **Note:** If the battery is known to be fully charged; the ignition light comes on, and the starter motor fails to turn the engine check the tightness of the leads on the battery terminals and also the security of the earth lead to its connection to the body. It is quite common for the leads to have worked loose, even if they look and feel secure. If one of the battery terminal posts gets very hot when trying to work the starter motor this is a sure indication of a faulty connection to that terminal.

2   One of the commonest reasons for bad starting is wet or damp spark plug leads and distributor. Remove the distributor cap. If condensation is visible internally, dry the cap with a rag and also wipe over the leads. Replace the cap.

3   If the engine still fails to start, check that current is reaching the plugs, by disconnecting each plug lead in turn at the spark plug end, and hold the end of the cable about 3/16 in (4.7 mm) away from the cylinder block. Spin the engine on the starter motor.

4   Sparking between the end of the cable and block should be fairly strong with a regular blue spark. (Hold the lead with rubber to avoid electric shocks). If current is reaching the plugs, then remove them and clean and regap them. The engine should now start.

5   If there is no spark at the plug leads take off the HT lead from the centre of the distributor cap and hold it to the block as before. Spin the engine on the starter once more. A rapid succession of blue sparks between the end of the lead and the block indicate that the coil is in order and that the distributor cap is cracked, the rotor arm faulty, or the carbon brush in the top of the distributor cap is not making good contact with the spring on the rotor arm. Possibly the points are in bad condition. Clean and reset them as described in this Chapter.

6   If there are no sparks from the end of the lead from the coil, check the connections at the coil end of the lead. If it is in order start checking the low tension circuit.

7   Use a 12v voltmeter or a 12v bulb and two lengths of wire. With the ignition switch on and the points open test between the low tension wire to the coil (it is marked +) and earth. No reading indicates a break in the supply from the ignition switch. Check the connections at the switch to see if any are loose. Refit them and the engine should run. A reading shows a faulty coil or condenser, or broken lead between the coil and the distributor.

8   Take the condenser wire off the points assembly and with the points open, test between the moving point and earth. If there now is a reading, then the fault is in the condenser. Fit a new one and the fault is cleared.

9   With no reading from the moving contact breaker point to earth, take a reading between earth and the (–) terminal of the coil. A reading

sufficient to separate the points with a piece of dry paper while testing with the points open.

Engine misfires

10   If the engine misfires regularly run it at a fast idling speed. Pull or unscrew each of the plug caps in turn and listen to the note of the engine. Hold the plug cap in a dry cloth or with a rubber glove as additional protection against shock from the HT supply.

11   No difference in engine running will be noticed when the lead from the defective circuit is removed. Removing the lead from the good cylinder will accentuate the misfire or stop the engine.

12   Remove the plug lead from the end of the defective plug and hold it about 3/16 in (5 mm) away from the block. Restart the engine. If the sparking is fairly strong and regular the fault must lie in the spark plug.

13   The plug may be loose, the insulation may be cracked, or the point may have burnt away giving too wide a gap for the spark to jump. Worse still, one of the points may have broken off. Either renew the plug, or clean it, reset the gap, and then test it.

14   If there is no spark at the end of the plug lead, or if it is weak and intermittent, check the ignition lead from the distributor to the plug. If the insulation is cracked or perished, renew the lead. Check the connection at the distributor cap.

15   If there is still no spark, examine the distributor cap carefully for tracking. This can be recognised by a very thin black line running between the two contacts, or between a contact and some part of the distributor. These lines are paths which now conduct electricity across the cap thus letting it run to earth. The only answer is a new distributor cap.

16   Apart from the ignition timing being incorrect, other causes of misfiring have already been dealt with under the Section dealing with the failure of the engine to start. To recap - these are that:

a)   The coil may be faulty giving an intermittent misfire.
b)   There may be a damaged wire or loose connection in the low tension circuit.
c)   The condenser may be short circuiting.
d)   There may be a mechanical fault in the distributor (broken driving spindle or contact breaker spring)

17   If the ignition timing is too far retarded, it should be noted that engine will tend to overheat, and there will be a quite noticeable drop in power. If the engine is overheating and the power is down, and the ignition timing is correct, then the carburettor should be checked, it is likely that this is where the fault lies.

Chapter 5 Clutch

Contents

Specifications

Type	Single dry plate, diaphragm spring with cable actuation

Drive plate diameter	6.1 in (155 mm)

Pedal free-movement	1.1 in (28 mm)

Torque wrench settings	lb f ft	Nm
Release fork lockbolt	18	25
Pressure plate cover bolts to flywheel	12	16
Bellhousing bolts to engine	18	25

1 General description

1 The clutch is of single dry plate, diaphragm spring type.
2 Clutch actuation is by cable from a pendant type foot pedal.

2 Clutch - adjustment

1 The free-movement at the clutch pedal should be maintained at just over 1 in (28 mm).
2 Measure the free-movement carefully by holding a rule against the side of the clutch pedal and depressing the pedal with the fingers until resistance can be felt. The distance over which the pedal has moved from the fully released position to the point where resistance is felt is the free-movement.
3 The free-movement can be increased, or decreased, by releasing the locknut on the threaded part at the end of the clutch cable within the engine compartment and turning the adjuster nut in the appropriate direction (Fig. 5.1).
4 Re-check the free-movement, and then tighten the locknut without altering the position of the adjuster nut.
5 Always keep the threaded end of the clutch cable well smeared with grease to prevent corrosion of the threads.

3 Clutch cable - renewal

1 Disconnect the threaded end of the clutch cable from the release lever on the clutch bellhousing by unscrewing the adjuster nut and locknut (Fig. 5.2).
2 Disconnect the outer cable bracket adjacent to the release lever.

3 Disconnect the opposite end of the cable from the clutch pedal by extracting the split pin and the cotter pin.
4 Working within the car, remove the heater duct from the floorpan, as described in Chapter 2, Section 6.
5 The clutch cable is now accessible and can be withdrawn through its sealing grommets and a new one installed.
6 Adjust the cable to provide the correct pedal free-movement, as described in the preceding Section.

Fig. 5.1. Clutch cable adjusting nuts

1 Release lever   3 Return spring
2 Adjusting nuts   4 Cable

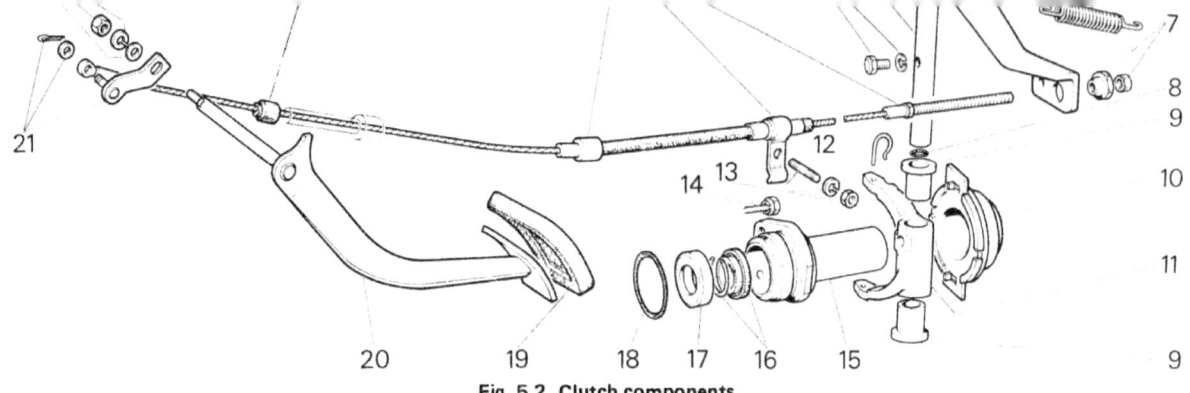

Fig. 5.2. Clutch components

1	Pivot nut and washers	7	Adjuster nut and locknut	12	Spring clip	17	Bush
2	Boot	8	Seal	13	Bracket stud and nut	18	Seal
3	Cable assembly	9	Bush	14	Bearing hub securing bolt	19	Pedal rubber
4	Lockbolt	10	Release bearing	15	Release bearing mounting hub	20	Clutch pedal
5	Release lever/shaft	11	Fork	16	Oil seal	21	Relay lever assembly
6	Return spring						

4 Clutch pedal - removal and installation

1   The pendant type clutch pedal is supported by a pivot bolt attached to a bracket assembly under the fascia panel.

2   To remove the pedal, disconnect the clutch cable from the lever on the end of the pedal pivot bolt.

3   Unscrew the nut which secures the lever to the flats on the end of the pivot bolt and remove the lever and washers. Withdraw the pedal/pivot bolt assembly.

4   Install the pedal by reversing the removal operations, but apply grease to the pivot bolt.

5   There is no provision for adjusting the pedal height and a fixed backstop is incorporated in the pedal arm but adjust the free-movement after installation, as described in Section 2.

5 Clutch - removal

1   Access to the clutch is attained by removing the gearbox as described in Chapter 6, Section 3.

2   Should the engine have to be removed for major overhaul, always take the opportunity to check the clutch components.

3   With the gearbox removed, unbolt and remove the clutch pressure plate from the flywheel. Unscrew the bolts evenly and in diagonally opposite sequence.

4   Withdraw the pressure plate/cover assembly and catch the driven plate which will be released.

6 Clutch - inspection and renovation

1   Examine the clutch disc friction linings for wear and loose rivets and the disc for rim distortion, cracks, and worn splines. The surfaces of the friction linings may be highly glazed, but as long as the clutch material pattern can be clearly seen this is satisfactory. Compare the amount of lining wear with a new clutch disc at the stores in your local garage, and if the linings are more than three quarters worn renew the disc (Fig. 5.3).

2   It is always best to renew the clutch driven plate as an assembly to preclude further trouble but if it is wished to merely renew the linings, the rivets should be drilled out and not knocked out with a punch. The manufacturers do not advise that only the linings are renewed and personal experience dictates that it is far more satisfactory to renew the driven plate complete than to try to economise by only fitting new friction linings.

3   Check the machined faces of the flywheel and the pressure plate. If either are grooved they should be renewed.

4   If the pressure plate is cracked or split it is essential that an exchange unit is fitted, also if the pressure of the diaphragm spring suspect. It is not practical to dismantle the pressure plate assembly it will have been accurately set up and balanced to very fine limits.

5   If a new clutch disc is being fitted, it is a false economy not to renew the release bearing at the same time. This will preclude havin replace it at a later date when wear on the clutch linings is still very small.

6   Check the release bearing for smoothness of operation. There should be no harshness and no slackness in it. It should spin reason freely bearing in mind it has been pre-packed with grease.

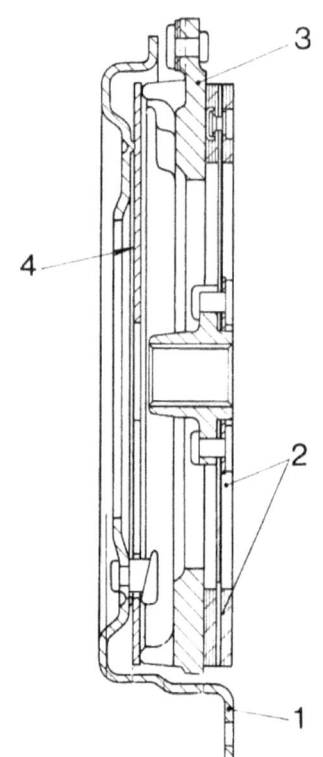

Fig. 5.3. Sectional view of clutch assembly

1	Clutch cover	3	Pressure plate
2	Driven plate	4	Diaphragm spring

clips which secure the release bearing to the release fork (photo).

2 Withdraw the release bearing from the hub on which it slides.

3 If there is any evidence of oil leakage within the clutch bellhousing, this is probably coming from a defective oil seal in the release bearing hub.

4 The bush and oil seal are both renewable and can be drifted from the release bearing hub using a suitable drift after the hub has been unbolted (photo).

5 Wear in the release fork shaft bushes can be rectified if the release fork/shaft assembly is removed. To do this, turn the fork right-over to expose the lockbolt, unscrew the bolt and withdraw the shaft and fork (photo).

6 Extract the old bushes and press in new ones.

7 Reassembly is a reversal of dismantling, but apply grease to the release shaft bushes and to the outer surface of the release bearing mounting hub, also to the contact area between release fork and bearing.

8 It is recommended that new spring clips are used to retain the release bearing to the fork.

9 Renew the spigot bush in the centre of the flywheel mounting flange of the crankshaft if it is worn as described in Chapter 1, Sec 18.

to the flywheel, a centralising guide tool must be obtained or made up. This may be either an old input shaft from a dismantled gearbox or a stepped mandrel.

2 Locate the driven plate against the face of the flywheel ensuring that its flatter side is against the flywheel.

3 Offer up the pressure plate assembly to the flywheel aligning the marks made prior to dismantling and insert the retaining bolts finger-tight only. Where a new pressure plate assembly is being fitted, locate it to the flywheel in a similar relative position to the original by reference to the index marking and dowel positions.

4 Insert the guide tool through the splined hub of the driven plate so that the end of the tool locates in the flywheel spigot bush. This action of the guide tool will centralise the driven plate by causing it to move in a sideways direction (photo).

5 Insert and remove the guide tool two or three times to ensure that the driven plate is fully centralised and then tighten the pressure plate securing bolts a turn at a time and in a diametrically opposite sequence to the specified torque in order to prevent distortion of the pressure plate cover.

6 Refit the gearbox, after reference to Chapter 6, and then adjust the clutch pedal free-movement.

7.1 Clutch release bearing installed

7.4 Clutch release bearing hub

7.5 Clutch release fork showing lockbolt

8.4 Assembling and centralising the clutch driven plate

Judder when taking up drive	Loose engine or gearbox mountings. Badly worn friction surfaces or contaminated with oil. Worn splines on gearbox input shaft or driven plate hub. Worn input shaft spigot bush in flywheel.
Clutch spin (failure to disengage) so that gears cannot be meshed	Incorrect release bearing to pressure plate clearance. Rust on splines. (May occur after vehicle standing idle for long perio Damaged or misaligned pressure plate assembly. Incorrect pedal free-movement.
Clutch slip (increase in engine speed does not result in increase in vehicle road speed - particularly on gradients)	Incorrect release bearing to diaphragm spring finger clearance caused by wrong pedal free-movement. Friction surfaces worn out or oil contaminated.
Noise evident on depressing clutch pedal	Dry, worn or damaged release bearing. Insufficient pedal free-travel. Weak or broken pedal return spring. Weak or broken clutch release lever return spring. Excessive play between driven plate hub splines and input shaft splines.
Noise evident as clutch pedal released	Distorted driven plate. Insufficient pedal free-travel. Weak or broken clutch pedal return spring. Weak or broken release lever return spring. Distorted or worn input shaft. Release bearing loose on retainer hub.

Chapter 6 Gearbox and final drive

Contents

Specifications

Gearbox type ... ... Four forward speeds and reverse. Synchromesh on upper three ratios. Final drive incorporated in gearcase.

Ratios

1st	3.250 : 1
2nd	2.067 : 1
3rd	1.300 : 1
4th	0.872 : 1
Reverse	4.024 : 1

Final drive ... ... 4.875 : 1 (8/39)

Lubrication

Oil type/specification ... ... Multigrade engine oil, viscosity SAE 15W/40 (Duckhams Hypergrade)
Oil capacity ... ... 2 Imp. pts (2.3 US pts/1.1 litres)

Torque wrench settings

	lb f ft	Nm
Gearcase to bellhousing bolt	25	35
Bellhousing to engine bolt	18	25
Pinion shaft and countershaft castillated nuts	36	50
Crownwheel bolts	33	46
Gearbox mounting stud nut	18	25

---

1 General description

1 The gearbox is of four forward speed type with reverse gear. Synchromesh is incorporated on the upper three ratios.
2 The gearshift lever is floor-mounted.
3 The differential/final drive assembly is incorporated in the gear casing.
4 Power is transmitted to the rear roadwheels through open driveshafts (see Chapter 7) (Fig. 6.1).
5 The engine, gearbox and final drive are mounted as one assembly at the rear of the car but the gearbox/final drive can be removed independently leaving the engine in position in the car.
Note: Throughout the text - rear of the gearbox or its components denotes the 'in car' position, that is at the flywheel/differential/bellhousing end.

2 Gearshift lever and linkage - adjustment and overhaul

1 If the gears fail to engage properly, adjustment of the gearshift lever may be required. Always check this before assuming that the fault lies within the gearbox.
2 Working inside the car, slacken the screws which secure the gearshift lever support to the centre tunnel. The screw holes are elongated to enable the lever support to be moved fore or aft (Fig. 6.2).
3 Move the lever support forward if lack of engagement has been evident with 1st or 3rd gears.

4 Move the lever support to the rear if it has been found that 2nd, 4th or reverse gears have not been engaging correctly.
5 Re-tighten the lever support screws and check engagement of the gears on the road.
6 To renew worn components, unscrew the self-locking nut which secures the gearshift lever to its support (Fig. 6.3). The ball, socket or spring can be renewed if any of them are worn or damaged.
7 The connecting linkage under the car incorporates a link with flexible joint which may require renewal if it has deteriorated (Fig. 6.4).
8 Reassembly is a reversal of dismantling, but always apply grease to the shift lever ball and socket and to the other linkage rubbing surfaces.

3 Gearbox/final drive - removal and installation

1 Place the car over an inspection pit or raise the rear end by backing it up a pair of ramps. Alternatively, jack-up the rear of the car and support it securely on axle stands placed under the body frame side members. Check that the clearance under the rear of the car is in excess of the diameter of the clutch bellhousing, otherwise the gearbox cannot be withdrawn from under the car.
2 Disconnect the flanges at the outer ends of the driveshafts by unscrewing and removing the securing bolts.
3 Disconnect the clutch operating cable from the release lever on the clutch bellhousing and then release the outer conduit from its support bracket.

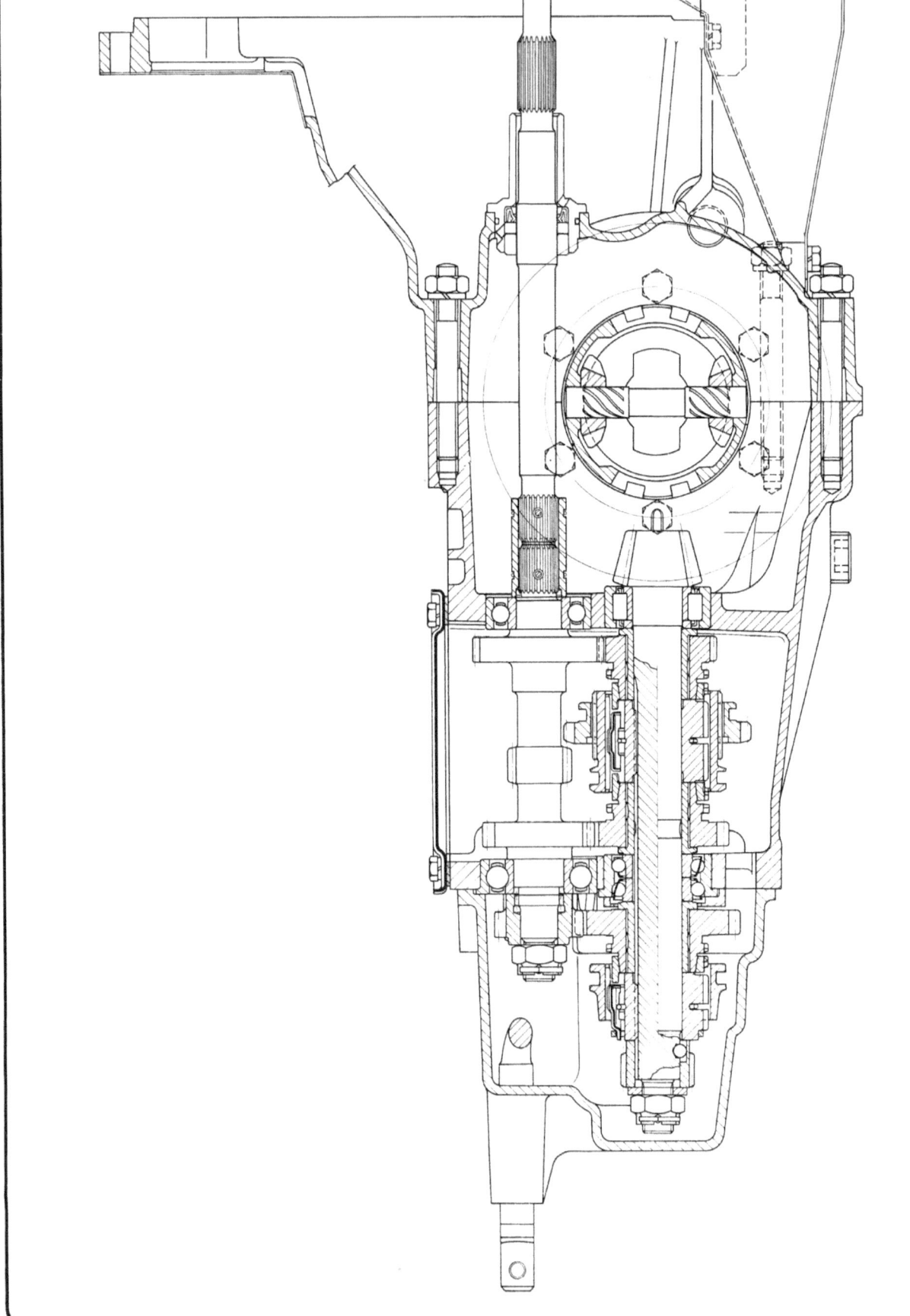

Fig. 6.1. Sectional view of transmission unit

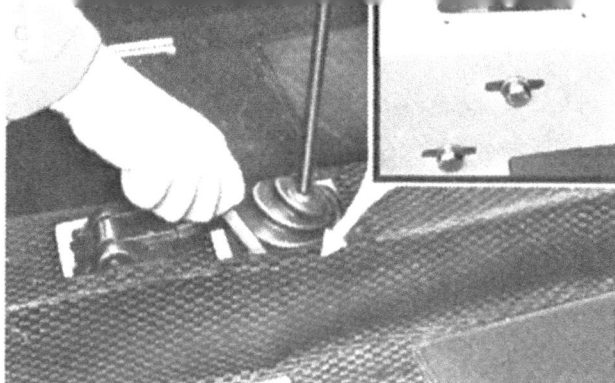

Fig. 6.2. Gearshift lever support bracket

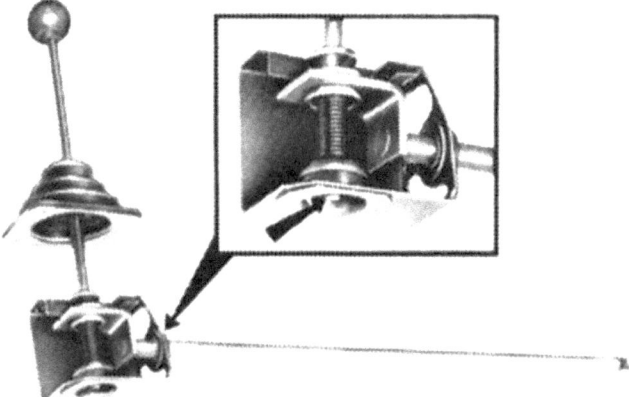

Fig. 6.3. Gearshift lever support and self-locking nut

Fig. 6.4. Gearshift linkage under car

1 Remote control rod	3 Connecting rod to gearshift
2 Link with flexible joint	lever
	4 Flexible boot
	5 Shouldered bolts

Disconnect the leads from the starter motor and unbolt and remove the starter.

6 Still working beneath the car, unbolt and remove the long tapering torsion plate from the bottom of the gearbox and from the body-frame box member (photo).

7 Reach up at the rear of the gearbox extension housing and disconnect the speedometer cable by unscrewing the knurled ring (photo).

8 Disconnect the gearshift flexible link from the gearbox remote control rod by removing the special shouldered bolt (photo).

9 Support the engine sump on a jack and a wooden block as an insulator and then place a second jack under the gearbox.

10 Unbolt and remove the 'U' shaped support bracket (complete with flexible mounting pads) from its attachment to the bodyframe (photo).

11 Unscrew and remove the bolts which secure the clutch bellhousing to the engine. Some of these are accessible from below the car while the others are reached from within the engine compartment.

12 Lower the two jacks simultaneously so that the rear of the gearbox is below the floor pan and then withdraw the gearbox towards the front of the car, making ure that the outer ends of the two drive-shafts are depressed rearwards and down to clear the undersides of the suspension lower arms. On no account allow the weight of the gearbox to hang upon the input shaft while the latter is still engaged with the clutch mechanism (Fig. 6.5).

13 Installation is a reversal of removal, but if the clutch mechanism has been dismantled, make sure that the driven plate has been centralised as described in Chapter 5. Check and adjust the clutch pedal free-movement also as described in that Chapter.

Fig. 6.5. Removing gearbox/final drive from under car in a forward direction

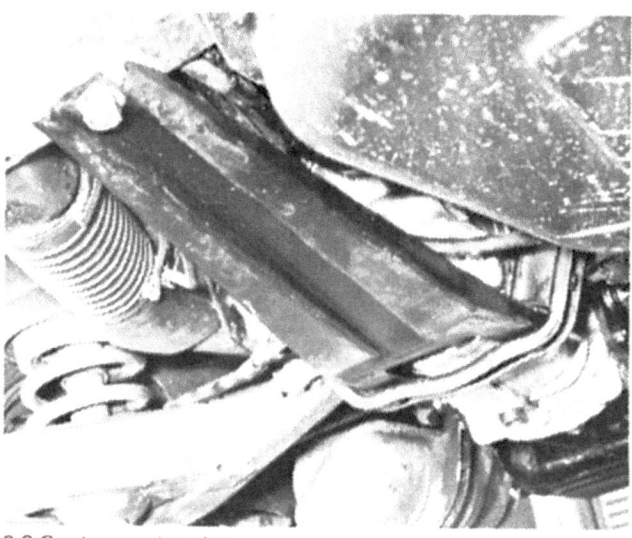

3.6 Gearbox torsion plate

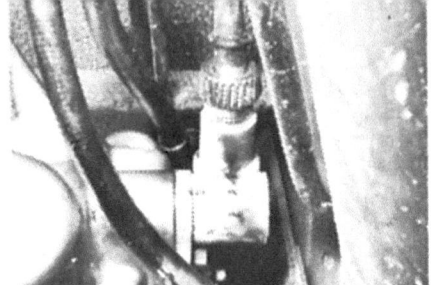
3.7 Speedometer cable connection to gearbox

3.8 Gearshift flexible link

3.10 Gearbox U-shaped support bracket

4 Gearbox - dismantling and inspection

1 With the gearbox removed from the car, drain the oil and then unbolt and remove the top cover.

2 Within the bellhousing, extract the spring clips and remove the clutch release bearing.

3 Mark the position of the driveshaft inner flanges in relation to the gear case.

4 Unscrew the bolts which secure the oil sealing boots at the inner ends of the driveshafts.

5 Withdraw the locking ring now exposed (photo).

6 Mark the position of the adjuster in relation to the bearing retainer.

7 Unscrew and remove the nuts which secure the bearing retainers and then prise the retainers from the gear case. Slide the inner flange components down the driveshafts (photo).

8 Unscrew and remove the six bolts from within the clutch bell-housing and separate the bellhousing from the gear case.

9 Lift the differential complete with driveshafts from the gearcase.

10 Extract the circlip from the rear end of the input shaft, push out the lockpin and withdraw the input shaft from the gearcase (Fig. 6.6).

11 Unscrew and remove the single retaining bolt and withdraw the speedometer driven gear assembly (photo).

12 Unbolt and remove the extension housing.

13 Withdraw the gearshift remote control rod from the extension housing.

14 Unbolt and remove the 'U' shaped support complete with flexible mountings, from the gear case.

15 Unbolt and remove the plate and gasket which covers the detent springs.

16 Extract the three detent springs and balls.

17 Pull out the split pins from the castellated nuts on the ends of the countershaft and the pinion shaft..

18 Unscrew and remove the locking bolt from reverse shift fork.

19 Push 3rd/4th selector shaft to engage 3rd gear and then move reverse shift fork to lock up the gears in the box so that the pinion and countershaft nuts can be unscrewed. With the gearbox in its normally installed attitude, the upper selector shaft is REVERSE, the middle one is 3rd/4th, and the lower one is 1st/2nd.

20 Unscrew and remove the two shaft castellated nuts.

21 Move the 3rd/4th selector shaft and the reverse shift fork back to their original positions so that the gearbox will again be in the neutral

mode.

22 Unscrew and remove the locking bolts from the remaining shift forks.

23 Withdraw 2nd gear from the end of the countershaft (Fig. 6.7).

24 Withdraw 3rd/4th selector shaft but catching the interlock plun as it is removed.

25 With draw the speedometer drive gear from the pinion shaft and pick out the locking ball from the depression in the shaft.

26 Withdraw the 2nd gear synchro unit complete with 1st/2nd sele shaft and shift fork from the pinion shaft. Make sure the synchro u is kept in engagement otherwise it will fall to pieces and have to be reassembled (photo).

27 Turn the gearbox on its side and shake out the remaining interlo plungers.

28 Using two screwdrivers, lever out the counterhsaft front bearing

29 Remove the countershaft rear bearing and then withdraw the countershaft.

30 Unscrew and remove the locking bolt from the side of reverse id shaft and then tap the shaft out towards the front of the gearbox a remove the reverse idler gear from it.

31 Stand the gearbox on its front face and withdraw the pinion sha Retain any shims and the thrust washers which are fitted behind th pinion shaft rear bearing.

32 Remove the gears which remain in the gearcase.

33 Remove the pinion shaft front bearing assembly which comprise two races and an outer track. This is achieved by removing the two countersunk screws with an impact screwdriver.

34 With the gearbox completely dismantled, clean all components suitable solvent and check the gear teeth for wear or chipping and t shafts for scoring.

35 Inspect the gearcase for cracks especially around the bolt and st holes.

36 Check the bearings for noisy operation when turned with the fingers.

37 Renew the synchroniser units if noisy gearchanges have been ev or the synchromesh could be easily 'beaten' when changing gear.

38 Any faults arising from this examination should be overcome renewal of the components concerned.

39 Any wear in the pinion shaft can only be rectified by installing new matched set of pinion shaft and crownwheel, as described in Section 6.

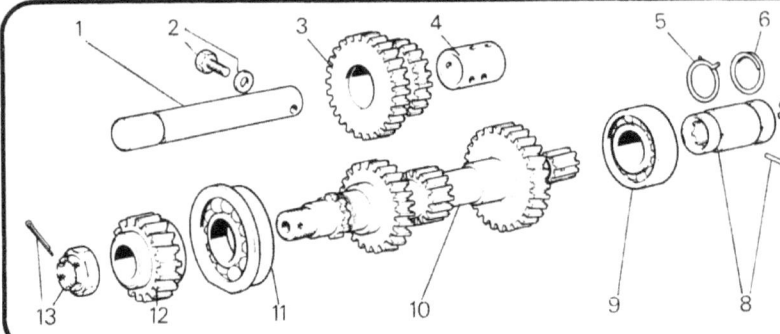

Fig. 6.6. Reverse shaft and countershaft components

1 Reverse idler shaft	8 Sleeve and pin
2 Lockbolt and washer	9 Rear bearing
3 Reverse idler gear	10 Countergear assembly w
4 Bush	1st, 3rd and 4th gears
5 Circlip	11 Front bearing
6 Circlip	12 2nd speed gear
7 Input shaft	13 Castellated nut and spli

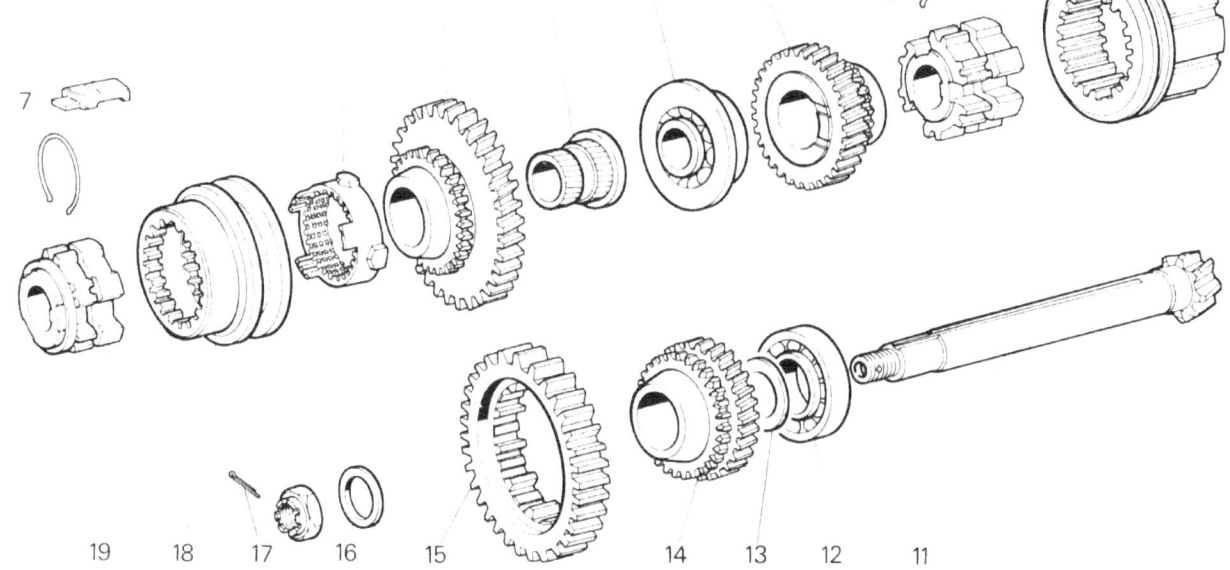

Fig. 6.7. Pinion shaft components

1 Synchro sliding key	6 3rd speed driven gear	11 Pinion shaft	16 Plain washer
2 2nd speed synchro ring	7 Synchro spring	12 Rear bearing	17 Castellated nut and split pin
3 2nd speed driven gear	8 Sliding key	13 Adjustment shim	18 2nd speed synchro sleeve
4 Bush	9 3rd/4th synchro hub	14 4th speed driven gear	19 2nd speed synchro hub
5 Front bearing	10 3rd/4th synchro sleeve	15 1st/reverse gear	

4.5 Driveshaft bearing retainer and adjuster lockring

4.7 Driveshaft inner flange components

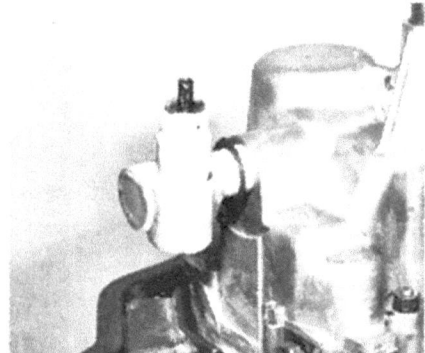

4.11 Speedometer driven gear assembly

4.26 2nd gear and synchro unit

5 Gearbox - reassembly

1 During reassembly, lubricate the components with the specified gear oil.

2 Lower the pinion shaft gear train (correctly assembled) into the bottom of the gearcase (Fig. 6.8 and photo).

3 Install the pinion shaft complete with bearing and bushes and the original shims (photos).

4 Install the bearing to the front end of the pinion shaft (photo).

5 Install the bearing retainer noting that the position of the cutout on the retainer is provided to allow installation of the countershaft bearing (photo).

6 Tighten the retainer countersunk screws using an impact screwdriver. If this tool is not available, use a heavy screwdriver and apply leverage to the shaft of the screwdriver with a Stillson wrench.

9 Install the countershaft bearings (photos).

10 Fit 2nd gear to the part of the countershaft which lies outside the main gearcase (photo).

11 Screw the castellated nut onto the front end of the countershaft using the fingers to do this.

12 Fit 2nd gear synchro unit to the front end of the pinion shaft and at the same time install the 1st/2nd selector shaft and 2nd gear shift fork, the latter taking up a position outside the main gearcase (photo).

13 Locate the locking ball and fit the speedometer drive gear to the front end of the pinion shaft (photo).

14 Fit the plain washer and then screw the castellated nut onto the front end of the pinion shaft.

15 Screw in and tighten the 1st gear shift fork lock bolt.

16 Drop in the interlock plunger which locates between 1st/2nd and 3rd/4th selector shafts (photo).

17 Install the relay interlock plunger into its hole in the 3rd/4th selector shaft. Use a dab of thick grease to retain it (photo).

18 Install 3rd/4th selector shaft, passing it through the 3rd/4th shift fork in the process (photo).

19 Screw in and tighten the lockbolt which secures 3rd/4th shift fork to its selector shaft (photo).

20 Install the reverse idler shaft and gear (photo).

21 Screw in and tighten reverse idler shaft lockbolt from outside the gearcase.

22 Insert the interlock plunger which locates between reverse and 3rd/4th selector shafts.

23 Install reverse gearshift fork and selector rod but do not screw in its lockbolt at this stage as the shift fork must be free to move when the gears are to be locked up later in order to tighten the pinion shaft and countershaft castellated nuts (photo).

24 Insert the three detent balls into the holes in the side of the gearcase (photo).

25 Insert the three detent springs and then fit the retaining plate and gasket. Use only one bolt to retain the plate (photo).

27 Lock the gears by moving 3rd/4th selector shaft to engage 3rd gear and then push the (still free) reverse shift fork to lock up the gears in the box.

28 Tighten the pinion and countershaft castellated nuts to the spec torque and insert new split pins (photos).

29 Unlock the gears and then screw in and tighten the lock bolt on reverse shift fork.

30 Fit a new extension housing gasket.

31 Install the gearshift remote control rod into the extension hous noting the sealing 'O' ring in the rod groove (photo).

32 Install the extension housing to the gearcase making sure that th dog on the remote control rod engages correctly with the cutouts i the ends of the selector shafts (photo).

33 Screw on and tighten the extension housing nuts and bolts.

34 Fit the gearbox top cover using a new gasket (photo).

35 Fit the input shaft to the rear end of the countershaft so that th splines engage and the lockpin can be pushed into place. Push the locking clip into its groove so that it retains the lockpin (photo).

36 Install the differential complete with driveshafts into the gearca (photo).

37 Smear the mating faces of the clutch bellhousing and the gearca with jointing compound and position the two together.

38 Screw in the bolts which secure the bellhousing and the gearcase together noting that the bolts are of two different lengths (photo).

39 Refit the inner flanges of the driveshafts noting that there are sealing 'O' rings on the bearing housings. Make sure that all marks made before dismantling are in alignment. This is particularly important with the bearing adjuster rings (photo).

40 Install the clutch release bearing and the spring clip and return spring to the release lever.

41 The gearbox is now ready to be refitted to the car and it is best wait until it is installed before filling it with the correct grade and quantity of oil.

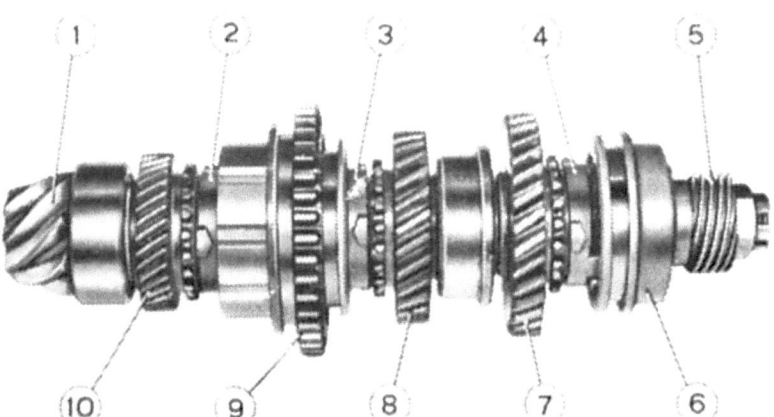

Fig. 6.8. Pinion shaft with gears correctly assem

1 Pinion
2 4th speed synchro ring
3 3rd speed synchro ring
4 2nd speed synchro ring
5 Speedometer drive gear
6 2nd speed synchro sleeve
7 2nd speed driven gear
8 3rd speed driven gear
9 1st/reverse gear
10 4th speed driven gear

5.2 Pinion shaft geartrain in bottom of casing

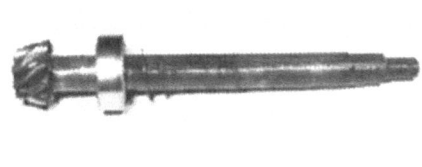

5.3a Pinion shaft with bearing and shims

5.3b Installing pinion shaft

5.4 Installing pinion shaft bearing

5.5 Installing pinion shaft bearing retainer

5.7 3rd/4th and 1st gearshift forks installed

5.8 Countershaft assembly installed

5.9a Countershaft rear bearing installed

5.9b Countershaft front bearing (upper) installed

5.10 2nd gear installed to countershaft

5.12 2nd gear synchro unit, 1st/2nd selector shaft and 2nd gearshift fork fitted to front end of pinion shaft

5.13 Locking ball and speedometer drivegear

5.16 Inserting interlock plunger between 1st/2nd and 3rd/4th selector shafts

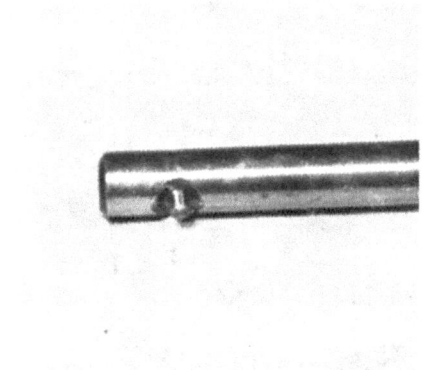

5.17 Relay interlock plunger fitted to 3rd/4th selector shaft

5.18 Installing 3rd/4th selector shaft

5.19 Tightening 3rd/4th shift fork lock bolt

5.20 Installing reverse idler shaft and gear

5.23 Installing reverse gearshift fork and selector shaft

5.24 Detent balls installed

5.25 Detent springs installed

5.28a Tightening pinion shaft castellated

5.28b Pinion shaft and countershaft nuts tightened and locked with split pins

5.31 Gearshift remote control rod installed

5.32 Installing extension housing

5.34 Installing top cover

5.35 Fitting input shaft lock pin

5.36 Installing differential/driveshaft assembly

assembly, it is recommended that the components are renewed by your Fiat dealer as the meshing of crownwheel and pinion shaft requires the use of special tools and gauges.

2 If any of the gears or bushes on the pinion shaft have been renewed then have your Fiat dealer determine the thickness of the shims which are required between the shaft rear roller bearing and the 4th gear bush. To be able to do this, he will require the new pinion shaft, all the pinion shaft components and the gearcase.

3 If only the pinion shaft and crownwheel are to be renewed (supplied in matched sets) or any other differential components then proceed in the following way.

4 Remove the pinion shaft, as described in Section 4.

5 On the end of the pinion shaft will be found two sets of figures. The upper ones are the matching numbers repeated on the crownwheel while the lower ones indicate the differential (+ or −) between the nominal distance of 2.95 in (75 mm) from the centre-line of the differential to the shoulder at the back of the pinion gearteeth.

6 Compare the lower sets of figures on the old and new pinion shafts and by simple calculation, increase or decrease the thickness of the shims required. Shims are available in thicknesses from 0.0039 to 0.0059 in (0.10 to 0.15 mm).

7 Install the pinion shaft, new shims and gear components, as described in Section 5.

8 To dismantle the differential case and crownwheel, first remove it complete with driveshafts from the gearcase, as described in Section 4, paragraphs 1 to 9.

9 Unscrew and remove the bolts which secure the crownwheel to the differential case.

10 Remove the crownwheel and then slide off the side gear followed by the joint blocks (photo).

11 Withdraw the driveshaft.

12 The opposite driveshaft can be removed after bending up the tabs of the pinion shaft retainer and sliding the retainer from the differential case.

13 Remove the planet gears and differential pinion shaft (photo).

14 Renew any worn components and the bearings if they appear rough or noisy when turned with the fingers.

15 On no account interchange any of the original components from one side of the differential unit to the other.

16 If a new crownwheel is being fitted, make sure that the numbers engraved upon it match those on the pinion shaft.

17 Reassemble the differential case and driveshafts by reversing the dismantling procedure. Make sure that the lubrication channels on the joint blocks are against the inside faces of the grooves in the side gears.

18 Provided the differential side gears and differential case have not been changed, the original side gear thrust washers can be refitted. Where these components have been renewed then it may be necessary to alter the thickness of the thrust washers in order to obtain a turning torque of the differential gears of between 2 and 5 lb f ft (3 and 7 Nm). Use a suitable torque gauge or spring balance to check this. Thrust washers are available in the following thicknesses:

setting and remember to bend down the locking tabs of the differential pinion shaft retainer.

20 Install the differential assembly into the gearcase.

21 Install the clutch bellhousing, having applied jointing compound to the mating flanges of the gearcase and bellhousing, and then tighten the securing bolts to the specified torque.

22 If the original components are being refitted then set the side adjusters to their original (marked) positions.

23 If new components have been fitted, a dial gauge should be used to check the backlash between the teeth of the gearbox pinion shaft and the teeth of the crownwheel. The backlash should be between 0.003 and 0.005 in (0.08 and 0.13 mm). Turn the bearing side adjusters to obtain the specified backlash. In the absence of the correct wrench, use a pair of narrow-nosed pliers to turn the adjusters (Fig. 6.10).

24 Now the turning torque of the differential roller bearings must be checked. Using either a spring balance and cord attached to a driveshaft or a torque gauge, the force required to rotate the bearings should be between 1 and 1.5 lb f ft (1.3 and 1.95 Nm). If a correction is needed, move one adjuster slightly in the appropriate direction and then turn the other adjuster in the opposite direction. Failure to do this will upset the previously set backlash.

25 With the final drive assembly correctly set, fit the driveshaft inner flanges with new 'O' ring seals, and then the adjuster lock rings taking care not to alter the position of the adjusters.

26 Fit the oil retaining boots and their retaining flanges. Make sure that the driveshaft inner oil seals and retainers are in good condition.

5.38 Tightening a clutch bellhousing to gearcase bolt

5.39 Refitting a driveshaft inner flange

6.10 Differential side gear, driveshaft and joint blocks

6.13 View of planet gears and a differential side gear (driveshaft removed)

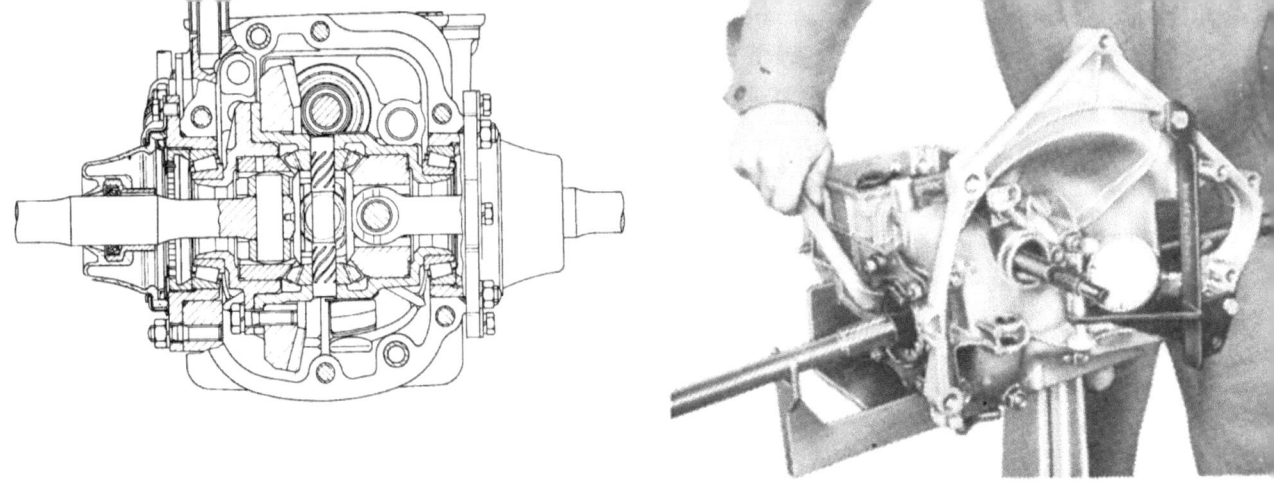

Fig. 6.9. Cross-sectional view of final drive/differential

Fig. 6.10. Using a dial gauge to check crownwheel backlash. Probe dial gauge passes through input shaft hole in bellhousing to contact crownwheel tooth

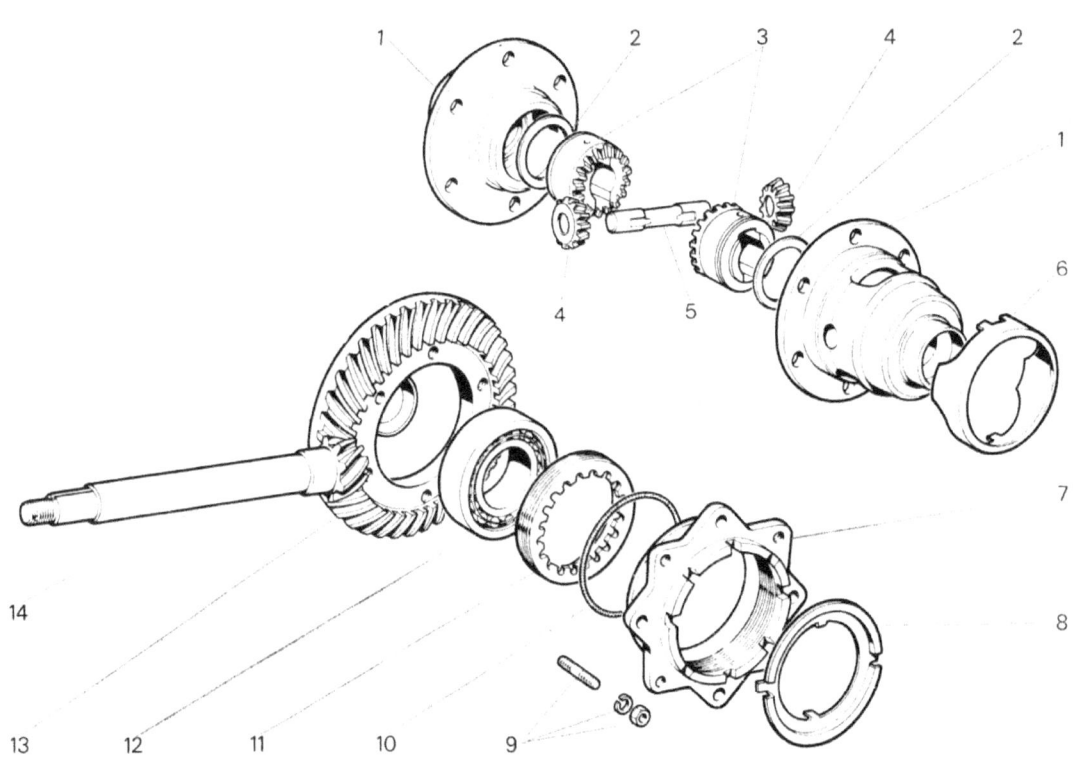

Fig. 6.11. Exploded view of the final drive/differential

1	Differential case	5	Differential pinion shaft	8	Bearing adjuster lock ring
2	Side gear thrust washer	6	Differential pinion shaft	9	Stud, nut and washer
3	Side gears		retainer	10	'O' ring
4	Differential pinions	7	Bearing housing	11	Adjuster

12	Roller bearing
13	Crownwheel
14	Pinion shaft

Weak or ineffective synchromesh	Synchro. cones worn or damaged.
	Baulk rings worn.
	Defective synchro unit.
Jumps out of gear	Worn interlock plunger.
	Worn detent ball.
	Weak or broken detent spring.
	Worn shift fork or synchro sleeve groove.
	Worn gear.
Excessive noise	Incorrect oil grade.
	Oil level too low.
	Worn gear teeth.
	Worn pinion shaft bearings.
	Worn thrust washers.
	Worn input or pinion shaft splines.
Difficult gear changing or selection	Incorrect clutch free-movement.

8   Fault diagnosis - final drive and differential

Symptom	Reason/s
Noisy differential:	
a) During normal running	Lack of oil, damaged or worn gears, incorrect adjustment.
b) During deceleration	Incorrect adjustment or damage to drive pinion bearings.
c) During turning of vehicle	Worn or damaged driveshaft bearing, worn differential gears.

Specifications

Torque wrench settings

						lb f ft	Nm
Driveshaft outer flange to flexible joint	...	...	...	...	...	18	25
Driveshaft inner flange to gearcase	...	...	...	...	...	11	15

1 General description

1 The driveshafts are of open type, having a sliding joint at their inner ends and a flexible joint at their outer ends (Fig. 7.1).
2 Power is transmitted from the differential side gears through the driveshafts to the outer flexible joints which are in turn splined to short axle stubs which run in double taper roller hub bearings (Fig. 7.2).
3 The brake drums are bolted to the flanges on the outer ends of these axle stubs and the roadwheels are bolted to the brake drums.

2 Driveshaft - joint seals and boots - removal and refitting

1 Place the car over an inspection pit or on ramps to provide access to the underside of the car.
2 Unscrew and remove the four bolts which secure the driveshaft outer flange to the flexible joint (photo).
3 Disconnect the outer flange from the flexible joint. Take care not to lose the small coil spring from inside the end of the driveshaft (photos).
4 Mark the relative positions of the driveshaft inner flange to the gearcase also the oil sealing boot retainer to the inner flange. Unbolt the driveshaft inner flange boot retainer (photo).
5 Extract the circlip from the outer end of the driveshaft and slide off the outer joint, the flexible boot followed by the flexible boot retainer from the inner end of the driveshaft, the boot itself, the oil seal and seal retainer.
6 Renew any worn seals or split flexible boots. The seal/sleeve assembly can be prised out of the inner flexible boot (photo).
7 Reassembly and refitting are reversals of removal and dismantling.

3 Driveshafts - removal and installation

1 Remove the gearbox complete with driveshafts, as described in Section 3, Chapter 6.
2 Remove the final drive/differential and driveshafts from the gearcase, as described in Section 4, paragraphs 1 to 9 of Chapter 6.
3 The crownwheel must now be unbolted and the driveshafts removed, as described in Section 6, paragraphs 8 to 12 of Chapter 6.
4 Installation is a reversal of removal, but tighten the crownwheel bolts to the specified torque of 33 lb f ft (46 Nm), make sure that the grooves in the joint blocks are in contact with the inner faces of the channels in the side gears to provide proper lubrication and that the

tabs of the differential pinion shaft retainer are correctly bent down.

4 Rear hub and axle stubs - dismantling, reassembly and adjustment

1 Disconnect the outer flanges of the driveshaft from the flexible joint by unscrewing and removing the four securing bolts.
2 Push the driveshaft to one side to expose the staked nut on the inner end of the axle stub.
3 Relieve the staking on the nut, apply the handbrake fully and unscrew the nut.
4 Jack-up the rear of the car and support it securely under the bodyframe side members and the suspension arm.
5 Remove the roadwheels.
6 Release the handbrake and unbolt and remove the brake drum.
7 Tap the axle stub out of the hub bearings, taking great care not damage the threads at the inner end of the stub. Use a brass drift or screw an old nut for a few threads to take the impact of the hammer blows.
8 With the axle stub removed, prise out the outer oil seal, extract spacer and circlip and remove the outer tapered roller bearing race.
9 Repeat the removal operations for the inner oil seal and circlip and inner tapered roller bearing.
10 If the bearings are in good condition, pack them with fresh multi purpose grease and reassemble using new inner and outer oil seals.
11 If the bearings must be renewed due to wear, extract the collapsible spacer and discard it, then drive out the bearing outer tracks.
12 Drive in the new bearing outer tracks, fit a new collapsible space fit the tapered roller bearings, the circlips, outer spacer and new inner and outer oil seals. Make sure that the new bearings are well packed with grease but not over lubricated.
13 Install the axle stub and screw on a new nut finger-tight.
14 Refit the brake drum and then wind a cord round the outside of the drum and attach it to a spring balance.
15 The nut on the inner end of the axle stub must now be tightened a fraction of a turn at a time until the pull required to start the brake drum turning is 1 lb. (0.45 kg) as recorded on the spring balance. On no account back off the nut in an attempt to rectify overtightening the compressible spacer will have been over-compressed and a new must be fitted and the adjustment started all over again.
16 When adjustment is correct, stake the nut, reconnect the driveshaft having first applied plenty of grease to the axle stub splines and to little coil spring which is located in the end of the driveshaft coupling flange.
17 Refit the roadwheel and lower the car to the ground.

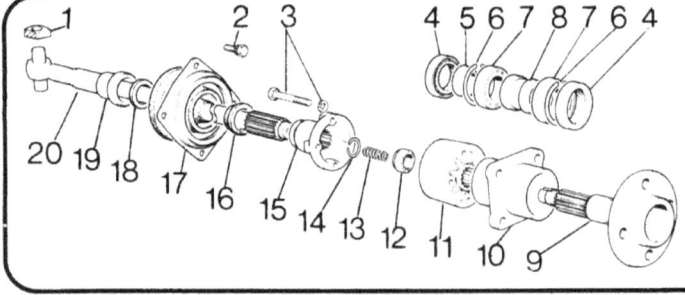

Fig. 7.1. Driveshaft and rear hub components

1	Joint block	11	Flexible joint
2	Driveshaft inner flange bolt	12	Axle stub nut
3	Driveshaft outer flange bolt	13	Spring
4	Hub oil seals	14	Circlip
5	Spacer	15	Outer coupling flange
6	Circlips	16	Flexible boot sleeve
7	Roller bearings	17	Inner boot retainer
8	Collapsible spacer	18	Oil seal
9	Axle stub	19	Oil seal retainer
10	Hub	20	Driveshaft

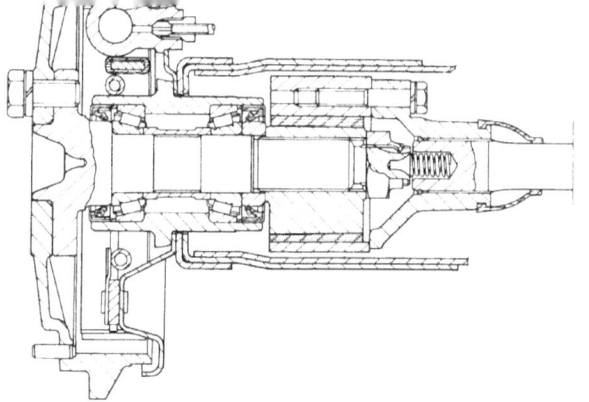

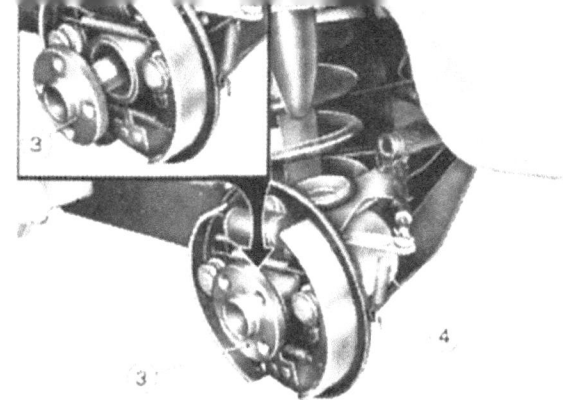

Fig. 7.2. Sectional view of a rear hub

Fig. 7.3. Withdrawing an axle stub from a rear wheel hub

2.1 Removing driveshaft outer coupling flange bolts

2.3a Driveshaft outer flexible coupling

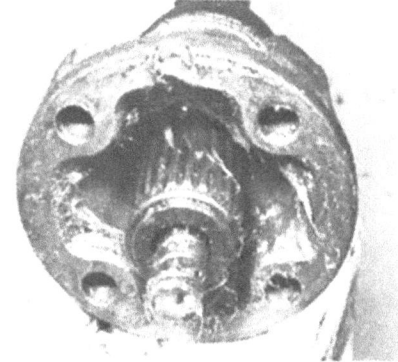

2.3b Outer end of driveshaft showing coupling flange and internal spring (well greased)

2.4 Driveshaft inner flexible boot

2.6a Driveshaft inner flexible boot with oil seal/sleeve

2.6b Oil seal/sleeve removed from driveshaft inner flexible boot

5 Fault diagnosis - driveshafts and rear hubs

Symptom	Reason/s
Noisy rear hub	Worn bearings. Incorrect adjustment. Buckled roadwheel. Defective tyre/s Worn splines on axle stub.
'Clunk' on taking up drive or on overrun	Worn shaft splines. Loose flange bolts. Worn grooves in side gear.

Chapter 8 Braking system

For modifications, and information applicable to later models, see Supplement at end of manual

Contents

Specifications

System	Hydraulic, four wheel drum dual circuit. Handbrake mechanical rear wheels
Brake fluid type/specification	Hydraulic fluid to FMVSS 116 DOT 3 and SAE J1703 (Duckham Universal Brake and Clutch Fluid)
Drum diameter	6.697 to 6.708 in (170.1 to 170.4 mm)
Maximum increase in internal diameter after refacing	0.04 in (1 mm)
Brake lining dimension	7.08 x 1.18 x 0.17 in (180.0 x 30.0 x 4.3 mm)
Minimum lining thickness before renewal	0.059 in (1.5 mm)
Master cylinder bore (diameter)	0.75 in (19.05 mm)

Wheel cylinder bore (diameter)

Front	15/16 in (23.80 mm)
Rear	5/8 in (15.70 mm)

Torque wrench settings	lb f ft	Nm
Rear drum securing bolt	60	83
Rear brake backplate	40	55
Master cylinder flange nut	12	16
Wheel cylinder to backplate bolt	7	10

1 General description

1 The braking system is of hydraulic, dual circuit, four wheel drum type with the handbrake operating mechanically on the rear wheels only (Fig. 8.1).
2 All brakes incorporate self-adjusting shoes.
3 The master cylinder is mounted on the front bulkhead just below the luggage compartment floor and adjacent to the steering box.
4 The fluid reservoir is located within the luggage boot.
5 A pendant type footbrake pedal is used with a stoplamp switch mounted on the pedal support bracket (photo).

2 Brake shoes - description of automatic adjusters

1 The automatic adjustment of the brake shoes is based upon the following arrangement.
2 Each shoe is located on a steady post (which is secured to the backplate) by means of a blind bush (Fig. 8.4).
3 The hole in the shoe web is larger in diameter than the outside diameter of the bush and the internal diameter of the bush is larger

than the diameter of the steady post.
4 When the brakes are applied, the shoes move outward into contact with the drum which also allows the web of the shoe to sl relation to the bush.
5 Through an assembly of friction washers and a heavy coil sprir the shoe does not fully return when the brake pedal is released, b shoe lining retracts from the drum only by the clearance which ex between the steady post and the bore of the bush, so providing minimum lining to drum clearance with short pedal travel.
6 It will be appreciated that the system depends upon the pressu the coil springs being greater than the retracting tension of the sh return springs and this will normally apply unless the friction was or shoe web have become contaminated with oil or grease.
7 **On no account apply oil to the friction washers or shoe web d brake overhaul.**
8 It has been found in practice that after a distance of about 4,0 miles (6,400 km) has been covered, the efficiency of the automati adjustment device leaves something to be desired and this is indica by lengthening of the foot brake pedal travel. When this occurs, d the car in reverse gear and apply the brakes very sharply. This will bring the shoes back to the closest adjustment. Repeat periodicall the need arises.

1   Jack-up the front of the car and support it securely.
2   Remove the roadwheel.
3   Tap off the grease cap and then relieve the staking on the nut at the end of the stub axle.
4   Unscrew and remove the nut and take off the thrust washer. The nut on the right-hand stub axle has a left-hand thread.
5   Support the weight of the brake drum and pull it directly from the stub axle, catching the outer taper roller bearing as the drum is withdrawn (photo).
6   Brush any accumulations of dust taking care not to inhale it and then inspect the thickness of the friction material. With bonded type linings, renew them if the thickness of the remaining material is 0.06 in (1.5 mm) or less. With rivetted linings, the shoes must be renewed if the linings have worn down to, or nearly down to the rivet heads.
7   To remove the shoes, unhook the shoe retracting springs and lift the shoes from the brake backplate. Twist a piece of wire or engage a rubber band round the wheel cylinder pistons to prevent them falling out while the shoes are missing. On no account depress the brake pedal (photo).
8   A compressor is now required to compress the spring on the shoe self-adjusting mechanism so that the circlip can be extracted. A valve spring compressor will often serve the purpose (Fig. 8.3).
9   Remove the self-adjusting components, keeping them in strict order and then reassemble them to the new shoes (Fig. 8.4).
10 Compress the spring again and engage the circlip (photo).
11 Remove the wire or band from the wheel cylinder pistons, locate the shoes on the brake backplate and reconnect the shoe retracting springs.
12 Refit the brake drum, adjust the hub bearings, as described in Chapter 10, using a new nut on the end of the stub axle and staking it securely.
13 Refit the roadwheel and lower the car to the ground.
14 Repeat the operations on the opposite front wheel.

Rear brakes
15 Jack-up the rear of the car and remove the roadwheels.
16 Unbolt and remove the brake drum (photo).
17 Repeat the operations described in paragraphs 6 to 11 of this Section, noting that the handbrake lever strut must be removed from between the upper ends of the shoe webs (photo).
18 Refit the drum and roadwheel and lower the car to the ground.
19 When all the shoes have been renewed, apply the footbrake several times to position the shoes and actuate the automatic adjuster mechanism.

---

4   Wheel cylinder - removal, overhaul and refitting

1   Remove the brake drum and shoes, as described in the preceding Section.
2   Disconnect the flexible brake hose at its union with the rigid pipeline at the support bracket. Plug the open end of the line to prevent loss of fluid.
3   The flexible hose can now be unscrewed from the wheel cylinder.
4   Unbolt and remove the wheel cylinder from the brake backplate.
5   Clean away all external dirt and pull off the boots and extract the pistons (photo).
6   Push out the reaction spring, thrust washers and seals.
7   At this stage inspect the condition of the piston and cylinder surfaces. If they are scored or scratched or show 'bright' wear areas, then renew the wheel cylinder complete.
8   If these components are in good condition, extract the seals and discard them. Clean the components in hydraulic fluid or methylated spirit - nothing else!
9   Obtain a repair kit and manipulate the new seals into position using the fingers only for the purpose.
10 Dip the components in clean hydraulic fluid before assembling them into the cylinder.
11 Refit the boots, the shoes and drum.
12 Reconnect the hydraulic hose and then bleed the circuit, as described in Section 8.

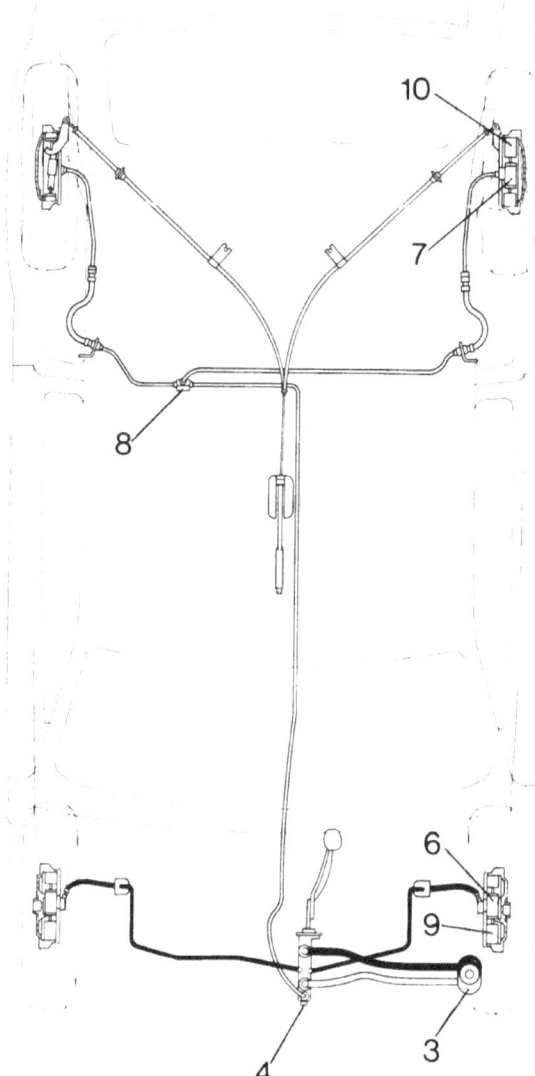

Fig. 8.1. Hydraulic circuits and handbrake linkage

3   Fluid reservoir   8   Three way connector
4   Master cylinder   9   Brake shoes
6   Wheel cylinder   10 Brake shoes
7   Wheel cylinder

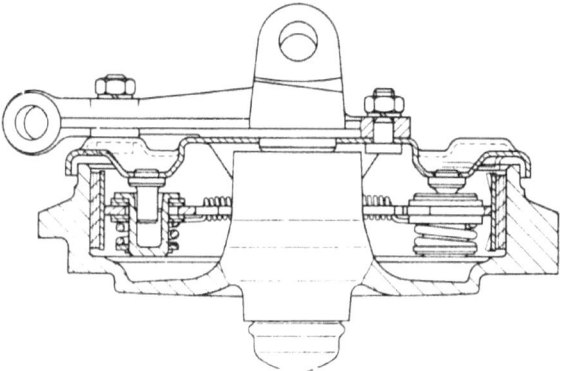

Fig. 8.2. Cut away view of a front brake assembly

1.5 Brake and clutch pedals showing stop lamp switch

3.5 Front hub outer bearing and thrust washer

3.7 Front brake assembly

3.10 An automatic adjuster showing retaining circlip

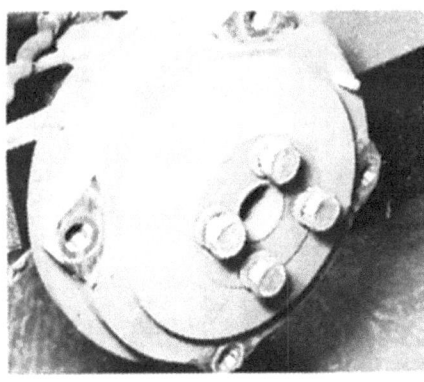

3.16 Rear brake drum showing securing bolts

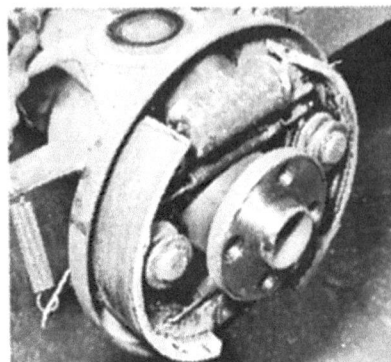

3.17 Rear brake assembly

13 Although the wheel cylinder seals can be renewed without removing the cylinder from the brake backplate, this is not advised; as apart from the possibility of dirt entering the cylinder it is very difficult to inspect the interior of the cylinder, which is essential if the seal has been deformed or cut and has been operating in this condition for any length of time and may have caused the piston to tilt and scrape the cylinder walls.

---

5 Master cylinder - removal, overhaul and refitting

1 Open the lid of the luggage boot and remove the cover from the boot floor which gives access to the brake master cylinder.

2 Disconnect the fluid supply pipes from the master cylinder and let the fluid drain from the reservoir into a suitable container. Take great care not to let the fluid come into contact with the paintwork as it will act as an effective paint stripper!

3 Disconnect the rigid pipelines from the master cylinder by unscrewing their unions. Cap the open ends of the lines to prevent entry of dirt (Fig. 8.5).

4 Working either through the opening in the luggage boot floor or by raising the front of the car and reaching upwards next to the steering box, unscrew the master cylinder flange mounting nuts and withdraw the unit.

5 Clean away external dirt and then insert a rod into the pushrod hole at the end of the cylinder and depress the pistons two or three times to expel the hydraulic fluid.

6 Secure the master cylinder body in the jaws of a vice and pull off the dust excluder (Fig. 8.6).

7 Depress the pistons against their spring pressure and unscrew and remove the stop bolts. Gently release the pressure applied to the pistons and then extract first the primary piston components followed by the secondary piston components (Fig. 8.7).

8 At this stage, examine the surfaces of the pistons and cylinder bore for scoring or 'bright' wear areas. If these are evident, renew the master cylinder complete.

9 If the components are in good condition, discard the seals and obtain a repair kit which will contain all the renewable components.

Clean each part in hydraulic fluid or methylated spirit - nothing else

10 Manipulate the new seals into position using the fingers only. Di the components in clean hydraulic fluid before inserting them into the cylinder.

11 Install the secondary components first and then depress the pist with a rod so that the stop bolt can be screwed into engagement wi the secondary piston. Note that the stop bolt engages in the groo in the piston.

12 Install the primary piston components and again depress the pist so that the second stop bolt can be screwed in. Fit the new dust excluding boot.

13 Refitting is a reversal of removal, but as the master cylinder is offered into position, remember to engage the pedal pushrod into t end of the cylinder body.

14 On completion, bleed both hydraulic circuits, as described in Section 8.

---

6 Flexible hydraulic hoses - inspection and renewal

1 Inspect the flexible hoses for rubbing, chafing or general deterioration at regular intervals. Bend each hose double with the fingers. If tiny cracks can be seen then the rubber is perished and th hose must be renewed.

2 Disconnect a flexible hose at its union with the rigid brake line a the support bracket.

3 Hold the end fitting on the flexible hose quite still while the uni nut is unscrewed. Now using two spanners, unscrew the locknut wh secures the flexible hose and fitting to the support bracket.

4 Remove the flexible hose from the end fitting and unscrew it fro the wheel cylinder (front brake) or the rigid pipe connecting union (rear brake).

5 When installing a flexible hose, make sure that it takes on a similar curve to that followed by the original one. If necessary, the hose end fitting can be rotated in the support bracket by not more than a quarter turn to achieve this.

6 Always bleed the appropriate hydraulic circuit on completion o the work.

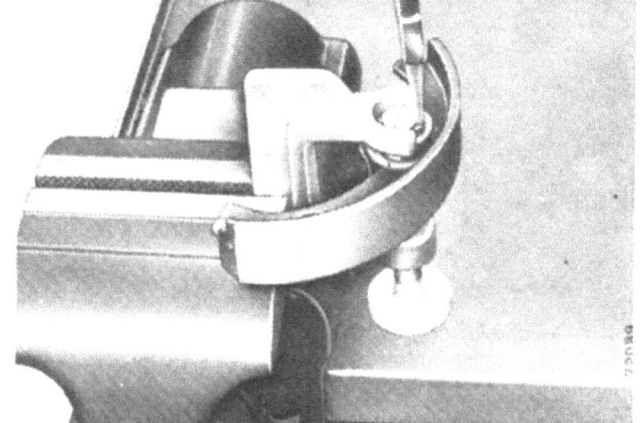

Fig. 8.3. Extracting a circlip from shoe automatic adjuster

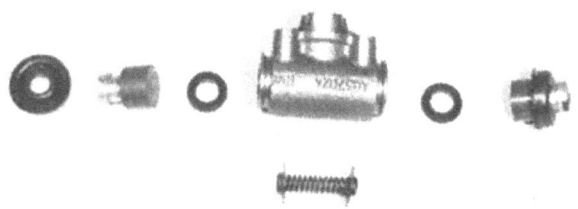

4.5 Exploded view of a wheel cylinder

Fig. 8.4. Brake shoe automatic adjuster components

1 Circlip
2 Plain washer
3 Spring
4 Friction washers
5 Brake shoe
6 Blind bush

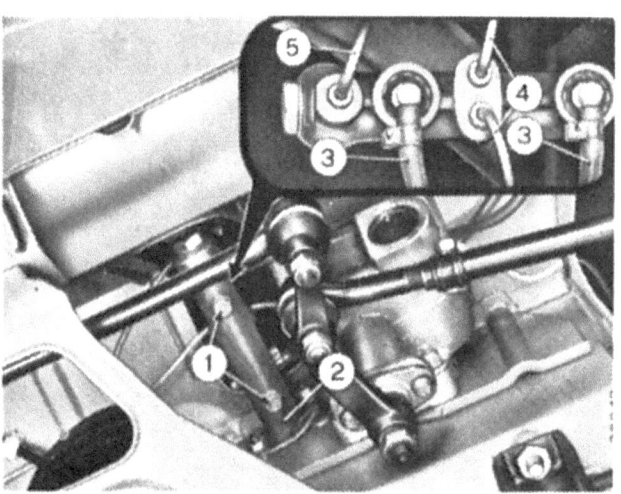

Fig. 8.5. Location of brake master cylinder. Inset, view through luggage boot floor aperture

1 Stop bolts
2 Master cylinder
3 Fluid feed from reservoir
4 Hydraulic line to front brakes
5 Hydraulic line to rear brakes

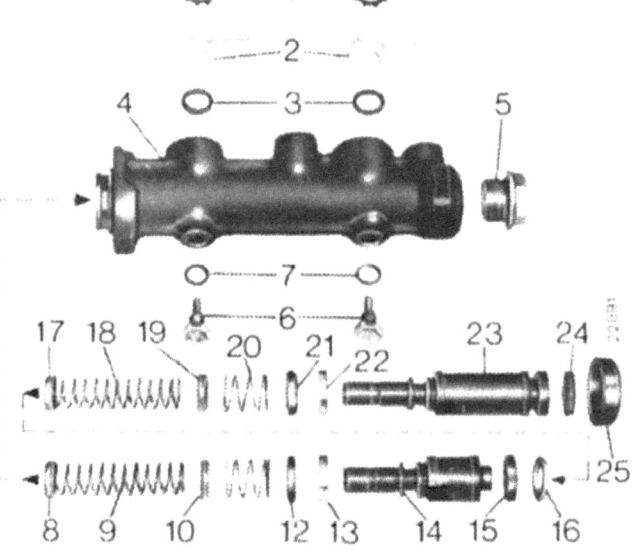

Fig. 8.6. Exploded view of the master cylinder

1 Spring washer
2 Fluid feed elbow
3 Seal
4 Master cylinder body
5 End plug
6 Stop bolt
7 Seal
8 Spring seat
9 Spring
10 Spring cup
11 Spring
12 Seal
13 Spacer
14 Secondary piston
15 Seal
16 Spacer
17 Spring seat
18 Spring
19 Spring cup
20 Spring
21 Seal
22 Spacer
23 Primary piston
24 Seal
25 Dust excluding boot

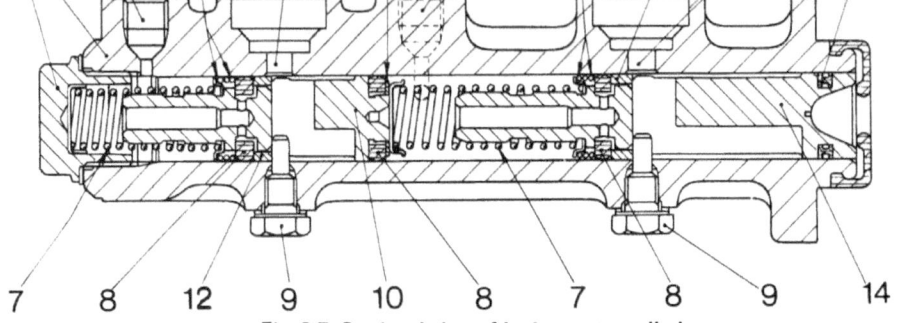

Fig. 8.7. Sectional view of brake master cylinder

1	Master cylinder body and end plug	4	Fluid outlet to front brakes	8	Seal
2	Fluid outlet to rear brakes	5	Fluid inlet from reservoir	9	Stop bolt
3	Fluid inlet from reservoir	6	Seal	10	Secondary piston
		7	Spring	11	Washer

12 Spacers
13 Spring and cup
14 Primary piston

7 Rigid brake lines - inspection and renewal

1   At regular intervals wipe the steel pipes clean and examine them for signs of rust or denting caused by flying stones.

2   Examine the securing clips. Bend the tongues of the clips if necessary to ensure that they hold the brake pipes securely without letting them rattle or vibrate.

3   Check that the pipes are not touching any adjacent components or rubbing against any part of the vehicle. Where this is observed, bend the pipe gently away to clear.

4   Any section of pipe which is rusty or chafed should be renewed. Brake pipes are available to the correct length and fitted with end unions from most Fiat dealers and can be made to pattern by many accessory suppliers. When installing the new pipes use the old pipes as a guide to bending and do not make any bends sharper than it is necessary.

5   The system will of course have to be bled when the circuit has been reconnected.

8 Hydraulic system - bleeding

1   Removal of all the air from the hydraulic system is essential to the correct working of the braking system, and before undertaking this examine the fluid reservoir cap to ensure that both vent holes, one on top and the second underneath but not in line, are clear; check the level of fluid and top up if required.

2   Check all brake line unions and connections for possible seepage, and at the same time check the condition of the rubber hoses, which may be perished.

3   If the condition of the wheel cylinders is in doubt, check for possible signs of fluid leakage.

4   If there is any possibility of incorrect fluid having been put into the system, drain all the fluid out and flush through with methylated spirit. Renew all piston seals and cups since these will be affected and could possibly fail under pressure.

5   Gather together a clean glass jar, a length of tubing which fits tightly over the bleed nipples, and a tin of the correct brake fluid.

6   To bleed the system if the master cylinder has been disturbed, clean dirt from the bleed nipples and start on the rear brakes by removing the rubber cap over the bleed valve, and fitting a rubber tube in position.

7   Place the end of the tube in a clean glass jar containing sufficient fluid to keep the end of the tube submerged during the operation (Fig. 8.8).

8   Open the bleed valve with a spanner and have an assistant quickly depress the brake pedal. After slowly releasing the pedal, pause for a moment to allow the fluid to recoup in the master cylinder and then depress again. This will force air from the system. Continue until no more air bubbles can be seen coming from the tube. At intervals make certain that the reservoir is kept topped-up otherwise air will enter at this point again.

9   Once the rear brakes have been bled, bleed the front brake furth from the master cylinder followed by the remaining front brake.

10 Tighten the bleed screws when the pedal is in the fully depresse position.

11 If a component of one hydraulic circuit only has been disturbed then only that circuit need be bled.

12 Use only clean fluid for topping-up purposes and discard fluid from the bleed jar. Fluid used for topping-up should have been kep an air tight container and remained unshaken for the previous 24 hours.

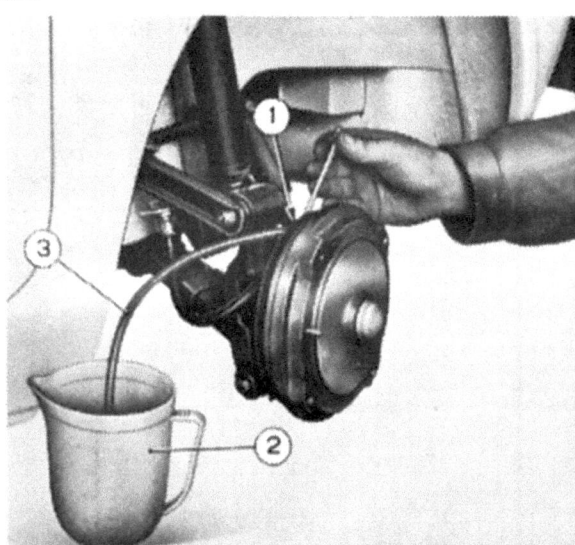

Fig. 8.8. Bleeding a front brake

1	Bleed nipple	3	Bleed tube
2	Container		

9 Brake drum - renovation

1   Whenever a brake drum is removed, examine its shoe lining rub surface for scoring or deep grooving.

2   After a considerable mileage the internal diameter of the drum wear oval in shape due to normal brake application characteristics. This can often be detected by juddering when the brakes are appli although it is known that the system is otherwise in first class condition.

3   Where any of these conditions are encountered, the interior of drum can be refaced provided that the internal diameter is not inc by more than 0.04 in (1 mm). This is a job for your dealer.

4   Where refacing would create drums of above the maximum internal diameter permissible, fit new ones.

1   The handbrake should normally be fully on after having passed over four or five teeth of its ratchet (Fig. 8.9).
2   Where handbrake travel is excessive, jack-up the rear of the car so that the roadwheels are free to turn.
3   Apply the handbrake control lever over three notches.
4   Release the locknuts at the cable abutment brackets.
5   Turn the cable adjustment nuts until each roadwheel just locks. Tighten the locknuts.
6   Release the handbrake and check that the two rear roadwheels are free to turn.

---

11 Handbrake cable - renewal

1   If the handbrake cable should break, or even show signs of age with fraying, it will need changing.
2   Remove the split pin from the pin holding each cable end fork to the lever on the handbrake mechanism on the rear of the brake drums (photo).
3   Having pulled out the pins from the forks undo the adjuster nuts and locknuts from the brackets on the rear suspension swinging arms. These are 'U' shaped brackets. The cable can be pulled along until the inner cable can pass through the slot in the bracket. Disconnect the conduit clamps.
4   Inside the car remove the two small bolts holding the tin cover to the panel just in front of the rear seat. Remove the tunnel trim and the seat.
5   Undo the bolts holding the handbrake bracket to the top of the tunnel. Now pull up the handbrake assembly until the pin through the wheel working the cable can be reached. Take out the split pin, remove the wheel's pin, and disengage the cable from the lever.

7   When fitting the new cable grease all the pivot pins.
8   Adjust the cable, as described in Section 10.

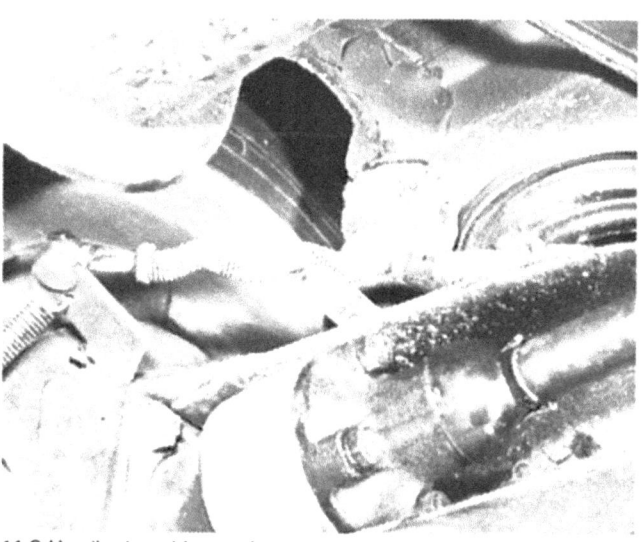

11.2 Handbrake cable attachment to rear brake

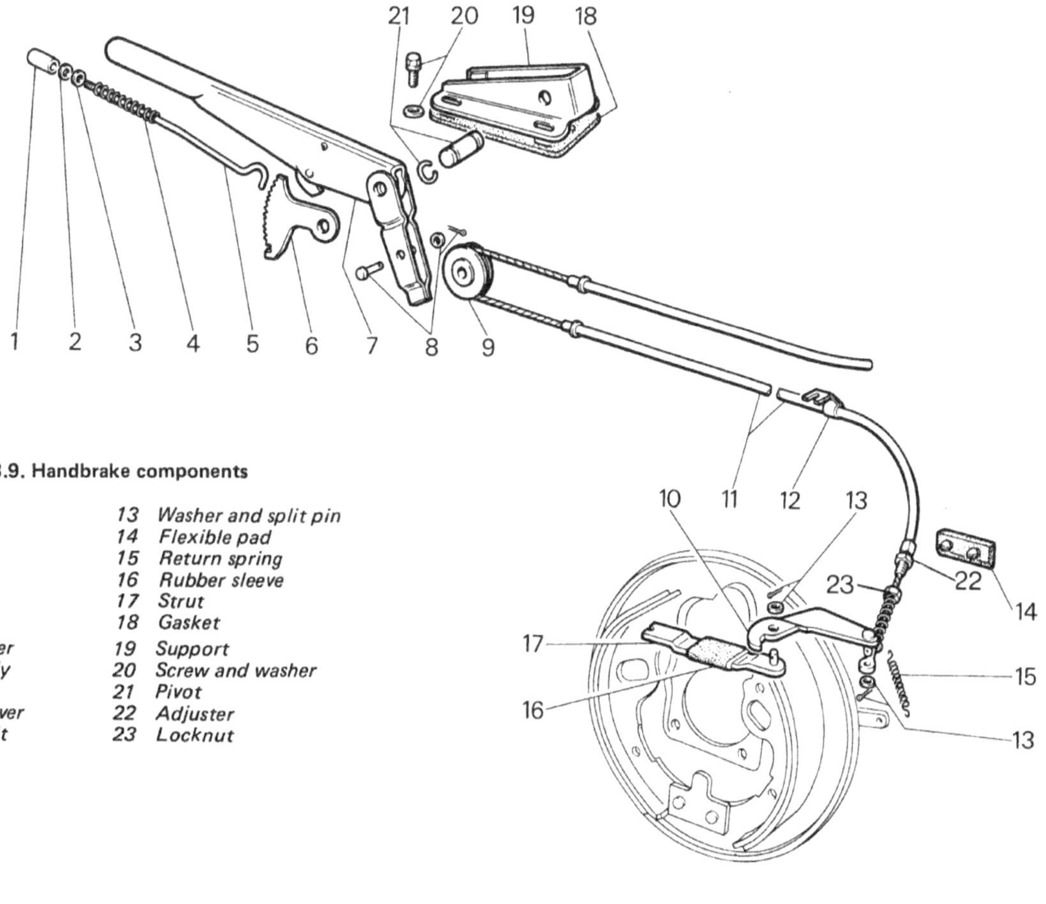

Fig. 8.9. Handbrake components

1	Release button	13	Washer and split pin
2	Grommet	14	Flexible pad
3	Washer	15	Return spring
4	Spring	16	Rubber sleeve
5	Rod	17	Strut
6	Ratchet	18	Gasket
7	Hand control lever	19	Support
8	Pivot pin assembly	20	Screw and washer
9	Pulley	21	Pivot
10	Shoe actuating lever	22	Adjuster
11	Cable and conduit	23	Locknut
12	Clamp		

Brake grab	Brake shoe linings not bedded-in.
	Contaminated with oil or grease.
	Scored drums.
Brake drag	Master cylinder faulty.
	Brake foot pedal return impeded.
	Blocked filler cap vent.
	Master cylinder reservoir or compartments overfilled.
	Seized wheel cylinder.
	Incorrect adjustment of handbrake.
	Weak or broken shoe return springs.
	Crushed or blocked pipelines.
Brake pedal feels hard	Friction surfaces contaminated with oil or grease.
	Glazed friction material surfaces.
	Seized wheel cylinder.
Excessive pedal travel	Low fluid level in reservoir.
	Automatic shoe adjusters faulty.
	Worn front wheel bearings.
	System requires bleeding.
	Worn linings.
Pedal creep during sustained application	Fluid leak.
	Faulty master cylinder.
Pedal 'spongy' or 'springy'	System requires bleeding.
	Perished flexible hose.
	Loose master cylinder.
	Cracked brake drum.
	Linings not bedded-in.
	Faulty master cylinder.
Fall in master cylinder fluid level	Normal lining wear.
	Leak.

Chapter 9 Electrical system

For modifications, and information applicable to later models, see Supplement at end of manual

Contents

Specifications

System type	12V negative earth
Battery	12V 34 A/h

Dynamo

Type	Fiat DSV 90/12/16/3S
Maximum steady output	230W
Maximum steady current	16A
Charing starts	120 rev/min (17 mph - 27 km/h in top gear)
Armature resistance	68°F (20°C) 0.145 ± 0.01 ohm
Field winding resistance	68°F (20°C) 7.7 to 8.1 ohm

Regulator unit

Type	Fiat GN 2/12/16

Starter motor

Type	Fiat B 76-05/12S pre-engaged
Rated output	0.5 kW

Fuses

Number	Rating (Amps)	Circuit protected
1 - A	8	Direction indicators, fuel gauge, stop lamps Windscreen wiper, oil pressure warning lamp
2 - B	8	Horn, interior lamp
3 - C	8	Headlamp (L.H. main beam), main beam warning lamp
4 - D	8	Headlamp (R.H. main beam)
5 - E	8	Headlamp (L.H. dipped beam)
6 - F	8	Headlamp (R.H. dipped beam)
7 - G	8	Front parking lamp (L.H.), tail lamp (R.H.), rear number plate lamp (L.H.)
8 - H	8	Front parking lamp (R.H.), instrument panel lamps, tail lamps (L.H.) number plate lamp (R.H.)

	lb f ft	Nm
Front parking and direction indicator lamp	5/21W double filament	
Side repeater lamp	4W	
Tail and brake stoplamp	5/21W double filament	
Rear direction indicator lamp	21W	
Rear number plate lamp	5W	
Interior lamp	5W	
Instrument and parking lamp and indicator lamps	3W	
Warning and indicator lamps	1.2W	

Torque wrench settings

	lb f ft	Nm
Dynamo pulley flange nut	25	35
Fan to dynamo shaft nut	25	35
Dynamo pulley hub nut	100	138

1 General description

1 The electrical system is of 12V negative earth type.
2 The battery is mounted at the front of the car within the luggage compartment (photo).
3 The battery is charged by a dynamo which is driven by a drivebelt from the centrifugal oil filter/pulley which is mounted on the rear end of the crankshaft.
4 A regulator unit controls the charging rate.
5 A pre-engaged starter motor is fitted.

1.2 Location of the battery

2 Battery - removal and installation

1 The battery is located at the front on the right-hand side of the engine compartment.
2 Disconnect the lead from the negative terminal by unscrewing the clamp bolt.
3 Disconnect the lead from the positive terminal and remove the battery securing bolts and frame.
4 Lift the battery carefully from its tray and avoid spilling electrolyte on the paintwork.
5 Installation is a reversal of removal, but when connecting the terminals, clean off any corrosion or white deposits which may be present and when the clamp bolts are tight, smear the terminal and clamp with petroleum jelly to prevent corrosion recurring.

3 Battery - maintenance

1 Carry out the regular weekly maintenance described in the Routine Maintenance Section at the front of this manual.
2 Clean the top of the battery, removing all dirt and moisture.
3 As well as keeping the terminals clean and covered with petroleum jelly, the top of the battery, and especially the top of the cells, should be kept clean and dry. This helps prevent corrosion and ensures that the battery does not become partially discharged by leakage through dampness and dirt.
4 Once every three months, remove the battery and inspect the battery securing bolts, the battery clamp plate, tray and battery leads

for corrosion (white fluffy deposits on the metal which are brittle touch). If any corrosion is found, clean off the deposits with ammonia and paint over the clean metal with an anti-rust/anti-aci paint.
5 At the same time inspect the battery case for cracks. If a crack found, clean and plug it with one of the proprietary compounds marketed for this purpose. If leakage through the crack has been excessive then it will be necessary to refill the appropriate cell wit fresh electrolyte as detailed later. Cracks are frequently caused to top of the battery cases by pouring in distilled water in the middl winter *after* instead of *before* a run. This gives the water no chanc mix with the electrolyte and so the former freezes and splits the battery case.
6 If topping-up the battery becomes excessive and the case has b inspected for cracks that could cause leakage, but none are found battery is being over-charged and the voltage regulator will have t checked and reset.
7 With the battery on the bench at the three monthly interval ch measure its specific gravity with a hydrometer to determine the st of charge and condition of the electrolyte (Fig. 9.1). There shoulc be very little variation between the different cells and if a variatio excess of 0.025 is present it will be due to either:

a) Loss of electrolyte from the battery at some time caused b spillage or a leak, resulting in a drop in the specific gravity electrolyte when the deficiency was replaced with distilled water instead of fresh electrolyte.
b) An internal short circuit caused by buckling of the plates o a similar malady pointing to the likelihood of total battery failure in the near future.

8 The specific gravity of the electrolyte for fully charged condit at the electrolyte temperature indicated, is listed in Table A. The gravity of a fully discharged battery at different temperatures of electrolyte is given in Table B.

Table A
Specific Gravity - Battery Fully Charged

1.268 at 100°F or 38°C electrolyte temperature
1.272 at 90°F or 32°C electrolyte temperature
1.276 at 80°F or 27°C electrolyte temperature
1.280 at 70°F or 21°C electrolyte temperature
1.284 at 60°F or 16°C electrolyte temperature
1.288 at 50°F or 10°C electrolyte temperature
1.292 at 40°F or 4°C electrolyte temperature
1.296 at 30°F or -1.5°C electrolyte temperature

Table B
Specific Gravity - Battery Fully Discharged

1.098 at 100°F or 38°C electrolyte temperature
1.102 at 90°F or 32°C electrolyte temperature
1.106 at 80°F or 27°C electrolyte temperature
1.110 at 70°F or 21°C electrolyte temperature
1.114 at 60°F or 16°C electrolyte temperature
1.118 at 50°F or 10°C electrolyte temperature
1.112 at 40°F or 4°C electrolyte temperature
1.126 at 30°F or -1.5°C electrolyte temperature

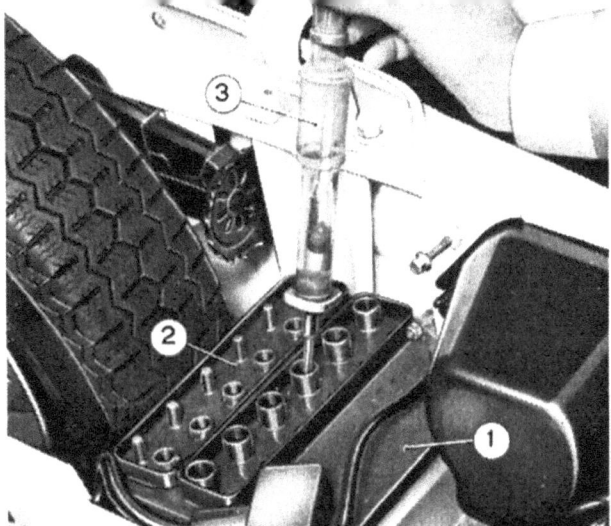

Fig. 9.1. Measuring specific gravity of battery electrolyte

1 Battery casing   3 Hydrometer
2 Call cover

---

4 Electrolyte - replenishment

1 If the battery is in a fully charged state and one of the cells maintains a specific gravity reading which is 0.025 or more lower than the others, and a check of each cell has been made with a voltage meter to check for short circuits (a four to seven second test should give a steady reading of between 1.2 to 1.8 volts), then it is likely that electrolyte has been lost from the cell with the low reading at some time.

2 Top-up the cell with a solution of 1 part sulphuric acid to 2.5 parts of water. If the cell is already fully topped-up draw some electrolyte out of it with a hydrometer.

3 When mixing the sulphuric acid and water **never add water to sulphuric acid** - always pour the acid slowly onto the water in a glass container. **If water is added to sulphuric acid it will explode.**

4 Continue to top-up the cell with the freshly made electrolyte and then recharge the battery and check the hydrometer readings.

---

5 Battery - charging

1 In winter time when heavy demand is placed upon the battery, such as when starting from cold, and much electrical equipment is continually in use, it is a good idea to occasionally have the battery fully charged from an external source at the rate of 3.5 or 4 amps.

2 Continue to charge the battery at this rate until no further rise in specific gravity is noted over a four hour period.

3 Alternatively, a trickle charger charging at the rate of 1.5 amps can be safely used overnight.

4 Specially rapid 'boost' charges which are claimed to restore the power of the battery in 1 to 2 hours are most dangerous as they can cause serious damage to the battery plates.

---

6 Dynamo - testing in the car

1 There can be two types of faults. The charging rate may become low, or the output may stop completely. A low output is difficult to detect unless an ammeter is fitted. The first symptoms are likely to be a flat battery, but a complete failure will be shown by the ignition warning lamp coming on. Normally the lamp goes out immediately the dynamo starts to charge.

2 If, with the engine running, no charge comes from the dynamo, or the charge is low, first check that the fan belt is in place and is not

3 If wiring has recently been disconnected, check that the leads have not been incorrectly fitted.

4 Make sure none of the electrical equipment such as the lights or radio, is on, and then take the leads off the dynamo terminals. Join the terminals together with a short length of wire.

5 Attach to the centre of this length of wire the positive clip of a 0-20 volts voltmeter and run the other clip to earth on the dynamo yoke. Start the engine and allow it to idle at approximately 1500 rev/min. At this speed the dynamo should give a reading of about 15 volts on the voltmeter. This speed is a fast idle: Do not run the engine faster or the field winding may be overloaded.

6 If no reading is recorded, then check the brushes and brush connections. If a very low reading of approximately 1 volt is observed then the field winding may be suspect.

7 If a reading of between 4 to 6 volts is recorded it is likely that the armature winding is at fault.

8 If a satisfactory reading is obtained, then the fault is either in the wiring or the control box. Reconnect the two wires onto the generator. They have different sized terminals, so cannot be muddled.

9 Take off the leads on terminals 51 and 67, the left two on the regulator. These can be muddled, so make sure they are marked to prevent this.

10 Again join the two leads together and repeat the same test. If again it is successful, and there is full generator voltage, then those leads must be alright, and the fault is in the control box or the wiring beyond. Refit the leads and refer to Section 9.

---

7 Dynamo - removal and refitting

1 Disconnect the lead from the battery negative terminal.

2 Unbolt and remove the front flange of the dynamo pulley and detach the drivebelt. Retain any belt adjustment shims.

3 Disconnect the leads from the dynamo terminals (photo).

4 Reaching round behind the engine, disconnect the air inlet ducting from the rear of the fan cooling casing.

5 The nut which secures the fan to the extension of the dynamo armature shaft will now be exposed and it should be unscrewed. In order to prevent the armature turning as the nut is unscrewed, hold the flange still at the opposite end of the dynamo using a ring spanner on the nut and lever it against a stud (photos).

6 Release the dynamo mounting strap by unscrewing the clamp bolt.

7 Unscrew the two nuts which secure the dynamo flange to the fan cooling casing.

8 Withdraw the dynamo at the same time holding the fan within the casing and taking care not to let the Woodruff key (which secures the fan to the shaft) drop into the fan casing. Should this happen, retrieve it with a magnet.

9 As the dynamo is withdrawn, tilt it to the left and upwards to disengage the plastic positioning dowel which locates it on the support cradle of the engine crankcase.

10 Refit the dynamo by reversing the removal operations, but if the drivebelt requires tensioning, refer to Chapter 2, Section 5.

---

8 Dynamo - overhaul

1 With the dynamo removed from the car, grip the pulley flange in the jaws of a vice and unscrew the securing nut (Fig. 9.2 and photo).

2 Remove the pulley and Woodruff key from the armature shaft (photo).

3 Unscrew and remove the tie-bolts and withdraw the fan end frame and the commutator end frame (photos).

4 If the dynamo has seen considerable service, the brushes will almost certainly require renewal.

5 If the shaft bearings are worn, they can be renewed after unbolting the bearing retainers.

6 Examine the commutator segments. If the armature has some burned out windings with short circuits there will be burns, and the windings may show signs of overheating.

7 Test the resistance of the windings by checking the resistance from segment to segment. A replacement armature may be difficult to get, and one from a vehicle breaker may have a bad commutator, so

Specification, then a short circuit is indicated. If the field windings are faulty, unless a visual inspection discloses an easily mended defect, a reconditioned unit will probably be needed. Replacement windings are unlikely to be available quickly and are difficult to fit. It should be possible to get a serviceable body complete at a breakers, and put your armature into the other body.

9 If the armature is in good condition, clean the commutator with a fuel moistened rag and note whether the segments are clearly defined and free from pitting or burned areas.

10 Scrape the dirt out of the undercut gaps of insulator between the metal segments with a narrow screwdriver.

11 If, after the commutator has been cleaned, pits and burnt spots are still present, wrap a strip of fine glass paper round the commutator. Rub the patches off. Keep moving the paper along and turning the armature so that the rubbing is spread evenly all over. Finally repolish the commutator with metal polish, then reclean the gaps.

12 In extreme cases of wear the commutator can be mounted in a lathe. With the lathe turning fast, take a very fine cut. Then polish with fine glass paper, followed by metal polish.

13 If the commutator is badly worn or has been skimmed the segments may be worn till level with the insulator in between. In this case the insulator must be undercut. This is done to a depth of 0.04 in (1 mm). The best tool is a hacksaw blade, if necessary ground down to make it thinner. The under cutting must take the full width of the insulator away, right out to the metal segments on each side (Fig. 9 3).

14 Again clean all thoroughly when finished, and ensure no rough edges are left. Any roughness will cause excessive brush wear. In all this work it must also be remembered that the commutator should be treated reasonably carefully.

15 Commence reassembly by installing to the armature, first the brush endplate, with the brushes in place, pushing them back with clean fingers against the springs to get them over the commutator (photo).

16 Now lower down the body of the dynamo over the armature. Slide

17 Now fit the other endplate. Again locate the dowel. These dowels are very small peenings on the body, locating with grooves in the end plate.

18 Guide the ends of the tie bolts through the holes in the endplate. Do this with the dynamo upright so that the bolts will hang vertical and find their way through the holes.

19 Fit the flat washers and the self locking nuts to the bolts.

9 Regulator unit - description and testing

1 The regulator unit is located on the left-hand side of the engine compartment and comprises a cut out, a voltage regulator and a current regulator (Fig. 9.4 and photo).

2 The purpose of the cut out is to prevent the battery discharging through the dynamo once the engine is switched off and the dynamo stops charging.

3 The two regulator relays by their combination of voltage and current control regulate the output to suit the electrical load, such lights that might be switched on, and to suit the state of charge of battery.

4 If the control box has a complete failure the ignition warning light will come on. If there is partial failure, unless an ammeter is fitted, there will be no warning. Undercharging may become apparent as flat battery. Minor overcharging will give the need for frequent topping-up of the battery. Gross overcharging may blow light bulbs and perhaps result in a smell of burning, from the overloaded dynamo.

5 Major defects are likely to be the burning of the points on the relays.

6 Special instruments are required to test the regulator for faults it is recommended that such work is left to your Fiat dealer, also a resetting which may be necessary.

7.3 Dynamo terminals and leads

7.5a Removing the fan securing nut

7.5b Method of locking dynamo prior to removing fan securing nut

8.1 Unscrewing dynamo pulley mounting flange nut

8.2 Removing dynamo pulley mounting flange and Woodruff key

8.3a Unscrewing a dynamo tie bolt nut

8.3b Removing dynamo brush end plate

8.15 Reassembling brush end plate to dynamo armature

9.1 Location of regulator unit

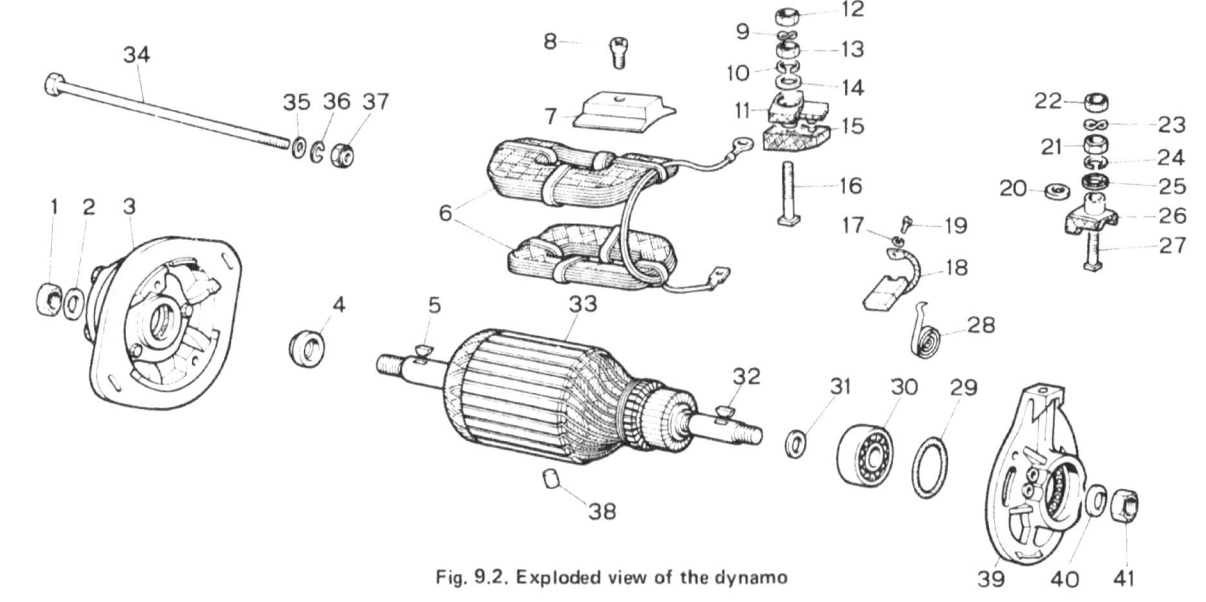

Fig. 9.2. Exploded view of the dynamo

1	Cooling fan nut	12	Terminal nut	22	Terminal nut	32	Woodruff key
2	Lockwasher	13	Terminal nut	23	Spring washer	33	Armature
3	Fan end frame	14	Plain washer	24	Lockwasher	34	Tie-bolt
4	Shouldered spacer	15	Insulator	25	Insulator	35	Plain washer
5	Woodruff key	16	Terminal	26	Insulator	36	Lockwasher
6	Field coils	17	Lockwasher	27	Terminal	37	Nut
7	Pole shoe	18	Brush	28	Brush spring	38	Locating dowel
8	Pole shoe screw	19	Brush terminal screw	29	Seal	39	Commutator end frame
9	Spring washer	20	Plain washer	30	Bearing	40	Plain washer
10	Lockwasher	21	Terminal nut	31	Plain washer	41	Pulley hub nut
11	Insulator						

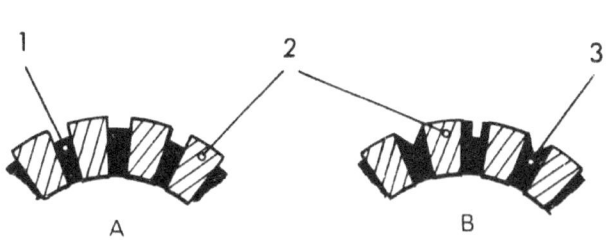

Fig. 9.3. Commutator undercutting diagram

A	Correct	B	Incorrect
1	Mica insulators	3	Mica insulators
2	Segments		

Fig. 9.4. Regulator unit with cover removed

1	Voltage regulator contact bracket	6	Cut-out relay contact bracket
2	Voltage regulator armature	7	Connecting wire to series resistor on voltage regulator
3	Current regulator armature		
4	Cut-out relay armature	8	Current regulator contact bracket
5	Cut-out relay armature stop		

1 The starter is of the pre-engaged type (Fig. 9.5).

2 When the cable is pulled by the lever beside the driver an arm on the top of the starter does two things. A fork at the bottom of the actuating lever on the starter body slides the drive gear on the starter shaft towards the gear ring on the outside of the flywheel. If the teeth happen to be lined up it goes into mesh. If not lined up, the starter's gear slides on its mounting against a spring, which will push it into mesh as soon as the starter begins to turn and lines up the teeth. Once the lever has got near the end of its travel the gears are ready for the motor to turn. In the last bit of its movement the lever pushes on a switch and completes the electrical circuit.

3 Once the engine fires, the starter motor could run too fast as the engine picks up, so there is a freewheel in the drive.

---

11 Starter motor and operating cable – removal and refitting

Starter motor

1 Disconnect the lead from the battery negative terminal.

2 Open the engine compartment lid and disconnect the operating cable from the switch lever on the top of the starter motor by extracting the split pin (photo).

3 Disconnect the electrical lead from the starter motor terminal.

4 Unbolt the support plate from the front end of the starter motor. This is secured under one of the driveshaft flange nuts (photo).

5 Unbolt the starter from the clutch bellhousing and lift it from the engine compartment.

6 Installation is a reversal of removal. Adjust the cable as described in paragraph 11.

Operating cable

7 Raise the rear of the car on ramps or axle stands and chock the front wheels.

8 Remove the cover from the operating lever and disconnect the cable by removing the split pin. It may be necessary to remove the bolt securing the choke and starter levers to gain access. The outer cable bush lugs are released by turning it through 90° and pushing it through the floor.

9 Open the engine compartment lid and disconnect the operating cable from the switch lever on the top of the starter motor by extracting the split pin.

10 The cable can now be detached from its retaining clips under the car.

11 Refit the cable to the switch and operating levers before reattaching it to the underside of the car. Adjustment is by using one of three holes at the starter end of the cable – put the split pin through the hole which allows minimum slack in the cable without tending to operate the switch.

1 Remove the two Phillips headed screws that hold the starter switch to the top of the body, and take off the switch (photo and Fig. 9.6).

2 Undo the screw clamping the shield over the apertures for the brushes and remove the shield (photo).

3 Undo the two nuts on the long bolts that clamp the whole starter together, at the brush end (photo).

4 From the other end pull off the starter drive, with its engaging mechanism (photo).

5 At the windows for the brushes, undo the terminal securing the field coils in the starter body to the brush endplate. Then take off the endplate (photos).

6 To dismantle the drive mechanism, first remove the dirt shield. It is a rubber boot held by the pin of the actuating lever.

7 Remove the lever's pin (photo).

8 Push the drive pinion as far as it will go into the housing. Disconnect the forks of the engaging arm from the groove in the drive pinion, and then bring out the engaging lever fork-end first. The components of the drive can now be lifted out (photo).

9 Unscrew the switch from the top of the starter body.

10 Check the brushes for wear. It is best to renew them in any case at the time of major overhaul.

11 Clean the commutator with a fuel-soaked rag and if necessary, undercut the insulators, as described for the dynamo in Section 8.

12 Clean the bearings of the armature shaft and relubricate them after checking them for signs of wear.

13 Clean all the components of the drive, and check them for wear. Lubricate with a molybdenum - disulphide grease.

14 If any of the major components are badly worn, it may be best to get a replacement unit.

15 The bearings are self-lubricating. Place them in engine oil, allowing it time to soak in before reassembly.

16 Check the switch contacts for burning. If the starter control lever has been pulled gently too often the switch will have been burned. With gentle operation the two contacts are not firmly pressed against each other, so sparking takes place. This can lead either to the starter failing to work, or worse, not stopping when the control is released. Should the latter happen, switch off the ignition, and take off the battery lead quickly.

17 Commence reassembly with the starter drive assembly. Insert the drive pinion into the end of the housing and then engage the shift lever so that its lug is correctly located for actuating the switch.

18 Install the spring between the forks of the lever and insert the pivot pin. Make sure that the ends of the spring are holding the shift lever in the 'OFF' position.

19 Fit a new split pin into the pivot pin and then install the flexible dust excluding boot. If the boot is deformed or has deteriorated, then it should be renewed.

20 Fit the flat washer to the armature shaft at the commutator end.

21 Push the brush endplate over the commutator holding the brushes in their retracted position with the fingers.

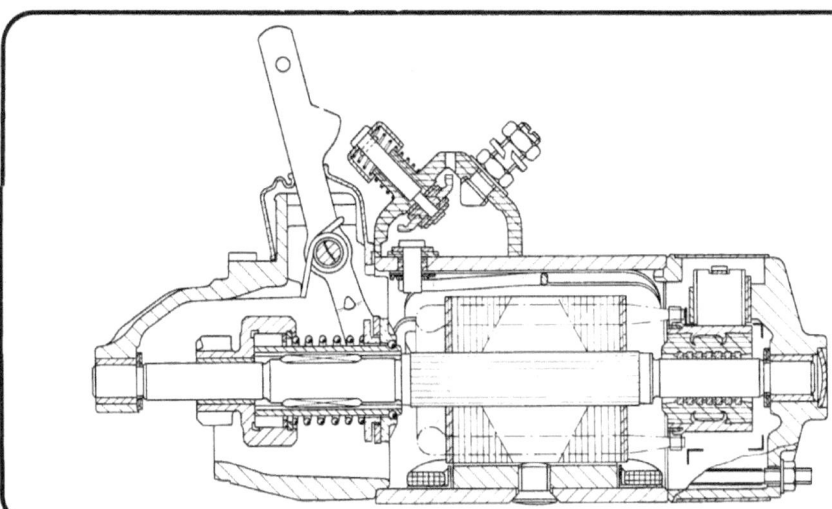

Fig. 9.5. Sectional view of starter motor

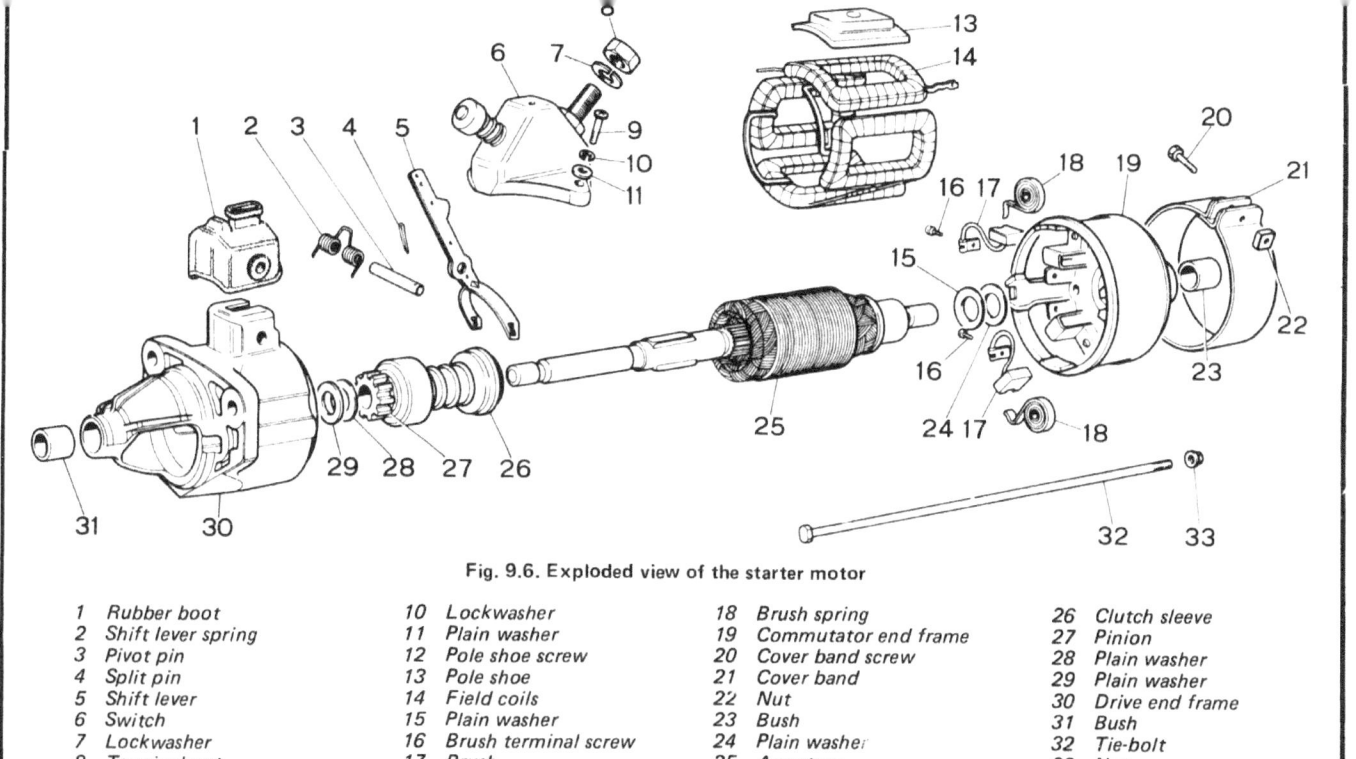

Fig. 9.6. Exploded view of the starter motor

1	Rubber boot	10	Lockwasher	18	Brush spring	26	Clutch sleeve
2	Shift lever spring	11	Plain washer	19	Commutator end frame	27	Pinion
3	Pivot pin	12	Pole shoe screw	20	Cover band screw	28	Plain washer
4	Split pin	13	Pole shoe	21	Cover band	29	Plain washer
5	Shift lever	14	Field coils	22	Nut	30	Drive end frame
6	Switch	15	Plain washer	23	Bush	31	Bush
7	Lockwasher	16	Brush terminal screw	24	Plain washer	32	Tie-bolt
8	Terminal nut	17	Brush	25	Armature	33	Nut
9	Switch retaining screw						

11.2 Starter switch operating cable

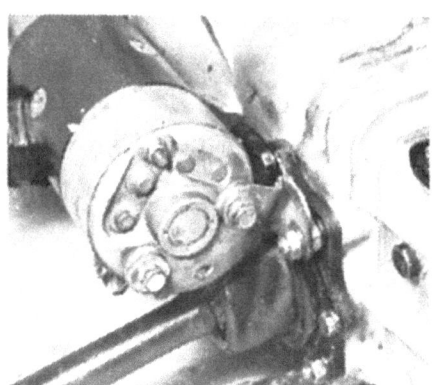

11.4 Starter motor front end mounting plate

12.1 Starter motor switch securing screw (arrowed)

12.2 Removing starter motor cover band

12.3 Removing starter motor tie bolt nut

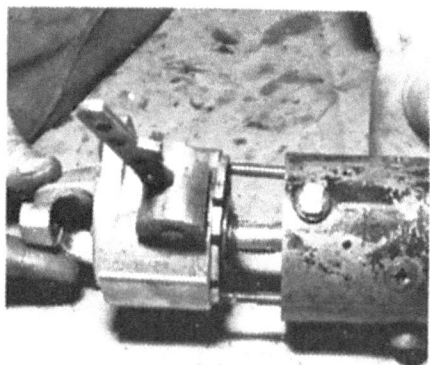

12.4 Removing starter drive assembly

12.5a Disconnecting starter motor field winding terminals

12.5b Separating starter motor brush end cover from body

12.5c Removing brush end cover from starter motor armature

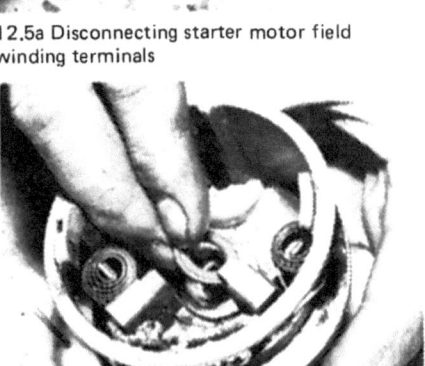

12.5d Extracting thrust washer from starter motor brush end cover

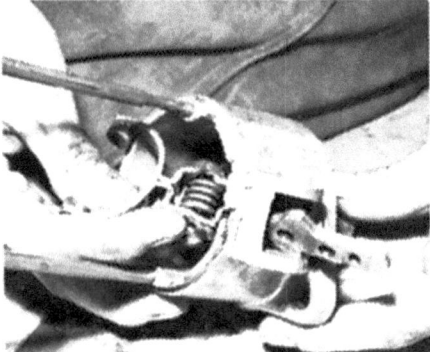

12.7 Removing starter motor shift lever and spring

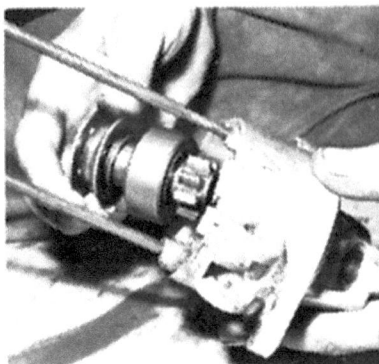

12.8 Extracting starter pinion/clutch assembly

22 Fit the body over the armature, sliding it down towards the brush-end plate with the field winding terminal lined up with its fixing in the endplate. Put the screw through the connecting tag for the brush and the terminal for the field winding, and screw it into the post on the endplate.

23 Fit the drive end. Note that the two long bolts that will hold the whole starter together are covered with insulating sleeves. As the drive unit is slid on it will be necessary to turn the drive pinion to line up the splines.

24 Put the flat washers on the ends of the long bolts, and fit the self locking nuts and tighten them.

25 Slide the dirt shield over the brush end to cover the body apertures. Fix it so that the slit at the end is not in alignment with any of the apertures.

26 Refit the switch to the top of the starter.

13 Fuses - general

1 The fuses are located on a block within the luggage compartment.

2 In the event of failure of an electrical component always check the fuse to ensure that it has not blown before blaming the component (Fig. 9.7).

3 Fuses generally blow very infrequently, but may do so simultaneously when a lamp bulb fails.

4 Always renew a fuse with one of similar rating and if it blows again immediately, trace the source of the trouble instead of fitting yet another new fuse.

5 Most causes of fuses blowing are due to a breakdown in the insulation of the wiring due to age or to cutting through the cable covering on sharp edges of body or underframe. These factors will cause the cable to short circuit to earth.

14 Direction indicator flasher unit

1 The unit is located behind the instrument centre panel.

2 Remove the centre panel as described in Section 23 if access to the sealed cylindrical flasher canister is required.

3 In the event of failure of the direction indicators, first check that

the connecting wiring is secure and that the bulbs (including the pil warning) are not blown.

4 If everything is in order, renew the canister.

15 Bulbs - renewal

Headlamps

1 Access to the double filament bulbs used in the headlamps is obtained through the luggage compartment.

2 Take off the plastic shield from the back of the headlamp (pho

3 Slide out the plug connector and remove the rubber boot from rear of the lamp (photo).

4 Withdraw the bulb and holder by depressing the two ends of th spring ring and turning it in a clockwise direction (photo).

5 When fitting the new bulb, install the spring ring and check that the positioning dowel on the bulb aligns with the cut out on its holder.

6 If the headlamp unit is to be removed, simply pull it from the front of the car by giving it a sharp jerk to disengage its ball and socket type fixings (photo).

Front parking lamp

7 The bulb holder is pulled from the lower section of the headlam reflector casing and the bulb extracted (photo).

Front direction indicator lamp

8 The bayonet fixing type bulb is accessible after having removed lamp lens (two screws) (photo).

Rear lamp cluster

9 Access to the direction indicator bulb and to the double filame stop/tail bulb is obtained after removing the lens from the rear lam cluster (three screws) (photo).

Rear number plate lamp

10 This lamp is located underneath the rear bumper. To gain acces the screws, depress the locking tabs at each end of the lamp unit an withdraw it from the lamp body.

Courtesy lamp

11 This lamp is a combined lamp and switch.

12 To renew the festoon type bulb, pull off the snap-on type lens.

14 Disconnect the lamp leads and prise out the lamp using a screw-driver as a lever.

Instrument warning and indicator lamps

15 The lamp holders which are plugged into the back of the instru-ment panel are accessible from within the luggage compartment.
16 Twist the bulb holders from their locations and then extract the bulbs.
17 Refit the bulbs and push the holders into position.

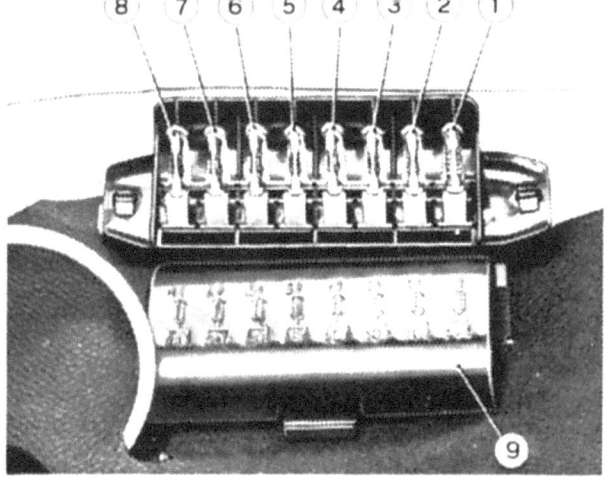

Fig. 9.7. Fuse block with cover (9) removed

16 Headlamp - beam setting

1 It is recommended that this job is carried out by your dealer, but if you wish to do the job yourself, observe the following procedure.
2 Place the car (during the hours of darkness) 16 ft (5 metres) from and square to, a wall or screen.
3 Measure the height and distance apart of the centres of the head-lamps and transpose these measurements as crosses onto the wall or screen in precise alignment with the headlamp centres.
4 Switch the headlamps to dipped beam and note if the brightest points of the beams are 1.4 in (35 mm) below the crosses.
5 If this is not the case, adjust the beams by means of the adjuster screws at the back of the headlamps within the luggage boot.

17 Horn and switch

1 If the horn fails to work first check whether it is the horn button or the actual horn.
2 The horn button is a push fit in the steering wheel. If the problem is here it may be burned points due to sparking as the button makes contact.
3 The circuit from the button is to a contact by the indicator stalk on the steering column. This contact must be good. A failure here is normally given away by the horn working fitfully when the steering wheel is wiggled. The contact should be coated with petroleum jelly (Vaseline).
4 The horn button is the earth return, and is the black/yellow wire. Find which it is at the horn. Check that the other lead is live with a voltmeter or test lamp. Then earth the earth contact with an odd length of wire, to prove the horn itself is working.
5 The horn is mounted up underneath the luggage boot and in the event of it becoming faulty it must be renewed as a unit as it cannot be repaired (photo).

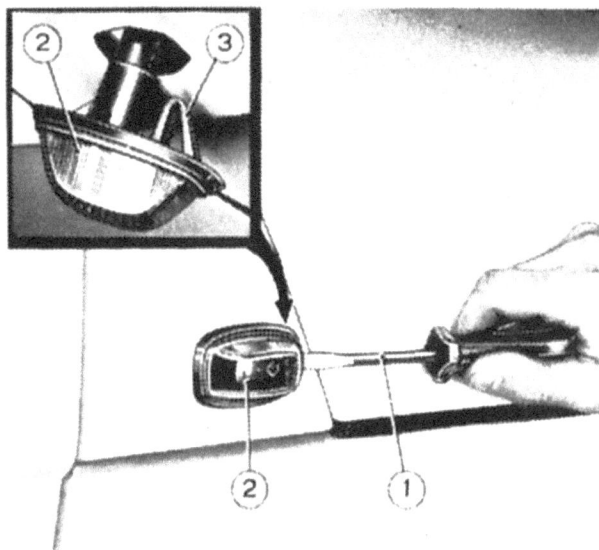

Fig. 9.8. Direction indicator side repeater lamp

1 Screwdriver   3 Snap fastener
2 Lamp assembly

18 Steering column switches - removal and refitting

1 Disconnect the lead from the battery negative terminal.
2 Remove the horn button (preceding Section) at the steering wheel (Chapter 10).
3 Insert a screwdriver through the hole in the steering column shroud and release the screw which secures the direction indicator switch to the steering shaft support (Fig. 9.9).
4 Draw off the switches as required and disconnect the wiring at the multi-pin plugs.
5 Refitting is a reversal of removal, but install the steering wheel, as described in Chapter 10.

19 Windscreen wiper blades and arms - removal and refitting

1 Whenever the wiper blades fail to clean the screen effectively, renew them.
2 To do this, pull the arm away from the glass until it locks.
3 Pull the small tag to release the peg which secures the blade to the wiper arm and slide the blade off the arm (photo).
4 Install the new blade by pushing it onto the arm until the securing peg locks in the hole in the wiper blade carrier. Push the arm/blade assembly into contact with the windscreen glass.
5 To remove a wiper arm, pull the blade/arm assembly fully away from the screen until it locks and then pull the arm from the splines of the driving spindle. If any difficulty is encountered, use a small screw-driver to lever it off (photo).
6 When refitting the arm, do not push it fully home on the splines until the position of the blades on the screen has been checked. They

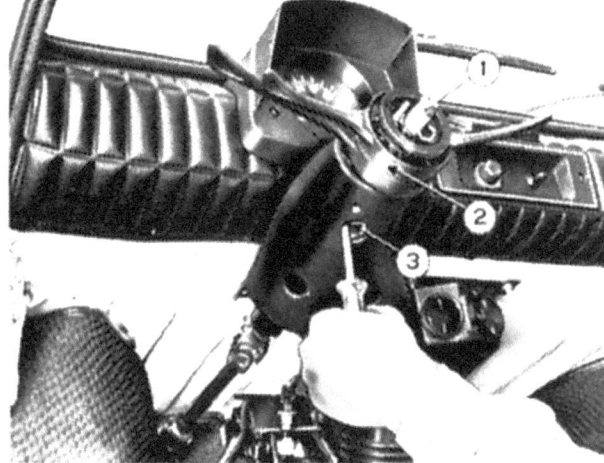

Fig. 9.9. Releasing the direction indicator switch

1 Steering shaft   3 Switch securing screw
2 Direction indicator switch

15.2 Removing headlamp rear cover

15.3 Removing rubber boot from rear of headlamp

15.4 Removing headlamp bulb and holder

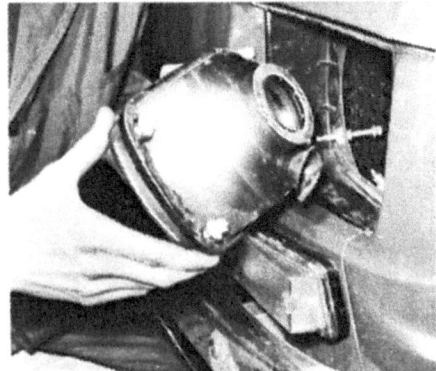

15.6 Removing headlamp unit from front of car

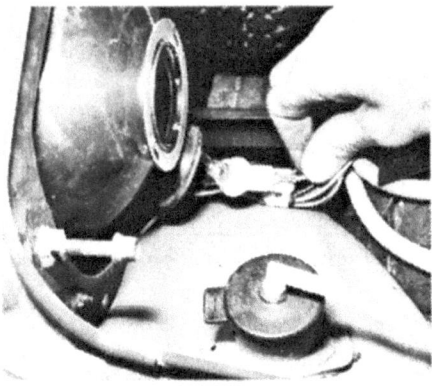

15.7 Removing front parking lamp and holder from headlamp

15.8 Front direction indicator lamp

15.9 Rear lamp cluster

15.10 Rear number plate lamp bulb holder

17.5 Location of horn

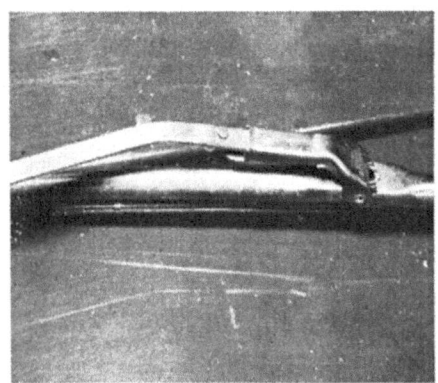

19.3 Windscreen wiper blade attachment

19.5 Removing a windscreen wiper arm

20.1 Location of windscreen wiper motor and linkage

1   The windscreen wiper motor and linkage is accessible within the luggage compartment after the covering panel has been pulled away (photo).
2   First remove the wiper blades and arms, as described in the preceding Section.
3   Unscrew and remove the securing nuts, flanges and seals which hold the driving spindles in position.
4   Unbolt the wiper motor support bracket from the body and then withdraw the complete motor linkage from the rear bulkhead of the luggage compartment far enough to be able to disconnect the electrical harness.
5   The crankarm can be unbolted from the motor and the linkage dismantled if new components are required. A faulty motor should be renewed as it is unlikely that the individual components to repair it can be obtained.
6   Installation is a reversal of removal.

Fig. 9.10. Instrument panel securing screws

21 Speedometer cable - renewal

1   Open the luggage compartment lid and withdraw the cover panel from the rear of the compartment.
2   Unscrew the knurled ring which secures the speedometer cable to the back of the speedometer (photo).
3   Normally, the inner cable can now be extracted but if it has broken, the cable assembly may have to be detached from the extension housing of the gearbox and the inner cable lower section which has broken off, pulled out from the bottom of the conduit.
4   When installing a new inner cable, apply a smear of grease to the lower two thirds of its length before pushing it into its conduit.
5   If a complete cable assembly has been installed, make sure that it follows the same route as the original with no sharp bends.

22 Instruments - removal and installation

1   Working within the luggage compartment, disconnect the speedometer cable and the electrical connectors from the back of the instruments.
2   Extract the two screws from the front face of the instrument panel and withdraw the panel (Fig. 9.10).
3   Individual instruments and lamps can then be removed from the panel (Fig. 9.11).
4   Installation is a reversal of removal.

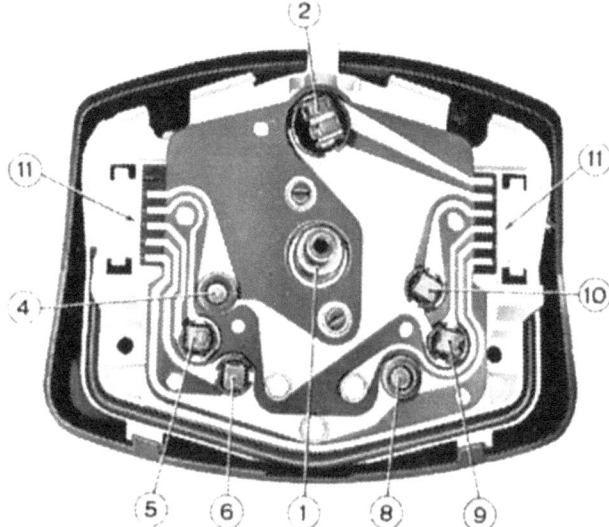

Fig. 9.11. Reverse side of instrument panel

1 Speedometer	8 Low fuel level lamp
2 Parking lamp indicator lamp	(Nov 1974 onwards)
4 Spare position for	9 Main beam warning lamp
indicator lamp	10 Direction indicator warning
5 Ignition warning lamp	lamp
6 Oil pressure warning lamp	11 Circuit connections

23 Centre panel - removal and installation

1   Extract the two screws which secure the panel (Fig. 9.12).
2   Pull the panel far enough towards you to be able to disconnect the washer hoses from the washer pump and the connector plug from the back of the lighting switch. Remove the panel.
3   Installation is a reversal of removal.

24 Windscreen washer assembly

1   A manually-operated washer assembly is fitted and comprises, a curiously shaped fluid reservoir within the luggage compartment, a pump mounted on the centre panel of the fascia and the necessary pipes and jets (Fig. 9.13).
2   The stream of washer fluid ejected from the jets should strike the screen at the top of the glass which is swept by the wiper blades. Adjust if necessary with a screwdriver.
3   Keep the interior of the fluid bag clean and if the jets become blocked, they can be cleaned with a pin.
4   Periodically clean the filter screen of the reservoir pick-up tube with a stiff brush.
5   Always use solvent in the washer reservoir water and in cold weather add methylated spirit to prevent it freezing.

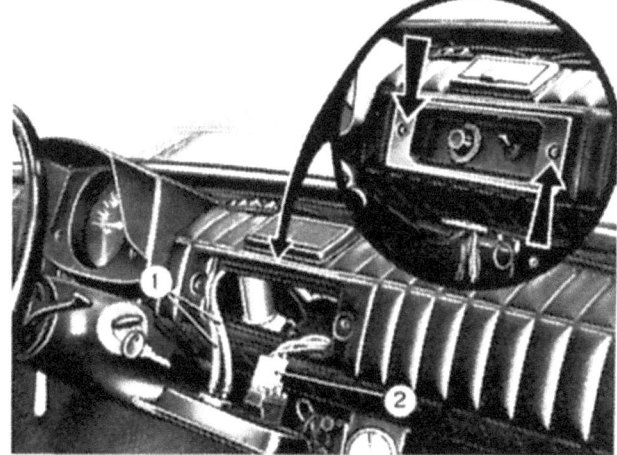

Fig. 9.12. Centre panel removal

1   Washer hoses
2   Lighting switch multi-pin connector
3   Flasher unit

2.1 Rear view of instrument panel

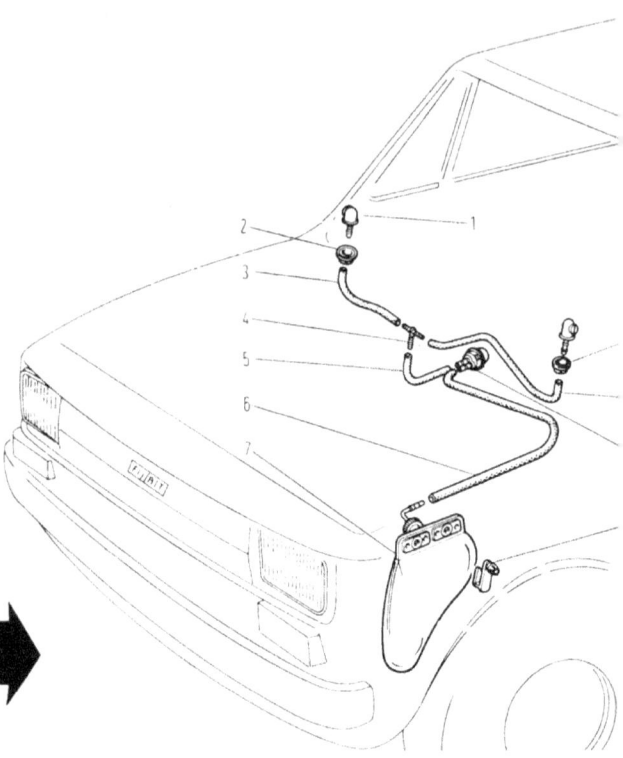

Fig. 9.13. Windscreen washer components

1 Jet nozzle
2 Bush
3 Hose
4 Three-way connector
5 Hose
6 Hose
7 Fluid reservoir
8 Reservoir securing hook
9 Pump

25 Fault diagnosis - electrical system

Symptom	Reason/s
Starter motor fails to turn engine	
No electricity at starter motor	Battery discharged.
	Battery defective internally.
	Battery terminal leads loose or earth lead not securely attached to b
	Loose or broken connections in starter motor circuit.
	Starter motor switch faulty.
Electricity at starter motor: faulty motor	Starter brushes badly worn, sticking, or brush wires loose.
	Commutator dirty, worn or burnt.
	Starter motor armature faulty.
	Field coils earthed.
Starter motor turns engine very slowly	
Electrical defects	Battery in discharged condition.
	Starter brushes badly worn, sticking, or brush wires loose.
	Loose wires in starter motor circuit.
Starter motor operates without turning engine	
Mechanical damage	Pinion or flywheel gear teeth broken or worn.
Starter motor noisy or excessively rough engagement	
Lack of attention or mechanical damage	Pinion or flywheel gear teeth broken or worn.
	Starter motor retaining bolts loose.
Battery will not hold charge for more than a few days	
Wear or damage	Battery defective internally.
	Electrolyte level too low or electrolyte too weak due to leakage.
	Plate separators no longer fully effective.
	Battery plates severely sulphated.

Dynamo not charging.
Short in lighting circuit causing continual battery drain.
Regulator unit not working correctly.

Ignition light fails to go out, battery runs flat in a few days
Dynamo not charging

Fanbelt loose and slipping or broken.
Brushes worn, sticking, broken or dirty.
Brush springs weak or broken.
Commutator dirty, greasy, worn or burnt.
Dynamo field coils burnt, open, or shorted.
Commutator worn.
Pole pieces very loose.

Regulator or cut-out fails to work correctly

Regulator incorrectly set.
Cut-out incorrectly set.
Open circuit in wiring of cut-out and regulator unit.

Horn
Horn operates all the time

Horn push either earthed or stuck down.

Horn fails to operate

Blown fuse.
Cable or cable connection loose, broken or disconnected.
Horn has an internal fault.

Horn emits intermittent or unsatisfactory noise

Cable connections loose.
Horn incorrectly adjusted.

Lights
Lights do not come on

If engine not running, battery discharged.
Lamp bulbs broken.
Wire connections loose, disconnected or broken.
Light switch shorting or otherwise faulty.

Lights come on but fade out

If engine not running battery discharged.
Light bulb filament burnt out.
Wire connections loose, disconnected or broken.
Light switch shorting or otherwise faulty.

Lights give very poor illumination

Lamp glasses dirty.
Lamp badly out of adjustment.

Lights work erratically - flashing on and off, especially over bumps

Battery terminals or earth connection loose.
Light not earthing properly.
Contacts in light switch faulty.

Wipers
Wiper motor fails to work

Blown fuse.
Wire connections loose, disconnected, or broken.
Brushes badly worn.
Armature worn or faulty.
Field coils faulty.

Wiper motor works very slowly and takes excessive current

Commutator dirty, greasy or burnt.
Armature bearings dirty or unaligned.
Armature badly worn or faulty.

Wiper motor works slowly and takes little current

Brushes badly worn.
Commutator dirty, greasy or burnt.
Armature badly worn or fault,

Wiper motor works but wiper blades remain static

Wiper motor gearbox parts badly worn.

Wipers do not stop when switched off or stop in wrong place

Auto-stop device faulty.

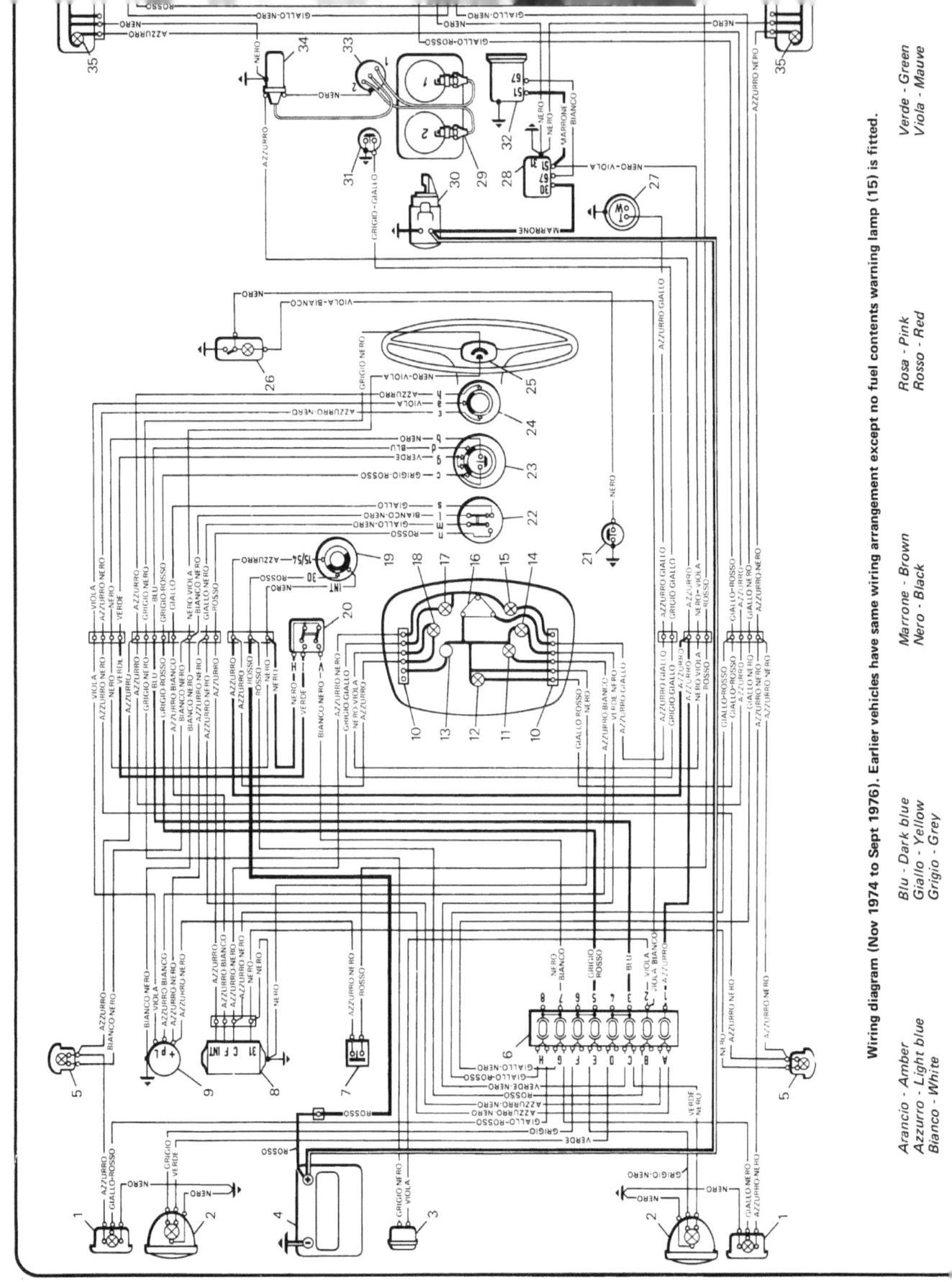

Wiring diagram (Nov 1974 to Sept 1976). Earlier vehicles have same wiring arrangement except no fuel contents warning lamp (15) is fitted.

Arancio - Amber
Azzurro - Light blue
Bianco - White

Blu - Dark blue
Giallo - Yellow
Grigio - Grey

Marrone - Brown
Nero - Black

Verde - Green
Viola - Mauve
Rosa - Pink
Rosso - Red

Key to Wiring Diagram

1 Front parking and turn signal lights
2 High/low beam headlights
3 Horn
4 Battery
5 Turn signal side repeaters
6 Protection fuses
7 Stop light press switch
8 Windshield wiper motor
9 Turn signal flasher
10 Junctions in instrument cluster
11 Turn signal indicator (green)
12 Parking light indicator (green) and
   instrument cluster light
13 Spare indicator
14 High beam indicator (blue)
15 Fuel warning light (red)
   [Starting from chassis N. 4231505 onward]
16 Fuel gauge
17 Low oil pressure warning light (red)
18 No-charge warning light (red)
19 Ignition and starting key switch

20 Exterior lighting switch
21 Courtesy light press switch, on driver's side
   door pillar
22 Windshield wiper lever switch
23 High/low beam change-over switch and
   signal flasher
24 Turn signal switch
25 Horn button
26 Courtesy light with built-in switch, above
   rear view mirror
27 Fuel gauge sending unit
28 Generator regulator unit
29 Spark plugs
30 Starting motor
31 Low oil pressure sending unit
32 Generator
33 Ignition distributor
34 Ignition coil
35 Rear turn signal lights
36 Tail and stop lights
37 License plate lights

Chapter 10 Suspension and steering

For modifications, and information applicable to later models, see Supplement at end of manual

Contents

Specifications

Front suspension

Type	Independent with transverse leaf spring and telescopic shock absorbers
Number of spring leaves	5
Front hub bearing endfloat	0.001 to 0.004 in (0.025 to 0.10 mm)
Camber *	0° 30' to 1° 30' positive
Castor *	8° to 10° positive
Steering axis inclination	6° positive
Toe-in *	0 to 0.12 in (0 to 3 mm)
Wheel bearing grease type	Multi-purpose lithium based grease (Duckhams LB 10)
Kingpin lubricant type	Multi-purpose lithium based grease (Duckhams LB 10)

* Set with car loaded with equivalent of four people

Rear suspension

Type	Independent with triangular shaped control arms, coil springs an telescopic shock absorbers
Wheel bearing grease type	Multi-purpose lithium based grease (Duckhams LB 10)

Spring identification **

Yellow	Height 6.22 in (158 mm) under load of 875 lb (397 kg)
Green	Height greater than 6.22 in (158 mm) under a load of 875 lb (39

* * Rear coil springs must always be fitted in pairs with the same colour coding

Camber (non-adjustable):	
Up to 1974	0° 20' to 1° 20' negative
1974 on	0° 22' to 1° 22' negative
Toe-in	0.197 to 0.354 in (5 to 9 mm)

Steering

Type	Worm and sector with three section universally-jointed shaft
Ratio	13 : 1
Turning circle	28 ft 2 in (8.6 m)
Number of steering wheel turns (lock-to-lock)	3
Steering lock angles:	
Inner wheel	33°
Outer wheel	25° 40'
Oil type/specification	Hypoid gear oil, viscosity SAE 90EP (Duckhams Hypoid 90)
Oil capacity	4.2 fluid oz (0.12 litres)

Wheels and tyres

Wheels	Pressed steel 4.00 x 12 in
Tyres	Radial ply 135 SR 12
Pressures:	
Front	20 lb/sq in (1.4 kg/sq cm)
Rear	28 lb/sq in (1.97 kg/sq cm)

1 General description

1 *The front suspension* is of independent type having a transverse leaf spring and upper wishbones (Fig. 10.1).
2 The spring is attached to the bodyframe and also serves as a stabiliser bar.
3 Telescopic type shock absorbers are fitted.
4 *The rear suspension* is also of independent type but comprises semi-trailing arms and coil springs (Fig. 10.2).
5 Telescopic shock absorbers are also fitted at the rear, inside the spring coils.
6 *The steering gear* is of worm and sector type with a three section universally jointed steering column (Fig. 10.3).
7 *Roadwheels* are of pressed steel type having 4 in (102 mm) rims and are fitted with radial ply tyres.

2 Maintenance and inspection

1 At the intervals recommended in 'Routine Maintenance' apply the grease gun to the nipples on the stub axle carriers.
2 At the specified intervals, check the oil level in the steering box after having removed the side plug.
3 At the specified intervals, check the front wheel bearing adjustment and repack them with fresh grease, as described in Section 4.
4 The safety of the vehicle depends more on the steering and suspension than anything else and regular inspection of these components should be carried out.
5 Have an assistant lift the rear of the vehicle body up and down and check any movement in the top and bottom rear shock absorber mountings. Renew the bushes as necessary.
6 Also check for movement in the transverse spring bushes and eyes and for a broken or cracked spring leaf and renew as described later in this Chapter.
7 Any signs of oil on the outside of the rear shock absorber bodies will indicate that the seals have started to leak and the units must be renewed as assemblies. Where the shock absorber has failed internally, this is more difficult to detect. When a shock absorber is suspected to have failed, remove it from the vehicle and holding it in a vertical position operate it for the full length of its stroke eight or ten times. Any lack of resistance in either direction will indicate the need for renewal.
8 Any movement of the steering wheel which is not followed by corresponding movement of the front roadwheels will indicate one of

the following:

   a) *Wear in the steering box internal components.*
   b) *Wear in the steering linkage balljoints.*
   c) *Slackness or wear in the steering column universal joints or splines or slack pinch bolts.*

9 Regularly check the balljoint flexible boots for splits or deterioration and renew as necessary.
10 Periodically check the torque wrench settings of all suspension and steering nuts and bolts.
11 Wear in the front suspension stub axle carrier bushes or any of the suspension flexible bushes can be detected if an assistant rocks the car or roadwheels and the movement of adjacent components in relation to each other is observed.

3 Shock absorbers and rear coil spring - removal and installation

1 *To remove a front shock absorber,* raise the car on a jack and remove the roadwheel.
2 The suspension should now be compressed before disconnecting the upper mounting of the shock absorber. To do this, either have an assistant push down on the top of the front wing or place a second jack under the stub axle carrier and raise the jack until the transverse leaf spring takes on a horizontal appearance at the end being worked on.
3 Working within the luggage boot, hold the flats on the top of the shock absorber spindle still, while the locknut is unscrewed (Fig. 10.4).
4 Remove the upper mounting components and then contract the shock absorber to release it from the wing inner valance.
5 Disconnect the shock absorber lower mounting in a similar way and withdraw it from under the wing (Fig. 10.5).
6 *To remove a rear shock absorber,* first lift the front of the rear seat cushion to disengage it from its locating dowels. Withdraw the seat cushion forward to expose the shock absorber upper mountings (Fig. 10.6).
7 Place a jack under the suspension arm and raise it until the roadwheel leaves the ground. Now sit in the rear seat cushion pan as close as possible to the shock absorber mounting which will have the effect of compressing the rear suspension coil spring.
8 Hold the flats on the shock absorber spindle quite still with one spanner while the locknut is released.
9 Climb out of the car; as your weight in removed, the shock absorber

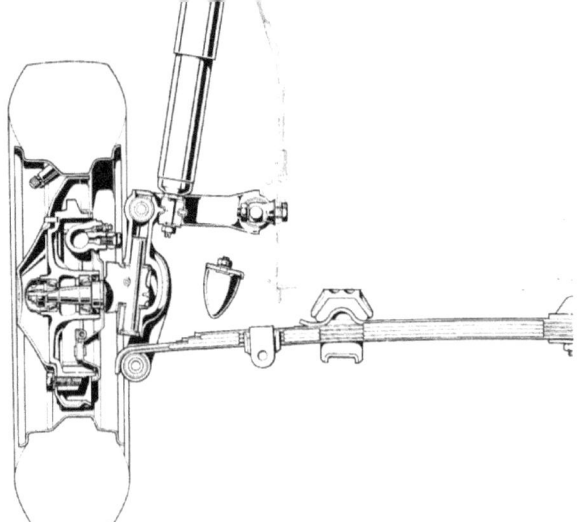

Fig. 10.1. Cross sectional view of one side of the front suspension

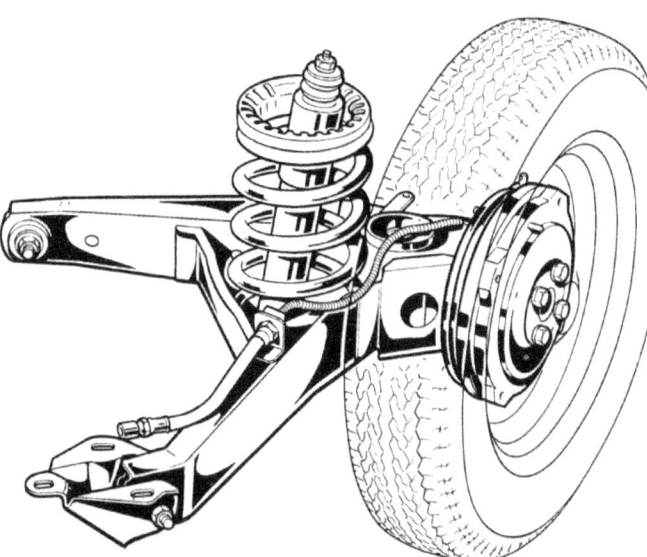

Fig. 10.2. Rear suspension layout (one side)

the shock absorber removed from the car (Fig. 10.7).

11 Installation of the front and rear shock absorbers is a reversal of removal operations, but make sure that the spindle is held still while the locknut is tightened to the specified torque wrench setting.

4   Front hubs - overhaul and adjustment

1   Jack-up the front of the car and remove the roadwheel.

2   Tap off the grease cap from the end of the stub axle.

3   Relieve the staking on the nut and unscrew and remove it togeth with the thrust washer (photo). The right-hand nut has a left-hand thread.

4   Pull the brake drum towards you and catch the outer taper rolle bearing. Remove the brake drum.

5   Provided the bearings are in good condition and the oil seal show no sign of seepage, clean away all the old grease and repack the bearings and hub interior with fresh multi-purpose lubricant.

6   The brake drum and hub can now be refitted.

7   If the bearings are worn or the oil seal is leaking, then the components will have to be renewed.

8   If only the oil seal is to be renewed, it can be extracted by levering it from its seat and a new one tapped squarely into position (photo).

9   If the outer bearing is to be renewed, draw out the bearing track from the centre of the brake drum and then press or drive in the ne one squarely.

10 If the inner tapered roller bearing is to be renewed, then it will mean destroying the oil seal in order to extract the bearing and trac

11 If the bearings are worn, never attempt to renew just the races leaving the old tracks in position. If both front wheels are being dismantled at the same time, never mix the new bearing races and tracks but keep them in their boxes until required. The bearing components are matched in production and are not interchangeable

12 Install the reassembled drum/hub, well packed with grease, fit t outer bearing race and the thrust washer.

13 Screw on a new nut to a torque wrench setting of 5lb f ft (7 Nm Where a torque wrench covering this range is not available, tighten nut as hard as you can gripping it with the hands only. Now unscre the nut through 30° which will give the correct endfloat of the dru hub of between 0.001 and 0.004 in (0.025 and 0.100 mm). This ca measured using a dial gauge or feeler blades.

14 When the adjustment is correct, stake the nut into the cut out in the end of the stub axle using a narrow punch. Take care not to damage the threads on the stub axle. Remember that the right-hanc has a left-hand thread.

15 Refit the grease cap, the roadwheel and lower the car to the gro

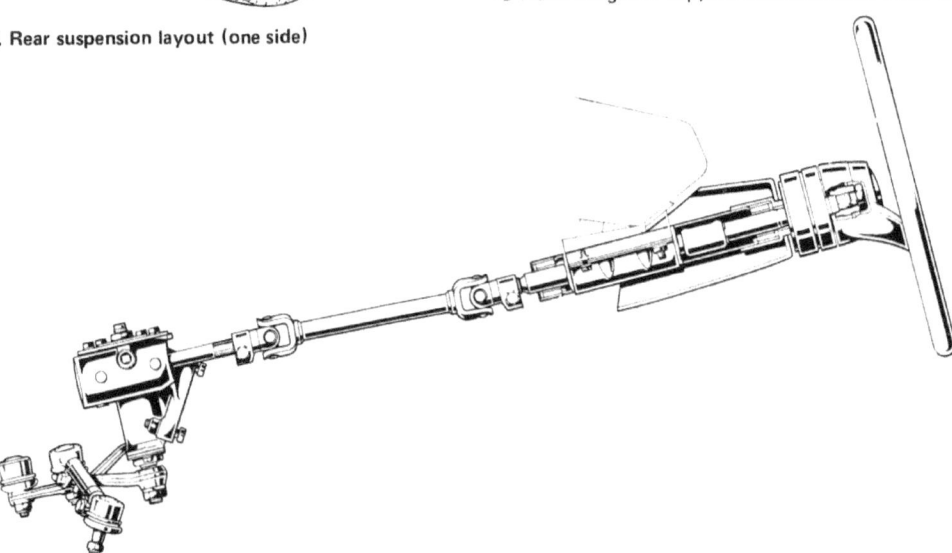

Fig. 10.3. Steering column and box

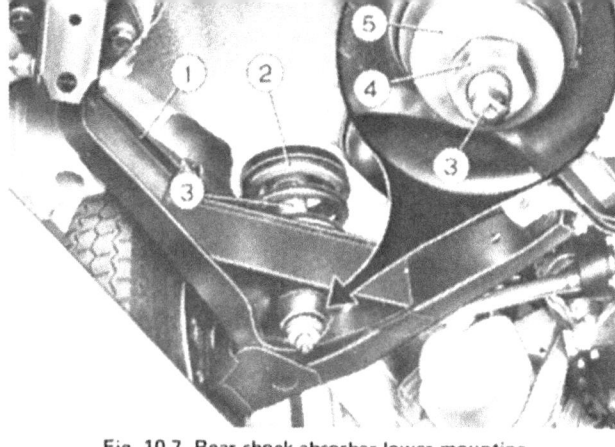

Fig. 10.4. Front shock absorber upper mounting

1 Spanner
2 Spanner
3 Rubber bush
4 Cup
5 Shock absorber spindle
6 Locknut
7 Lockwasher

Fig. 10.7. Rear shock absorber lower mounting

1 Suspension control arm
2 Coil spring
3 Shock absorber spindle
4 Locknut
5 Plain washer
6 Rubber cushion

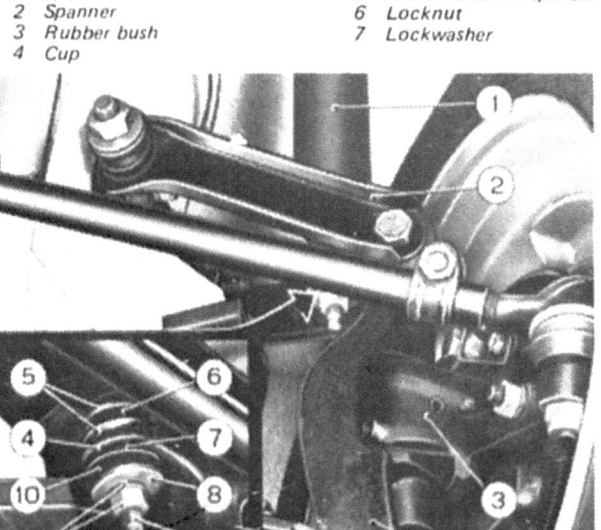

Fig. 10.5. Front shock absorber lower mounting

1 Shock absorber spindle
2 Suspension upper control arm
3 Steering arm
4 Stub axle carrier
5 Cups
6 Rubber cushion
7 Cup
8 Flat washer
9 Locknut and lockwasher
10 Lower cushion

4.3 Staking of front stub axle nut

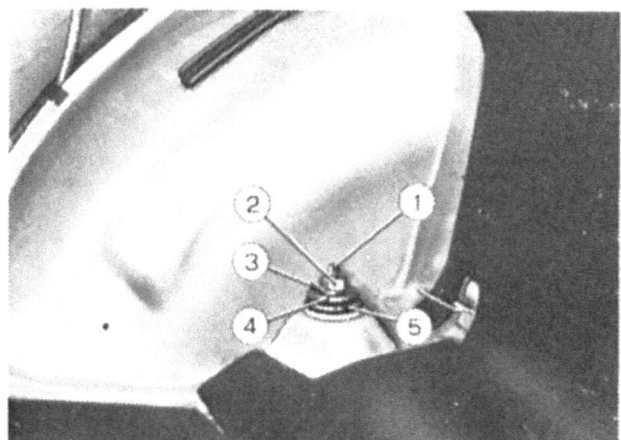

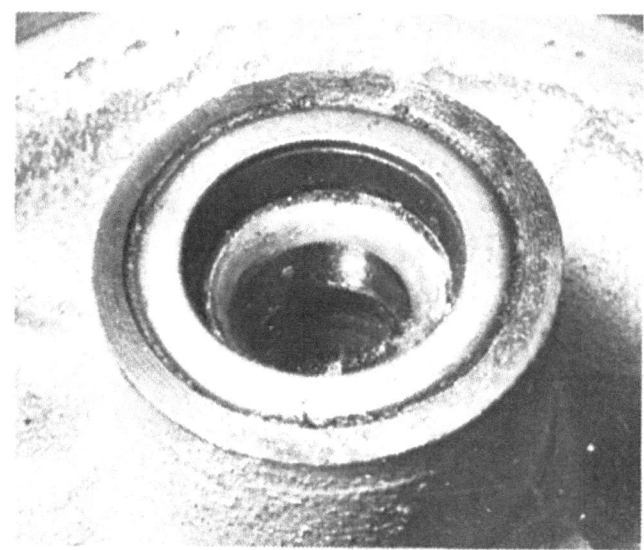

Fig. 10.6. Rear shock absorber upper mounting

1 Shock absorber spindle
2 Locknut
3 Lockwasher
4 Plain washer
5 Rubber cushion

4.8 Front brake drum showing oil seal

6 Front leaf spring - removal, overhaul and refitting

1 Jack-up the front of the car and support it securely under the bodyframe side members.

2 Place a jack under one end of the leaf spring and take its weight off the stub axle carrier.

3 Unscrew the pivot bolt from the spring eye and disconnect the spring from the stub axle carrier (Fig. 10.8).

4 Lower the jack gently from under the spring and repeat the operations at the opposite end of the spring.

5 Release the clamps which secure the spring to the bodyframe and remove the spring from the car.

6 Clean the spring leaves and examine for cracks. If any are found, the complete spring must be renewed as individual leaves are not supplied.

7 Examine the flexible bushes. If these appear to have deteriorated or if their centre sleeves are no longer central or have worn oval, then the bushes should be pressed out of the spring eyes and new ones installed. If a press is not available, remove the bushes with a long bolt, nuts, washers and suitable tubular distance pieces.

8 Check the condition of the spring to bodyframe clamp and rebound stops. Renew if necessary.

9 Install the spring by reversing the removal method using a jack to apply leverage to the spring eye.

7 King pins and bushes - renewal

1 The stub axle and king pin housing assembly can be removed quite simply.

2 Jack-up the front of the car. Transfer the weight to blocks under the body, spreading the weight broadly, and making sure that the car is very secure.

3 Move the jack to the outer end of the spring, and take some of the weight on this, so that the shock absorber is telescoped.

4 Remove the roadwheel, brake drum/hub and the brake backplate. This is held by one nut on a stud through the steering arm, and another to the rear of the king pin. Lift off the backplate, still with the brake shoes on it, and the hydraulic pipe connected. Take care the hydraulic pipe is not strained by pulling or twisting. Tie the backplate up out of the way, or prop it up.

5 Disconnect the balljoint taper pin of the trackrod-end from the

7 Telescope the shock absorber as far as it will go and take off the lower mounting components.

8 Remove the nut from the pivot bolt through the spring eye at the bottom of the king pin housing. Drive out the bolt (Fig. 10.9 and photo).

9 Lower the jack under the spring. Pull the king pin housing clear the spring, so that it is hanging from the wishbone at the top.

10 Repeat for the bolt through the top of the king pin housing and wishbone. Now pull the whole king pin housing and stub axle assem away.

11 Note all the washers, and where they came from.

12 The king pin is pegged to the stub axle carrier. To remove it ham out the pin with a punch. Prise out the disc peened into the bottom the stub axle carrier closing the bottom bush.

13 Press out the rubber bush from the top of the stub axle carrier. Drive out the king pin from above through the space vacated by the rubber bush. If the disc at the bottom could not be removed, provic it has been loosened, it can be driven out with the king pin.

14 As the king pin comes out of its housing and the stub axle carrie is removed, note the position of all the washers. There is a load carrying washer and rubber dirt seal above. Below is a spacer.

15 The king pin replacement kit should include a pin for locking th stub axle carrier to the king pin, and all the washers and seals neede but there are many different thicknesses of spacers; but the original ones should not need changing.

16 Take the old bushes out of the housing. If difficulty is found in pressing them out they can be collapsed by cutting with a hack saw downwards to split them.

17 Press in the new bushes.

18 The bushes must now be in-line reamed to an internal diameter c between 0.5911 to 0.5922 in (15.016 to 15.043 mm). If a suitable reamer is not available, have your Fiat dealer do this for you.

19 For reassembly, grease the king pin and bushes. Get the stub axl into place in the carrier. Put all the washers in place, holding them with grease.

20 Fit the new king pin, lining up its groove with the hole in the stu axle for the locking pin.

21 Hammer in the locking pin firmly. Fit the disc to the bottom bu and peen it into place, being careful not to damage the disc.

22 Reassemble by reversing the dismantling operations but do not fully tighten the pivot bolts at the top and bottom of the stub axle carrier until the weight of the car is again on the roadwheels. This w prevent distortion of the flexible bushes.

23 Always check the front wheel alignment after major overhaul of front suspension (see Section 17).

Fig. 10.8. The front suspension

1 Shock absorber lower mounting	3 Shock absorber lower mounting	5 Stub axle carrier	8 Stub axle carrier
2 Rebound stops	4 Leaf spring eye pivot	6 Leaf spring clamps	9 Spring eye pivot bolt
		7 Spring	

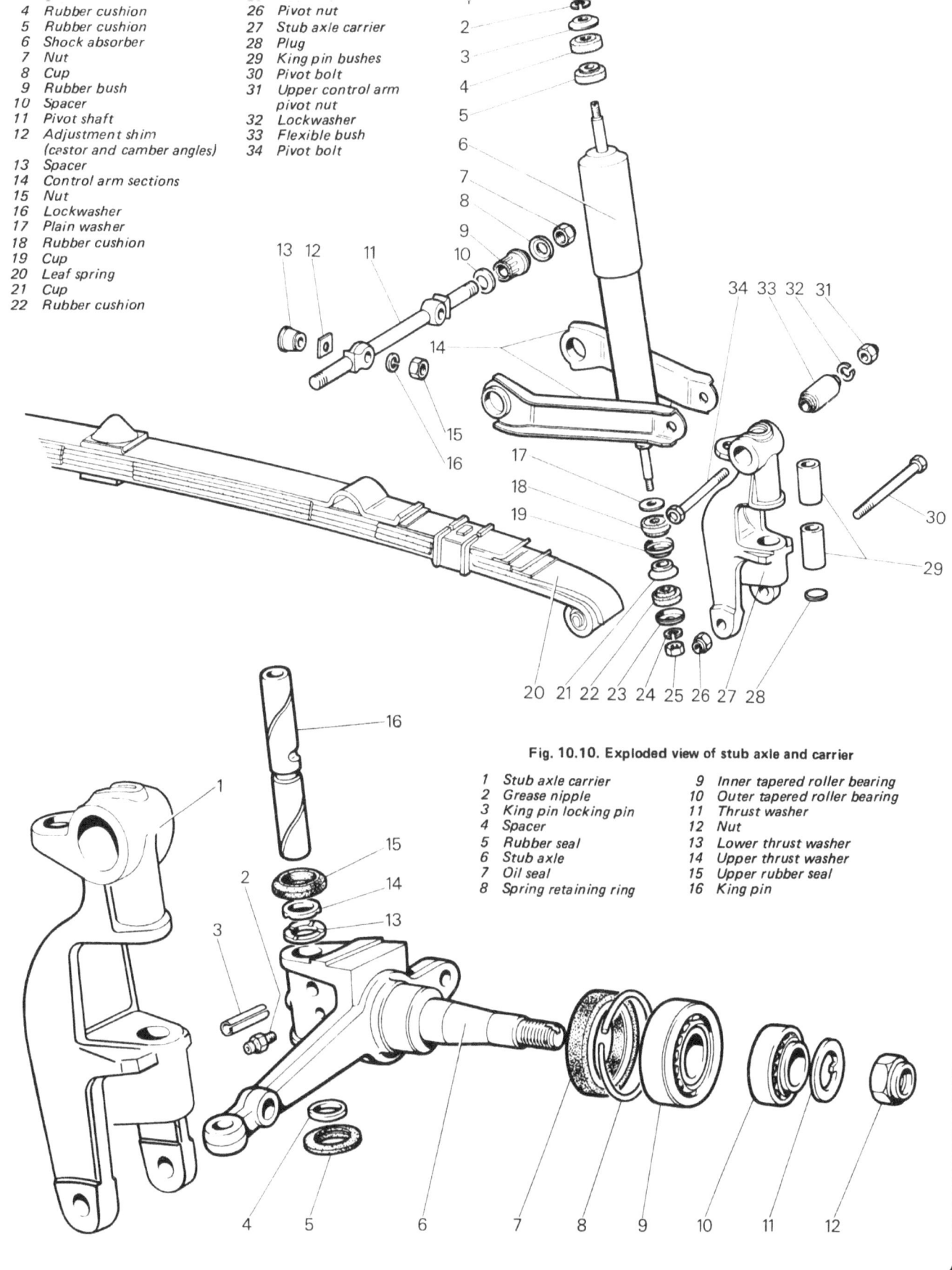

4 Rubber cushion
5 Rubber cushion
6 Shock absorber
7 Nut
8 Cup
9 Rubber bush
10 Spacer
11 Pivot shaft
12 Adjustment shim
    (castor and camber angles)
13 Spacer
14 Control arm sections
15 Nut
16 Lockwasher
17 Plain washer
18 Rubber cushion
19 Cup
20 Leaf spring
21 Cup
22 Rubber cushion

26 Pivot nut
27 Stub axle carrier
28 Plug
29 King pin bushes
30 Pivot bolt
31 Upper control arm
    pivot nut
32 Lockwasher
33 Flexible bush
34 Pivot bolt

Fig. 10.10. Exploded view of stub axle and carrier

1 Stub axle carrier
2 Grease nipple
3 King pin locking pin
4 Spacer
5 Rubber seal
6 Stub axle
7 Oil seal
8 Spring retaining ring

9 Inner tapered roller bearing
10 Outer tapered roller bearing
11 Thrust washer
12 Nut
13 Lower thrust washer
14 Upper thrust washer
15 Upper rubber seal
16 King pin

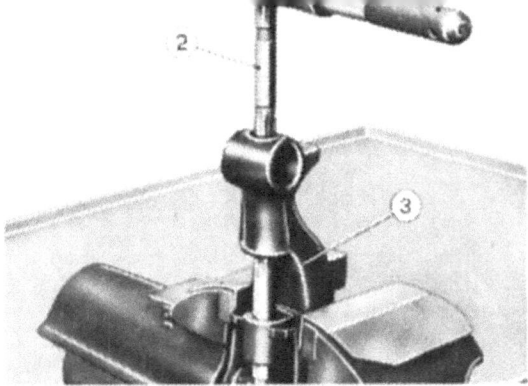

Fig. 10.11. Reaming king pin bushes

1 *Reamer holder*   3 *Stub axle carrier*
2 *Reamer*

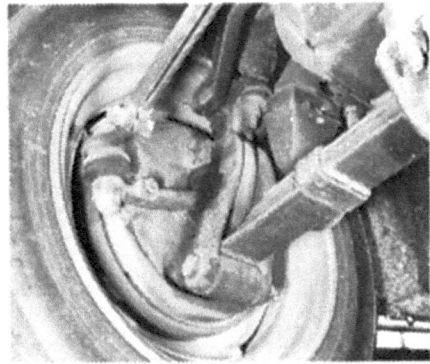

7.8 One side of the front suspension

8 Front suspension upper control arm bushes - renewal

1 Jack-up the front of the car, remove the roadwheel and disconnect the shock absorber lower mounting, while keeping the underside of the leaf spring eye supported on a second jack.
2 Support the brake drum in the vertical attitude and unscrew and remove the pivot bolt which secures the outer end of the control arm to the top of the stub axle carrier.
3 Remove the nuts which secure the control arm inner pivot shaft to the bodyframe.
4 Withdraw the control arm but identify in respect of location and retain the shims which are fitted on the studs behind the pivot shafts. These shims control the castor and camber angles.
5 Renew the bushes in the control arm with a press or by using a bolt, washers and distance pieces to draw them out and to refit them. Renew the bush at the top of the stub axle carrier in the same way.
6 Reassembly is a reversal of removal and dismantling.

9 Front suspension - removal, overhaul and installation

1 When all the king pin bushes have to be renewed or the upper track control arm bushes require attention, it is recommended that the complete front suspension is removed as an assembly. This will be just as quick and provide better access than removing individual suspension components.
2 Jack-up the front of the car and support it securely on axle stands placed under the bodyframe side members.
3 Remove the roadwheels.
4 Disconnect the trackrod-end balljoints from the steering arms of the stub axles. A ball joint taper pin separator will be required for this, or forked wedges (Fig. 10.12).
5 Disconnect the shock absorber upper mountings (see Section 3) and then the lower mountings.

camber angles (Fig. 10.13).
7 Disconnect the brake hydraulic hoses at the support brackets a◼ plug or cap the hose ends to prevent loss of fluid or the entry of di◼ (photo).
8 Support the centre of the transverse leaf spring on a trolley jack◼ and then disconnect the spring clamps from the bodyframe.
9 Remove the front suspension complete from under the car (Fig. 10.14).
10 Dismantle the upper control arm by withdrawing both pivot sha◼
11 Disconnect the stub axle carrier from the leaf spring by removir◼ the spring eye pivot bolt.
12 Remove the drum/hub components, as described in Section 4.
13 Service the king pin bushes, as described in Section 7.
14 Service the control arm bushes, as described in Section 8.
15 Reassembly and installation are reversals of removal and dismantling, but make sure that the shims which control camber ar◼ castor are returned to their original locations and bleed the front b◼ hydraulic circuit on completion.

9.7 Front brake hose attachment

Fig. 10.12. Disconnecting a track rod balljoint

1 *Extractor*   3 *Balljoint*
2 *Trackrod*

1 Raise the rear of the car and support securely under the bodyframe members. Remove the roadwheels.

2 Disconnect the shock absorber upper mountings, as described in Section 3, having a second jack under the suspension control arm.

3 Disconnect the driveshaft outer coupling from the flexible joint of the axle stub.

4 Push the coupling aside and extract the small coil spring from its open end (Fig. 10.15).

5 Disconnect the brake hydraulic flexible hose at the attachment bracket on the control arm. Plug or cap the hose and pipe to prevent loss of fluid (Fig. 10.16).

6 Disconnect the handbrake cable from the lever on the brake back-plate.

7 Lower the jack under the control arm, compress the shock absorber and slide out the coil spring with its two rubber insulators.

8 Before unscrewing the bolts which secure the suspension control arm bracket to the bodyframe, mark the exact position of the bracket on the bodyframe. This can either be done by marking round the edge of the bracket or by giving a quick spray with paint from an aerosol. This will leave the position of the bracket clearly defined on the bodyframe once it has been removed (Fig. 10.17).

attachment point (Fig. 10.18).

11 Withdraw the control arm assembly complete with brake drum and axle stub (Fig. 10.19).

12 The control arm flexible bushes can be renewed by extracting and installing them with a press or by using a bolt and nut, washers and suitable distance pieces.

13 Dismantling of the axle stub and hub bearings is described in Chapter 7, Section 4.

14 Repeat the foregoing operations on the opposite suspensions assembly if required.

15 Reassembly and installation are reversals of removal and dismantling. Make sure that the control arm support bracket is refitted in exactly its previously marked position, also the shims are returned to their original positions on the inner control arm pivot. Failure to observe either of these points will upset the rear wheel alignment.

16 Tighten the control arm pivot and bracket bolts to the specified torque wrench settings.

17 Bleed the brake hydraulic circuit for the rear brakes.

18 Although the rear wheel alignment should not have been altered if the suspension control arm has been attached in its original position, it

Fig. 10.13. Front suspension upper control arm detail

1 Flexible bush
2 Castor and camber adjusting shims
3 Control arm
4 Pivot shaft
5 Pivot shaft
6 Stub axle carrier
7 Shock absorber lower mounting
8 Shock absorber spindle

Fig. 10.15. View of right-hand rear suspension assembly

1 Driveshaft outer coupling bolts
2 Flexible joint
3 Splined sleeve
4 Suspension control arm
5 Shock absorber lower mounting
6 Driveshaft

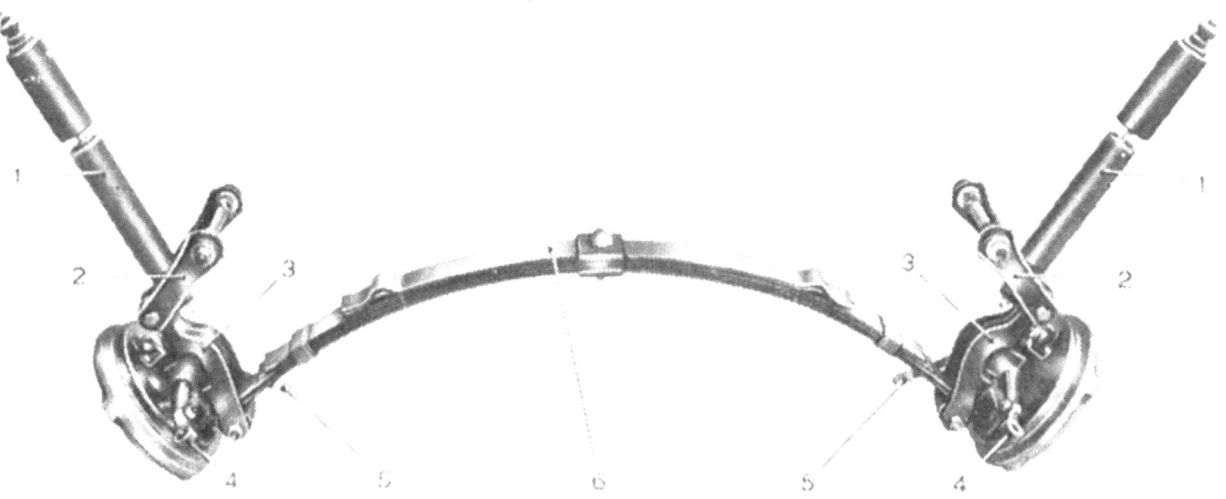

Fig. 10.14. Complete front suspension removed from car

1 Shock absorbers
2 Suspension upper control arm
3 Stub axle carriers
4 Steering arm
5 Flexible brake hoses
6 Leaf spring

Fig. 10.16. View of left-hand rear suspension assembly

1   Brake hose connection   3   Handbrake cable
2   Coil spring

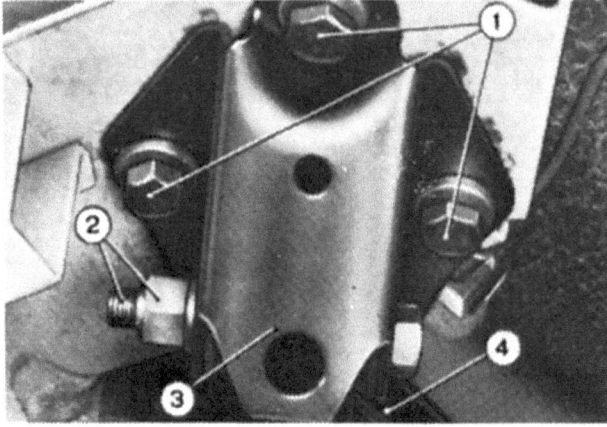

Fig. 10.17. Rear suspension attachment to bodyframe

1   Securing bolts   3   Bracket
2   Pivot bolt and nut   4   Control arm

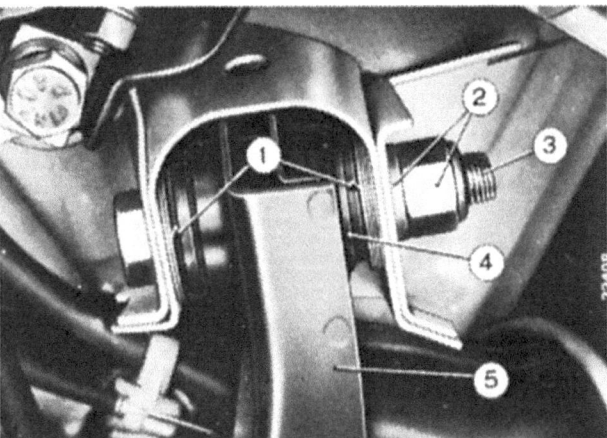

Fig. 10.18. Attachment of inner end of rear suspension control
arm to bodyframe

1   Adjustment shims   4   Rubber bush
2   Nut and lockwasher   5   Control arm
3   Pivot bolt

11 Trackrod-end ball joints - removal and refitting

1   The steering linkage comprises a centre and two outer trackrod
sections (Fig. 10.20).
2   The trackrod-end ball joint assemblies on the outer trackrods are
renewable but the ones at each end of the centre rod are integral with
the rod and must be renewed as a complete assembly.
3   Any wear in the ball joints must be rectified immediately by
renewal of the components.
4   To disconnect a ball joint taper pin from the stub axle carrier
steering arm, the idler drop arm or the steering drop arm, first
unscrew the securing nut and then separate the ball joint from the eye
of the arm using a ball joint extractor or forked wedges. If these tools
are not available they can often be hired. Do not waste time using the
old fashioned idea of hitting the eye with two club hammers as
damage is likely to be done to adjacent components.
5   With the taper pin separated from the eye, in the case of the outer
trackrod joints, mark the number of exposed threads so that the new
ball joint assembly can be positioned in the same relative position as
the original one.
6   Release the clamp pinch bolt and unscrew the trackrod-end ball
joint from the track rod.
7   Grease the threads of the new balljoint assembly and screw it into
the trackrod until the equivalent number of exposed threads as there
were originally are showing. The outer trackrod ball joint assemblies
are supplied in pairs (LH and RH) so that when installed, the hollow
trackrod tube can be rotated to effectively increase or decrease the
length of the rod assembly in order to vary the front wheel alignment
(toe-in).
8   Locate the balljoint taper pin in the eye of the arm and tighten the
nut to the specified torque. If there is a tendency for the ball joint pin
to rotate as the nut is tightened, apply pressure to force it further
into its seat. Do not apply grease to the taper pin when assembling as
this will aggravate this problem.
9   Set the ball joint in its correct attitude at the centre of its arc of
travel and then position the clamp so that its slot is in alignment with
the slot in the trackrod tube. Tighten the pinch bolt.
10 Even though the greatest care may have been taken to install the
new trackrod-end ball joints in the same relative position as the
original ones, always have the front wheel alignment (toe-in) checked
as soon as possible by your Fiat dealer or by reference to Section 17.
This applies even if the centre trackrod assembly only has been
renewed as there may be slight manufacturing tolerance differences
which could affect the steering alignment dimensions.

12 Steering idler - inspection and overhaul

1   If movement is detected between the idler arm shaft and the
rubber bushes which are pressed into the idler shaft carrier, then the
unit must be dismantled and new components fitted (photo).
2   Disconnect the trackrod-end and centre rod ball joints from the
idler arm as described in the preceding Section.
3   Unbolt and remove the idler assembly from the bodyframe.
4   Unscrew the nut from the base of the idler shaft and withdraw the
shaft. Inspect the surface of the shaft for scoring and if evident renew
the shaft.
5   Press the bushes from the carrier and install new ones.
6   Reassemble the shaft, but do not fully tighten the nut at this stage.
7   Bolt the idler assembly to the bodyframe and reconnect the
steering trackrod to the idler arm while the roadwheels are in the
'straight-ahead' position. This will mean that the idler arm will also be
positioned so that it faces towards the front of the car parallel with the
car centre-line.
8   Now tighten the idler shaft nut to a torque wrench setting of
50 lb f ft (69 Nm).
9   Where other new steering linkage components have been fitted, do
not tighten the idler shaft nut until the front wheel alignment has been
checked and adjusted and the front roadwheels set in the 'straight-
ahead' position.

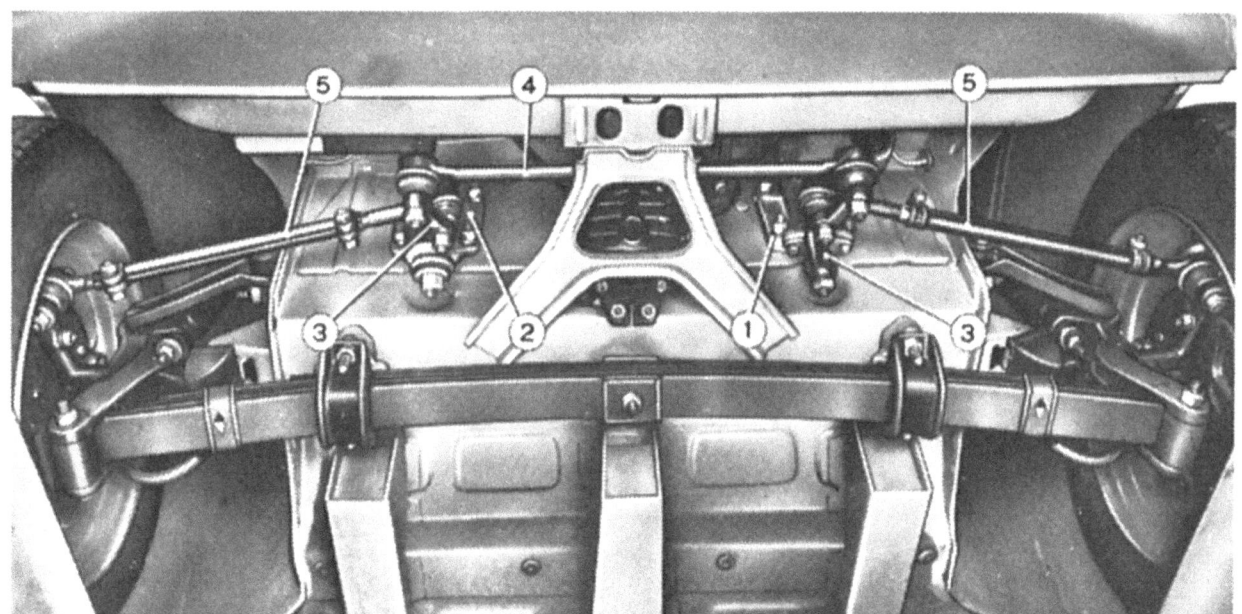

2	Seat	16	Lockwasher
3	Spring	17	Plain washer
4	Control arm	18	Rebound stop
5	Bracket	19	Nut
6	Pivot bolt	20	Lockwasher
7	Plain washer	21	Plain washer
8	Plain washer	22	Cushion
9	Lockwasher	23	Shock absorber
10	Bolt	24	Plain washer
11	Plain washer	25	Cushion
12	Flexible bush	26	Plain washers
13	Lockwasher	27	Lockwasher
14	Nut	28	Nut

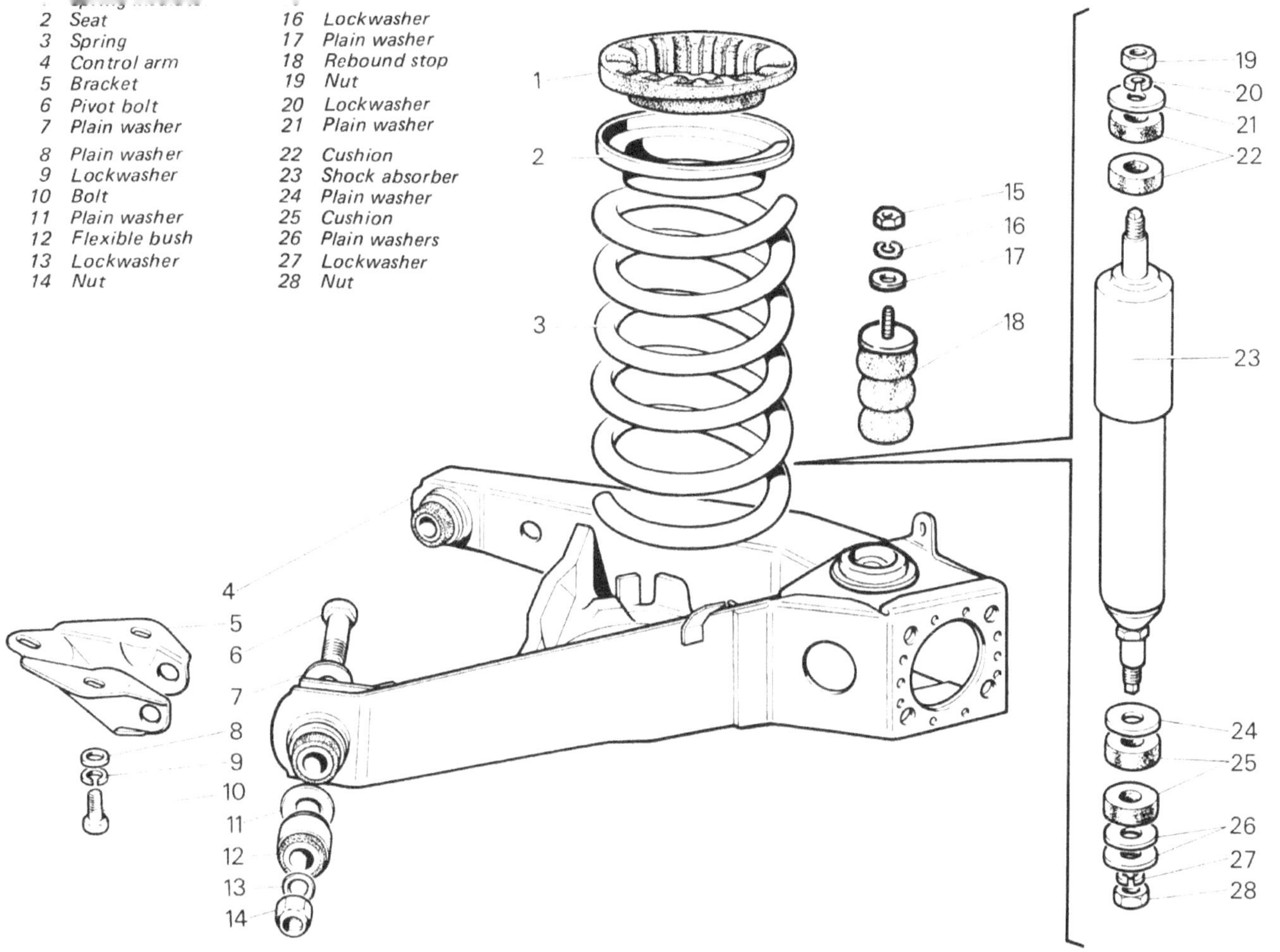

Fig. 10.20. Steering linkage (left-hand drive pinion)

1	Steering box	3	Steering and idler drop arms	4	Centre track rod
2	Idler arm assembly				

5   Outer track rods

1 Disconnect the lead from the battery negative terminal.

2 Prise off the horn button from the centre of the steering wheel.

3 Relieve the staking on the now exposed nut and unscrew and remove it.

4 Turn the steering wheel if necessary to set the roadwheels in the 'straightahead' position and then pull the wheel from the steering shaft splines. If it is stuck tight, jar it off using the palms of the hands on the rear of the spokes.

5 Before refitting the steering wheel, apply a little grease to the shaft splines. Push the wheel into position and tighten a new nut using hand-pressure on the socket wrench only.

6 Reconnect the battery and drive the car along a straight section of road and check that the steering wheel spokes are horizontal or at least in an attitude to suit the driver.

7 Now tighten the nut to a torque wrench setting of 36 lb f ft (50 Nm) and stake the nut.

8 Refit the horn button.

---

14 Steering column - removal and installation

---

1 Set the roadwheels in the 'straight-ahead' position and disconnect the battery.

2 Working within the car, mark the position of the steering shaft upper and lower universal joint couplings in relation to the shaft. Use quick drying paint or scribe lines to do this (photo).

3 Remove the steering wheel, as described in the preceding Section.

4 Insert a screwdriver into the hole on the lower surface of the steering column shroud and release the screw which secures the direction indicator switch.

5 Disconnect the wiring harness multipin plugs and withdraw the column switches.

6 Extract the securing screws from the steering column shroud and withdraw it upwards.

7 Unscrew and remove the pinch bolt from the steering shaft upper coupling.

8 Unscrew and remove the nuts which secure the steering column upper bracket to the instrument panel (Fig. 10.21).

9 Withdraw the steering column.

10 The steering shaft lower coupling can be released if required by removing its pinch bolt and the lower shaft assembly detached from the steering box pinion shaft.

11 Installation is a reversal of removal, but do not tighten the upper bracket nuts until the universal coupling pinch bolts are fully engaged in their grooves in the splined sections of the shafts and the nuts tightened.

rectified by renewal of the complete shaft assembly (Fig. 10.22).

2 The rubber bushes in the upper bracket can be renewed, but wh installing the new ones, make sure that the slots in them are not in alignment with the staking tags of the bracket.

3 If the steering column lock assembly must be removed because fault, or if the keys have been lost, then the shear type bolts must drilled out or the bolts cut by carefully inserting a hacksaw blade between the joint of the lock half sections. When installing the new lock assembly do not fully tighten the securing bolts until the key been turned to check that the lock tongue is in correct alignment the notch in the steering upper shaft.

4 When the operation of the steering lock is satisfactory, fully tig the shear bolts to break off their heads.

Fig. 10.21. Steering column securing nuts (1) and upper couplin pinch bolt (2)

12.1 Steering idler assembly

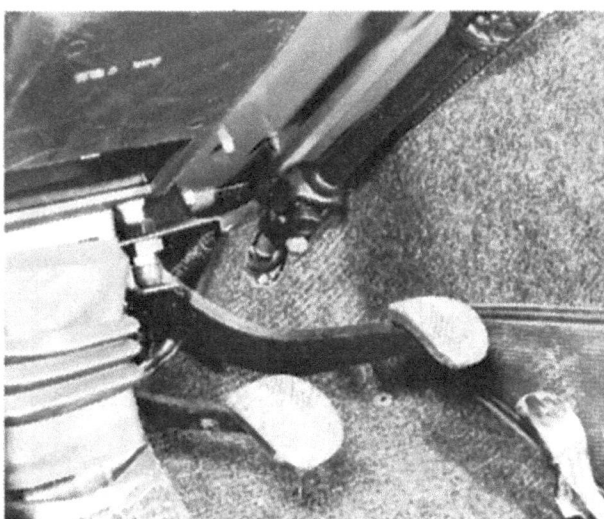

14.2 Steering column shaft

1 Set the roadwheels in the 'straight-ahead' position with the car over an inspection pit or the front of it raised on ramps or stands.

2 Working inside the car, mark the alignment of the steering shaft lower coupling to the splined pinion shaft of the steering box and then extract the coupling pinch bolt.

3 Working under the car, disconnect the centre and outer trackrod-end ball joints from the steering drop arm (photo).

4 Unscrew and remove the steering box mounting nuts and remove the box from the bodyframe. If it appears stuck, carefully prise the jaws of the steering shaft lower coupling apart with a large screwdriver.

5 Clean away external dirt, unscrew the combined oil filler/level plug and drain the oil.

6 Secure the steering box in the jaws of a vice.

7 Undo the bolt holding the drop arm to the drop arm shaft and pull it off. An extractor will be needed for this (Fig. 10.23).

8 Remove the screws holding the steering box cover and remove that (Fig. 10.29).

9 Take out the sector attached to the drop arm shaft. With it may come the eccentric bush. Between the sector and the casing is a thick thrust washer. Note the small peg that prevents the thrust washer from turning, sticking out from the body of the steering box. Also there are likely to be shims between the thrust washer and the steering box.

10 Remove the split pin from the castellated cap at the bottom of the worm shaft.

11 Unscrew the castellated cap. Long nosed pliers can be used for this if the special tool is not available. With the cap removed the worm should be tapped very gently on the end of the shaft where the steering column is attached. This will drive out the race for the bottom taper roller bearing. Once this is removed the worm with the two inner races can be removed. Note there is a seal inside the top race mounted in the steering box. This stops oil coming out upwards to the shaft. The seal for the bottom is the castellated cap.

12 Inspect all components and renew any that are worn.

13 Reassemble the steering box by reversing the dismantling operations but observe the following precautions and adjustment.

14 Before installing the worm, check that the upper oil seal is in good condition, otherwise renew it.

15 Before fitting the thrust washer for the sector, put in shims as needed to get the centre line of the sector's teeth level with the centre line of the worm. Then put in the thrust washer, locating its cut out with the peg in the box.

16 An oil seal goes round the drop arm shaft at the bottom of the

eccentric bush. The bush is moved by the adjuster plate which should be turned within the limits of its elongated bolt holes. This action moves the sector on top of the drop arm shaft closer to the worm. If the range of adjustment provided by the holes in the adjuster plate is insufficient, lift the plate and move it round a few splines (photo).

18 The ideal setting is for the sector to have all free-play eliminated when the steering drop arm is in the 'straight-ahead' position. The drop arm will of course have been removed but this position can be determined by reference to the master spline on the drop arm shaft.

19 The endfloat in the drop arm shaft is corrected by a peg screwed into the top of the steering box. This is held by a locknut. Slacken the locknut. Screw in the peg until it is in light contact with the sector underneath the cover. Hold it there and tighten the locknut. Note this adjustment must also be done with the steering in the 'straight-ahead' position. On the road, the need for this adjustment can be detected sometimes by a clonking heard or felt in the steering wheel on bad bumps taken slowly. It can be felt in bad cases when pulling or pushing the drop arm from beneath the car (photo).

20 The endfloat in the worm, which is the extension of the steering column in the box, is adjusted by the castellated cap in the bottom of the box (photo).

21 Take out the split pin. Screw up the cap, using long nosed pliers opened wide, till all endfloat goes. But do not overtighten. There should be no stiffness.

22 Insert the split pin into whichever of the two holes lines up best.

23 This endfloat should not need resetting in service, but will need adjustment after the box is stripped.

24 Install the steering box, engaging the lower coupling of the steering shaft in the previously marked alignment position while the steering drop arm shaft master spline is also in the 'straight-ahead' attitude.

25 Tighten the steering box mounting nuts and the coupling pinch bolt.

26 Refit the drop arm. This can only go on in one position as it has a master spline/groove arrangement.

27 Reconnect the trackrod-end ball joints to the steering drop arm.

28 Refill the steering box to the correct level with the specified oil.

Note: The adjustments described in this Section can be carried out if necessary at times when overhaul is not required and without removing the box from the car. It is important however, to disconnect the trackrod-end ball joints from the drop arm if worm to sector backlash is being checked in order to remove any external influence on the precise setting which must be achieved.

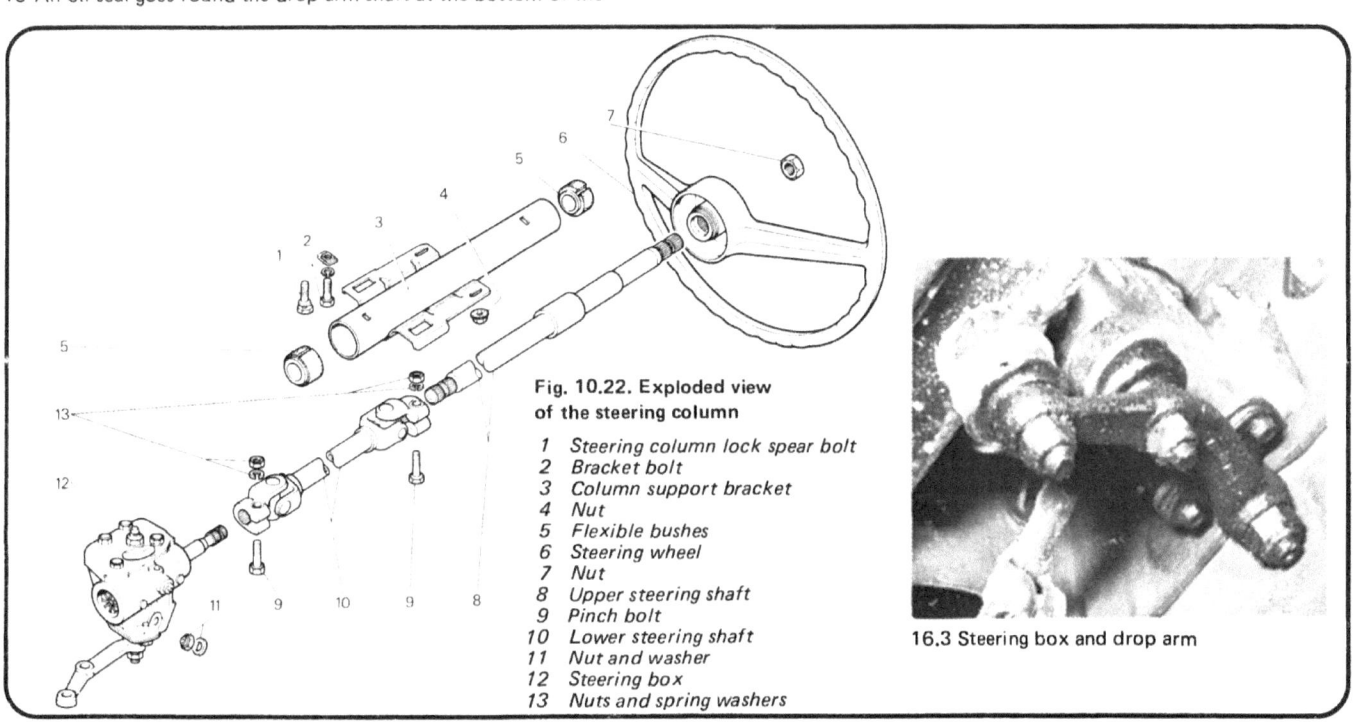

Fig. 10.22. Exploded view
of the steering column

1 Steering column lock spear bolt
2 Bracket bolt
3 Column support bracket
4 Nut
5 Flexible bushes
6 Steering wheel
7 Nut
8 Upper steering shaft
9 Pinch bolt
10 Lower steering shaft
11 Nut and washer
12 Steering box
13 Nuts and spring washers

16.3 Steering box and drop arm

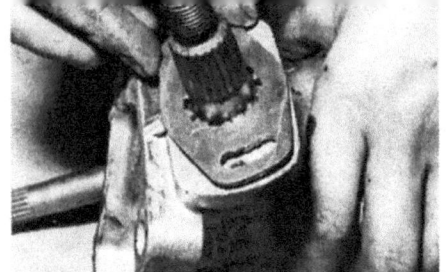

16.17 Steering worm and sector backlash adjuster plate

16.19 Steering box cover, adjuster and locknut

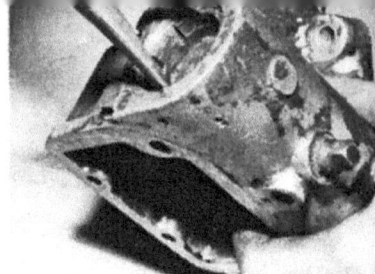

16.20 Turning the worm endfloat adjust cap

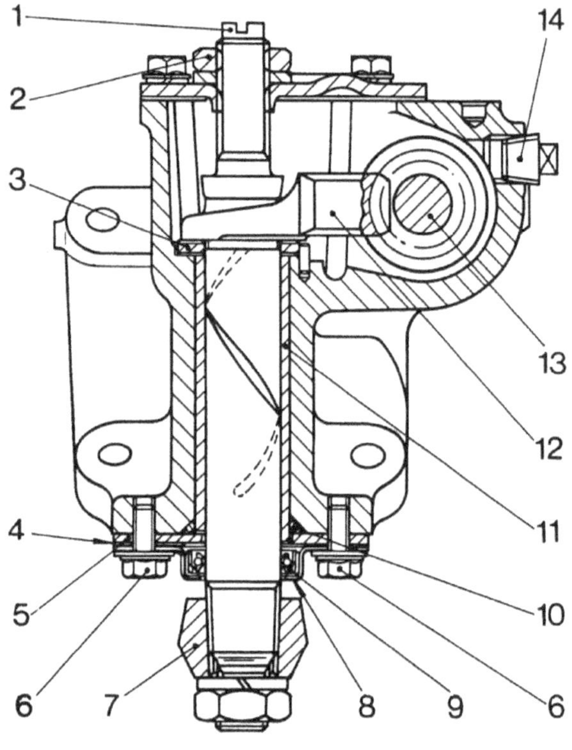

Fig. 10.23. Sectional view of steering box

1 Sector adjusting screw
2 Locknut
3 Shim
4 Gasket
5 Bush
6 Adjuster plate screws
7 Drop arm
8 Oil seal cover
9 Seal
10 Upper seal
11 Eccentric bush
12 Sector
13 Worm
14 Oil filler/level plug

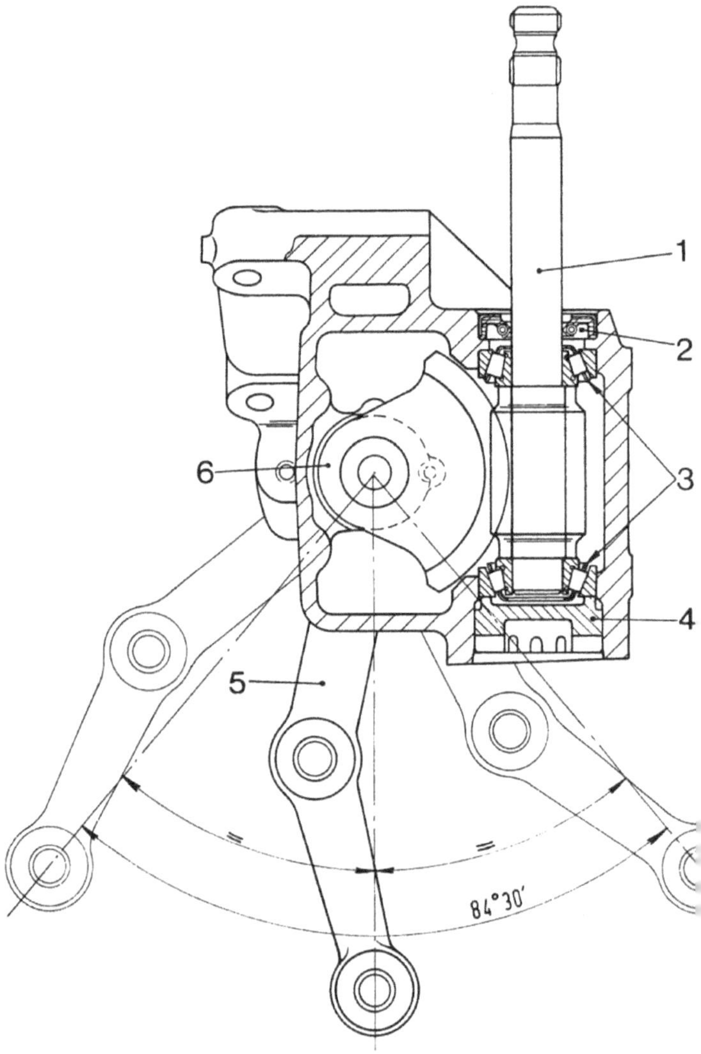

Fig. 10.14. Sectional view of steering box worm components

1 Worm
2 Oil seal
3 Tapered roller bearings
4 Lower bearing retainer worm adjusting ring nu
5 Drop arm
6 Sector

84°30'

1 Accurate front wheel alignment is essential for good steering and
tyre wear. Before considering the steering angle, check that the tyres
are correctly inflated, that the front wheels are not buckled, the hub
bearings are not worn or incorrectly adjusted and that the steering
linkage is in good order, without slackness or wear at the joints.
2 Wheel alignment consists of four factors:

Camber, which is the angle at which the front wheels are set from
the vertical when viewed from the front of the car. Positive camber is
the amount (in degrees) that the wheels are tilted outwards at the top
from the vertical.

Castor is the angle between the steering axis and a vertical line when
viewed from each side of the car. Positive castor is when the steering
axis is inclined rearward.

Steering axis inclination is the angle, when viewed from the front of
the car, between the vertical and an imaginary line drawn through the
king pins.

Toe-in is the amount by which the distance between the front
inside edges of the roadwheels (measured at hub height) is less than the
diametrically opposite distance measured between the rear inside edges
of the front roadwheels.
3 It is recommended that steering angles other than toe-in are checked
and adjusted by your Fiat dealer as special gauges are required.
However, it is worth knowing the method of adjusting the camber and
castor angles.
4 To adjust the camber angle, release the suspension upper control
arm pivot shaft from the bodyframe as fully described in Section 8 of
this Chapter and add or remove an equal number of shims from each
securing stud. Adding shims increases the camber angle.
5 To adjust the castor angle, again release the suspension upper
control arm pivot shaft from the bodyframe and transfer shims from
one securing stud to the other. To increase the castor angle, transfer
shims from the rear to the front stud.
6 To adjust the front wheel toe-in, place the car on level ground, with
the tyres correctly inflated and loaded with the weight of four people.
An alternative to this is to load the car with the equivalent weight of
concrete blocks placed on the floor of the car and evenly distributed.
7 Obtain or make a toe-in (tracking) gauge. One can be made from a
length of tubing having an adjustable setscrew and nut at one end.
8 With the gauge, measure the distance between the two inner rims of
the front roadwheels, at hub height and at the rear of the wheels.
9 Pull or push the vehicle so that the roadwheel turns through half a
turn (180°) and measure the distance between the two inner rims at
hub height at the front of the wheel. This last measurement should be
less than the first by the specified toe-in (see Specifications Section).
10 When the toe-in is found to be incorrect, slacken the clamp nuts on
each outer trackrod and rotate each trackrod an equal amount but in
opposite directions, until the correct toe-in is obtained. Tighten the
clamp nuts ensuring that the ball joints are held in the centre of their
arc of travel during tightening. If new trackrods or ball joints have
been fitted, a starting point for adjusting the front wheel alignment is
to set each outer trackrod so that the distance measured between the
centres of the ball joint taper pins is equal with the roadwheels in the
'straight-ahead' position.

18 Steering lock angles

1 These angles are not adjustable, but should conform to the angles
given in the Specifications Section.
2 In the event of the front tyres scraping on the suspension or
bodywork during full lock, this will be due to one of three causes and
should be rectified immediately.

   a) *Collision damage to components.*
   b) *Severe wear in suspension or steering components*
   c) *Grossly inaccurate steering angles or front wheel
      alignment (toe-in).*

19 Rear wheel alignment

1 The rear roadwheels toe-in by the amount given in the Specifications
Section.

upsetting the toe-in.
3 Special equipment is needed to check the rear wheel toe-in and
this is best left to your dealer. In an emergency, an approximate
setting can be obtained if the front wheels are set exactly in the
'straight-ahead' position and a straight edge is then placed in contact
with the front and rear tyre walls on one side of the car. Load the car
with (or the equivalent of) four people.
4 Adjust the rear wheel toe-in so that the wall of the tyre at the front
of the rear roadwheel shows a gap between it and the straight edge of
half of the specified toe-in. Adjustment is carried out by releasing the
control arm to bodyframe bolts and moving the control arm within the
limits of the elongated bolt holes. If the range of adjustment is
insufficient, then the adjustment shims which are located on either side
of the control arm pivot bolt will have to be transferred from one side
to the other as required (Fig. 10.25).
5 Repeat the operations on the opposite rear roadwheel.

20 Wheels and tyres

1 The roadwheels are of pressed steel type.
2 Periodically remove the wheels, clean dirt and mud from the inside
and outside surfaces and examine for signs of rusting or rim damage
and rectify as necessary.
3 Apply a smear of light grease to the wheel bolts before screwing
them in and finally tighten them to the specified torque.
4 The tyres fitted are of radial ply construction. Never mix tyres of
different construction and always check and maintain the pressures
regularly.
5 If the wheels have been balanced on the vehicle then it is important
that the wheels are not moved round the vehicle in an effort to
equalise tread wear. If a wheel is removed, then the relationship of the
hub to the holes in the wheel should be marked to ensure exact
replacement otherwise the balance of wheel, hub and tyre will be
upset.
6 Where the wheels have been balanced off the vehicle, then they may
be moved round to equalise wear. Include the spare wheel in any
rotational pattern. With radial ply tyres, do not move the wheels from
side to side but only interchange the front and rear wheels on the
same side.
7 Balancing of the wheels is an essential factor in good steering and
road holding. When the tyres have been in use for about half their
useful life the wheels should be rebalanced to compensate for the lost
tread rubber due to wear.
8 Inspect the tyre walls and treads regularly for cuts and damage and
where evident, have them professionally repaired.

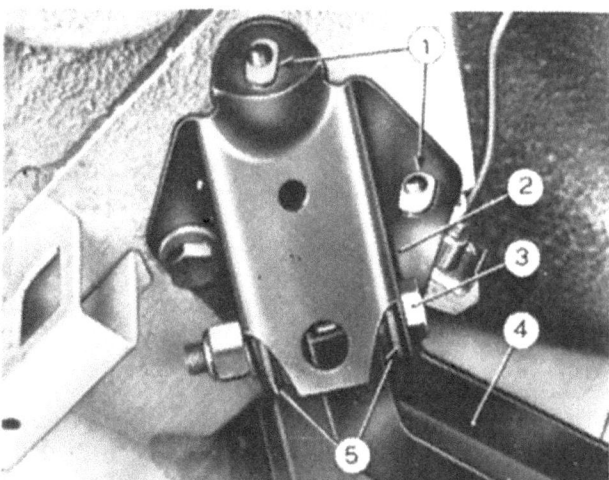

Fig. 10.25. Rear suspension control arm bracket showing elongated
bolt holes for toe-in adjustment

1 Holes   4 Control arm
2 Bracket   5 Adjustment shims
3 Pivot bolt

Steering feels vague, car wanders and floats at speed	Tyre pressure uneven.
	Shock absorbers worn.
	Spring broken.
	Steering gear balljoints badly worn.
	Suspension geometry incorrect.
	Steering mechanism free play excessive.
	Front suspension and rear control arm pick-up points out of alignme
Stiff and heavy steering	Tyre pressures too low.
	No grease in king pin bushes.
	Seized steering and suspension balljoints.
	Front wheel toe-in incorrect.
	Suspension geometry incorrect.
	Steering gear incorrectly adjusted too tightly.
Wheel wobble and vibration	Wheel bolts loose.
	Front wheels and tyres out of balance.
	Steering balljoints badly worn.
	Hub bearings badly worn.
	Steering gear free play excessive.
	Front spring weak or broken.

Chapter 11 Body and fittings

For modifications, and information applicable to later models, see Supplement at end of manual

Contents

1 General description

1 The Fiat 126 is produced in one body style - a two door four seater saloon.

2 Construction is of welded, all steel integral body and underframe or floorpan.

3 General trim and equipment is adequate without luxury features and the keynote of controls and accessories is one of simplicity.

4 Apart from the engine compartment and luggage boot lids and the doors, no other body panels are detachable and in the event of damage of a serious nature, the panel will have to be cut away and a new one welded into place.

2 Maintenance - bodywork and underframe

1 The general condition of a car's bodywork is the one thing that significantly affects its value. Maintenance is easy but needs to be regular and particular. Neglect, particularly after minor damage, can lead quickly to further deterioration and costly repair bills. It is important also to keep watch on those parts of the car not immediately visible, for instance, the underside, inside all the wheel arches and the lower part of the engine compartment.

2 The basic maintenance routine for the bodywork is washing - preferably with a lot of water, from a hose. This will remove all the loose solids which may have stuck to the car. It is important to flush these off in such a way as to prevent grit from scratching the finish. The wheel arches and underbody need washing in the same way to remove any accumulated mud which will retain moisture and tend to encourage rust. Parodoxically enough, the best time to clean the underbody and wheel arches is in wet weather when the mud is thoroughly wet and soft. In very wet weather the underbody is usually cleaned of large accumulations automatically and this is a good time for inspection.

3 Periodically it is a good idea to have the whole of the underside of the car steam cleaned, engine compartment included, so that a thorough inspection can be carried out to see what minor repairs and renovations are necessary. Steam cleaning is available at many garages and is necessary for removal of accumulation of oily grime which sometimes is allowed to cake thick in certain areas near the engine, gearbox and back axle. If steam facilities are not available, there are one or two excellent grease solvents available which can be brush applied. The dirt can then be simply hosed off.

4 After washing paintwork, wipe off with a chamois leather to give an unspotted clear finish. A coat of clear protective wax polish will give added protection against chemical pollutants in the air. If the paintwork sheen has dulled or oxidised, use a cleaner/polish combination to restore the brilliance of the shine. This requires a little more effort, but is usually caused because regular washing has been neglected. Always check that door and ventilator opening drain holes and pipes are completely clear so that water can drain out. Bright work should be treated the same way as paintwork. Windscreens and windows can be kept clear of the smeary film which often appears, if a little ammonia is added to the water. If they are scratched, a good rub with a proprietary metal polish will often clear them. Never use any form of wax or other body or chromium polish on glass.

3 Maintenance - upholstery and carpets

1 Mats and carpets should be brushed or vacuum cleaned regularly to keep them free of grit. If they are badly stained remove them from the car for scrubbing or sponging and make quite sure they are dry before replacement. Seats and interior trim panels can be kept clean by a wipe over with a damp cloth. If they do become stained (which can be more apparent on light coloured upholstery) use a little detergent and a soft nail brush to scour the grime out of the grain of the material. Do not forget to keep the head lining clean in the same way as the upholstery. When using liquid cleaners inside the car do not over-wet the surface being cleaned. Excessive damp could get into the seams and padded interior causing stains, offensive odours or even rot. If the inside of the car gets wet accidentally it is worthwhile taking some trouble to dry it out properly, particularly where carpets are involved. **Do not** leave oil or electric heaters inside the car for this purpose.

Repair of minor scratches in the car's bodywork

If the scratch is very superficial, and does not penetrate to the metal of the bodywork repair is very simple. Lightly rub the area of the scratch with a paintwork renovator, or a very fine cutting paste, to remove loose paint from the scratch and to clear the surrounding bodywork of wax polish. Rinse the area with clean water.

Apply touch-up paint to the scratch using a thin paint brush; continue to apply thin layers of paint until the surface of the paint in the scratch is level with surrounding paintwork. Allow the new paint at least two weeks to harden; then, blend it into the surrounding paintwork by rubbing the paintwork in the scratch area with a paintwork renovator or a very fine cutting paste. Finally apply wax polish.

Where a scratch has penetrated, right through to the metal of the bodywork, causing the metal to rust, a different repair technique is required. Remove any loose rust from the bottom of the scratch with a penknife, then apply rust inhibiting paint to prevent the formation of rust in the future. Using a rubber or nylon applicator fill the scratch with bodystopper paste. If required, this paste can be mixed with cellulose thinners to provide a very thin paste which is ideal for filling narrow scratches. Before the stopper-paste in the scratch hardens, wrap a piece of smooth cotton rag around the tip of the finger; dip the finger in cellulose thinners and then quickly sweep it across the surface of the stopper-paste in the scratch; this will ensure that the surface of the stopper-paste is slightly hollowed. The scratch can now be painted over as described earlier in this Section.

Repair of dents in the car's bodywork

When deep denting of the car's bodywork has taken place, the first task is to pull the dent out, until the affected bodywork almost attains its original shape. There is little point in trying to restore the original shape completely, as the metal in the damaged area will have stretched on impact and cannot be reshaped fully to its original contour. It is better to bring the level of the dent up to a point which is about 1/8 in (3 mm) below the level of the surrounding bodywork. In cases where the dent is very shallow anyway, it is not worth trying to pull it out at all.

If the underside of the dent is accessible, it can be hammered out gently from behind, using a mallet with a wooden or plastic head. Whilst doing this, hold a suitable block of wood firmly against the outside of the dent. This block will absorb the impact from the hammer blows and thus prevent a large area of bodywork from being 'belled-out.'

Should the dent be in a section of the bodywork which has a double skin or some other factor making it inaccessible from behind, a different technique is called for. Drill several small holes through the metal inside the dent area - particularly in the deeper sections. Then screw long self-tapping screws into the holes just sufficiently for them to gain a good purchase in the metal. Now the dent can be pulled out by pulling on the protruding heads of the screws with a pair of pliers.

The next stage of the repair is the removal of the paint from the damaged area, and from an inch or so of the surrounding 'sound' bodywork. This is accomplished most easily by using a wire brush or abrasive pad on a power drill, although it can be done just as effectively by hand using sheets of abrasive paper. To complete the preparations for filling, score the surface of the bare metal with a screwdriver or the tang of a file, or alternatively, drill small holes in the affected area. This will provide a really good 'key' for the filler paste.

To complete the repair see the Section on filling and respraying.

Repair of rust holes or gashes in the car's bodywork

Remove all paint from the affected area and from an inch or so of the surrounding 'sound' bodywork, using an abrasive pad or a wire brush on a power drill. If these are not available a few sheets of abrasive paper will do the job just as effectively. With the paint

expensive as most people think and it is often quicker and more satisfactory to fit a new panel than to attempt to repair areas of corrosion.

Remove all fittings from the affected area, except those which will act as a guide to the original shape of the damaged bodywork (eg. head lamp shells etc). Then, using tin snips or a hacksaw blade, remove all loose metal and any other metal badly affected by corrosion. Hammer the edges of the hole inwards in order to create a slight depression for the filler paste.

Wire brush the affected area to remove the powdery rust from the surface of the remaining metal. Paint the affected area with rust inhibiting paint, if the back of the rusted area is accessible treat this also.

Before filling can take place it will be necessary to block the hole in some way. This can be achieved by the use of aluminium plastic mesh, or aluminium tape.

Aluminium or plastic mesh is probably the best material to use for a large hole. Cut a piece to the approximate size and shape of the hole to be filled, then position it in the hole so that its edges below the level of the surrounding bodywork. It can be retained in position by several blobs of filler paste around its periphery.

Aluminium tape should be used for small or very narrow holes. Pull a piece off the roll and trim it to the approximate size and shape required, then pull off the backing paper (if used) and stick the tape over the hole; it can be overlapped if the thickness of one piece is insufficient. Burnish down the edges of the tape with the handle of screwdriver or similar, to ensure that the tape is securely attached to the metal underneath.

Bodywork repairs - filling and re-spraying

Before using this Section, see the Sections on dent, deep scratch, rust hole, and gash repairs.

Many types of bodyfiller are available, but generally speaking the proprietary kits which contain a tin of filler paste and a tube of resin hardener are best for this type of repair. A wide, flexible plastic or nylon applicator will be found invaluable for imparting a smooth and well contoured finish to the surface of the filler.

Mix up a little filler on a clean piece of card or board - use the hardener sparingly (follow the maker's instructions on the packet), otherwise the filler will set very rapidly.

Using the applicator, apply the filler paste to the prepared area; draw the applicator across the surface of the filler to achieve the correct contour and to level the filler surface. As soon as a contour that approximates the correct one is achieved stop working the paste. If you carry on too long the paste will become sticky and begin to 'pick-up' on the applicator. Continue to add thin layers of filler paste at twenty-minute intervals until the level of the filler is just 'proud' of the surrounding bodywork.

Once the filler has hardened, excess can be removed using a metal plane or coarse file. From then on, progressively finer grades of abrasive paper should be used, starting with a 40 grade production paper and finishing with 400 grade wet or dry paper. Always wrap the abrasive paper around a flat rubber, cork, or wooden block - otherwise the surface of the filler will not be completely flat. During the smoothing of the filler surface the wet or dry paper should be periodically rinsed in water; this will ensure that a very smooth finish is imparted to the filler at the final stage.

At this stage the 'dent' should be surrounded by a ring of bare metal, which in turn should be encircled by a finely 'feathered' edge the good paintwork. Rinse the repair area with clean water, until all the dust produced by the rubbing-down operation is gone.

Spray the whole repair area with a light coat of grey primer - this will show up any imperfections in the surface of the filler. Repair the imperfections with fresh filler paste or bodystopper, and once more smooth the surface with abrasive paper. If bodystopper is used, it can be mixed with cellulose thinners to form a really thin paste which is ideal for filling small holes. Repeat this spray and repair procedure until you are satisfied that the surface of the filler, and the feathered edge of the paintwork are perfect. Clean the repair area with clean

condition can be created artificially if you have access to a large indoor working area, but if you are forced to work in the open, you will have to pick your day very carefully. If you are working indoors, dousing the floor in the work area with water will 'lay' the dust which would otherwise be in the atmosphere. If the repair area is confined to one body panel, mask off the surrounding panels; this will help to minimise the effect of a slight mis-match in paint colours. Bodywork fittings (eg. chrome strips, door handles etc) will also need to be masked off. Use genuine masking tape and several thicknesses of newspaper for the masking operation.

Before commencing to spray, agitate the aerosol can thoroughly, then spray a test area (an old tin, or similar) until the technique is mastered. Cover the repair area with a thick coat of primer; the thickness should be built up using several thin layers of paint rather than one thick one. Using 400 grade wet or dry paper, rub down the surface of the primer until it is really smooth. While doing this, the work area should be thoroughly doused with water, and the wet or dry paper periodically rinsed in water. Allow to dry before spraying on more paint.

Spray on the top coat, again building up the thickness by using several thin layers of paint. Start spraying in the centre of the repair area and then, using a circular motion, work outwards until the whole repair area and about 2 inches of the surrounding original paintwork is covered. Remove all masking material 10 to 15 minutes after spraying on the final coat of paint.

Allow the new paint at least 2 weeks to harden fully; then, using a paintwork renovator or a very fine cutting paste, blend the edges of the new paint into the existing paintwork. Finally, apply wax polish.

---

5 Major body damage - repair

Where serious damage has occurred or large areas need renewal due to neglect, it means certainly that completely new sections or panels will need welding in and this is best left to professionals. If the damage is due to impact it will also be necessary to completely check the alignment of the bodyshell structure. Due to the principle of construction the strength and shape of the whole can be affected by damage to a part. In such instances the services of a Fiat dealer with specialist checking jigs are essential. If a body is left misaligned it is first of all dangerous as the car will not handle properly and secondly uneven stresses will be imposed on the steering, engine and transmission causing abnormal wear or complete failure. Tyre wear may also be excessive.

---

6 Maintenance - hinges and locks

1   Oil the hinges of the engine compartment lid, boot and doors with a drop or two of light oil periodically. A good time is after the car has been washed.
2   Oil the luggage boot release catch pivot pin and the safety catch pivot pin periodically.
3   Do not over lubricate door latches and strikers. Normally a little oil on the rotary cam spindle alone is sufficient.

---

7 Door interior trim panel - removal and refitting

1   Open the door wide and prise off the escutcheon plate from the door interior handle (photo).
2   Insert a piece of wire with a hook at the end behind the window regulator handle and pull out the handle securing clip. Remove the regulator handle (photo).
3   Unscrew and remove the two upper securing screws from the map pocket (photo).
4   Insert the fingers between the trim panel and the door at its upper edge and pull the panel away to disengage the securing clips. Work the fingers all round the edge of the panel until it can be removed from the door. Pull away the waterproof sheet (photo).
5   Refitting is a reversal of removal, but when installing the window

---

8 Door lock - removal, refitting and adjustment

1   Open the door wide and remove the interior trim panel as described in the preceding Section.
2   Unscrew and remove the knob from the lock plunger (Fig. 11.1).
3   Unscrew and remove the screws which secure the door interior remote control handle and its baseplate.
4   Disconnect the link rod vibration insulator.
5   Disconnect the link rod from the door exterior handle.
6   Unscrew and remove the securing bolts which retain the lock assembly. These are accessible on the door edge.
7   The complete lock assembly can now be withdrawn from the door cavity, manoeuvring the link rods through the door apertures or bringing them to a position where their connecting clips can be detached.
8   If the exterior handle must be removed, the securing nuts can be reached through the access hole in the inner panel (photo).
9   Refitting is a reversal of removal, but any adjustment required to ensure smooth positive closure is carried out by moving the position of the striker on the door pillar after having released the securing and adjustment screws (Fig. 11.2).

---

9 Window regulator mechanism - removal and refitting

1   Remove the door interior trim panel, as previously described.
2   Before dismantling the cable assembly, cut two thin blocks of wood and insert them between the cable drum and its support bracket to prevent the cable unwinding from the drum (Fig. 11.3).
3   Disconnect the cable clamp at the glass lift channel. It is a good idea to mark the position of the cable at the clamp to assist when refitting (photo).
4   Push the glass well up and support it.
5   Unbolt the regulator unit from the door and then release the cable from the pulleys. Withdraw the mechanism from the door cavity (Fig. 11.4).
6   If the cable is not to be renewed, the assembly can be refitted by reversing the removal operations. Refit the cable clamp in its original position and any retensioning which may be necessary can be carried out by releasing the securing screw and moving the position of the tensioner pulley.
7   If a new cable is to be fitted, wind the new cable round the drum so that the part of the cable which leaves the drum in a downward direction is located in the groove of the drum nearest the door inner panel.
8   Engage the cable round the pulleys, bolt the regulator unit into position, tension the cable and then connect the cable clamp with the glass in its fully lowered position. Check the operation of the window by temporarily refitting the regulator handle and readjust the position of the cable clamp if necessary.

---

10 Door glass - removal and refitting

1   Remove the window regulator mechanism as described in paragraphs 1 to 5 of the preceding Section.
2   Push the window glass fully up and unbolt and remove the glass front channel (Fig. 11.5).
3   Lower the glass carefully and withdraw it downwards and outwards from the door cavity.
4   If a new door glass is being installed, make sure that the lift channel is located directly in the centre of the glass and the rubber insulator between channel and glass is firmly stuck in position.
5   Install the glass and regulator by reversing the removal operations.

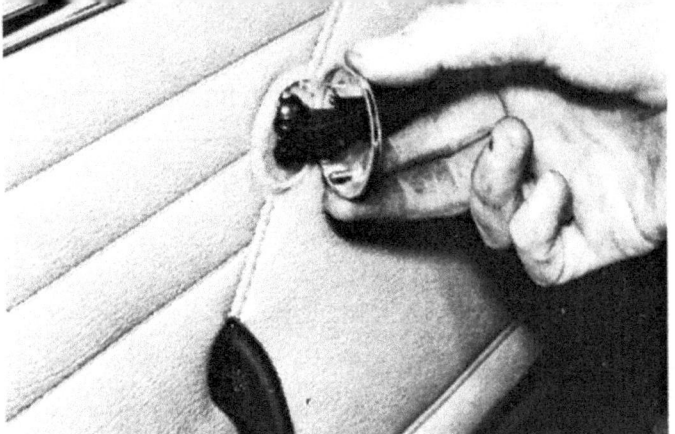

7.1 Removing door remote control handle escutcheon

7.2 Removing window regulator handle

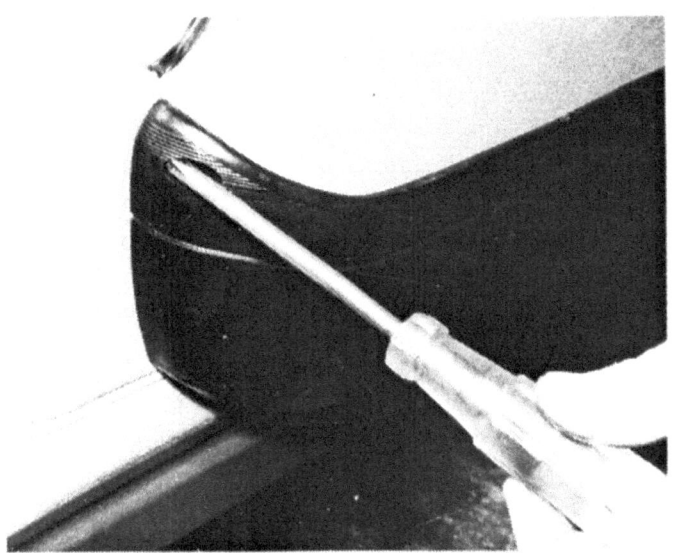

7.3 Removing a map pocket screw

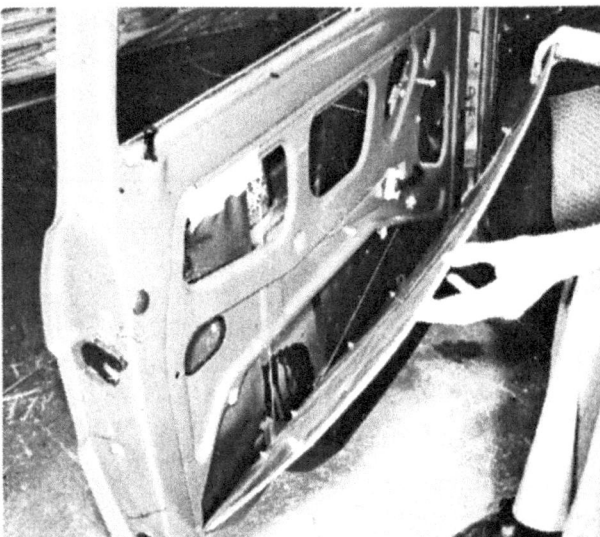

7.4 Removing the door interior trim panel

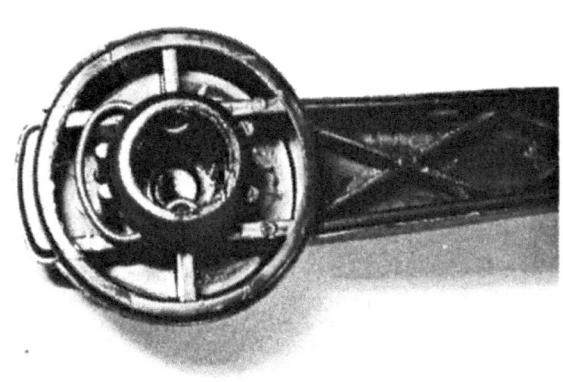

7.5 Window regulator handle securing clip

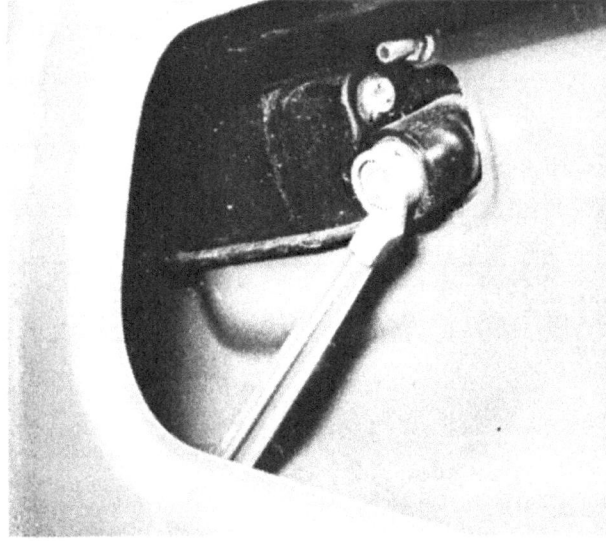

8.8 View of door exterior handle from within door cavity

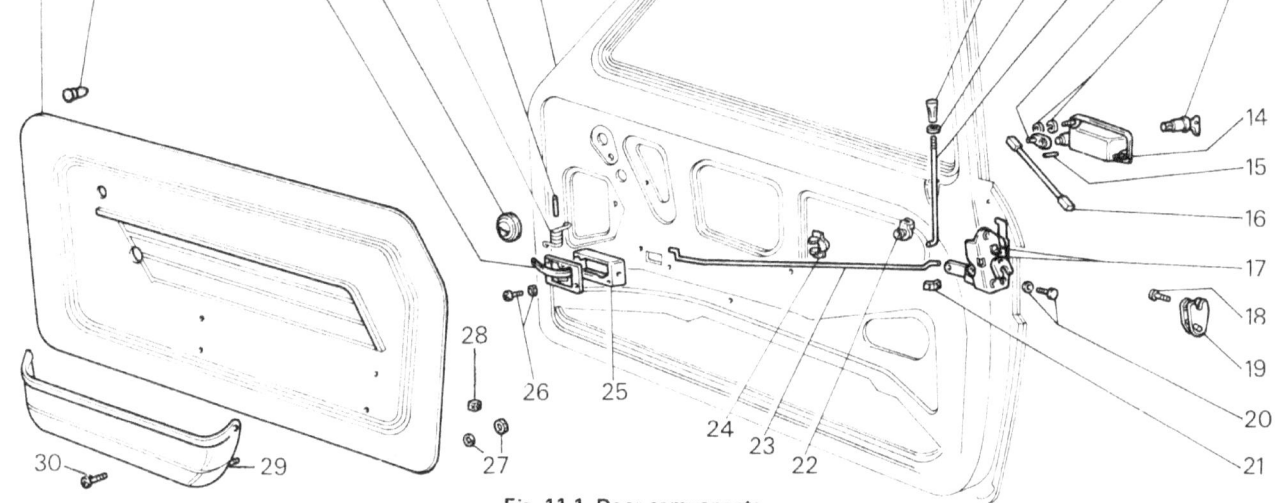

Fig. 11.1. Door components

1	Trim panel	7	Door	13	Lock cylinder	23	Remote control rod
2	Panel clip	8	Plunger knob	14	Exterior door handle	24	Control rod guide
3	Lock remote control handle	9	Grommet	15	Pin	25	Handle baseplate
4	Escutcheon plate	10	Lock control rod	16	Connecting rod	26	Screw
5	Return springs	11	Link plate	17	Lock assembly	27	Map pocket lower
6	Pivot pin	12	Washers	18	Screw		nut and washer
				19	Striker	28	Captive nut
				20	Screw and washer	29	Map pocket
				21	Connecting clips	30	Map pocket upper screw
				22	Connecting clips		

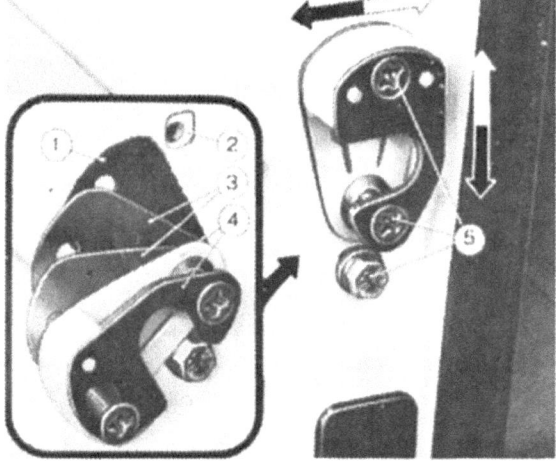

Fig. 11.2. Door striker assembly

1 Gasket
2 Captive tapped plate
3 Spacers
4 Striker
5 Securing screws and bolt

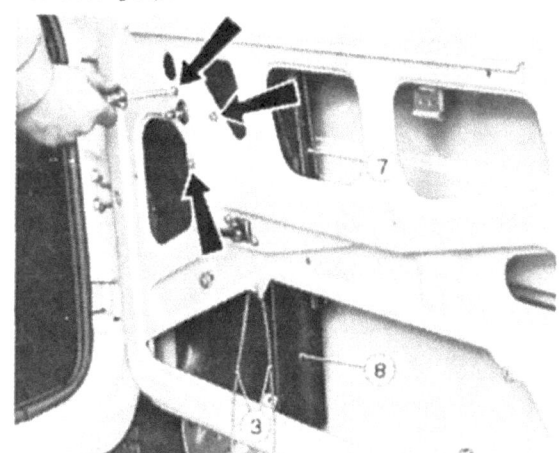

Fig. 11.4. Window regulator securing bolts (7) cable (3) and waterproof deflector (8)

Fig. 11.3. Window winding mechanism. Temporary cable retaining blocks (arrowed)

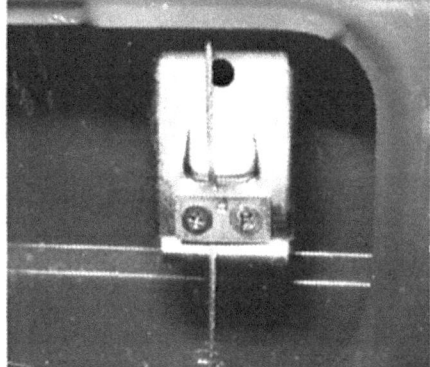

9.3 Window operating cable clamp

Fig. 11.5. Door glass front guide channel

5	Glass lift channel	7	Front guide channel
6	Glass	8	Waterproof deflector

---

11 Swivel ventilators - removal and refitting

1 Remove the main door glass, as described in the preceding Section.
2 Extract the two ventilator frame screws from the upper front door edge (Fig. 11.6).
3 Remove the main door glass rear guide channel which is secured to the inside of the door by two screws accessible on the door edge. This will enable the main glass rubber channel to be slid back by about 2 inches (50.8 mm) from its abutment with the ventilator vertical frame (Fig. 11.7).
4 Push in a wooden wedge to expand the weatherstrip and then move the ventilator assembly rearwards by tilting it at the top. Withdraw the ventilator from the door.
5 The ventilator upper hinge is rivetted and if the glass is to be renewed then it will have to be drilled out.
6 Refitting is a reversal of removal.

---

12 Window mouldings - removal and refitting

1 The window exterior mouldings can be removed after first prising off the clip from the butt joint (Fig. 11.9).
2 Pull the moulding from its retaining clips working carefully round the window frame.
3 If the interior mouldings are to be removed, note that their securing clips also retain the plastic sheeting which is used as a protective barrier inside the door cavity (Fig. 11.10).

---

13 Door - removal and installation

1 Open the door and using a pair of pliers, compress the two legs of the check link towards each other so that they can be released from the body pillar (photo).
2 Support the bottom edge of the door on blocks or a jack suitably insulated with pads of rag to prevent damage to the paintwork.
3 Mark the location of the hinge plates on the door pillar and then unbolt the hinges and remove the door (Fig. 11.11).
4 Installation is a reversal of removal. Any adjustment needed to set the door square within its frame or flush with the outer body panels can be carried out by moving the position of the hinges on the body pillar.
5 Check the door for smooth positive closure and if necessary, move the lock striker to achieve this, as described in Section 8.

1 This is one of the few jobs best left to the professionals. However where it is decided to do the work yourself, carry out the following operations.
2 If the glass has been broken, carefully knock out all the crystals which remain attached to the rubber surround. Protect the surface of the paintwork of the luggage boot lid and cover the vents on the fascia panel. Retrieve your tax disc.
3 If the glass is intact but is to be removed for renewal of the rubber weathersealing surround then first disconnect the wiper arms.
4 Using a small screwdriver, prise out the bright moulding from the rubber windscreen surround.
5 Remove the interior mirror and then prise the rubber surround lip (at the inside top centre) from the body frame edge. Work in both directions and exert even pressure along the top part of the screen until it moves outwards. Have an assistant help with this work.
6 Thoroughly clean the windscreen recess of the bodyframe and examine the rubber surround. If it is cut or has perished or hardened old pieces of sealant cannot easily be removed, then renew it.
7 Commence installation of the windscreen by locating the rubber surround to the glass. Fit a thin cord to the body seating groove of the rubber surround so that the two ends overlap at the top centre (Fig. 11.12).
8 Locate the windscreen accurately at the lower edge of its aperture with the two ends of the pull cord hanging inside the vehicle
9 Have an assistant press on the glass from the outside and pull the two ends of the fitting cord evenly so that the combination of pressure and cord withdrawal will engage the rubber surround lip with the body flange (Fig. 11.13).
10 With the windscreen installed, inject black sealant into the space between the rubber and the glass and between the rubber and the body
11 Refit the bright trim preferably using a tool similar to the one shown which has the effect of opening the lips of the rubber channel just before the rear part of the tool presses the trim into it (Fig. 11.
12 Clean off any excess sealant with a rag soaked in paraffin or white spirit.
13 Locate the lead to the interior lamp using a screwdriver to engage behind the lip of the rubber surround (Fig. 11.15).

Fig. 11.6. Swivel ventilator upper fixing screws

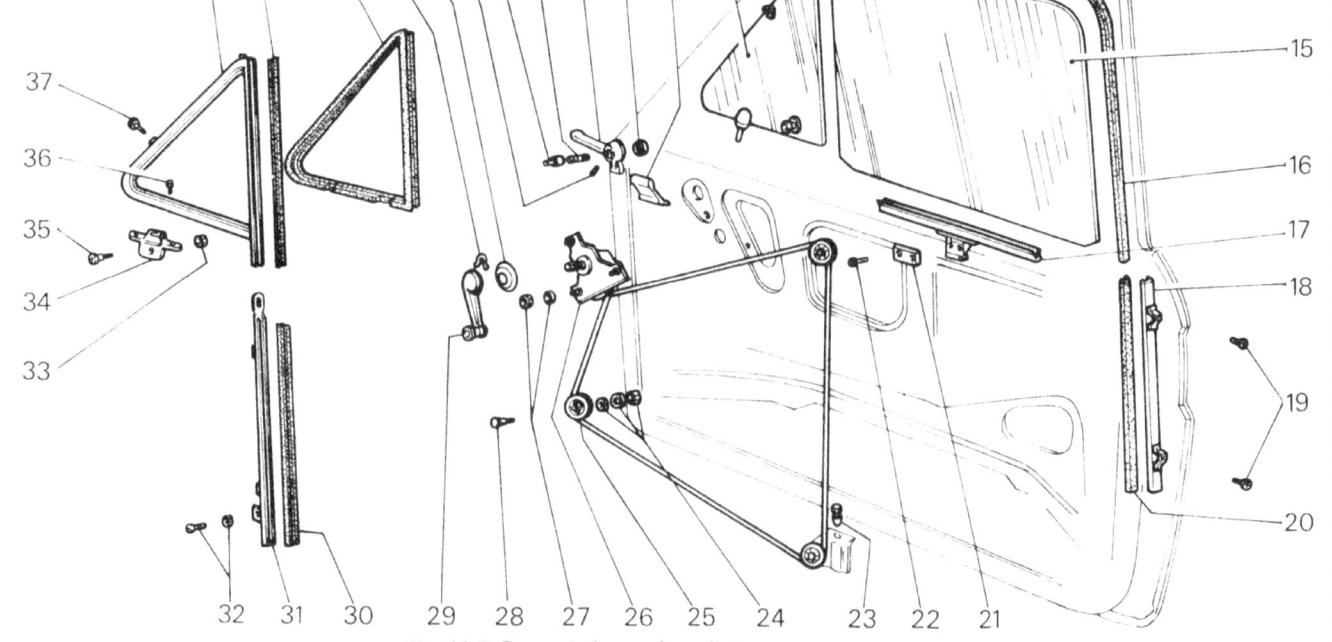

Fig. 11.7. Door window and ventilator components

1	Ventilator frame	10	Lockwasher
2	Rubber channel	11	Stop plate
3	Weather strip surround	12	Glass
4	Window regulator handle spring clip	13	Upper pivot
5	Escutcheon plate	14	Rivet
6	Dowel	15	Window glass
7	Lock button	16	Rubber channel
8	Spring	17	Glass lift channel
9	Lock lever	18	Rear guide channel
		19	Screws

20 Rubber channel	29 Regulator handle
21 Cable clamp plate	30 Rubber channel
22 Screw	31 Front glass guide channel
23 Glass lower stop	32 Screw and washer
24 Nut and washers	33 Nut
25 Tensioner pulley	34 Ventilator lower pivot
26 Regulator assembly	35 Screw and washer
27 Nut and washer	36 Rivet
28 Pivot pin	37 Frame securing screw

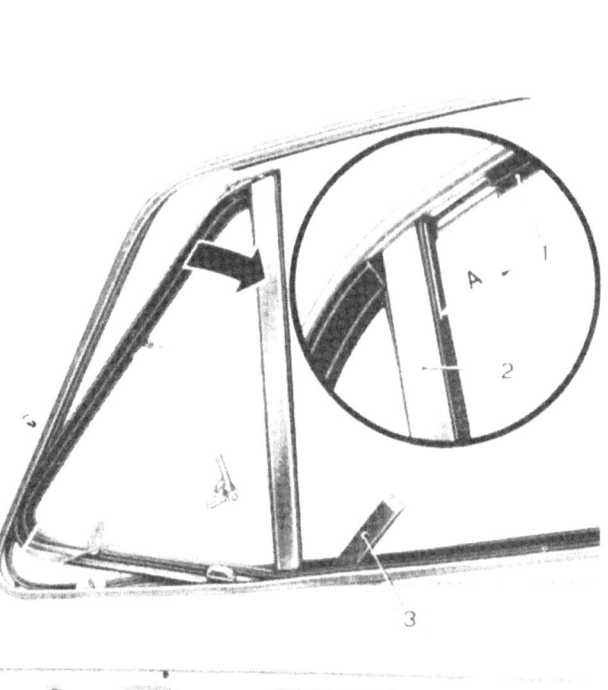

Fig. 11.8. Removing a swivel ventilator

1   Rubber channel   3   Temporary wooden wedge
2   Frame   A = 2.0 in (50.8 mm)

Fig. 11.9. Removing door window moulding

1   Retaining clips   3   Butt joint cover
2   Moulding

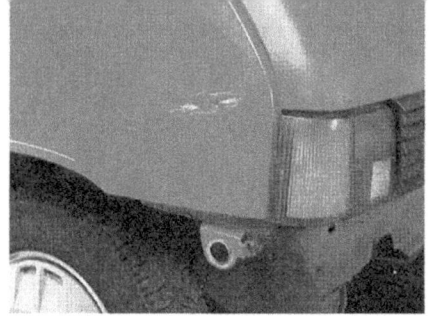

This photographic sequence shows the steps taken to repair the dent and paintwork damage shown above. In general, the procedure for repairing a hole will be similar; where there are substantial differences, the procedure is clearly described and shown in a separate photograph.

First remove any trim around the dent, then hammer out the dent where access is possible. This will minimise filling. Here, after the large dent has been hammered out, the damaged area is being made slightly concave.

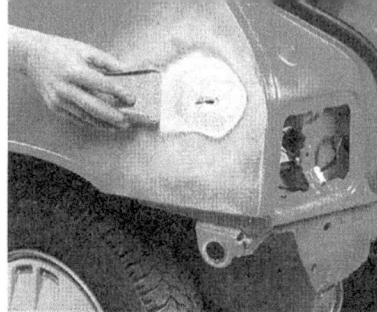

Next, remove all paint from the damaged by rubbing with course abrasive pape using a power drill fitted with a wire brus abrasive pad. 'Feather' the edge of boundary with good paintwork using a grade of abrasive paper.

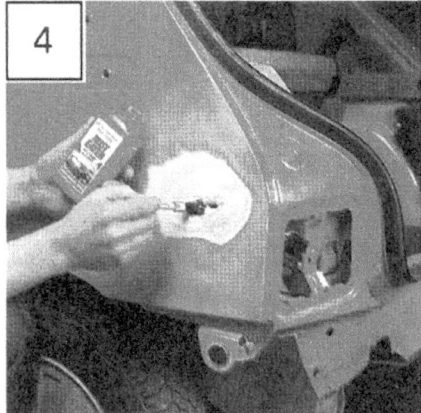

Where there are holes or other damage, the sheet metal should be cut away before proceeding further. The damaged area and any signs of rust should be treated with Turtle Wax Hi-Tech Rust Eater, which will also inhibit further rust formation.

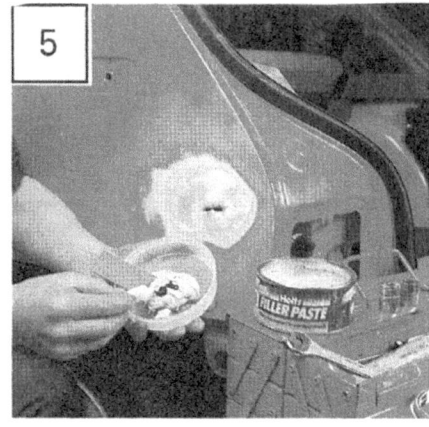

For a large dent or hole mix Holts Body Plus Resin and Hardener according to the manufacturer's instructions and apply around the edge of the repair. Press Glass Fibre Matting over the repair area and leave for 20-30 minutes to harden. Then ...

... brush more Holts Body Plus Resin Hardener onto the matting and leav harden. Repeat the sequence with tw three layers of matting, checking that the layer is lower than the surrounding a Apply Holts Body Plus Filler Paste as sh in Step 5B.

For a medium dent, mix Holts Body Plus Filler Paste and Hardener according to the manufacturer's instructions and apply it with a flexible applicator. Apply thin layers of filler at 20-minute intervals, until the filler surface is slightly proud of the surrounding bodywork.

For small dents and scratches use Holts No Mix Filler Paste straight from the tube. Apply it according to the instructions in thin layers, using the spatula provided. It will harden in minutes if applied outdoors and may then be used as its own knifing putting.

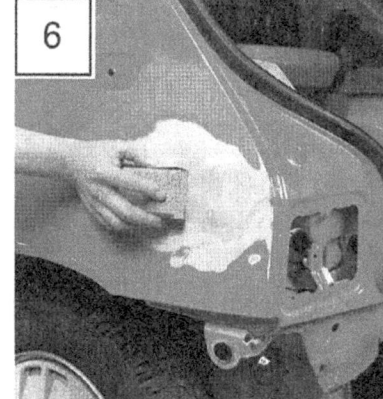

Use a plane or file for initial shaping. T using progressively finer grades of wet-dry paper, wrapped around a sanding b and copious amounts of clean water, down the filler until glass smooth. 'Fea the edges of adjoining paintwork.

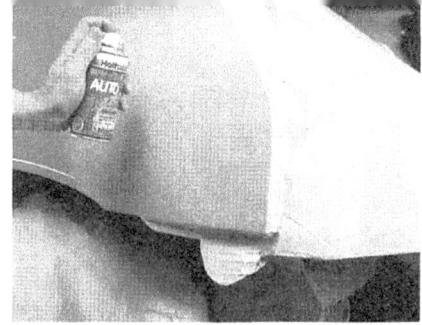

Protect adjoining areas before spraying the whole repair area and at least one inch of the surrounding sound paintwork with Holts Dupli-Color primer.

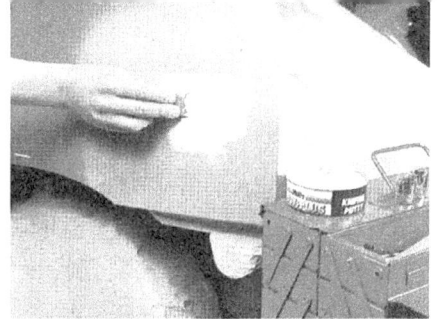

Fill any imperfections in the filler surface with a small amount of Holts Body Plus Knifing Putty. Using plenty of clean water, rub down the surface with a fine grade wet-and-dry paper - 400 grade is recommended - until it is really smooth.

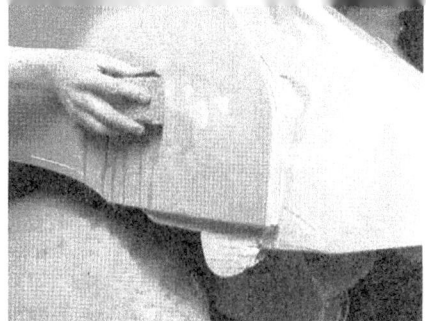

Carefully fill any remaining imperfections with knifing putty before applying the last coat of primer. Then rub down the surface with Holts Body Rubbing Compound to ensure a really smooth surface.

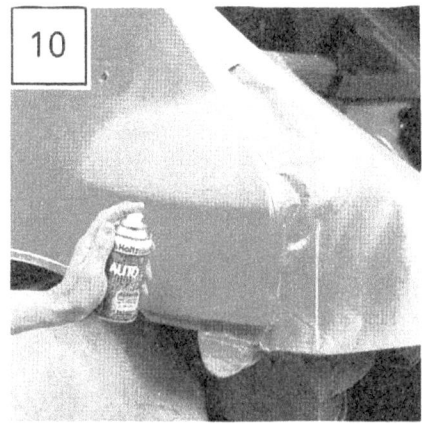

10

Protect surrounding areas from overspray before applying the topcoat in several thin layers. Agitate Holts Dupli-Color aerosol thoroughly. Start at the repair centre, spraying outwards with a side-to-side motion.

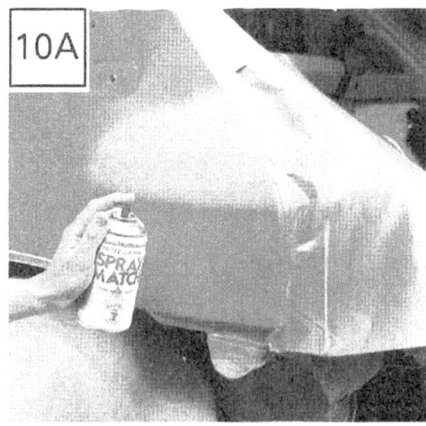

10A

If the exact colour is not available off the shelf, local Holts Professional Spraymatch Centres will custom fill an aerosol to match perfectly.

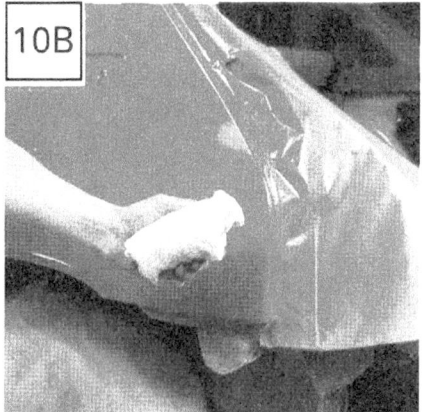

10B

To identify whether a lacquer finish is required, rub a painted unrepaired part of the body with wax and a clean cloth.

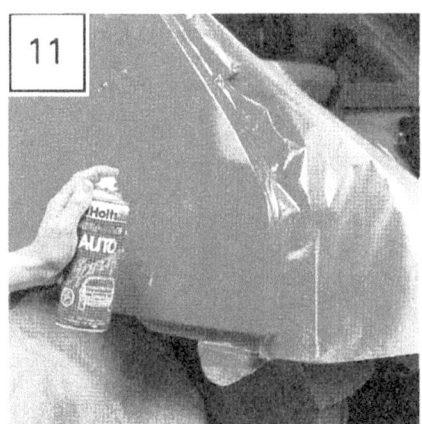

11

If no traces of paint appear on the cloth, spray Holts Dupli-Color clear lacquer over the repaired area to achieve the correct gloss level.

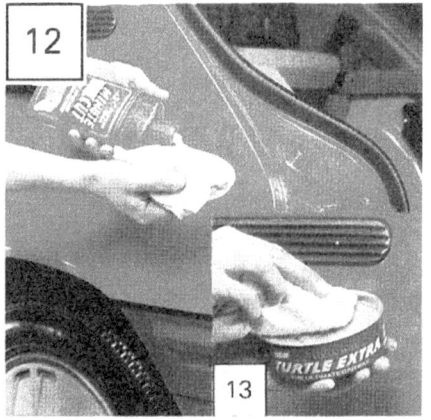

12

13

The paint will take about two weeks to harden fully. After this time it can be 'cut' with a mild cutting compound such as Turtle Wax Minute Cut prior to polishing with a final coating of Turtle Wax Extra.

14

When carrying out bodywork repairs, remember that the quality of the finished job is proportional to the time and effort expended.

Fig. 11.10. Door waterproof deflector and moulding retainers

13.1 A door check strap

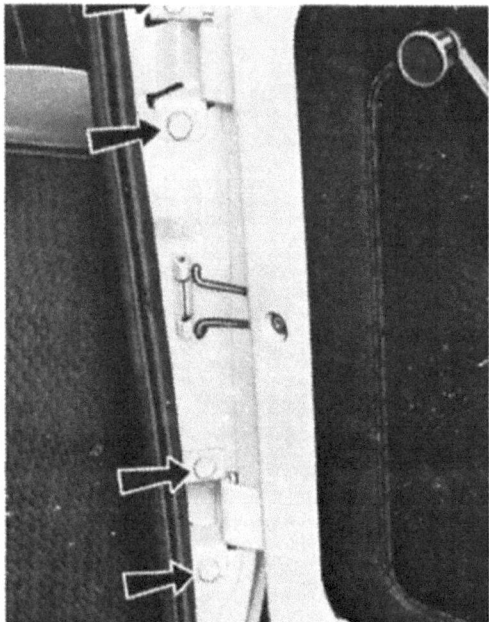

Fig. 11.11. Door ninge bolts on body pillar

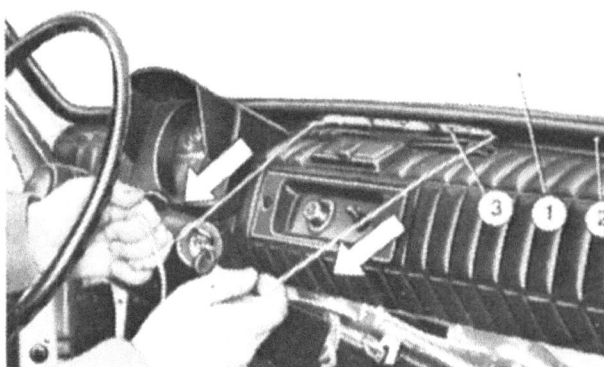

Fig. 11.13. Installing windscreen

1 Glass   3 Body
2 Rubber surround

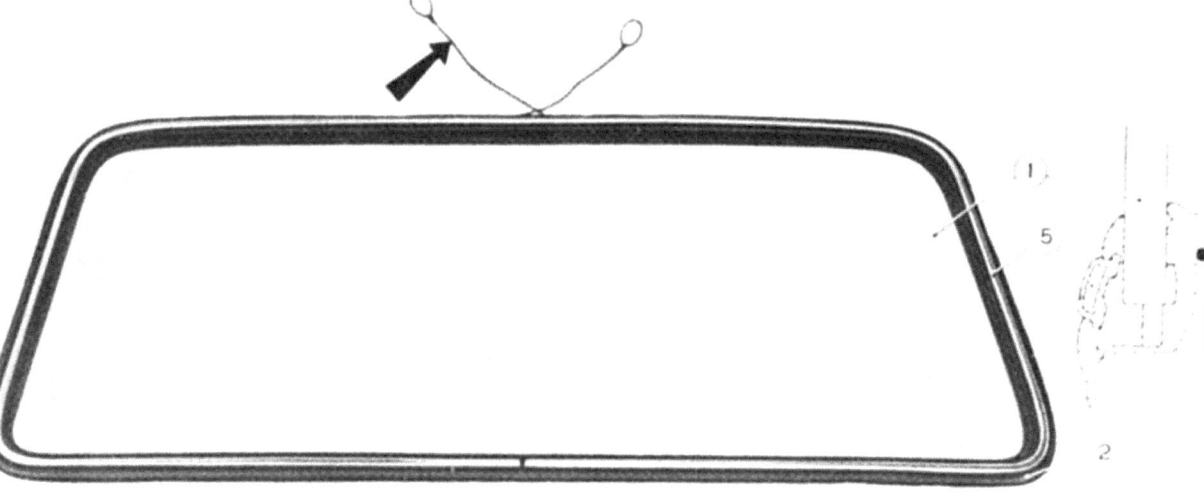

Fig. 11.12. Windscreen ready for installation

1 Glass   5 Fitting cord (arrowed)
2 Rubber surround

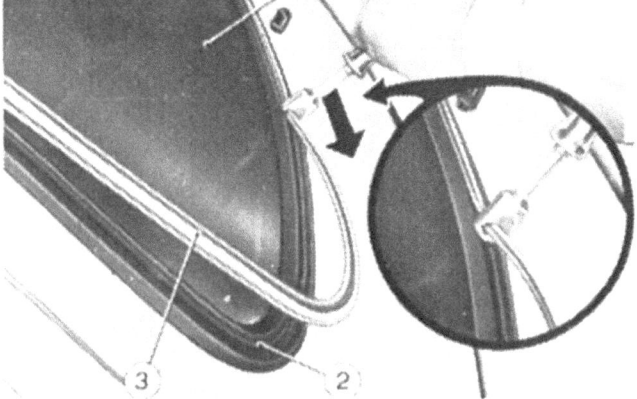

Fig. 11.14. Tool for installing bright trim to windscreen surround

1 Glass	3 Trim
2 Surround	

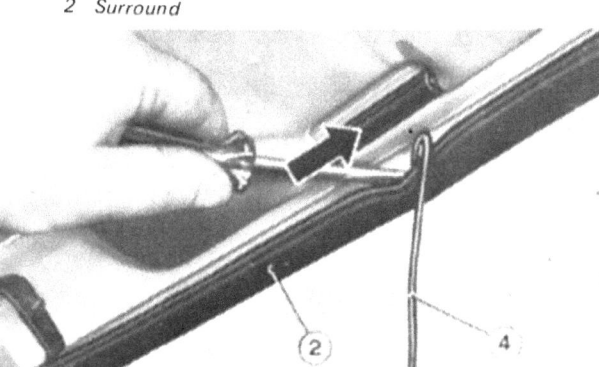

Fig. 11.15. Inserting lead to interior lamp under lip of windscreen rubber surround

2 Rubber surround	4 Lead

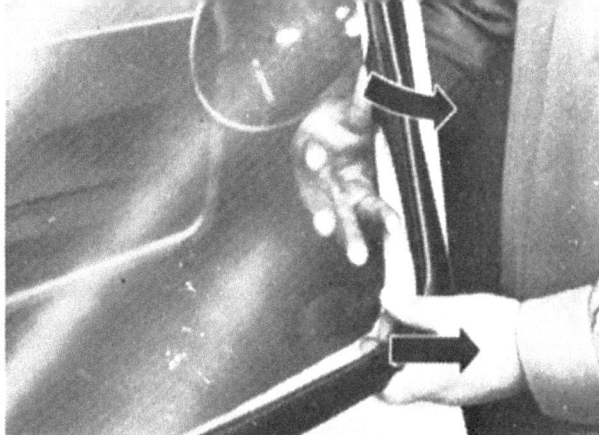

Fig. 11.16. Removing a side window

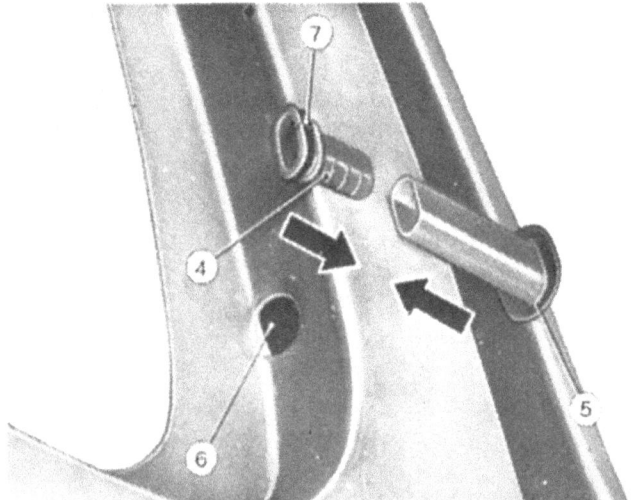

Fig. 11.17. Side window drain tube bushes

4 Bush component	6 Bush aperture
5 Bush component	7 Seal

15 Rear window glass - removal and installation

1   The operations are very similar to those for the windscreen but exert pressure at the bottom of the glass to remove it outwards.
2   Install the glass using the cord method described in the preceding Section, but locate the glass to the upper edge of the aperture first and then press it evenly into position.

16 Fixed side windows - removal and installation

1   Remove and install just as described for the windscreen in Section 14, but push the glass out from one of the lower corners (Fig. 11.16).
2   Refit it by engaging the top of the rubber surround first.
3   Note the fitting of the drain tube bushes which are used to drain water which may have accumulated in the groove of the rubber surround (Fig. 11.17).

17 Opening side windows - removal and installation

1   Working inside the car, extract the two screws which secure the lock toggle to the body (Fig. 11.18).
2   Open the window to the maximum extent and disengage the hinges from the rubber grommets in the door pillar and lift the glass away (Fig. 11.19).
3   The glass can be pulled from the hinge clips.
4   Install by reversing the removal operations.

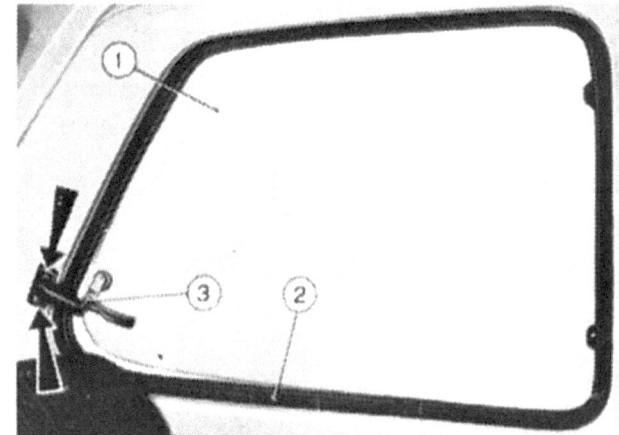

Fig. 11.18. Hinged type side window

1 Glass	3 Lock
2 Weather seal	

Fig. 11.19. Removing opening type window glass

1 Glass   *2 Weather seal*

18 Luggage boot lid - removal and refitting

1   Open the lid to its fullest extent and have an assistant support it in this position (Fig. 11.20).
2   Loosen, but do not remove, the hinge securing screws and slide the lid towards the rear of the car and remove it. This is possible as the hinge bolts pass through open-ended slots not holes in the hinge plates.
3   Refit the lid by reversing the removal operations.
4   Any adjustment needed to ensure positive closure can be carried

19 Engine compartment lid - removal and refitting

1   Unscrew and remove the single self-locking nut from the right-h hinge pin at the base of the lid (Fig. 11.21).
2   Open the lid and either prise up the tab of the check strap anch to release the strap or unscrew and remove the single screw which anchors the other end of the check strap (photo).
3   Slide the lid sideways from its hinge pins.
4   Refit the lid by reversing the removal operations but any adjust ment required to provide smooth positive closure should be carried out by releasing the bolts on the latch on the underside of the lid a moving the latch as necessary.

20 Fascia panel crash pad - removal and refitting

1   Remove the instrument cluster and the centre switch panel, as described in Chapter 9.
2   Remove the steering column shroud, unbolt the upper bracket and lower the column away from the fascia panel.
3   Extract the plastic clips from the lower edge of the crash pad, t peel the pad upwards and disengage its upper turned-over edge from anchorage (Fig. 11.22).
4   Refit by reversing the removal operations, but use new plastic c as the originals will be deformed during extraction.

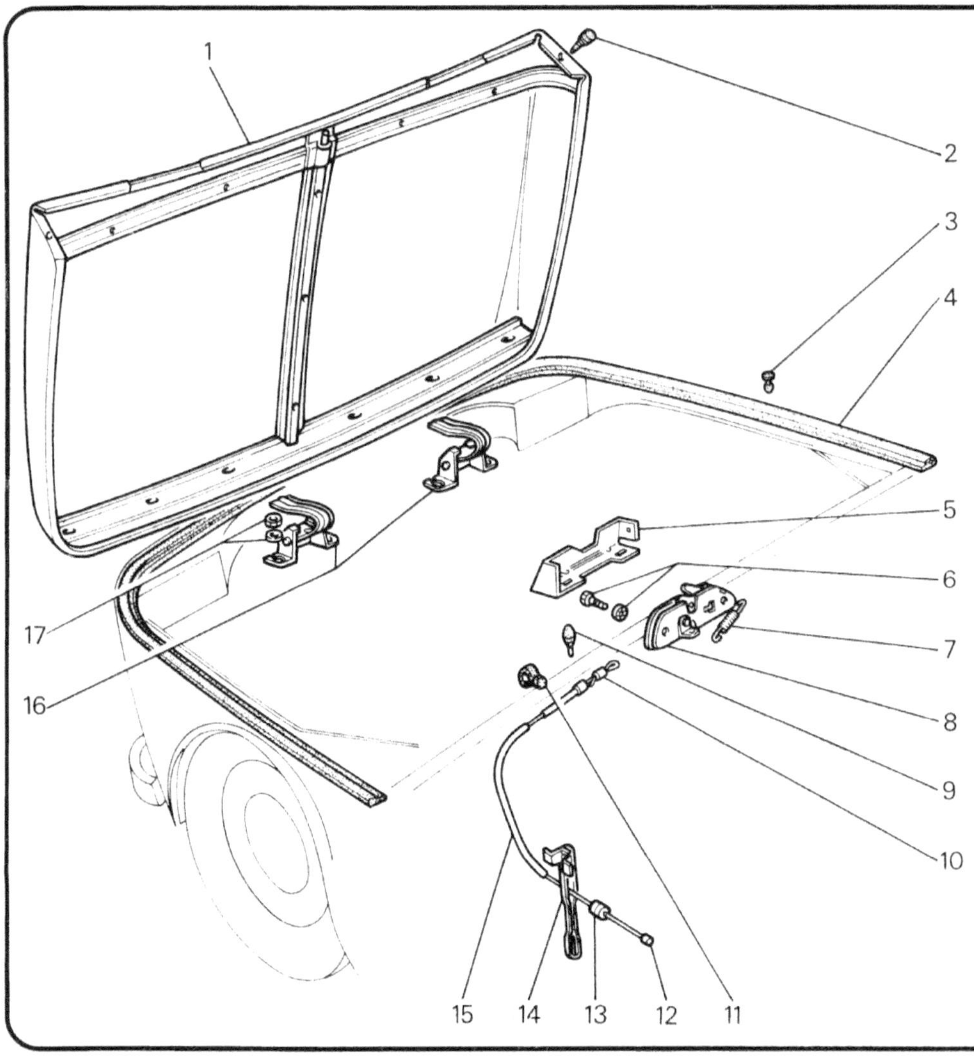

Fig. 11.20. Luggage boot components

1   Lid
2   Buffer
3   Weather seal clip
4   Weather seal
5   Latch guard
6   Screw and lockwasher
7   Return spring
8   Latch
9   Buffer
10 End loop
11 Cable retainer
12 Operating cable
13 Grommet
14 Lid release lever
15 Cable conduit
16 Hinges
17 Nut and lockwasher

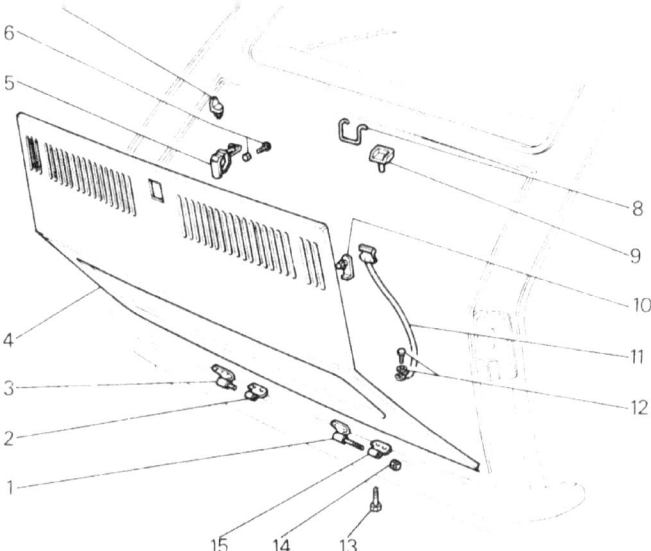

Fig. 11.21. Engine compartment lid components

1	Hinge with locknut	9	Buffer
2	Hinge plate	10	Check strap upper retainer
3	Hinge without nut	11	Check strap
4	Lid	12	Securing screw and washers
5	Latch	13	Hinge screw
6	Screw and washer	14	Self-locking nut
7	Buffer	15	Hinge plate
8	Striker		

Fig. 11.22. Instrument panel crash pad securing fasteners

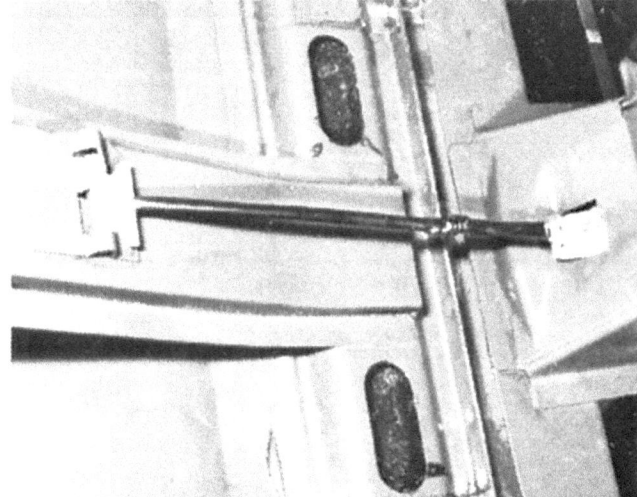

19.2 Engine compartment lid check strap

1   Removal of the sunroof for repair or renewal of the fabric is quite straight forward provided the means of access to the securing nuts and screws is understood.

2   Fold back the hood and using a screwdriver, prise the covers from the pivot nuts at the lower end of each side strut (Fig. 11.23).

3   Unscrew and remove the row of screws from the lower rear edge of the roof opening (Fig. 11.24).

4   Extract the two screws which are located one at each end of the rear anchor strip (Fig. 11.25).

5   Installation is a reversal of removal, but note that the pins which secure the covers on the strut nuts are pushed into place **after** the covers have been refitted.

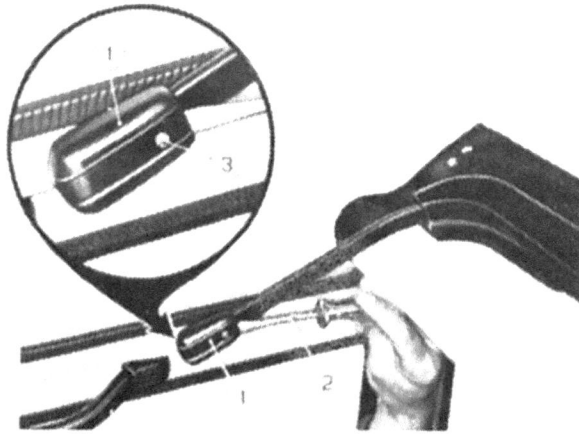

Fig. 11.23. Removing sun roof strut nut cover

1	Cover	3	Cover retaining pin
2	Screwdriver		

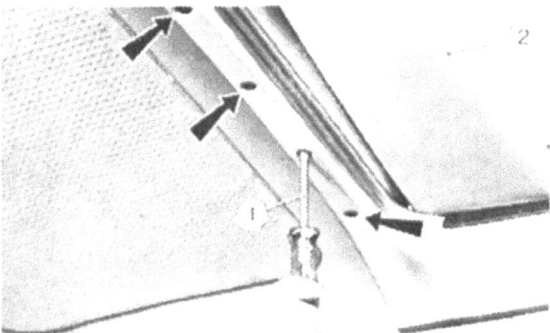

Fig. 11.24. Extracting screw from rear edge of sun roof

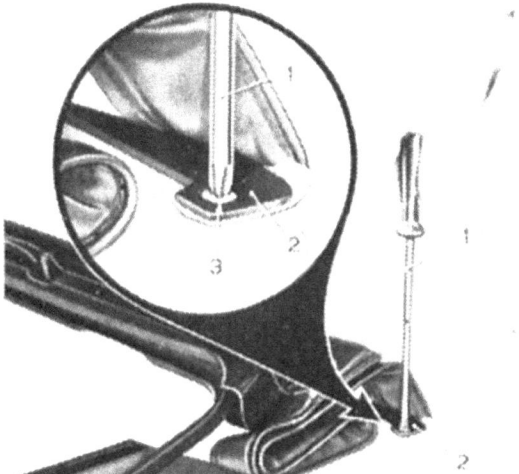

Fig. 11.25. Extracting screw from sun roof rear anchor strip

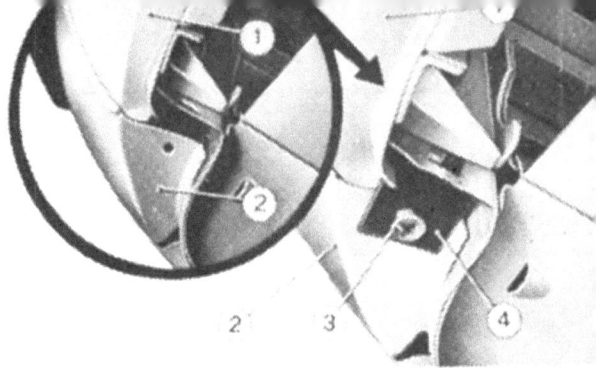

1 The engine air cooling inlet grilles can be removed from the rear sides of the body by first extracting the two retaining screws.

2 Using two screwdrivers as levers, prise the grille from its location. Reasonable leverage will be required for this as the resistance of the lips of the weatherseal must be overcome (Fig. 11.26).

3 The air inlet scoops can be removed from the upper corners of the engine compartment simply by extracting the securing screws.

4 The stale air outlets from the car interior are located on each (door closure) body pillar edge. To remove the grille, prise out the lower securing pin with a screwdriver and then pull the grille outwards and downwards to disengage its tag at the top edge from the bodywork (Fig. 11.27).

5 Refitting in all cases is a reversal of removal.

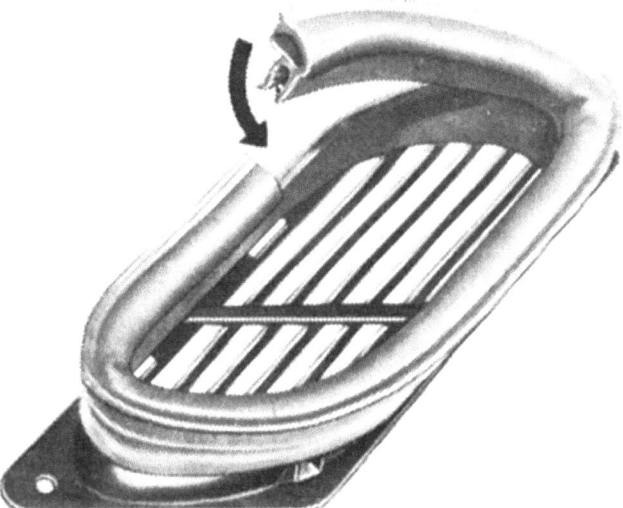

Fig. 11.26. Engine cooling air inlet grille removal

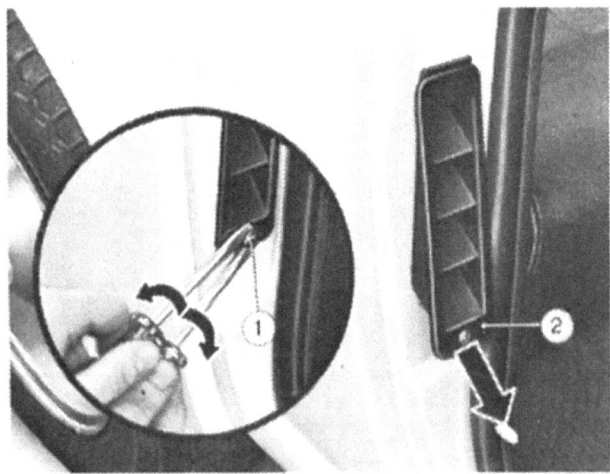

Fig. 11.27. Car interior air outlet

1 Lower retainer   2 Grille

23 Exhaust gas safety baffle

1 In order to obviate the possibility of exhaust gas being drawn back into the interior of the bodyframe box sections and subsequently entering the car interior, baffle plates are located below the rear body panel as shown (Fig. 11.28).

2 Keep the securing screws tight and renew the plates at once if they become perforated due to corrosion.

Fig. 11.28. Exhaust gas safety baffle

1 Rear body panel   3 Baffle securing screw
2 Body side panel   4 Baffle

24 Bumpers - removal and refitting

1 The front bumper mounting nuts are accessible from within the luggage boot.

2 Unscrew the nuts and withdraw the bumper bar complete with bolts, tubular spacers and brackets (Fig. 11.29).

3 Removal of the rear bumper is similar, the nuts being accessible the inside of the body rear panel. Before removing the bumper how disconnect the electrical connector on the lead to the rear number plate lamp (Fig. 11.30).

25 Rear seat - removal and refitting

1 To remove the rear seat cushion, grip the front edge of the seat lift it sharply upwards to disengage it from its securing dowels (Fig. 11.31).

2 Pull the seat forward and remove it from the car.

3 To remove the seat backrest, bend down the securing tags at th base of the upholstery trim and then push the backrest upwards to disengage the locating tongues from the loops on the backrest.

4 Refitting is a reversal of removal (Fig. 11.32).

26 Interior grab handle - removal and refitting

1 The grab handle is secured by two self-tapping screws. Removal the screw covers can sometimes prove baffling and they are in fact simply slid off the ends of the handle.

2 If they seem rather tight, persuade them gently by inserting a screwdriver blade at their open ends from which the grab handle emerges (Fig. 11.33).

27 Rear interior trim panels - removal and refitting

1 The trim panel is secured by plastic clips.

2 The clips should be withdrawn using a suitable blade to lever th out (Fig. 11.34).

3 The panel can then be lifted away.

4 A supply of new plastic clips should be on hand as the originals usually deformed or destroyed during removal.

28 Interior rear view mirror

1 The interior rear view mirror is integral with the interior lamp a the securing screws for the complete unit are accessible after remo the lamp lens. The screws engage in tapped holes in the bodywork

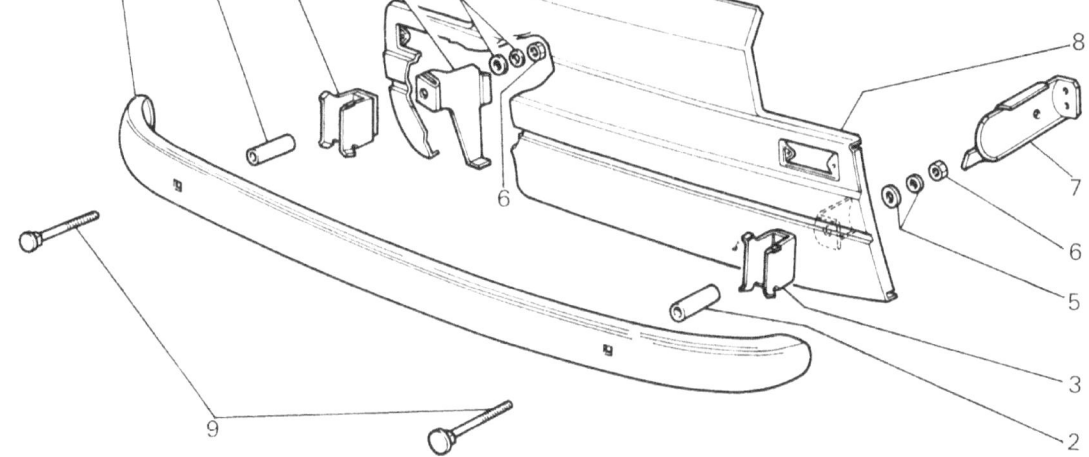

Fig. 11.29. Front bumper components

1 Bumper bar
2 Spacer tubes
3 Brackets

4 Plate
5 Washers

6 Nuts
7 Plate

8 Front body panel
9 Mounting bolts

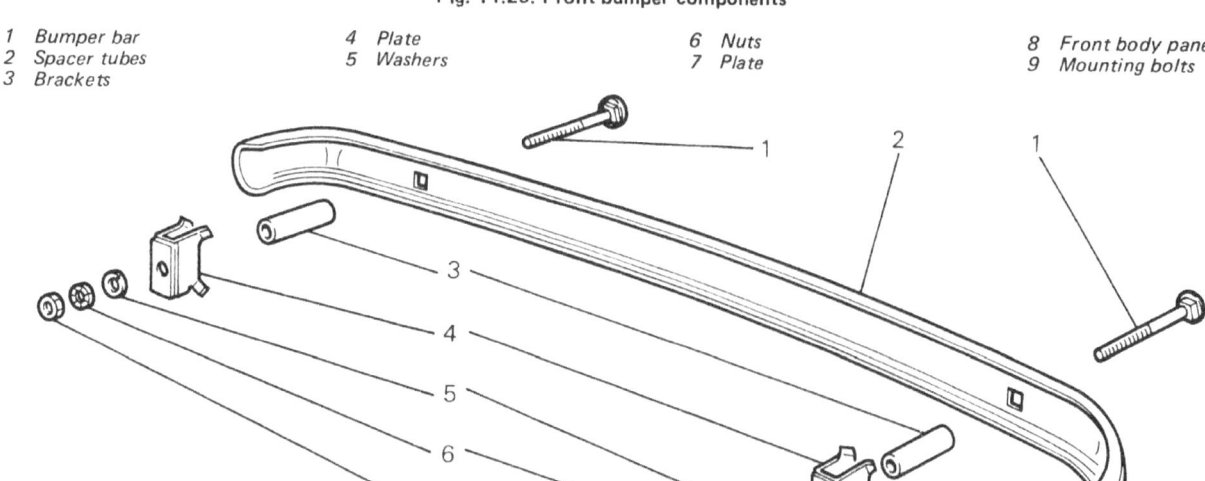

Fig. 11.30. Rear bumper components

1 Mounting bolts
2 Bumper bar

3 Spacer tubes
4 Brackets

5 Washers
6 Lockwashers

7 Nuts

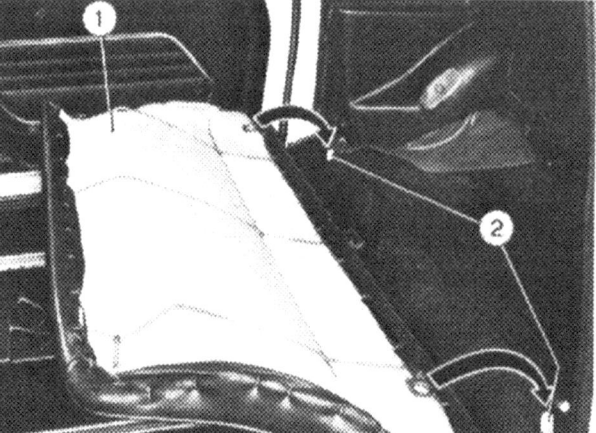

Fig. 11.31. Rear seat cushion removal

1 Cushion inverted

2 Positioning dowels

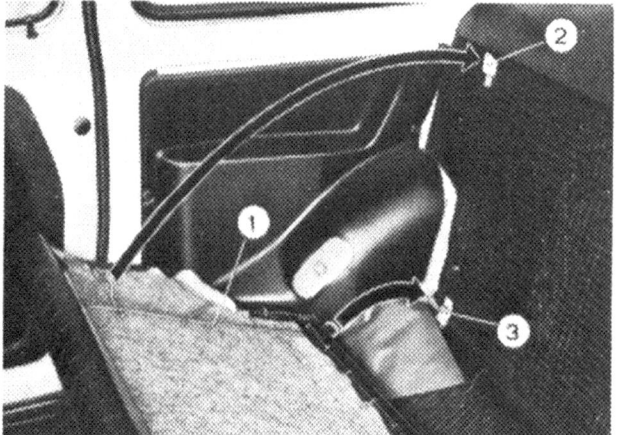

Fig. 11.32. Rear seat back removed

1 Seat back
2 Tongues for securing loops

3 Lower securing tabs

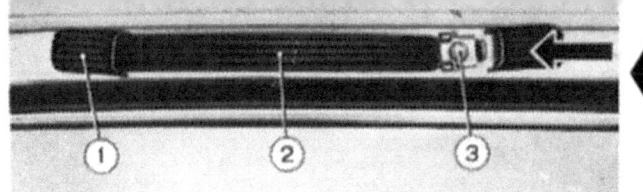

Fig. 11.33. Grab handle detail

1 *Securing screw cover*
2 *Grab handle*
3 *Securing screw*

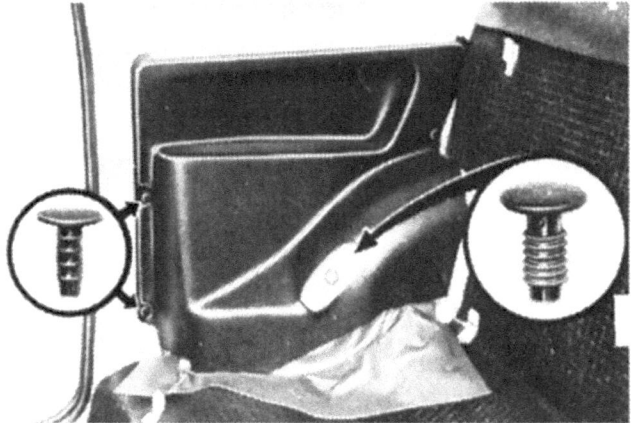

Fig. 11.34. Rear interior panel and fasteners

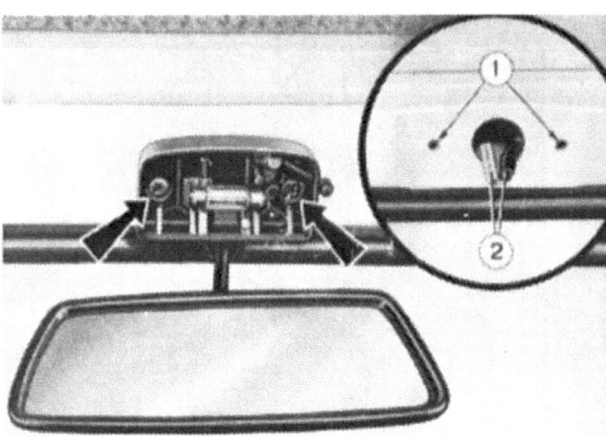

Fig. 11.35. Interior lamp/mirror assembly

1 *Screw holes*   2 *Lamp lead connectors*

Chapter 12 Supplement:
Revisions and information on later models

Contents

1 Introduction

The purpose of this Supplement is to cover the changes which have been made to the Fiat 126 since 1977. The major mechanical changes include the fitment of an increased capacity engine, rack and pinion steering and larger rear brakes. Body and trim changes have been largely confined to the instrument panel and facia.

Where no modifications have been made, the original material given in the relevent main Chapters should be used.

In order to use the Supplement to the best advantage, it is suggested that it is referred to before the main Chapters of the Manual. This will ensure that any relevant information can be incorporated into the procedures described in Chapters 1 to 11, and absorbed before starting work.

Project car
The vehicle used in the preparation of this Supplement, and appearing in many of the photographic sequences, was a 1987 model Fiat 126.

Engine (652 cc)
General
Identification code	126 A1 000
Bore	3.03 in (77.0 mm)
Compression ratio:	
Up to May 1985	7.5 : 1
May 1985 on	8.0 : 1
Maximum power (DIN)	24 bhp (17.7 kW) at 4500 rpm
Maximum torque	31 lbf ft (42 Nm) at 3000 rpm

Cylinder block and pistons
Cylinder bore diameter:	
Grade A	3.0315 to 3.0319 in (77.000 to 77.010 mm)
Grade B	3.0319 to 3.0323 in (77.010 to 77.020 mm)
Grade C	3.0323 to 3.0327 in (77.020 to 77.030 mm)
Piston diameter (measured 2.25 in/57.25 mm from piston crown):	
Grade A	3.0283 to 3.0287 in (76.920 to 76.930 mm)
Grade B	3.0287 to 3.0291 in (76.930 to 76.940 mm)
Grade C	3.0291 to 3.0295 in (76.940 to 76.950 mm)
Piston clearance in bore	0.0028 to 0.0035 in (0.070 to 0.090 mm)
Piston oversizes	0.008, 0.016, 0.024 in (0.20, 0.40, 0.60 mm)
Piston ring groove clearance:	
Top (compression)	0.0018 to 0.0030 in (0.045 to 0.077 mm)
Second (oil control)	0.0016 to 0.0028 in (0.040 to 0.072 mm)
Bottom (oil control)	0.0012 to 0.0024 in (0.030 to 0.062 mm)

Camshaft
Journal diameter:	
Timing gear end	1.6919 to 1.6929 in (42.975 to 43.000 mm)
Flywheel end	0.8653 to 0.8661 in (21.979 to 22.000 mm)
Cam lift:	
Up to May 1985	0.367 in (9.325 mm)
May 1985 on	0.409 in (10.380 mm)

Valves
Valve head diameter:	
Inlet	1.3 in (33.0 mm)
Exhaust	(28.0 mm)
Valve timing (up to May 1985):	
Inlet opens	26° BTDC
Inlet closes	57° ABDC
Exhaust opens	66° BBDC
Exhaust closes	17° ATDC
Valve timing (May 1985 on):	
Inlet opens	18° 30' BTDC
Inlet closes	53° 30' ABDC
Exhaust opens	72° BBDC
Exhaust closes	24° ATDC
Valve clearance for timing check	0.025 in (0.625 mm)
Rocker shaft diameter	0.7082 to 0.7087 in (17.988 to 18.000 mm)

Fuel system
Carburettor
Type:	
August 1977 to May 1985	Weber 28 IMB 5/250
May 1985 on	FOS (Weber) 28 IMB 12/250
Jets and settings:	
Venturi diameter (mm)	23.0
Auxiliary venturi diameter (mm):	
August 1977 to May 1985	4.0
May 1985 on	4.5
Main jet	115
Compensating jet:	
August 1977 to May 1985	190
May 1985 on	195
Slow running jet	50
Slow running air bleed	140
Fuel inlet needle valve diameter (mm)	1.25
Float level setting (mm)	7.0 ± 0.25 (gasket surface to float)
Idle speed	700 rpm
CO content at idle (%)	1.5 to 2.5

~~ing order/rotation~~	~~1-2/clockwise~~
Contact breaker gap	0.018 to 0.021 in (0.47 to 0.53 mm)
Ignition timing (dynamic)	10° BTDC at 700 rpm
Centrifugal advance commences	1400 rpm
Intermediate advance	14° at 3000 rpm
Maximum advance	21° at 3850 rpm

Spark plugs

Type	Champion L82YC or equivalent
Electrode gap	0.024 to 0.028 in (0.6 to 0.7 mm)

Braking system
Drum internal diameter

Front and rear	7.293 to 7.304 in (185.24 to 185.53 mm)
Refinishing limit	0.04 in (1.0 mm) oversize

Wheel cylinder bore diameter

Rear	0.75 in (19.05 mm)

Electrical system
Alternator

Type	Marelli or Polmot
Maximum output	33A
Regulated voltage	14.0 to 14.5V

Fuses

Number	Rating (A)	Circuit protected
1	8	Horn, courtesy lamp, direction indicator and hazard warning lamps, cigar lighter, radio
2	8	Direction indicator warning lamps, windscreen wipers, washers, fuel gauge and low level warning, handbrake and low brake fluid warning lamps, oil pressure warning lamp, brake stop-lamps, reversing lamp, heater fan
3	8	LH headlamp main beam and warning lamp
4	8	RH headlamp main beam and warning lamp
5	8	LH headlamp dipped beam
6	8	RH headlamp dipped beam, rear fog warning lamp
7	8	LH front parking, RH tail lamp, cigar lighter illumination
8	8	RH front parking, LH tail lamp, rear number plate lamp
In-line fuses		Heated rear window, headlamp circuit, ignition system

Suspension and steering
Steering gear

Type	Rack and pinion with safety column
Lubricant type	Molybdenum disulphide grease (Duckhams LBM 10)

Front suspension

Camber angle*	1° 10' to 2° 10' positive
Castor angle*	8° 0' to 10° 0' positive
King pin inclination	6°
Toe-in*:	
August 1977 to September 1979	0.28 to 0.43 in (7.0 to 11.0 mm)
September 1979 on	0.08 to 0.24 in (2.0 to 6.0 mm)

Set with car at kerb weight – no occupants

Rear suspension (non-adjustable)

Camber angle	1° 50' to 2° 50' positive
Toe-in	0.06 to 0.22 in (1.5 to 5.5 mm)

Dimensions, weights and capacities
Dimension

Overall length	122.5 in (3109 mm)

Weights

Kerb weight	1323 lbs (600 kg)
Maximum towing weight (braked)	882 lbs (400 kg)

Capacity

Engine oil – drain and refill (without filter)	4 pints (2.25 litres)

View of engine compartment (652 cc engine)

1 Air cleaner
2 Air intake duct
3 Oil filler cap

4 Carburettor
5 Fuel pump
6 Alternator

7 Engine mounting (coil spring type)
8 Exhaust manifold

9 Ignition coil
10 Distributor
11 Engine oil dipstick

View of front underside

1	Track rod end balljoint	3	Steering rack housing	5	Brake drum backplate
2	Steering gear bellows	4	Leaf spring	6	Horn unit

View of rear underside

1 Heater warm air duct	8 Cooling fan duct	15 Exhaust tail pipe
2 Driveshaft	9 Alternator	16 Handbrake actuating lever
3 Transmission	10 Engine-to-body earth strap	17 Drivebelt
4 Transmission oil drain plug	11 Reversing lamp	18 Clutch cable
5 Starter motor	12 Centrifugal oil filter	19 Clutch release lever return spring
6 Starter motor solenoid	13 Exhaust silencer	20 Rear lifting bracket
7 Engine oil drain plug	14 Rear foglamp	

Engine oil – topping up and renewal

1   The engine oil level should be checked when the engine is cold. If this is not possible, wait at least ten minutes after switching off the ignition.

2   Withdraw the dipstick, wipe it clean on a non-fluffy rag, insert it into its guide tube and withdraw it for the second time. The oil level should be between the MIN and MAX marks on the dipstick. Top up if necessary, but do not exceed the MAX mark.

3   When renewing the engine oil, always drain the old oil when the engine is hot. Unscrew the drain plug (photo) and allow the oil to drain into a suitable container for at least ten minutes.

4   Clean and refit the drain plug, and refill slowly with the specified grade and quantity of fresh oil.

---

4   Cooling and heating systems

Heater and controls – description

1   Later models are fitted with a redesigned heater.

2   The majority of modifications affect the controls. A floor-mounted lever, which replaces the starter motor control on earlier models, regulates the volume of heated air coming from the engine (photo).

3   Two push-pull levers located on the centre console (radio housing) control the 'mix' of fresh and heated air, and also the distribution of air between the car interior and the windscreen.

4   Increased airflow can be obtained by actuating the fan blower switch located at the top right-hand side of the instrument panel.

5   The fresh air grilles are fitted with independent controls to direct the airflow.

7   Remove the fixing nuts, release the clips and withdraw the duct, which incorporates the air distribution flap valve, until the valve control rod can be disconnected (photos).

8   Refitting is a reversal of removal.

Heater blower motor – removal and refitting

9   Disconnect the battery.

10   Working within the luggage boot, unscrew the blower mounting nuts, disconnect the wiring and remove the blower unit (photos).

11   Refitting is a reversal of removal.

---

5   Fuel system

Carburettors – later models

1   From August 1977 to May 1985, a Weber 28 IMB 5/250 carburettor was fitted in conjunction with the larger 652 cc engine. Refer to the Specifications at the start of this Chapter for details of modified calibration. Adjustment and overhaul procedures are as described for other Weber carburettors in Chapter 3.

2   From May 1985 on, an FOS (Weber) 28 IMB 12/250 carburettor is fitted, details of which are given in the following paragraphs.

Carburettor – FOS (Weber) 28 IMB 12/250
Description and maintenance

3   This carburettor is made under licence in Poland, and is very similar to the Weber 28 IMB 3 carburettor described in Chapter 3 (photo).

4   Certain detailed modifications have been made – for example, the mixture control screw has been redesigned.

3.3 Engine oil drain plug

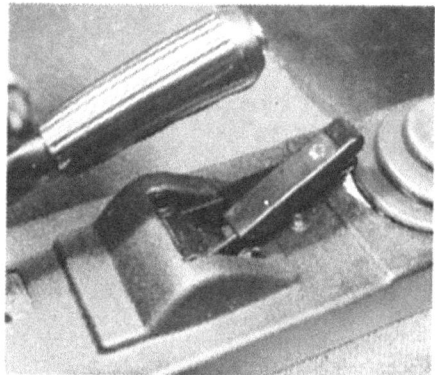

4.2 Floor-mounted warm air control lever

4.7A Heater duct upper frame nut and spring clip

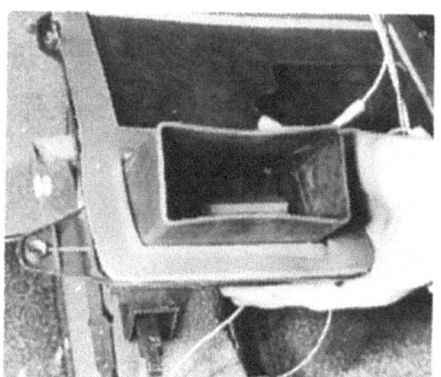

4.7B Removing heater duct

4.10A Unscrewing heater blower motor fixing nut

4.10B Blower motor casing removed showing deflector valve flap

6 One cause of stalling, or failure of the engine to run except on wide throttle openings may be clogging of the slow running jet. Should this happen, remove the jet and blow it clear, preferably using air from a type pump (photo).

Idle speed and mixture adjustment

7 Before adjusting, first ensure that the valve clearances and ignition are correctly set, and that the engine is at normal operating temperature.

8 Turn the idle speed screw until the specified idle speed is achieved (photo).

9 Prise out the tamperproof plug from the idle mixture screw hole and using a small screwdriver, turn the screw until the engine is idling smoothly. Re-adjust the idle speed if necessary.

10 Ideally, a tachometer and an exhaust gas analyser should be used to set the idle speed and mixture precisely in accordance with the specified figures.

Removal and refitting

11 The operations are similar to those described in Section 9 of Chapter 3 (photo).

Unleaded fuel

12 No Fiat 126 models covered by this Manual can be run successfully on unleaded petrol.

H.12694

Fig. 12.1 Later type ignition/starter switch markings (Se

ST	Steering locked, key removable	MAR	Ignition on
		AVV	Starter motor enga

---

6 Ignition system

Spark plugs – later models

1 The spark plugs on later models are of extended terminal connector type with carbon-cored (interference suppression) HT leads (photo). Dust seals are also fitted.

2 It is recommended that copper-cored type spark plugs are used on all models – see Specifications.

Distributor – rotorless type

3 The distributor on later models does not incorporate a rotor arm, or cap with HT lead connections. A conventional mechanical contact breaker set is still employed to interrupt the coil primary winding current flow, but the ignition coil is designed to induce a very high voltage in its secondary windings, and to distribute this to the spark plugs in the correct firing sequence (photos).

Ignition/starter switch – removal and refitting

4 On later models, a combined ignition/starter switch replaces the earlier ignition switch and separate floor-mounted starter motor lever.

5 To remove the later type of switch, first withdraw the steering column lock as described in Section 9 of this Supplement.

6 Extract the small roll pin (using an 'easy-out' or small self-tapping screw) which secures the chrome lock cover (photo).

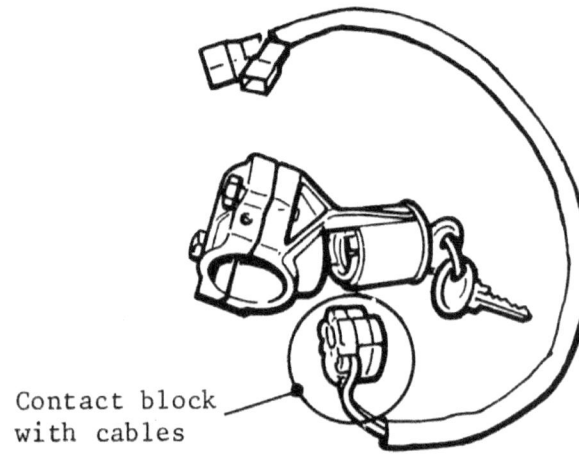

Contact block with cables

Fig. 12.2 Ignition switch/steering column lock compone (Sec 6)

5.3 Carburettor top cover removed – later models

5.5 Carburettor filter plug and gauze screen

5.6 Carburettor slow running jet (arrow

5.8 Carburettor adjustment screws
1   Idle speed screw
2   Idle mixture screw (tamper-
    proof plug removed)

5.11 Removing a carburettor mounting nut

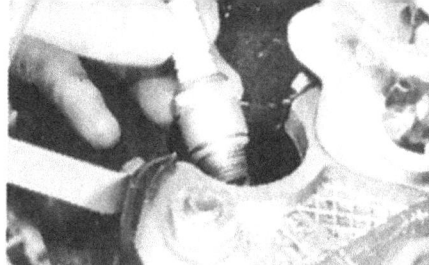

6.1 Spark plug showing extended HT lead terminal connector

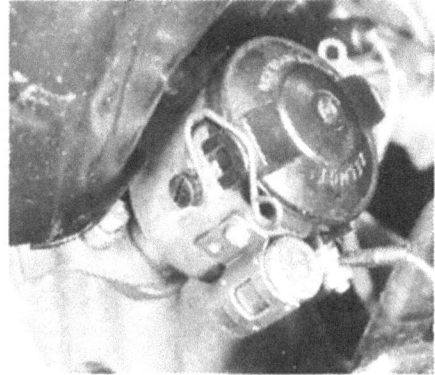

6.3A Distributor fitted to later models

6.3B Distributor with cap removed

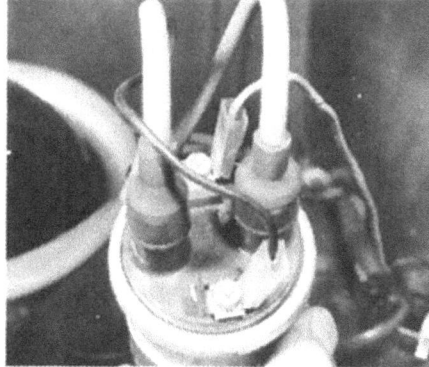

6.3C Ignition coil with HT lead connections

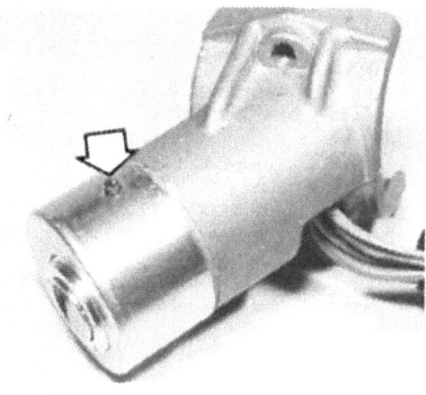

6.6 Steering column lock showing roll pin (arrowed) and chrome cover

6.7A Lock cylinder retaining screw (arrowed)

6.7B Lock cylinder partially withdrawn

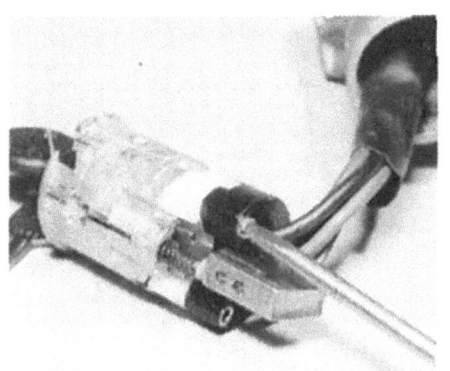

6.7C Extracting ignition/starter contact block screw

6.9 Ignition system ballast resistor

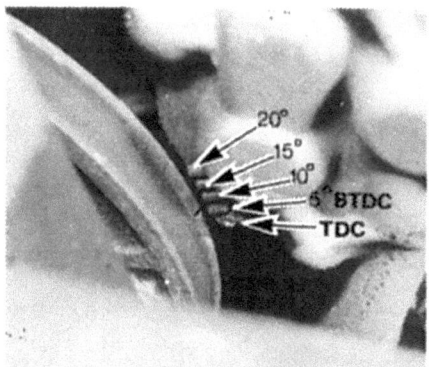

6.11 Ignition timing marks – later models

Ignition system ballast resistor – description

9 On later models a ballast/resistor is fitted under the edge of the luggage boot (photo). A protective relay is fitted in the circuit, see photo 8.72B.

10 The system functions in the following way. When the starter motor is operated, the ballast resistor is bypassed to allow full battery voltage through the ignition primary circuit. Once the engine has started and is running, the temperature of the ballast resistor rises, so increasing its resistance. This reduces the current flow through the primary circuit to the specified voltage level required for normal operations.

Ignition timing marks – later models

11 The ignition timing marks on later engines comprise a notch in the oil filter cover pulley rim and index marks on the engine casting (photo).

---

7 Braking system

Hydraulic system – additional bleeding methods

1 The following procedures may be used as alternatives to the method described in Chapter 8, Section 8.

Bleeding – using one way valve kit

2 There are a number of one-man, one-way brake bleeding kits available from the motor accessory shops. It is recommended that one of these kits is used wherever possible, as it will greatly simplify the bleeding operation and also reduce the risk of air or fluid being drawn back into the system, quite apart from being able to do the work without the help of an assistant.

3 To use the kit, connect the tube to the bleed screw and open the screw one half a turn.

4 Depress the brake pedal fully and slowly release it. The one-way valve in the kit will prevent expelled air from returning at the end of each pedal downstroke. Repeat this operation several times to be sure of ejecting all air from the system. Some kits include a translucent container which can be positioned so that air bubbles can actually be seen being ejected from the system.

5 Tighten the bleed screw, depress the brake pedal. If it still feels spongy repeat the bleeding operations as air must still be trapped in the system.

Bleeding – using a pressure bleeding kit

7 These kits too are available from motor accessory shops and are usually operated by air pressure from the spare tyre.

8 By connecting a pressurised container to the master cylinder fluid reservoir, bleeding is then carried out by simply opening each bleed screw in turn and allowing the fluid to run out, rather like turning on a tap, until no air is visible in the expelled fluid.

9 By using this method, the large reserve of hydraulic fluid provides a safeguard against air being drawn into the master cylinder during bleeding which often occurs if the fluid level in the reservoir is not maintained.

10 Pressure bleeding is particularly effective when bleeding 'difficult' systems or when bleeding the complete system at time of routine fluid renewal.

All methods

11 When bleeding is completed, check and top up the fluid level in the master cylinder reservoir.

12 Check the feel of the brake pedal. If it feels at all spongy, air must still be present in the system and further bleeding is indicated. Failure to bleed satisfactorily after a reasonable period of the bleeding operation, may be due to worn master cylinder seals.

13 Discard brake fluid which has been expelled. It is almost certain to be contaminated with moisture, air and dirt making it unsuitable for further use. Clean fluid should always be stored in an airtight container as it absorbs moisture readily (hygroscopic) which lowers its boiling point and could affect braking performance under severe conditions.

Hydraulic system – routine fluid renewal

14 When renewing the fluid every two years, first syphon out the old fluid from the master cylinder reservoir and refill it with fresh fluid.

hoses. Take care to keep the reservoir well topped up during bleeding operations.

Rear brake drums

15 Later models are fitted with larger diameter rear brake drums – Specifications.

16 It is very important when purchasing brake shoes or componen state exact details of the vehicle, indicating date of manufacture chassis type and number.

17 The brake drums are secured by one small setscrew and roadwheel locating spigot (photos).

18 The hubs now incorporate cut-outs to facilitate removal of brake shoes. The cut-outs provide clearance for the shoe self-adju as the shoes are worked up and off their backplate steady (photo).

Front brake drums

19 The front brake drums have been redesigned in a similar wa those fitted at the rear. They are now secured to the wheel hub setscrew and a roadwheel locating spigot.

20 The hub also incorporates cut-outs to provide clearance d removal of the brake shoes, as on the rear brakes (photo).

---

8 Electrical system

Alternator – description and precautions

1 As from August 1977, an alternator was fitted in place of dynamo.

2 From March 1979, the alternator is fitted with an integral vo regulator.

3 The alternator generates current at much lower revolutions th dynamo; the battery does not therefore discharge, even under idli slow motoring conditions.

4 The alternator develops its current in the stationary windings rotor carrying this field. The brushes therefore carry only a s current, so they last a long time, and only simple slip rings are ne instead of a commutator.

5 The AC voltage is rectified by a bank of diodes. These also pre battery discharge through the alternator. *To avoid damage to alternator, the following precautions should be observed.*

6 Disconnect the leads from the battery before connecting a m charger to the battery terminals.

7 Never stop the engine by pulling off one of the battery leads.

8 Disconnect the battery if electric welding is to be carried out o vehicle.

9 If using booster cables from another battery to start the car, sure that they are connected positive to positive and negativ negative.

10 Maintenance consists of keeping the outside of the altern clean, the electrical connections secure and the drivebelt corr tensioned.

Alternator drivebelt – tensioning and renewal

11 The operations are similar to those described in Chapter 2, Se 5. The belt deflection should be 3/8 in (10.0 mm).

Alternator – removal and refitting

12 Disconnect the battery negative lead.

13 Disconnect the leads from the alternator terminals (photo).

14 Unbolt the front section of the alternator pulley and detach drivebelt (photo).

15 Unbolt and remove the engine undershield.

16 Disconnect the large upper and lower clips and withdraw th trunking which is located at the rear of the alternator (photos).

17 Hold the large nut at the front end of the alternator shaft v reaching round with a socket wrench and unscrewing the nut a rear of the shaft which secures the cooling fan (photo).

18 Unbolt the fuel pump and place it to one side. There is no nee disconnect the fuel hoses (photo).

19 Unscrew the nuts which hold the alternator mounting flange t cooling fan casing.

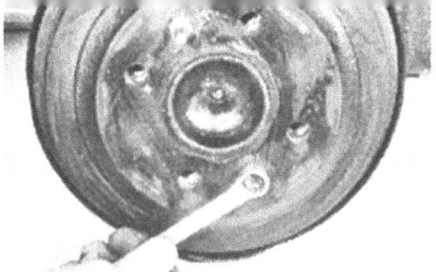
7.17A Removing a brake drum setscrew

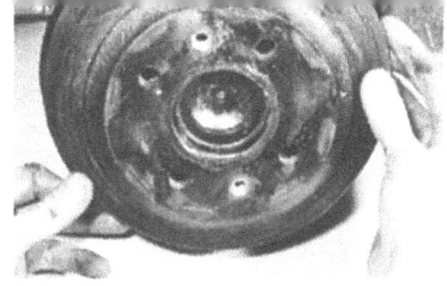
7.17B Removing a rear brake drum

7.18 Rear hub flange cut-out

7.20 Front brake assembly

8.13 Alternator connections

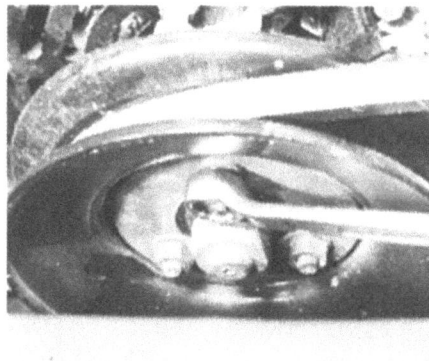
8.14 Unscrewing alternator pulley nuts

8.16A Air trunking upper clip

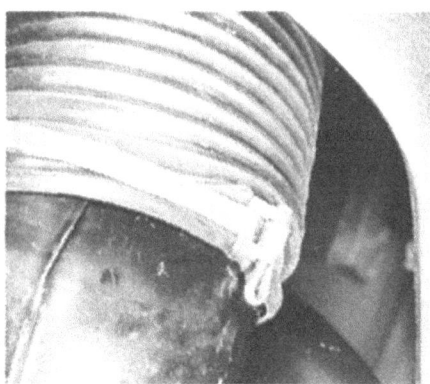
8.16B Air trunking lower clip

8.17 Cooling fan nut (arrowed)

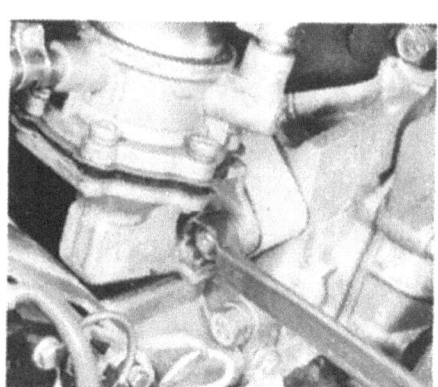
8.18 Unscrewing fuel pump mounting nut

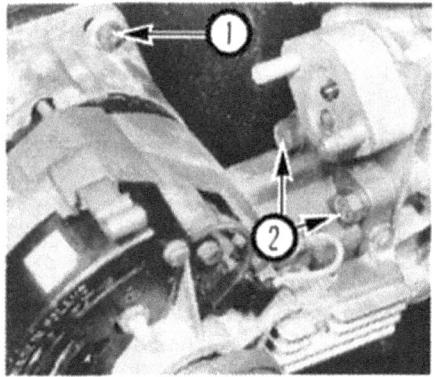
8.20A Alternator fixing mounting details
1   Alternator-to-fan casing nut
2   Alternator-to-engine bolts

8.20B Engine-to-body earth strap

21 Carefully prise the alternator away from the engine to release it from its locating dowels (photo). The mounting holes for the fan casing studs are elongated to allow for this sideways movement of the alternator.

22 Withdraw the alternator from the engine compartment (photos).

23 Refitting is a reversal of removal, but observe the following points.

24 Tension the drivebelt as previously described.

25 Do not overtighten the cooling fan nut. A plastic washer is used as an anti-locking device, and the nut will remain secure if it is tightened to the specified torque of 25 lbf ft (34 Nm).

Alternator – overhaul

26 The alternator is normally such a reliable unit that after a very high mileage when it becomes generally worn, it is preferable and more economical to exchange it for a new or reconditioned unit.

27 If only the brushes require renewing, this can be done in the following way, with the alternator either in or out of the car.

28 Extract the two screws and withdraw the brush holder. The holder, complete with brushes, is renewed as an assembly (photos).

29 The rectifier/regulator can be removed after extracting the two fixing screws (photo).

30 The diode pack is accessible after extracting the three screws which secure the plastic rear cover. Unbolt and remove the diode mounting plate (photos).

Starter motor (cable-operated type) – modification

31 Later models equipped with this type of starter motor have the operating cable attached to the floor-mounted control lever by means of a plastic clip. When purchasing a new cable, order the clip which is supplied as a separate item (part no. 4209712).

chanically-operated cable arrangement, for actuating the starter engagement lever.

33 In consequence of this, the floor-mounted starter control is no longer fitted. Instead, a combined starter/ignition switch with steering column lock is now used.

34 The ignition switch is of the type that if the engine fails to start when the key is turned to the start position, the key must be returned to the stop position before trying again.

35 Removal of the ignition switch and the steering column lock is described in Sections 6 and 9 of this Supplement.

Starter motor (ignition key operated type) – removal and refitting

36 Disconnect the battery negative lead.

37 Working within the engine compartment, remove the special starter motor top mounting bolt and the ordinary top bolt. Both bolts have nuts, the special bolt nut being towards the front of the car (photo).

38 Raise the rear of the car and support it securely on axle stands.

39 Unscrew the starter mounting flange lower bolt and then unbolt the rear support bracket (photos).

40 Disconnect the solenoid leads (photo).

41 Withdraw the starter motor, tilt it vertically and remove it downwards (photos). It may be necessary to prise the engine on its flexible mountings towards the rear of the car to increase the space available for the starter to pass downwards. Use a length of soft wood if this is necessary.

42 Refitting is a reversal of removal but remember to relocate the blanking plate (photo).

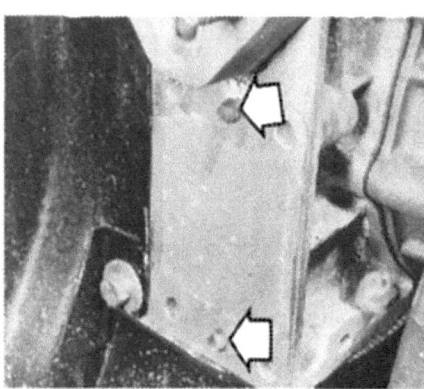

8.21 Alternator locating dowels (arrowed)

8.22A Withdrawing alternator from cooling fan casing

8.22B Cooling fan – alternator removed

8.28A Removing alternator brush holder screws

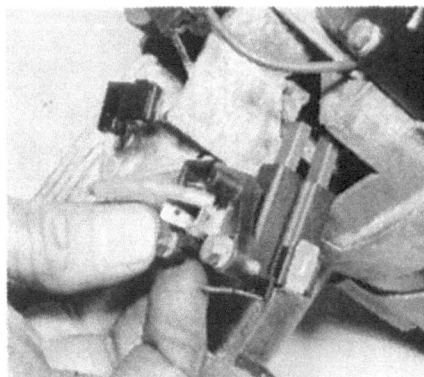

8.28B Removing brush holder assembly

8.29 Alternator rectifier/regulator

8.30A Alternator rear cover

8.30B Alternator diode mounting plate

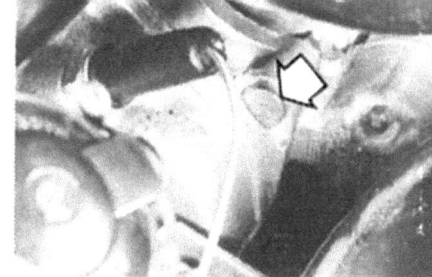

8.37A Starter motor special fixing bolt correctly located

8.37B Starter motor special bolt removed

8.39A Starter motor lower mounting bolt

8.39B Starter motor rear support bracket

8.40 Starter motor solenoid terminals

8.41A Withdrawing starter motor from flywheel housing

8.41B Withdrawing starter motor downwards

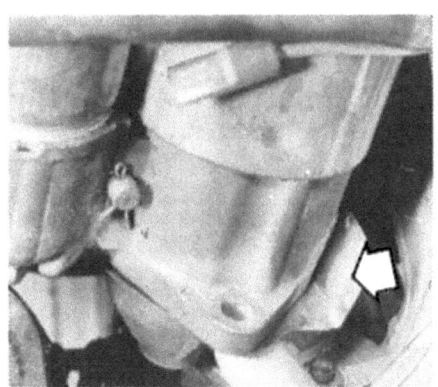

8.42 Starter motor blanking plate (arrowed)

8.45A Starter motor cover band screw

8.45B Starter motor cover band removed exposing brush spring (arrowed)

8.46 Extracting starter motor brush lead screw

8.50 Removing horn push button

8.52 Steering wheel removed

8.53 Unscrewing steering column switch clamp bolt

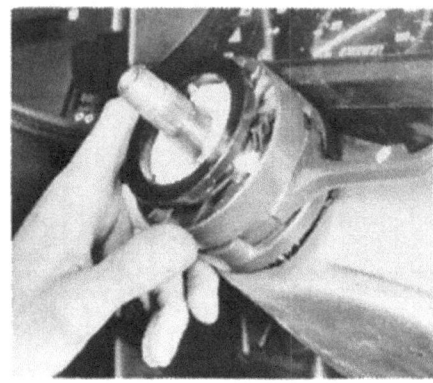

8.55 Removing steering column combination switches

8.59 Removing instrument panel surrou screw

Starter motor (ignition key operated type) – overhaul
43 As with the alternator, the starter motor is such a reliable unit that after a high mileage when it is generally worn, it is better to change it for a new or reconditioned exchange unit, rather than completely overhaul it. If it is only the brushes that are worn however, they may be renewed in the following way.
44 With the starter motor removed from the car, clean away any external dirt.
45 Loosen the cover band screw, slip the band from the yoke and recover the insulating strip which covers the field brushes (photos).
46 Unscrew the brush lead screws, prise up the brush springs and withdraw the brushes from their guides (photo).
47 Inspect the commutator and clean it with a fuel-soaked rag, or if badly discoloured, fine glass paper.
48 Fit the new brushes and then refit the cover band.

Steering column combination switches – removal and refitting
49 Disconnect the battery negative lead.
50 Prise off the horn pushbutton from the centre of the steering wheel and remove the horn contact springs (photo).
51 Unscrew the steering wheel retaining nut.
52 Check that the steering is in the straight ahead position and then grip the steering wheel and pull it from its splined tapered shaft (photo). If it is tight, thump the underside of the rim gently at opposite points using the palms of the hands. If this action does not release it, then a puller will have to be used.
53 Unscrew the clamp bolt which is visible through the top hole in the underside of the steering column shroud (photo).
54 Working within the luggage boot, disconnect the column switch wiring harness multi-plugs.
55 Withdraw the steering column combination switches from the steering shaft (photo). At the same time, ease the wiring harness through the steering column shroud.

56 Refitting is a reversal of removal, but check that the cancellin on the direction indicator switch engages correctly in the cut-out steering wheel hub.

Instrument panel (May 1985 on) – removal and refittin
57 Disconnect the battery negative lead.
58 Remove the steering wheel as previously described.
59 Extract the two screws from the lower edge of the instrument surround (photo).
60 Swivel the surround upwards to release its upper fixing hooks then withdraw the surround sufficiently to disconnect the wiring from the backs of the fingertip type switches (photo). Note location of the various plugs and connectors.
61 Remove the two other screws from the base of the instru panel and prise the panel upwards to release it (photo).
62 Working within the luggage boot, reach through the aperture bulkhead and unscrew the knurled ring to disconnect the speedo drive cable from the speedometer head (photo).
63 Withdraw the instrument panel sufficiently to disconnec multi-plugs, and then remove it (photo).
64 The various instruments may now be removed, together with components, for repair or renewal as necessary (photo).
65 Refitting is a reversal of removal.

Rocker switches – removal and refitting
Earlier models
66 To renew a switch, prise it carefully from its mounting panel us small screwdriver until the wiring plug can be disconnected.
Later models
67 These switches are of the 'fingertip' type. To remove a sw simply grip the switch operating lever and pull the switch fror panel.
68 The switch wiring connector plug will pass through the apert the panel and this can then be disconnected from the switch (ph
69 Refitting of both types of switch is a reversal of removal.

8.60 Withdrawing instrument panel surround with switches

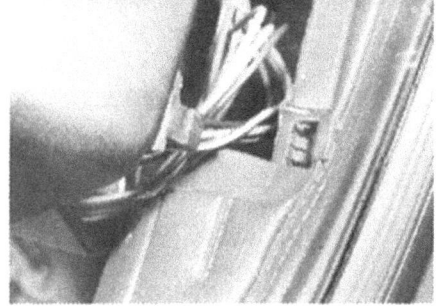
8.61 Instrument panel rear clip

8.62 Speedometer cable connecting ring (arrowed)

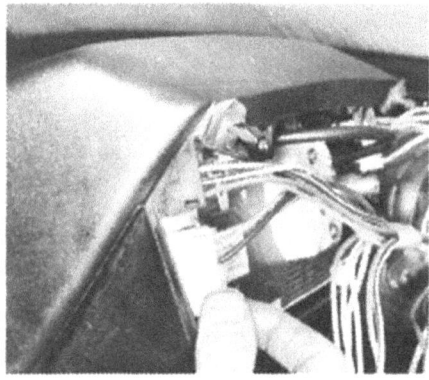
8.63 Disconnect instrument panel multi-plug

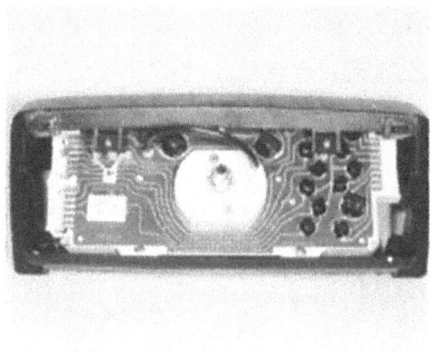
8.64 Rear view of the instrument panel

8.68 Removing a fingertip switch

Fuses and relays

70 The location of the fusebox is the same on all models, but later cars have modifications to the actual circuits protected – see Specifications.

71 In-line fuses are located below the fusebox (photo) and protect the following circuits:

Wiring colour	Fuse connection (Circuit protected)
Grey	Ballast resistor relay (Ignition system)
White	Headlamp relay (Headlamp circuit)
Orange/blue	Heated rear window relay (Heated rear window)

72 Later models have relays located on the bulkhead inside the luggage boot (photos).

Bulbs – renewal

Reversing light and rear foglamp

73 Later models are equipped with a reversing light and rear foglamp. The bulbs in either lamp can be renewed after extracting the two lens securing screws and removing the lens (photo).

Instrument panel lamps

74 The illumination and warning lamps on the rear of the instrument panel are accessible after having partially withdrawn the panel, as described earlier in this Section (photo).

Heated rear window – care and repair

75 Care should be taken to avoid damage to the element for the heated rear window.

76 Avoid scratching with rings on the fingers when cleaning, and do not allow luggage to rub against the glass.

77 Do not stick labels over the element on the inside of the glass.

78 A voltmeter or ohmmeter can be used to assist with location of defects. Look for an open-circuit or a sudden change in voltage, reading along the resistance wires.

79 If the element grids do become damaged, a special conductive paint is available from most motor factors to repair it.

80 To repair, degrease the affected area and wipe dry.

81 Apply tape at each side of the conductor, to mask the adjacent area.

82 Shake the repair paint thoroughly, and apply a thick coat with a fine paint brush. Allow to dry between coats, and do not apply more than three.

83 Allow to dry for at least one hour, before removing the tape.

84 Rough edges may be trimmed with a razor blade if necessary, after a drying time of some hours.

85 Do not leave the heated rear window switched on unnecessarily, as it draws a high current from the electrical system.

Headlamp dim-dip system – description

86 In order to meet current UK legislation, later models are equipped with a headlamp dim-dip system. The purpose of the system is to prevent driving of the car with only the sidelights illuminated.

87 The system operates through a relay (see paragraph 72 of this Section) which is energised when the ignition is switched on, and the light switch is in the 'on' position.

Sidelights – later models

88 Later models have the sidelights incorporated in the headlamp units (photo).

Windscreen washer – later models

89 Later models have an electrically operated windscreen washer system. The electric pump is incorporated in the base of the washer fluid reservoir (photo).

Mobile radio equipment – general

90 Earlier models were not fitted with in-car entertainment equipment as standard.

91 Owners wishing to fit such equipment should refer to the following Sections.

92 Later models may be fitted with a plug-in type radio which can be removed when leaving the car.

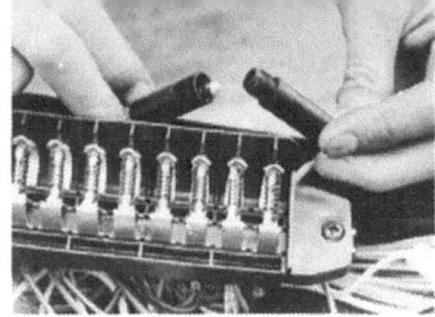

8.71 Renewing an in-line fuse

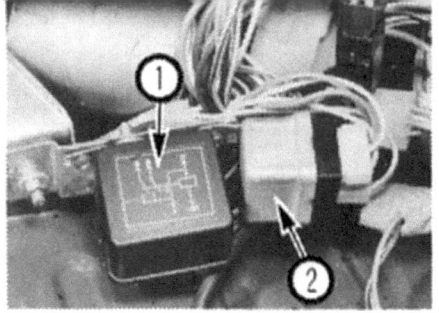

8.72A Relays on right-hand side of luggage boot
1 Hazard warning flasher
2 Intermittent wipe delay

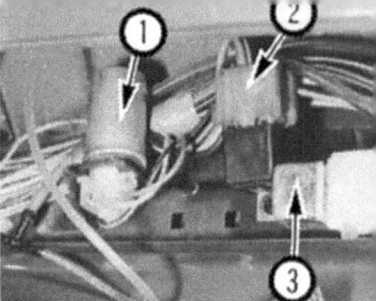

8.72B Relays on left-hand side of lugga boot
1 Direction indicator flasher
2 Ballast resistor
3 Headlamp dim/dip

8.73A Extracting lens securing screw from rear foglamp

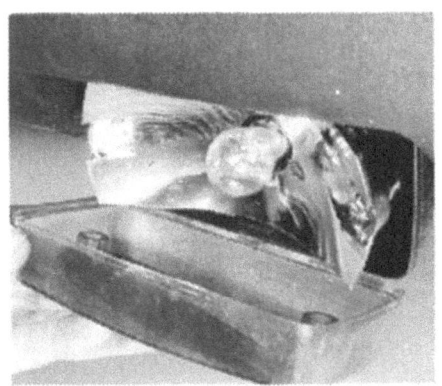

8.73B Rear foglamp bulb

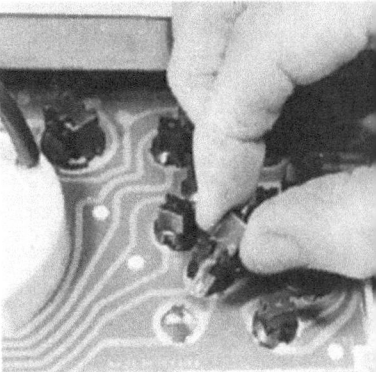

8.74 Instrument panel bulb and holder

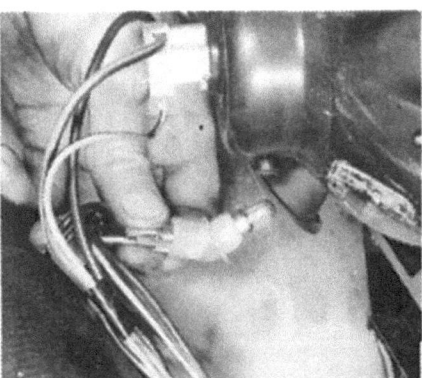

8.88 Sidelight bulb and holder

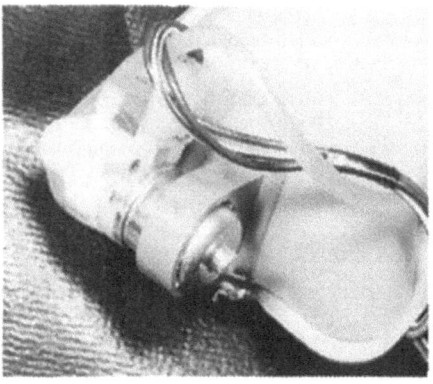

8.89 Washer pump

93 Certain models may be fitted with a power feed and earth lead behind the radio housing, but without aerial or speaker equipment.

Mobile radio equipment – interference-free installation
Aerials – selection and fitting
94 The choice of aerials is now very wide. It should be realised that the quality has a profound effect on radio performance, and a poor, inefficient aerial can make suppression difficult.
95 A wing-mounted aerial is regarded as probably the most efficient for signal collection, but a roof aerial is usually better for suppression purposes because it is away from most interference fields. Stick-on wire aerials are available for attachment to the inside of the windscreen, but are not always free from the interference field of the engine and some accessories.

96 Motorised automatic aerials rise when the equipment is sw on and retract at switch-off. They require more fitting space and s leads, and can be a source of trouble.
97 There is no merit in choosing a very long aerial as, for exampl type about three metres in length which hooks or clips on to the r the car, since part of this aerial will inevitably be located interference field. For VHF/FM radios the best length of aerial is one metre. Active aerials have a transistor amplifier mounted a base and this serves to boost the received signal. The aerial sometimes rather shorter than normal passive types.
98 A large loss of signal can occur in the aerial feeder cable, espe over the Very High Frequency (VHF) bands. The design of feeder is invariably in the co-axial form, ie a centre conductor surrounde flexible copper braid forming the outer (earth) conductor. Betwee

insulator, the loss usually being greater in a poor quality cable. The quality of cable used is reflected in the price of the aerial with the attached feeder cable.

99 The capacitance of the feeder should be within the range 65 to 75 picofarads (pF) approximately (95 to 100 pF for Japanese and American equipment), otherwise the adjustment of the car radio aerial trimmer may not be possible. An extension cable is necessary for a long run between aerial and receiver. If this adds capacitance in excess of the above limits, a connector containing a series capacitor will be required, or an extension which is labelled as 'capacity-compensated'.

100 Fitting the aerial will normally involve making a $^7/_8$ in (22 mm) diameter hole in the bodywork, but read the instructions that come with the aerial kit. Once the hole position has been selected, use a centre punch to guide the drill. Use sticky masking tape around the area for this helps with marking out and drill location, and gives protection to the paintwork should the drill slip. Three methods of making the hole are in use:

(a) Use a hole saw in the electric drill. This is, in effect, a circular hacksaw blade wrapped round a former with a centre pilot drill.

(b) Use a tank cutter which also has cutting teeth, but is made to shear the metal by tightening with an Allen key.

(c) The hard way of drilling out the circle is using a small drill, say $^1/_8$ in (3 mm), so that the holes overlap. The centre metal drops out and the hole is finished with round and half-round files.

101 Whichever method is used, the burr is removed from the body metal and paint removed from the underside. The aerial is fitted tightly ensuring that the earth fixing, usually a serrated washer, ring or clamp, is making a solid connection. *This earth connection is important in reducing interference.* Cover any bare metal with primer paint and topcoat, and follow by underseal if desired.

102 Aerial feeder cable routing should avoid the engine compartment and areas where stress might occur, eg under the carpet where feet will be located. Roof aerials require that the headlining be pulled back and that a path is available down the door pillar. It is wise to check with the vehicle dealer whether roof aerial fitting is recommended.

Loudspeakers

103 Speakers should be matched to the output stage of the equipment, particularly as regards the recommended impedance. Power transistors used for driving speakers are sensitive to the loading placed on them.

104 Before choosing a mounting position for speakers, check whether the vehicle manufacturer has provided a location for them. Generally door-mounted speakers give good stereophonic reproduction, but not all doors are able to accept them. The next best position is the rear parcel shelf, and in this case speaker apertures can be cut into the shelf, or pod units may be mounted.

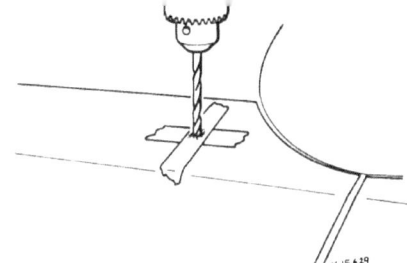

Fig. 12.3 Drilling the bodywork for aerial mounting

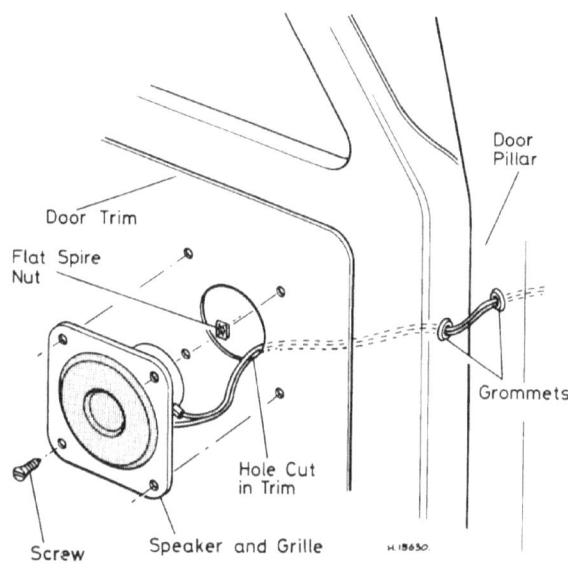

Fig. 12.4 Door-mounted speaker installation

105 For door mounting, first remove the trim, which is often held on by 'poppers' or press studs, and then select a suitable gap in the inside door assembly. Check that the speaker would not obstruct glass or winder mechanism by winding the window up and down. A template is often provided for marking out the trim panel hole, and then the four fixing holes must be drilled through. Mark out with chalk and cut cleanly with a sharp knife or keyhole saw. Speaker leads are then threaded through the door and door pillar, if necessary drilling 10 mm diameter holes. Fit grommets in the holes and connect to the radio or tape unit correctly. Do not omit a waterproofing cover, usually supplied with door speakers. If the speaker has to be fixed into the metal of the door itself, use self-tapping screws, and if the fixing is to the door trim use self-tapping screws and flat spire nuts.

106 Rear shelf mounting is somewhat simpler but it is necessary to find gaps in the metalwork underneath the parcel shelf. However, remember that the speakers should be as far apart as possible to give a good stereo effect. Pod-mounted speakers can be screwed into position through the parcel shelf material, but it is worth testing for the best position. Sometimes good results are found by reflecting sound off the rear window.

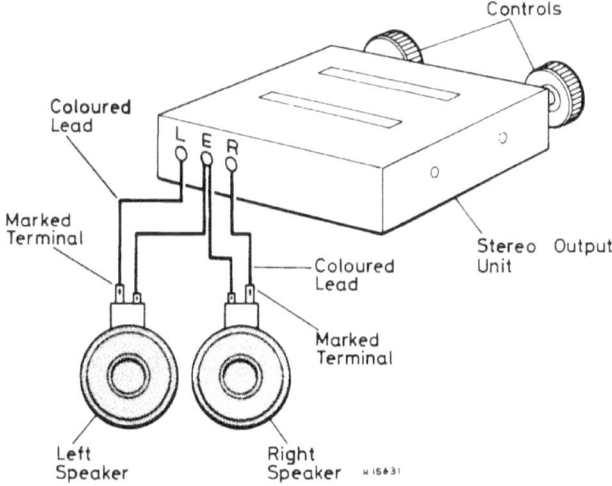

Fig. 12.5 Speaker connections must be correctly made as shown

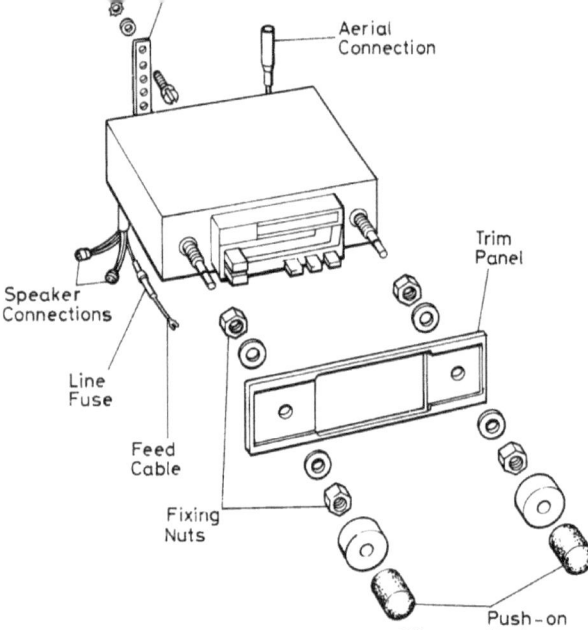

Fig. 12.6 Mounting component details for radio/cassette unit

Labels on figure: Aerial Connection, Trim Panel, Speaker Connections, Line Fuse, Feed Cable, Fixing Nuts, Push-on Knobs

Unit installation

107 Many vehicles have a dash panel aperture to take a radio/audio unit, a recognised international standard being 189.5 mm x 60 mm. Alternatively a console may be a feature of the car interior design and this, mounted below the dashboard, gives more room. If neither facility is available a unit may be mounted on the underside of the parcel shelf; these are frequently non-metallic and an earth wire from the case to a good earth point is necessary. A three-sided cover in the form of a cradle is obtainable from car radio dealers and this gives a professional appearance to the installation; in this case choose a position where the controls can be reached by a driver with his seat belt on.

108 Installation of the radio/audio unit is basically the same in all cases, and consists of offering it into the aperture after removal of the knobs *(not push buttons)* and the trim plate. In some cases a special mounting plate is required to which the unit is attached. It is worthwhile supporting the rear end in cases where sag or strain may occur, and it is usually possible to use a length of perforated metal strip attached between the unit and a good support point nearby. In general it is recommended that tape equipment should be installed at or nearly horizontal.

109 Connections to the aerial socket are simply by the standard plug terminating the aerial downlead or its extension cable. Speakers for a stereo system must be matched and correctly connected, as outlined previously.

Note: *While all work is carried out on the power side, it is wise to disconnect the battery earth lead.* Before connection is made to the vehicle electrical system, check that the polarity of the unit is correct. Most vehicles use a negative earth system, but radio/audio units often have a reversible plug to convert the set to either + or – earth. *Incorrect connection may cause serious damage.*

110 The power lead is often permanently connected inside the unit and terminates with one half of an in-line fuse carrier. The other half is fitted with a suitable fuse (3 or 5 amperes) and a wire which should go to a power point in the electrical system. This may be the accessory terminal on the ignition switch, giving the advantage of power feed with ignition or with the ignition key at the 'accessory' position. Power to the unit stops when the ignition key is removed. Alternatively, the lead may be taken to a live point at the fusebox with the consequence of having to remember to switch off at the unit before leaving the vehicle.

ensure that all sections are working, and check the tape u applicable. The aerial trimmer should be adjusted to give the stror reception on a weak signal in the medium wave band, at say metres.

Interference

112 In general, when electric current changes abruptly, unwa electrical noise is produced. The motor vehicle is filled with elec devices which change electric current rapidly, the most obvious b the contact breaker.

113 When the spark plugs operate, the sudden pulse of spark cu causes the associated wiring to radiate. Since early radio transm used sparks as a basis of operation, it is not surprising that the car will pick up ignition spark noise unless steps are taken to reduce acceptable levels.

114 Interference reaches the car radio in two ways:

(a) by conduction through the wiring.
(b) by radiation to the receiving aerial.

115 Initial checks presuppose that the bonnet is down and faste the radio unit has a good earth connection *(not* through the downlead outer), no fluorescent tubes are working near the ca aerial trimmer has been adjusted, and the vehicle is in a positic receive radio signals, ie not in a metal-clad building.

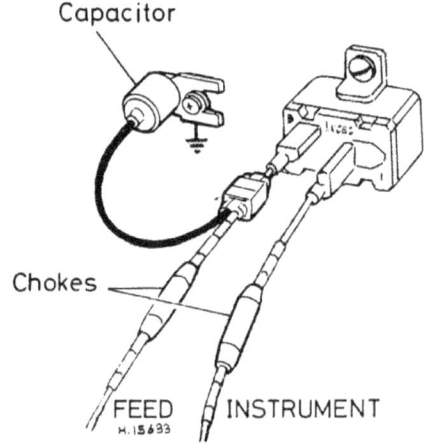

Fig. 12.7 Voltage stabiliser interference suppression

Labels on figure: Capacitor, Chokes, FEED, INSTRUMENT

116 Switch on the radio and tune it to the middle of the medium (MW) band off-station with the volume (gain) control set fairly Switch on the ignition (but do not start the engine) and wait to irregular clicks or hash noise occurs. Tapping the facia panel may produce the effects. If so, this will be due to the voltage stab which is an on-off thermal switch to control instrument voltage located usually on the back of the instrument panel, often attach the speedometer. Correction is by attachment of a capacitor and, troublesome, chokes in the supply wires.

117 Switch on the engine and listen for interference on the MW b Depending on the type of interference, the indications are as foll

118 A harsh crackle that drops out abruptly at low engine spee when the headlights are switched on is probably due to a vo regulator.

119 A whine varying with engine speed is due to the dynam alternator. Try temporarily taking off the fan belt – if the noise goe is confirmation.

120 Regular ticking or crackle that varies in rate with the engine s is due to the ignition system. With this trouble in particular and o in general, check to see if the noise is entering the receiver fror wiring or by radiation. To do this, pull out the aerial plug, (prefe shorting out the input socket or connecting a 62 pF capacitor a it). If the noise disappears it is coming in through the aerial a

indicators, stop lamps, etc is usually taken to the receiver by wiring, and simple treatment using capacitors and possibly chokes will solve the problem. Switch on each one in turn (wet the screen first for running wipers!) and listen for possible interference with the aerial plug in place and again when removed.

122 Electric petrol pumps are now finding application again and give rise to an irregular clicking, often giving a burst of clicks when the ignition is on but the engine has not yet been started. It is also possible to receive whining or crackling from the pump.

123 Note that if most of the vehicle accessories are found to be creating interference all together, the probability is that poor aerial earthing is to blame.

Component terminal markings

124 Throughout the following sub-sections reference will be found to various terminal markings. These will vary depending on the manufacturer of the relevant component. If terminal markings differ from those mentioned, reference should be made to the following table, where the most commonly encountered variations are listed.

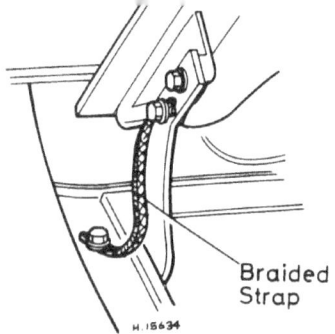

Fig. 12.8 Braided earth strap

Alternator	Alternator terminal (thick lead)	Exciting winding terminal
DIN/Bosch	B+	DF
Delco Remy	+	EXC
Ducellier	+	EXC
Ford (US)	+	DF
Lucas	+	F
Marelli	+B	F

Ignition coil	Ignition switch terminal	Contact breaker terminal
DIN/Bosch	15	1
Delco Remy	+	–
Ducellier	BAT	RUP
Ford (US)	B/+	CB/–
Lucas	SW/+	–
Marelli	BAT/+B	D

Voltage regulator	Voltage input terminal	Exciting winding terminal
DIN/Bosch	B+/D+	DF
Delco Remy	BAT/+	EXC
Ducellier	BOB/BAT	EXC
Ford (US)	BAT	DF
Lucas	+/A	F
Marelli		F

Suppression methods – ignition

125 Suppressed HT cables are supplied as original equipment by manufacturers and will meet regulations as far as interference to neighbouring equipment is concerned. It is illegal to remove such suppression unless an alternative is provided, and this may take the form of resistive spark plug caps in conjunction with plain copper HT cable. For VHF purposes, these and 'in-line' resistors may not be effective, and resistive HT cable is preferred. Check that suppressed cables are actually fitted by observing cable identity lettering, or measuring with an ohmmeter – the value of each plug lead should be 5000 to 10 000 ohms.

126 A 1 microfarad capacitor connected from the LT supply side of the ignition coil to a good nearby earth point will complete basic ignition interference treatment. *NEVER fit a capacitor to the coil terminal to the contact breaker – the result would be burnt out points in a short time.*

127 If ignition noise persists despite the treatment above, the following sequence should be followed:

(a) Check the earthing of the ignition coil; remove paint from fixing clamp.

(b) If this does not work, lift the bonnet. Should there be no change in interference level, this may indicate that the bonnet is not electrically connected to the car body. Use a proprietary braided strap across a bonnet hinge ensuring a first class electrical connection. If, however, lifting the bonnet increases the interference, then fit resistive HT cables of a higher ohms-per-metre value.

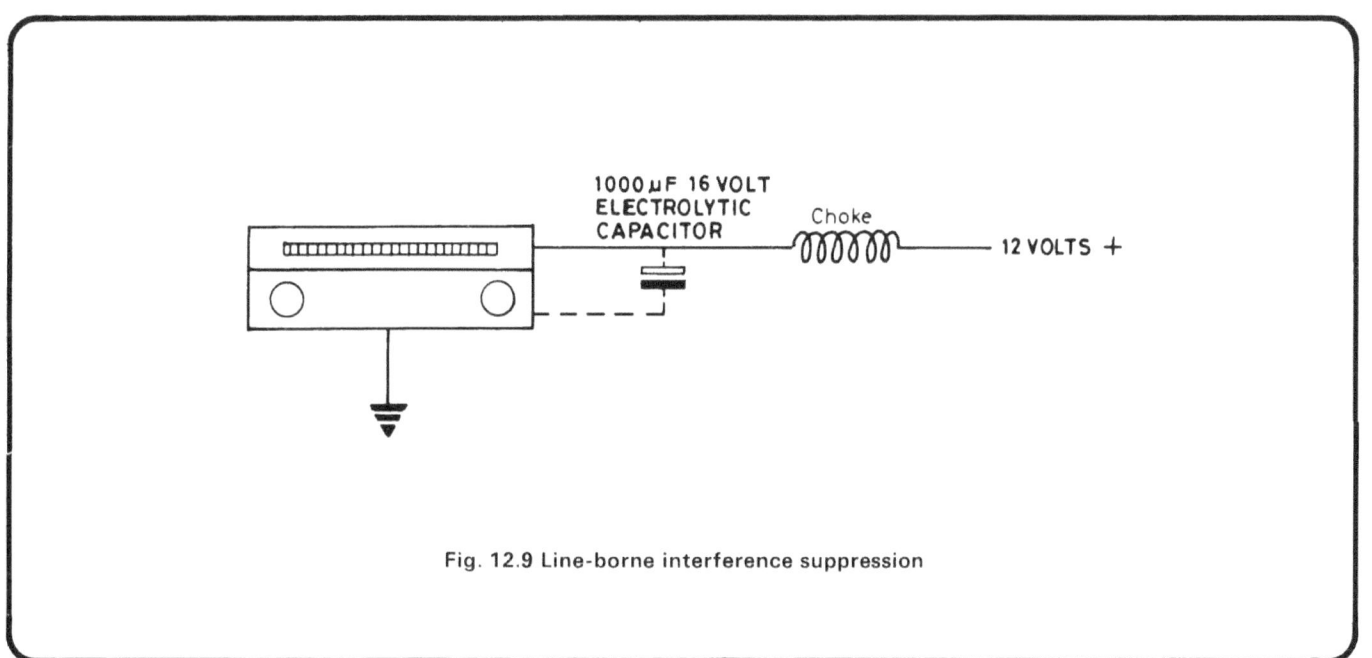

Fig. 12.9 Line-borne interference suppression

try the following: engine to body, exhaust system to body, front suspension to engine and to body, steering column to body (especially French and Italian cars), gear lever to engine and to body (again especially French and Italian cars), Bowden cable to body, metal parcel shelf to body. When an offending component is located it should be bonded with the strap permanently.

(d) As a next step, the fitting of distributor suppressors to each lead at the distributor end may help.

(e) Beyond this point is involved the possible screening of the distributor and fitting resistive spark plugs, but such advanced treatment is not usually required for vehicles with entertainment equipment.

128 Electronic ignition systems have built-in suppression components, but this does not relieve the need for using suppressed HT leads. In some cases it is permitted to connect a capacitor on the low tension supply side of the ignition coil, but not in every case. Makers' instructions should be followed carefully, otherwise damage to the ignition semiconductors may result.

Suppression methods – generators

129 For older vehicles with dynamos a 1 microfarad capacitor from the D (larger) terminal to earth will usually cure dynamo whine. Alternators should be fitted with a 3 microfarad capacitor from the B + main output terminal (thick cable) to earth. Additional suppression may be obtained by the use of a filter in the supply line to the radio receiver.

130 It is most important that:

(a) Capacitors are never connected to the field terminals of either a dynamo or alternator.

(b) Alternators must not be run without connection to the battery.

Suppression methods – voltage regulators

131 Voltage regulators used with DC dynamos should be suppressed by connecting a 1 microfarad capacitor from the control box D terminal to earth.

132 Alternator regulators come in three types:

(a) Vibrating contact regulators separate from the alternator. Used extensively on continental vehicles.

(b) Electronic regulators separate from the alternator.

(c) Electronic regulators built-in to the alternator.

133 In case (a) interference may be generated on the AM and FM (VHF) bands. For some cars a replacement suppressed regulator is available. Filter boxes may be used with non-suppressed regulators. But if not available, then for AM equipment a 2 microfarad or 3 microfarad capacitor may be mounted at the voltage terminal marked D+ or B+ of the regulator. FM bands may be treated by a feed-through capacitor of 2 or 3 microfarad.

134 Electronic voltage regulators are not always troublesome, but where necessary, a 1 microfarad capacitor from the regulator + terminal will help.

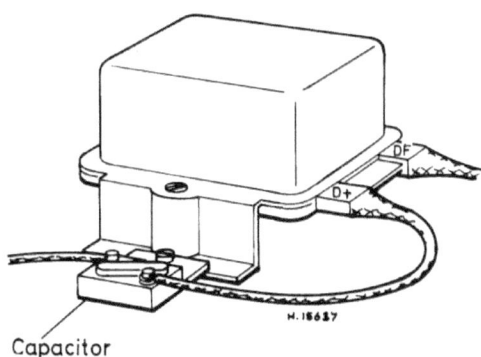

Capacitor

Fig. 12.11 Suppression of AM interference by vibrating contact voltage regulator (alternator equipment)

warning lamp (IND) terminal to earth for Lucas ACR alternator. Femsa, Delco and Bosch equivalents should cure the problem.

Suppression methods – other equipment

136 *Wiper motors* – Connect the wiper body to earth with a bo? strap. For all motors use a 7 ampere choke assembly inserted i? leads to the motor.

137 *Heater motors* – Fit 7 ampere line chokes in both leads, assis? necessary by a 1 microfarad capacitor to earth from both leads.

138 *Horn* – A capacitor and choke combination is effective if the? is directly connected to the 12 volt supply. The use of a relay? alternative remedy, as this will reduce the length of the interfere? carrying leads.

139 *Electrostatic noise* – Characteristics are erratic crackling a? receiver, with disappearance of symptoms in wet weather. ? shocks may be given when touching bodywork. Part of the probl? the build-up of static electricity in non-driven wheels anc? acquisition of charge on the body shell. It is possible ? spring-loaded contacts at the wheels to give good condu? between the rotary wheel parts and the vehicle frame. Changing

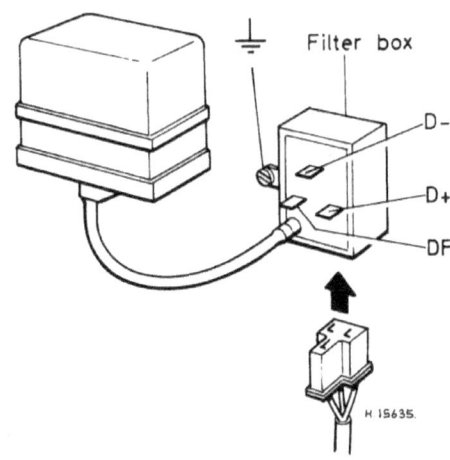

Fig. 12.10 Typical filter box for vibrating contact volta? regulator (alternator equipment)

sometimes helps – because of tyre varying resistances. In difficult? a trailing flex which touches the ground will cure the problem. If? not acceptable it is worth trying conductive paint on the tyre wa?

140 *Fluorescent tubes* – Vehicles used for camping/carava? frequently have fluorescent tube lighting. These tubes requ? relatively high voltage for operation and this is provided by an in? (a form of oscillator) which steps up the vehicle supply voltage? can give rise to serious interference to radio reception, and the ? themselves can contribute to this interference by the pulsating ? of the lamp discharge. In such situations it is important to mou? aerial as far away from a fluorescent tube as possible. The interfe? problem may be alleviated by screening the tube with fine wire ? spaced an inch (25 mm) apart and earthed to the chassis. Su? chokes should be fitted in both supply wires close to the inverte?

Radio/cassette case breakthrough

141 Magnetic radiation from dashboard wiring may be suffic? intense to break through the metal case of the radio/cassette p? Often this is due to a particular cable routed too close and shows? ignition interference on AM and cassette play and/or alternator ? on cassette play.

142 The first point to check is that the clips and/or screws are fix? parts of the radio/cassette case together properly. Assuming ? earthing of the case, see if it is possible to re-route the offending? – the chances of this are not good, however, in most cars.

143 Next release the radio/cassette player and locate it in dif? positions with temporary leads. If a point of low interference is f? then if possible fix the equipment in that area. This also confirm?

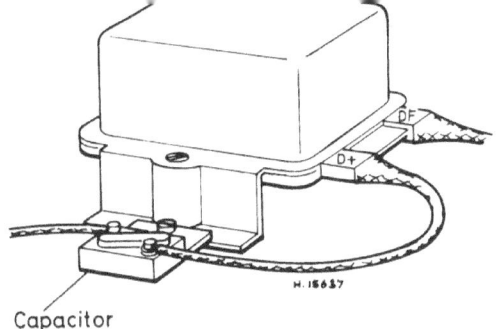

Capacitor

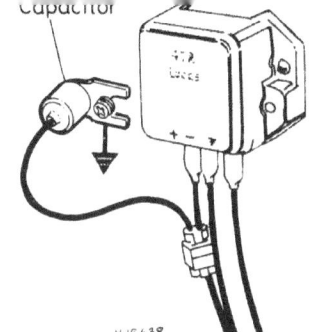

Fig. 12.12 Suppression of FM interference by vibrating contact voltage regulator (alternator equipment)

Fig. 12.13 Electronic voltage regulator suppression

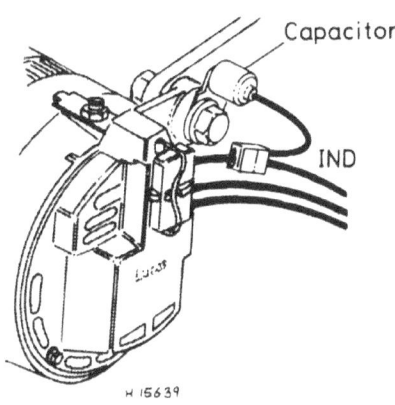

Capacitor

IND

Fig. 12.14 Suppression of interference from integral electronic voltage regulator (alternator equipment)

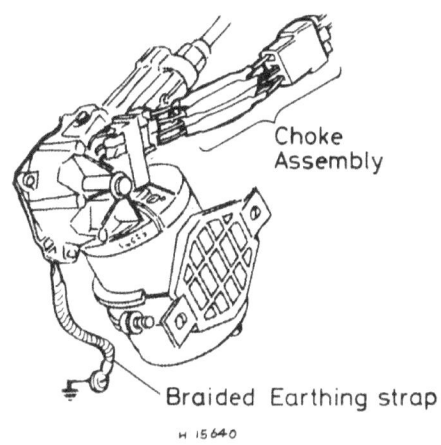

Choke Assembly

Braided Earthing strap

Fig. 12.15 Wiper motor suppression

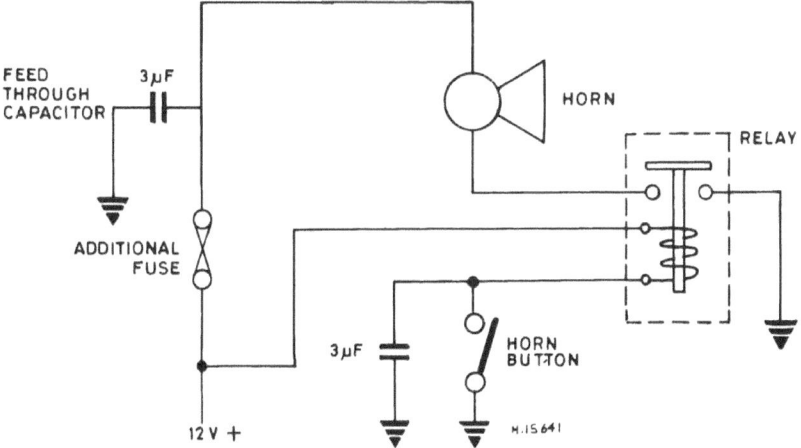

FEED THROUGH CAPACITOR

3 μF

ADDITIONAL FUSE

HORN

RELAY

3 μF

HORN BUTTON

12V +

Fig. 12.16 Use of relay to reduce horn interference

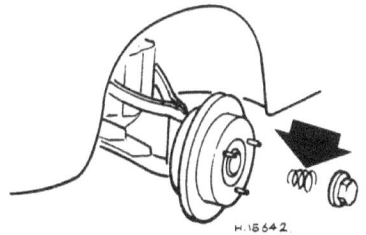

Fig. 12.17 Use of spring contacts at wheels

from the main charging cable which goes from the battery to the output terminal of the alternator, usually via the + terminal of the starter motor relay. In some vehicles this cable is routed under the dashboard, so the solution is to provide a direct cable route. Detach the original cable from the alternator output terminal and make up a new cable of at least 6 mm² cross-sectional area to go from alternator to battery with the shortest possible route. *Remember – do not run the engine with the alternator disconnected from the battery.*

145 Ignition breakthrough on AM and/or cassette play can be a difficult problem. It is worth wrapping earthed foil round the offending cable run near the equipment, or making up a deflector plate well screwed down to a good earth. Another possibility is the use of a suitable relay to switch on the ignition coil. The relay should be mounted close to the ignition coil; with this arrangement the ignition coil primary current is not taken into the dashboard area and does not flow through the ignition switch. A suitable diode should be used since it is possible that at ignition switch-off the output from the warning lamp alternator terminal could hold the relay on.

Connectors for suppression components

146 Capacitors are usually supplied with tags on the end of the lead, while the capacitor body has a flange with a slot or hole to fit under a nut or screw with washer.

147 Connections to feed wires are best achieved by self-stripping connectors. These connectors employ a blade which, when squeezed down by pliers, cuts through cable insulation and makes connection to the copper conductors beneath.

148 Chokes sometimes come with bullet snap-in connectors fitted to the wires, and also with just bare copper wire. With connectors, suitable female cable connectors may be purchased from an auto-accessory shop together with any extra connectors required for the cable ends after being cut for the choke insertion. For chokes with bare wires, similar connectors may be employed together with insulation sleeving as required.

VHF/FM broadcasts

149 Reception of VHF/FM in an automobile is more prone to problems than the medium and long wavebands. Medium/long wave transmitters are capable of covering considerable distances, but VHF transmitters are restricted to line of sight, meaning ranges of 10 to 50 miles, depending upon the terrain, the effects of buildings and the transmitter power.

150 Because of the limited range it is necessary to retune on a long journey, and it may be better for those habitually travelling long distances or living in areas of poor provision of transmitters to use an AM radio working on medium/long wavebands.

151 When conditions are poor, interference can arise, and some of the suppression devices described previously fall off in performance at very high frequencies unless specifically designed for the VHF band. Available suppression devices include reactive HT cable, resistive distributor caps, screened plug caps, screened leads and resistive spark plugs.

152 For VHF/FM receiver installation the following points should be particularly noted:

(a) Earthing of the receiver chassis and the aerial mounting is important. Use a separate earthing wire at the radio, and scrape paint away at the aerial mounting.

(b) If possible, use a good quality roof aerial to obtain maximum height and distance from interference generating devices on the vehicle.

(c) Use of a high quality aerial downlead is important, since losses in cheap cable can be significant.

(d) The polarisation of FM transmissions may be horizontal, vertical, circular or slanted. Because of this the optimum mounting angle is at 45° to the vehicle roof.

Citizens' Band radio (CB)

153 In the UK, CB transmitter/receivers work within the 27 MHz and 934 MHz bands, using the FM mode. At present interest is concentrated on 27 MHz where the design and manufacture of equipment is less difficult. Maximum transmitted power is 4 watts, and 40 channels spaced 10 kHz apart within the range 27.60125 to 27.99125 MHz are available.

154 Aerials are the key to effective transmission and reception. Regulations limit the aerial length to 1.65 metres including the loading

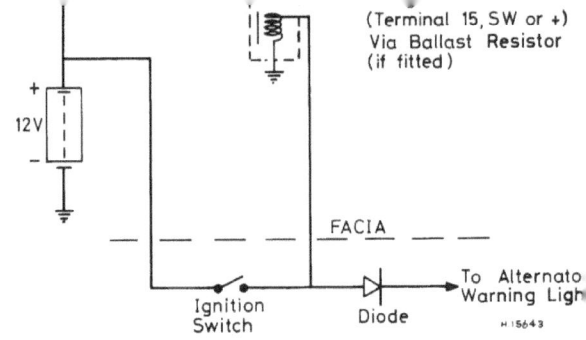

(Terminal 15, SW or +)
Via Ballast Resistor
(if fitted)

12V

FACIA

Ignition Switch

Diode

To Alternato
Warning Ligh

Fig. 12.18 Use of ignition coil relay to suppress case breakthrough

coil and any associated circuitry, so tuning the aerial is necess obtain optimum results. The choice of a CB aerial is depende whether it is to be permanently installed or removable, an performance will hinge on correct tuning and the location point c vehicle. Common practice is to clip the aerial to the roof gutter employ wing mounting where the aerial can be rapidly unscrewe alternative is to use the boot rim to render the aerial theftproof, popular solution is to use the 'magmount' – a type of mounting h a strong magnetic base clamping to the vehicle at any point, u the roof.

155 Aerial location determines the signal distribution for transmission and reception, but it is wise to choose a point away the engine compartment to minimise interference from v electrical equipment.

156 The aerial is subject to considerable wind and acceleration f Cheaper units will whip backwards and forwards and in so doin alter the relationship with the metal surface of the vehicle with w forms a ground plane aerial system. The radiation pattern will c correspondingly, giving rise to break-up of both incoming outgoing signals.

157 Interference problems on the vehicle carrying CB equipme into two categories:

(a) Interference to nearby TV and radio receivers when mitting.

(b) Interference to CB set reception due to electrical equip on the vehicle.

158 Problems of break-through to TV and radio are not frequer can be difficult to solve. Mostly trouble is not detected or rep because the vehicle is moving and the symptoms rapidly disapp the TV/radio receiver, but when the CB set is used as a base static trouble with nearby receivers will soon result in a complaint.

159 It must not be assumed by the CB operator that his equipm faultless, for much depends upon the design. Harmonics (th multiples) of 27 MHz may be transmitted unknowingly and thes fall into other user's bands. Where trouble of this nature occurs pass filters in the aerial or supply leads can help, and should be fit base station aerials as a matter of course. In stubborn cases it m necessary to call for assistance from the licensing authority, possible, to have the equipment checked by the manufacturers.

160 Interference received on the CB set from the vehicle equipm fortunately, not usually a severe problem. The precautions ou previously for radio/cassette units apply, but there are some points worth noting.

161 It is common practice to use a slide-mount on CB equi enabling the set to be easily removed for use as a base statio example. Care must be taken that the slide mount fittings are pr earthed and that first class connection occurs between the se slide-mount.

162 Vehicle manufacturers in the UK are required to p suppression of electrical equipment to cover 40 to 250 MHz to p TV and VHF radio bands. Such suppression appears to be adeq effective at 27 MHz, but suppression of individual items su alternators/dynamos, clocks, stabilisers, flashers, wiper motors

163 Besides CB radio already mentioned, a considerable increase in the use of transceivers (ie combined transmitter and receiver units) has taken place in the last decade. Previously this type of equipment was fitted mainly to military, fire, ambulance and police vehicles, but a large business radio and radio telephone usage has developed.

164 Generally the suppression techniques described previously will suffice, with only a few difficult cases arising. Suppression is carried

Wiring diagrams – later models

165 Wiring diagrams for later (May 1985 on) models were not available at the time of writing. In consequence, it is suggested that owners of later models use earlier diagrams as far as possible, in conjunction with the information contained in this Supplement regarding fuses and relays.

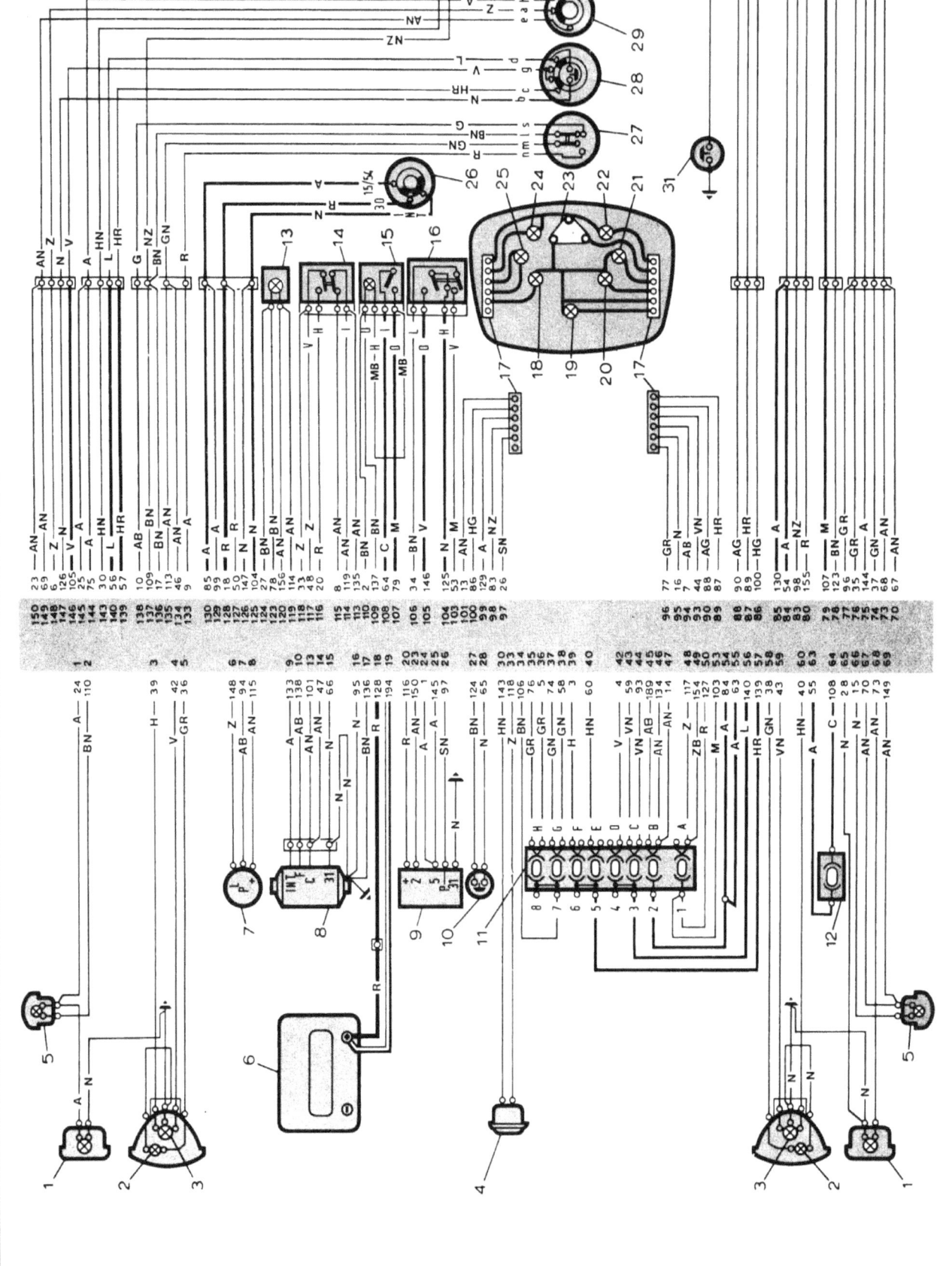

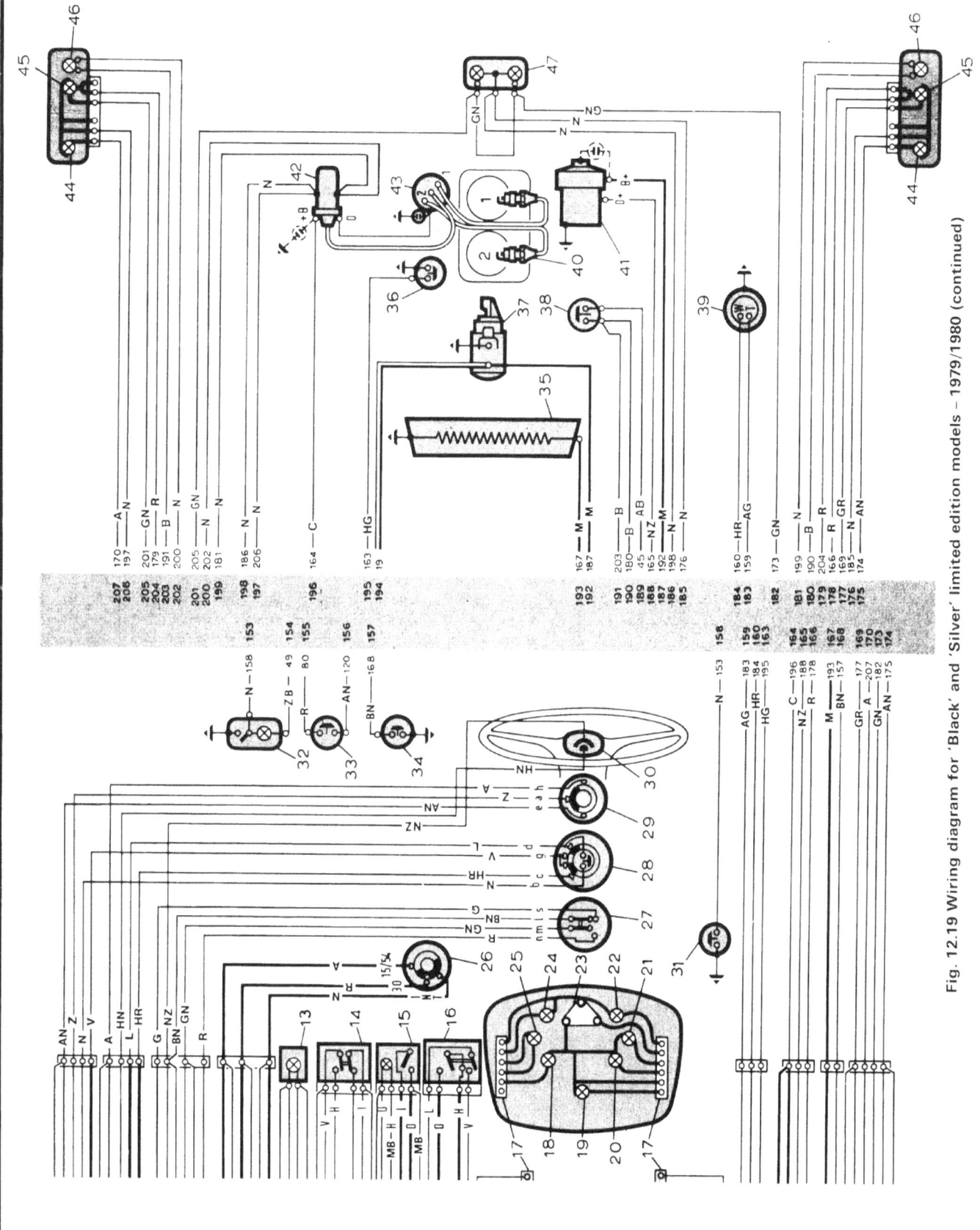

Fig. 12.19 Wiring diagram for 'Black' and 'Silver' limited edition models – 1979/1980 (continued)

Key to Fig. 12.19

No	Description	No	Description
1	Front direction indicators	25	Ignition warning light
2	Sidelights	26	Ignition switch
3	Headlamps	27	Wiper switch
4	Horn	28	Headlamp switch
5	Indicator side repeaters	29	Direction indicator switch
6	Battery	30	Horn switch
7	Direction indicator flasher relay	31	Courtesy light door switch
8	Windscreen wiper motor	32	Courtesy light/switch
9	Hazard warning flasher relay	33	Stop-light switch
10	Low brake fluid level warning switch	34	Handbrake 'on' switch
11	Fuses	35	Heated rear window
12	Heated rear window fuse	36	Oil pressure transmitter
13	Handbrake 'on'/low brake fluid level warning light	37	Starter motor
14	Hazard warning switch	38	Reversing light switch
15	Heated rear window switch and warning light	39	Fuel transmitter
16	Lighting/panel light switch	40	Spark plugs
17	Panel connectors	41	Alternator
18	Hazard flasher warning light	42	Ignition coil
19	Panel/sidelight warning light	43	Ignition distributor
20	Direction indicator warning light	44	Rear direction indicators
21	Headlamp warning light	45	Stop-lights
22	Low fuel level warning light	46	Reversing lights
23	Fuel gauge	47	Number plate lights
24	Oil pressure warning light		

Note: *Each wire section ends in an identification number. Actual wiring can be traced by looking for the wire number in the adjacent shaded strip, where wire path is resumed. Some items not fitted to all models*

Colour code

A	Light blue	H	Grey	R	Red
B	White	L	Blue	S	Pink
C	Orange	M	Brown	V	Green
G	Yellow	N	Black	Z	Mauve

Key to Fig. 12.20

No	Description	No	Description
1	Front direction indicators	24	Ignition warning light
2	Sidelights	25	Ignition switch
3	Headlamps	26	Windscreen wiper switch
4	Horn	27	Headlamp switch
5	Indicator side repeaters	28	Direction indicator switch
6	Battery	29	Horn switch
7	Direction indicator flasher relay	30	Courtesy light door switch
8	Windscreen wiper motor	31	Courtesy light/switch
9	Hazard warning flasher relay	32	Brake warning light check switch
10	Stop-light switch	33	Heated rear window
11	Fuses	34	Brake warning sender
12	Handbrake 'on'/low brake fluid level warning light	35	Oil pressure sender
13	Hazard warning switch	36	Starter motor
14	Heated rear window switch and warning light	37	Spark plugs
15	Lighting/panel light switch	38	Voltage regulator
16	Panel connectors	39	Fuel tank sender
17	Hazard flasher warning light	40	Alternator
18	Panel/sidelight warning light	41	Ignition coil
19	Direction indicator warning light	42	Ignition distributor
20	Headlamp warning light	43	Rear direction indicators
21	Low fuel level warning light	44	Stop-lights
22	Fuel gauge	45	Number plate lights
23	Oil pressure warning light		

For explanatory note on use of wiring diagrams, refer to key to Fig. 12.19

Colour code

Arancio	Amber	Giallo	Yellow	Rosa	Pink
Azzurro	Light blue	Grigio	Grey	Rosso	Red
Bianco	White	Marrone	Brown	Verde	Green
Blue	Blue	Nero	Black	Viola	Mauve

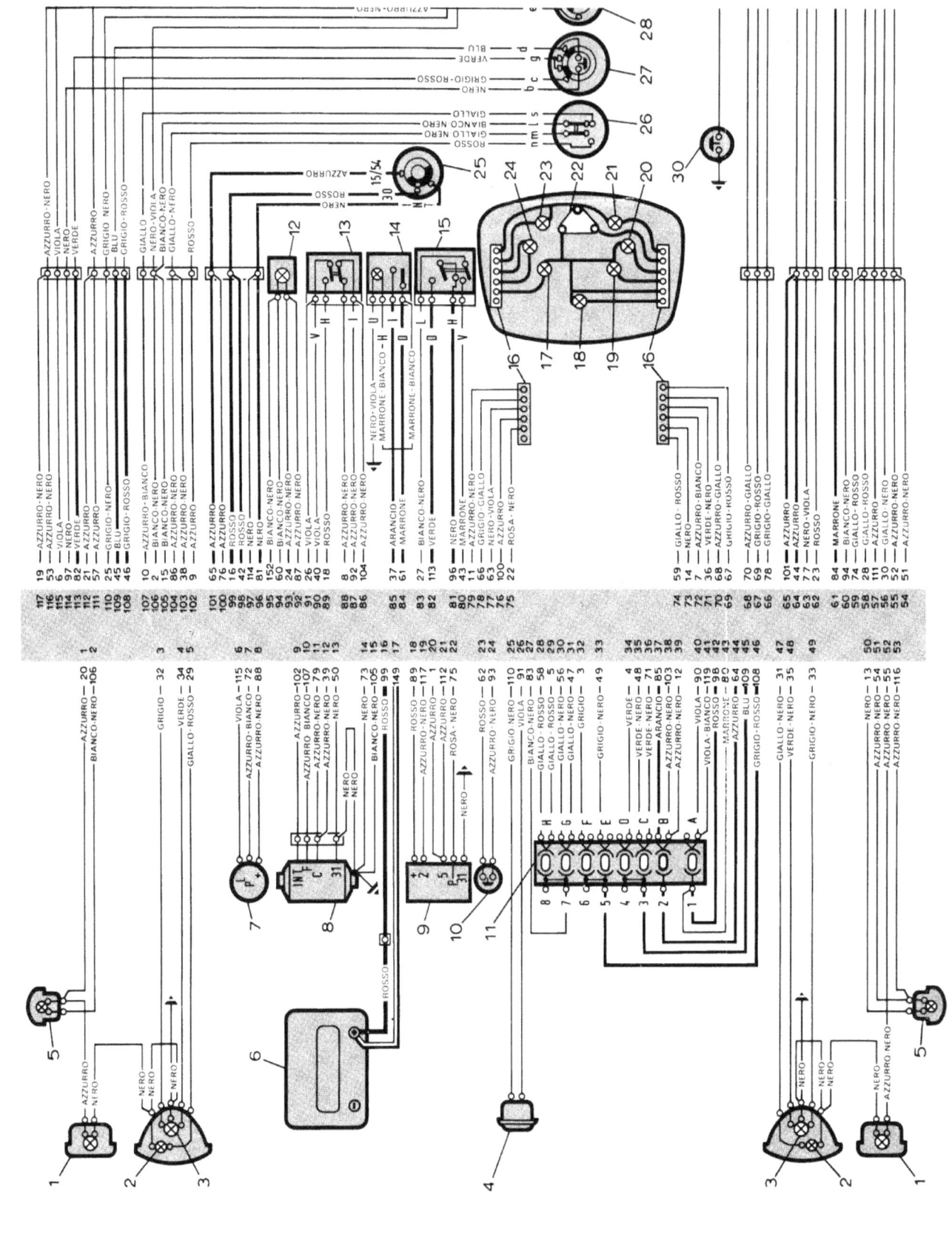

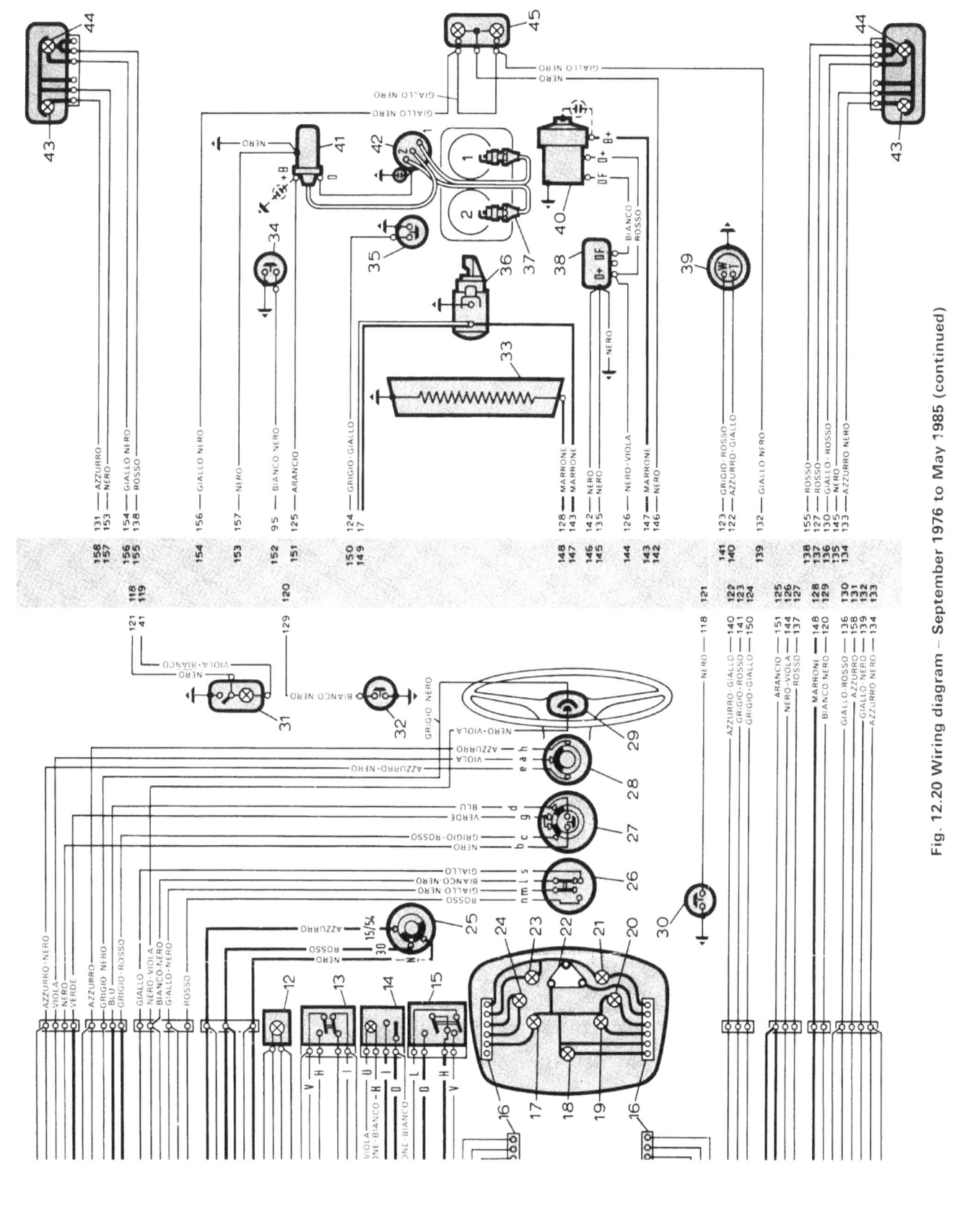

Fig. 12.20 Wiring diagram – September 1976 to May 1985 (continued)

1 Disconnect the battery negative lead.
2 Remove the steering wheel and column switches as described in Section 8 of this Supplement.
3 Insert a socket wrench into the lower hole in the underside of the steering column shroud, and unscrew the nut which holds the shroud and the column bracket to the bulkhead (photo).
4 Withdraw the steering column shroud (photo).
5 Drill out the steering column lock shear-bolts. It is sometimes possible to remove the bolts by tapping them round in an anti-clockwise direction with a sharply-pointed punch.
6 Disconnect the wiring multi-plug and withdraw the column lock/ignition switch (photo).
7 When refitting the new assembly, check the operation of the steering lock tongue in the column tube aperture using the ignition key. Tighten the new shear-bolts until their heads break off. Refitting is now a reversal of removal.

Steering gear (rack and pinion type) – bellows renewal

8 If as the result of close inspection, a split is discovered in the bellows, they must be renewed immediately.
9 Unscrew the track rod end balljoint taper pin nut and using a suitable balljoint splitter tool, disconnect the balljoint from the steering arm (photos).
10 Mark the track rod and the balljoint, so that when refitting, the balljoint can be screwed on in its original position, thus maintaining the correct wheel alignment.
11 Release the balljoint locknut a quarter of a turn (photo). Unscrew the balljoint and remove it from the track rod.
12 Release the bellows clips and withdraw the bellows from the end of the track rod.
13 Before fitting the new bellows the rack must be wiped clean of old lubricant to remove any grit or moisture.
14 Pack the new bellows one-third full with the specified grease and fit them. Fit and tighten the inboard clip.
15 Insert a small screwdriver between the outboard end of the bellows and the track rod to release any trapped air, or to destroy vacuum conditions, then withdraw the screwdriver and fit the outboard clip. Grease the track rod threads.
16 Screw the balljoint onto the track rod lining up the previously made marks, so that its locknut can be tightened by turning it through a quarter of a turn.
17 Connect the balljoint to the steering arm and tighten the nut to 25 lbf ft (35 Nm).
18 Check the front wheel alignment as described in Chapter 10, Section 17, referring to the Specifications at the start of this Supplement for setting details.

Track rod end balljoint (rack and pinion steering) – renewal

19 The operations are covered in the preceding paragraphs 9 to 11 and 16 to 18.

21 Remove the pinch-bolt from the lower coupling on the ste column shaft. This is accessible below the brake pedal inside th (photo). Raise the front of the car to give clearance.
22 Unscrew the nuts from both track rod end balljoint taper pin then using a balljoint splitter tool, disconnect the balljoints fron steering arms.
23 Unscrew and remove one balljoint and then measure betwee end of the track rod and a fixed point on the pinion housing. Re this dimension as a means of centralising the steering rack refitting it to the car.
24 Unscrew the rack housing clamp bolts and remove the clamps their insulators (photo).
25 Disconnect and remove the horn (photo).
26 Lower the steering gear and withdraw it sideways (photo).
27 It is not recommended that worn steering gear is repaired – a or factory-reconditioned unit should be fitted.
28 Turn the pinion shaft on the steering gear until the appro track rod is extended to the dimension recorded before removal. up the steering gear.
29 Connect the steering pinion shaft with the steering shaft cou If necessary, the jaws of the coupling clamp may be opened sl with a large screwdriver to ease fitting. Do not fit the cou pinch-bolt at this stage (photo).
30 Bolt the rack housing into position, locating the insu correctly.
31 Screw in the steering shaft coupling pinch-bolt.
32 Screw on the track rod end balljoints to the position where taper pins will drop straight into the eyes of the steering arms. Pro the roadwheels have not been removed from the straight-a position, the front wheel alignment (toe) will be within accep limits. Even so, the front wheel alignment should be checked as as possible, as described in Chapter 10, Section 17.
33 Screw on and tighten the balljoint taper pin nuts to 25 lbf Nm).
34 Tighten the balljoint locknuts.

Front wheel alignment (rack and pinion steering gear)

35 The information given in Chapter 10, Section 17 is gen applicable, except that locknuts are used to set the track ro relation to the balljoints instead of clamps.
36 The front wheel alignment and steering angles should be che and adjusted without occupants or other loading – just at norma weight.

Wheels and tyres – general care and maintenance

37 Wheels and tyres should give no real problems in use provided a close eye is kept on them with regard to excessive wear or dar To this end, the following points should be noted.
38 Ensure that tyre pressures are checked regularly and maint correctly. Checking should be carried out with the tyres cold an immediately after the vehicle has been in use. If the pressure checked with the tyres hot, an apparently high reading will be obt

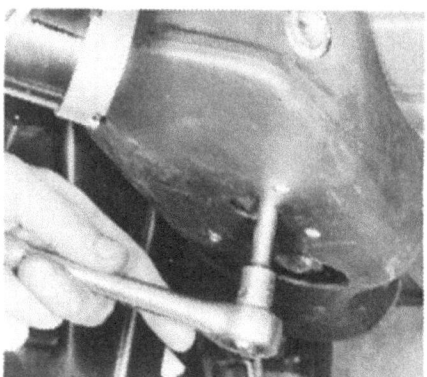

9.3 Unscrewing steering column shroud nut

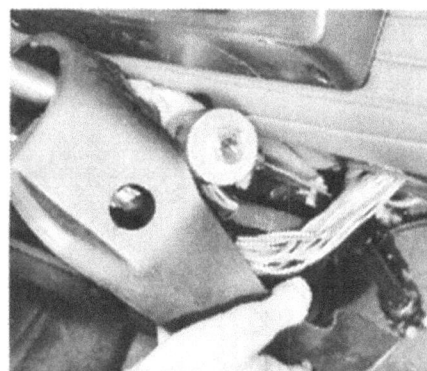

9.4 Withdrawing the steering column shroud

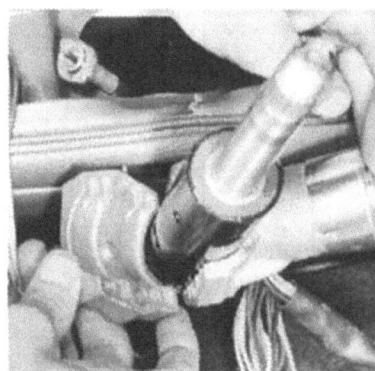

9.6 Removing the steering column lock ignition switch

9.9A Unscrewing track rod end balljoint taper pin nut

9.9B Disconnecting track rod end balljoint

9.11 Holding flats on track rod while balljoint locknut is released

9.21 Steering shaft coupling pinch-bolt (arrowed)

9.24 Steering rack housing clamp

9.25 Horn unit location (front underside of car)

9.26 Removing steering gear

9.29 Steering gear splined pinion shaft. Note coupling pinch-bolt groove

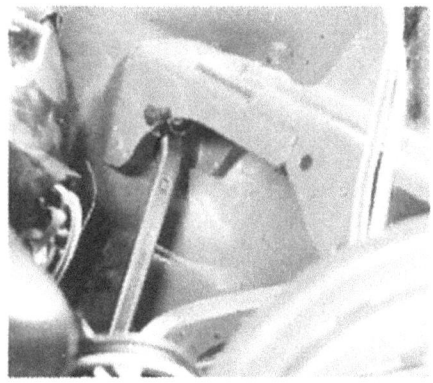

10.3 Unscrewing a front bumper mounting bracket nut

owing to heat expansion. Under no circumstances should an attempt be made to reduce the pressures to the quoted cold reading in this instance, or effective underinflation will result.

39 Underinflation will cause overheating of the tyre owing to excessive flexing of the casing, and the tread will not sit correctly on the road surface. This will cause a consequent loss of adhesion and excessive wear, not to mention the danger of sudden tyre failure due to heat build-up.

40 Overinflation will cause rapid wear of the centre part of the tyre tread coupled with reduced adhesion, harsher ride, and the danger of shock damage occurring in the tyre casing.

41 Regularly check the tyres for damage in the form of cuts or bulges, especially in the sidewalls. Remove any nails or stones embedded in the tread before they penetrate the tyre to cause deflation. If removal of a nail *does* reveal that the tyre has been punctured, refit the nail so that its point of penetration is marked. Then immediately change the wheel

and have the tyre repaired by a tyre dealer. Do *not* drive on a tyre in such a condition. In many cases a puncture can be simply repaired by the use of an inner tube of the correct size and type. If in any doubt as to the possible consequences of any damage found, consult your local tyre dealer for advice.

42 Periodically remove the wheels and clean any dirt or mud from the inside and outside surfaces. Examine the wheel rims for signs of rusting, corrosion or other damage. Light alloy wheels are easily damaged by 'kerbing' whilst parking, and similarly steel wheels may become dented or buckled. Renewal of the wheel is very often the only course of remedial action possible.

43 The balance of each wheel and tyre assembly should be maintained to avoid excessive wear, not only to the tyres but also to the steering and suspension components. Wheel imbalance is normally signified by vibration through the vehicle's bodyshell, although in many cases it is particularly noticeable through the steering wheel. Conversely, it

also fall into this category. Balancing will not usually cure vibration caused by such wear.

44 Wheel balancing may be carried out with the wheel either on or off the vehicle. If balanced on the vehicle, ensure that the wheel-to-hub relationship is marked in some way prior to subsequent wheel removal so that it may be refitted in its original position.

45 General tyre wear is influenced to a large degree by driving style – harsh braking and acceleration or fast cornering will all produce more rapid tyre wear. Interchanging of tyres may result in more even wear, but this should only be carried out where there is no mix of tyre types on the vehicle. However, it is worth bearing in mind that if this is completely effective, the added expense of replacing a complete set of tyres simultaneously is incurred, which may prove financially restrictive for many owners.

46 Front tyres may wear unevenly as a result of wheel misalignment. The front wheels should always be correctly aligned according to the settings specified by the vehicle manufacturer.

47 Legal restrictions apply to the mixing of tyre types on a vehicle. Basically this means that a vehicle must not have tyres of differing construction on the same axle. Although it is not recommended to mix tyre types between front axle and rear axle, the only legally permissible combination is crossply at the front and radial at the rear. When mixing radial ply tyres, textile braced radials must always go on the front axle, with steel braced radials at the rear. An obvious disadvantage of such mixing is the necessity to carry two spare tyres to avoid contravening the law in the event of a puncture.

48 In the UK, the Motor Vehicles Construction and Use Regulations apply to many aspects of tyre fitting and usage. It is suggested that a copy of these regulations is obtained from your local police if in doubt as to the current legal requirements with regard to tyre condition, minimum tread depth, etc.

Plastic components

1 With the use of more and more plastic body components b vehicle manufacturers (eg bumpers, spoilers, and in some cases body panels), rectification of damage to such items has beco matter of either entrusting repair work to a specialist in this fie renewing complete components. Repair by the DIY owner is not feasible owing to the cost of the equipment and materials requir effecting such repairs. The basic technique involves making a g along the line of the crack in the plastic using a rotary burr in a p drill. The damaged part is then welded back together by using a h gun to heat up and fuse a plastic filler rod into the groove. Any e plastic is then removed and the area rubbed down to a smooth fin is important that a filler rod of the correct plastic is used, as components can be made of a variety of different types polycarbonate, ABS, polypropylene).

2 If the owner is renewing a complete component himself, he w left with the problem of finding a suitable paint for finishing wh compatible with the type of plastic used. At one time the use universal paint was not possible owing to the complex ran plastics encountered in body component applications. Sta paints, generally speaking, will not bond to plastic or r satisfactorily. However, it is now possible to obtain a plastic body finishing kit which consists of a pre-primer treatment, a prime coloured top coat. Full instructions are normally supplied with but basically the method of use is to first apply the pre-primer 1 component concerned and allow it to dry for up to 30 minutes. the primer is applied and left to dry for about an hour before 1 applying the special coloured top coat. The result is a cor coloured component where the paint will flex with the plas rubber, a property that standard paint does not normally posses

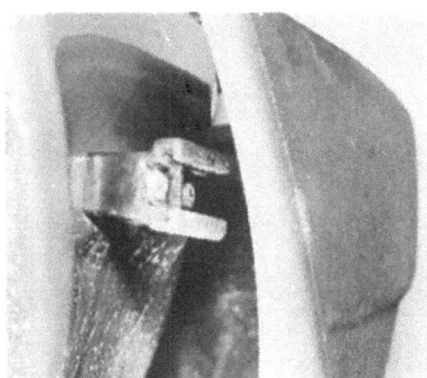

10.4 Bumper end locating slide

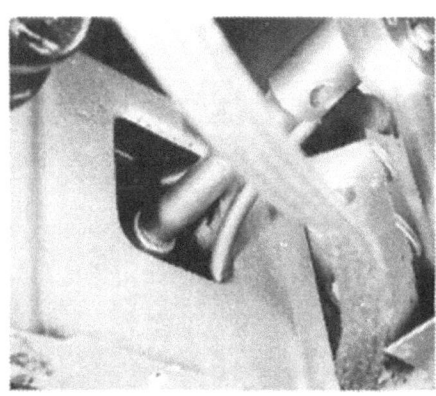

10.6 Unscrewing rear bumper mounting bracket nut

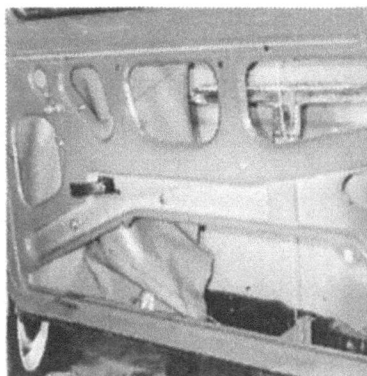

10.9A Later type door with trim panel removed

10.9B Extracting door check link fixing screw

10.9C Door check link removed

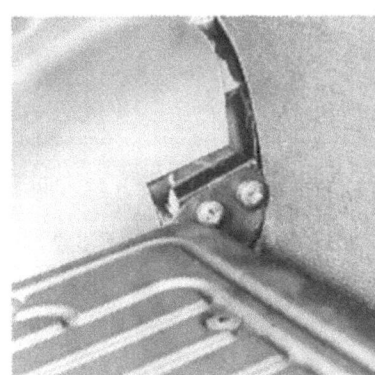

10.13 Rear seat back hinge screws

4 Grip the bumper and pull it from the body front panel. The bumper end locating slides will release, and the bumper can be removed (photo).

Rear bumper

5 Disconnect the leads from the rear number plate lamp.
6 Working through the apertures in the rear lower body panel, unscrew the bumper bracket mounting nuts (photo).
7 Grip the bumper and pull it from the body panel. The bumper end locating slides will release and the bumper can be removed.
8 Refitting of both the front and rear bumpers is a reversal of removal.

Doors – modifications

9 Slight modifications have been made to the door internal components on later models, and a redesigned door check link is used. Otherwise the operations described in Chapter 11 apply (photos).

Front seat – removal and refitting

10 The front seat can be removed by releasing its fore and aft adjustment lever and pushing the seat fully forward out of its slides.

Rear seat – removal and refitting

11 The rear seat on later models incorporates a hinged back which may be folded down to provide additional luggage space.
12 Grip the front edge of the seat cushion and pull it upwards to release it from its locating spigots. Remove the cushion.
13 Fold the seat back down and remove the screws from the side hinge plates (photo). Remove the seat back.
14 Refitting is a reversal of removal.

16 If a belt is damaged in any way, it should be renewed.
17 Periodically, the belts should be cleaned using warm water and detergent. Allow the belt to dry before it is retracted into its reel housing. Never use solvent or chemicals to clean a belt as this may weaken the filaments.
18 If the vehicle has been subjected to a front end collision, it is recommended that the seat belts are renewed if they were in use at the time of impact.
19 Whenever a seat belt anchor plate is detached from its mounting, make sure that the original sequence of washers and other components is maintained when refitting (photos).
20 The belt reels for the front seats are located behind the rear side trim panels. To remove a panel, take out the rear seat, unscrew the belt lower anchor bolt and pull the panel from its clips. The belt reel is now accessible (photos).
21 Refitting is a reversal of removal.

Door mirrors – later models

22 These are secured on later models by two self-tapping screws (photo).

Facia trim – removal and refitting
Glove compartment

23 Extract the fixing screws and withdraw the glove compartment (photos).
24 Refitting is a reversal of removal, but make sure when pushing the glove compartment into position that the locating tab is positively engaged (photo).

10.19A Seat belt anchor plate cover

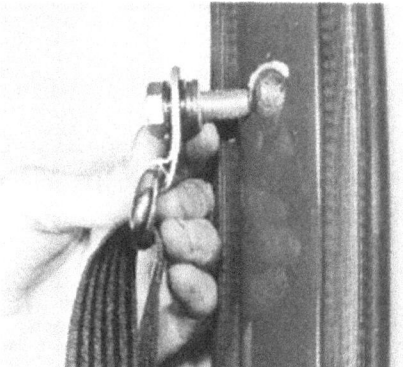

10.19B Seat belt anchor plate showing washers and spacers

10.19C Rear seat belt upper anchorage

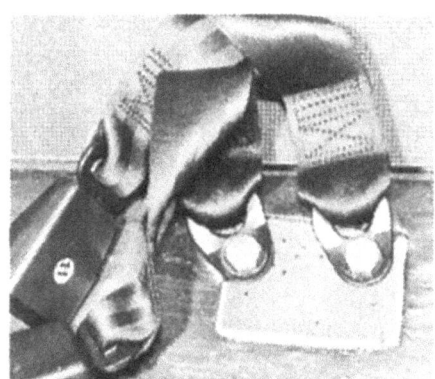

10.19D Rear seat belt anchorage under seat cushion

10.20A Rear side trim panel

10.20B Belt reel under side trim panel

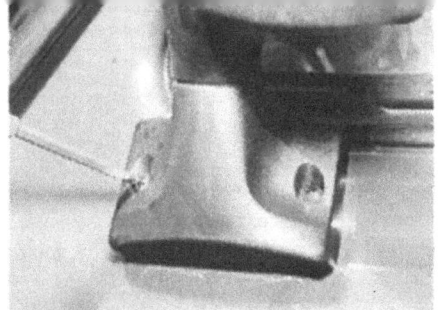

10.22 Door mirror screws

10.23A Removing glove compartment screw

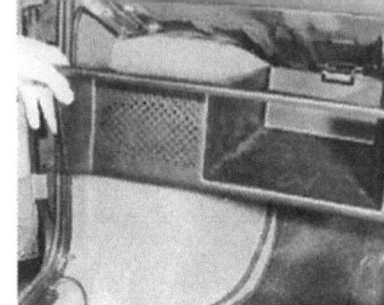

10.23B Removing glove compartment

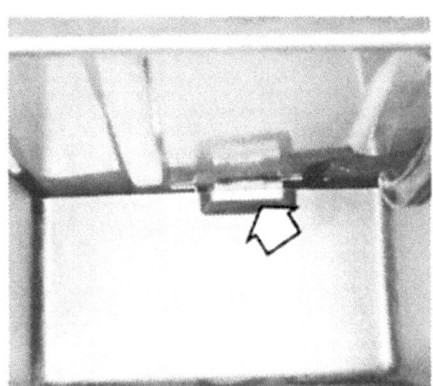

10.24 Glove compartment locating tab (arrowed)

10.26A Removing centre console screw (arrowed)

10.26B Removing centre console

Centre console
25 Remove the heater control knobs by gripping each knob and giving a sharp pull, at the same time supporting the control lever.
26 Extract the fixing screws and remove the console (photos). The screws on the right-hand side are more easily removed if the steering column shroud is first withdrawn as described in Section 9, paragraphs 3 and 4.
27 Refitting is a reversal of removal.
Facia padding
28 Remove the instrument panel as described in Section 8.

29 Remove the glove compartment and centre console as desc earlier in this Section.
30 Prise out the air inlet grilles and windscreen demister vents.
31 Release the upper metal fixing clips and remove the plastic from the lower edge. The latter are of the type which have a cent which requires tapping out before withdrawing the clip.
32 Peel off the facia padding.
33 Refitting is a reversal of removal.

General repair procedures

Whenever servicing, repair or overhaul work is carried out on the car or its components, it is necessary to observe the following procedures and instructions. This will assist in carrying out the operation efficiently and to a professional standard of workmanship.

Joint mating faces and gaskets

Where a gasket is used between the mating faces of two components, ensure that it is renewed on reassembly, and fit it dry unless otherwise stated in the repair procedure. Make sure that the mating faces are clean and dry with all traces of old gasket removed. When cleaning a joint face, use a tool which is not likely to score or damage the face, and remove any burrs or nicks with an oilstone or fine file.

Make sure that tapped holes are cleaned with a pipe cleaner, and keep them free of jointing compound if this is being used unless specifically instructed otherwise.

Ensure that all orifices, channels or pipes are clear and blow through them, preferably using compressed air.

Oil seals

Whenever an oil seal is removed from its working location, either individually or as part of an assembly, it should be renewed.

The very fine sealing lip of the seal is easily damaged and will not seal if the surface it contacts is not completely clean and free from scratches, nicks or grooves. If the original sealing surface of the component cannot be restored, the component should be renewed.

Protect the lips of the seal from any surface which may damage them in the course of fitting. Use tape or a conical sleeve where possible. Lubricate the seal lips with oil before fitting and, on dual lipped seals, fill the space between the lips with grease.

Unless otherwise stated, oil seals must be fitted with their sealing lips toward the lubricant to be sealed.

Use a tubular drift or block of wood of the appropriate size to install the seal and, if the seal housing is shouldered, drive the seal down to the shoulder. If the seal housing is unshouldered, the seal should be fitted with its face flush with the housing top face.

Screw threads and fastenings

Always ensure that a blind tapped hole is completely free from oil, grease, water or other fluid before installing the bolt or stud. Failure to do this could cause the housing to crack due to the hydraulic action of the bolt or stud as it is screwed in.

When tightening a castellated nut to accept a split pin, tighten the nut to the specified torque, where applicable, and then tighten further to the next split pin hole. Never slacken the nut to align a split pin hole unless stated in the repair procedure.

When checking or retightening a nut or bolt to a specified torque setting, slacken the nut or bolt by a quarter of a turn, and then retighten to the specified setting.

Locknuts, locktabs and washers

Any fastening which will rotate against a component or housing in the course of tightening should always have a washer between it and the relevant component or housing.

Spring or split washers should always be renewed when they are used to lock a critical component such as a big-end bearing retaining nut or bolt.

Locktabs which are folded over to retain a nut or bolt should always be renewed.

Self-locking nuts can be reused in non-critical areas, providing resistance can be felt when the locking portion passes over the bolt or stud thread.

Split pins must always be replaced with new ones of the correct size for the hole.

Special tools

Some repair procedures in this manual entail the use of special tools such as a press, two or three-legged pullers, spring compressors etc. Wherever possible, suitable readily available alternatives to the manufacturer's special tools are described, and are shown in use. In some instances, where no alternative is possible, it has been necessary to resort to the use of a manufacturer's tool and this has been done for reasons of safety as well as the efficient completion of the repair operation. Unless you are highly skilled and have a thorough understanding of the procedure described, never attempt to bypass the use of any special tool when the procedure described specifies its use. Not only is there a very great risk of personal injury, but expensive damage could be caused to the components involved.

Fault diagnosis

Introduction

The vehicle owner who does his or her own maintenance according to the recommended schedules should not have to use this section of the manual very often. Modern component reliability is such that, provided those items subject to wear or deterioration are inspected or renewed at the specified intervals, sudden failure is comparatively rare. Faults do not usually just happen as a result of sudden failure, but develop over a period of time. Major mechanical failures in particular are usually preceded by characteristic symptoms over hundreds or even thousands of miles. Those components which do occasionally fail without warning are often small and easily carried in the vehicle.

With any fault finding, the first step is to decide where to begin investigations. Sometimes this is obvious, but on other occasions a little detective work will be necessary. The owner who makes half a dozen haphazard adjustments or replacements may be successful in curing a fault (or its symptoms), but he will be none the wiser if the fault recurs and he may well have spent more time and money than was necessary. A calm and logical approach will be found to be more satisfactory in the long run. Always take into account any warning signs or abnormalities that may have been noticed in the period preceding the fault – power loss, high or low gauge readings, unusual noises or smells, etc – and remember that failure of components such as fuses or spark plugs may only be pointers to some underlying fault.

The pages which follow here are intended to help in cases of failure to start or breakdown on the road. There is also a Fault Diagnosis Section at the end of each Chapter which should be consulted if the preliminary checks prove unfruitful. Whatever the fault, certain basic principles apply. These are as follows:

Verify the fault. This is simply a matter of being sure that you know what the symptoms are before starting work. This is particularly important if you are investigating a fault for someone else who may not have described it very accurately.

Don't overlook the obvious. For example, if the vehicle won't start, is there petrol in the tank? (Don't take anyone else's word on this particular point, and don't trust the fuel gauge either!) If an electrical fault is indicated, look for loose or broken wires before digging out the test gear.

Cure the disease, not the symptom. Substituting a flat battery with a fully charged one will get you off the hard shoulder, but if the underlying cause is not attended to, the new battery will go the same way. Similarly, changing oil-fouled spark plugs for a new set will get you moving again, but remember that the reason for the fouling (if it wasn't simply an incorrect grade of plug) will have to be established and corrected.

Don't take anything for granted. Particularly, don't forget a 'new' component may itself be defective (especially if it's rattling round in the boot for months), and don't leave component of a fault diagnosis sequence just because they are new or re fitted. When you do finally diagnose a difficult fault, you'll pro realise that all the evidence was there from the start.

Electrical faults

Electrical faults can be more puzzling than straightfo mechanical failures, but they are no less susceptible to logical an if the basic principles of operation are understood. Vehicle ele wiring exists in extremely unfavourable conditions – heat, vib and chemical attack -- and the first things to look for are loc corroded connections and broken or chafed wires, especially w the wires pass through holes in the bodywork or are subje vibration.

All metal-bodied vehicles in current production have one p the battery 'earthed', ie connected to the vehicle bodywork, a nearly all modern vehicles it is the negative (–) terminal. The va electrical components -- motors, bulb holders etc – are also conn to earth, either by means of a lead or directly by their moun Electric current flows through the component and then back t battery via the bodywork. If the component mounting is loo corroded, or if a good path back to the battery is not availabl circuit will be incomplete and malfunction will result. The e and/or gearbox are also earthed by means of flexible metal straps body or subframe; if these straps are loose or missing, starter n generator and ignition trouble may result.

Assuming the earth return to be satisfactory, electrical faults v due either to component malfunction or to defects in the c supply. Individual components are dealt with in Chapter 9. If s wires are broken or cracked internally this results in an open-c and the easiest way to check for this is to bypass the suspec temporarily with a length of wire having a crocodile clip or su connector at each end. Alternatively, a 12V test lamp can be us verify the presence of supply voltage at various points along the and the break can be thus isolated.

If a bare portion of a live wire touches the bodywork or earthed metal part, the electricity will take the low-resistance path formed back to the battery: this is known as a short-circuit. Hope short-circuit will blow a fuse, but otherwise it may cause burn the insulation (and possibly further short-circuits) or even a fire. T why it is inadvisable to bypass persistently blowing fuses with foil or wire.

Carrying a few spares may save a long wal' '

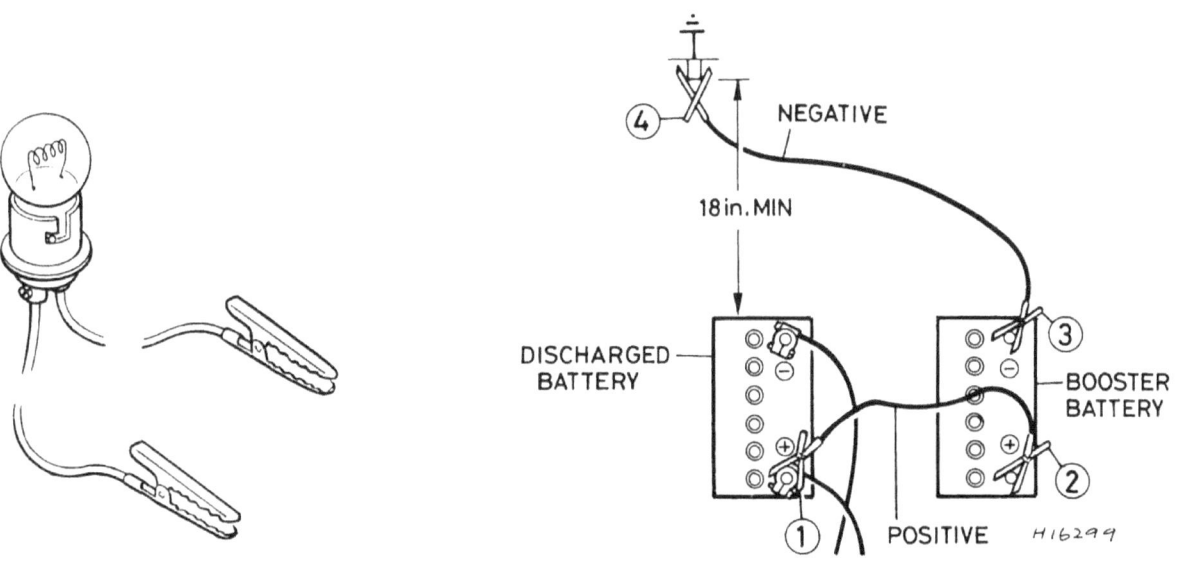

A simple test lamp is useful for tracing electrical faults

Jump start lead connections for negative earth vehicles –
connect leads in order shown

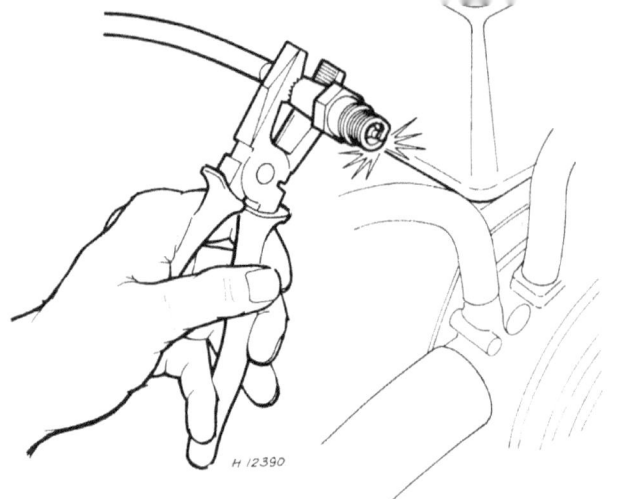

Crank engine and check for spark. Note use of insulated tool to hold plug lead

Spares and tool kit

Most vehicles are supplied only with sufficient tools for wheel changing; the *Maintenance and minor repair* tool kit detailed in *Tools and working facilities*, with the addition of a hammer, is probably sufficient for those repairs that most motorists would consider attempting at the roadside. In addition a few items which can be fitted without too much trouble in the event of a breakdown should be carried. Experience and available space will modify the list below, but the following may save having to call on professional assistance:

Spark plugs, clean and correctly gapped
HT lead and plug cap – long enough to reach the plug furthest from the distributor
Distributor rotor, condenser and contact breaker points
Drivebelt(s) – emergency type may suffice
Spare fuses
Set of principal light bulbs
Exhaust bandage
Roll of insulating tape
Length of soft iron wire
Length of electrical flex
Torch or inspection lamp (can double as test lamp)
Battery jump leads
Tow-rope
Ignition waterproofing aerosol
Litre of engine oil
Sealed can of hydraulic fluid
Emergency windscreen
Worm drive clips
Tube of filler paste

If spare fuel is carried, a can designed for the purpose should be used to minimise risks of leakage and collision damage. A first aid kit and a warning triangle, whilst not at present compulsory in the UK, are obviously sensible items to carry in addition to the above.

When touring abroad it may be advisable to carry additional spares which, even if you cannot fit them yourself, could save having to wait while parts are obtained. The items below may be worth considering:

Clutch and throttle cables
Cylinder head gasket
Dynamo or alternator brushes
Fuel pump repair kit
Tyre valve core

One of the motoring organisations will be able to advise on availability of fuel etc in foreign countries.

Engine fails to turn when starter operated

Flat battery (recharge, use jump leads, or push start)
Battery terminals loose or corroded
Battery earth to body defective
Engine earth strap loose or broken
Starter motor (or solenoid) wiring loose or broken
Ignition/starter switch faulty
Major mechanical failure (seizure)
Starter or solenoid internal fault (see Chapter 9)

Starter motor turns engine slowly

Partially discharged battery (recharge, use jump leads, or start)
Battery terminals loose or corroded
Battery earth to body defective
Engine earth strap loose
Starter motor (or solenoid) wiring loose
Starter motor internal fault (see Chapter 9)

Starter motor spins without turning engine

Flat battery
Starter motor pinion sticking on sleeve
Flywheel gear teeth damaged or worn
Starter motor mounting bolts loose

Engine turns normally but fails to start

Damp or dirty HT leads and distributor cap (crank engine check for spark)
Dirty or incorrectly gapped distributor points (if applicable)
No fuel in tank (check for delivery at carburettor)
Excessive choke (hot engine) or insufficient choke (cold eng)
Fouled or incorrectly gapped spark plugs (remove, clean regap)
Other ignition system fault (see Chapter 4)
Other fuel system fault (see Chapter 3)
Poor compression
Major mechanical failure (eg camshaft drive)

Engine fires but will not run

Insufficient choke (cold engine)
Air leaks at carburettor or inlet manifold
Fuel starvation (see Chapter 3)
Ballast resistor defective, or other ignition fault (see Chapter

---

Engine cuts out and will not restart

Engine cuts out suddenly – ignition fault

Loose or disconnected LT wires
Wet HT leads or distributor cap (after traversing water splash)
Coil or condenser failure (check for spark)
Other ignition fault (see Chapter 4)

Engine misfires before cutting out – fuel fault

Fuel tank empty
Fuel pump defective or filter blocked (check for delivery)
Fuel tank filler vent blocked (suction will be evident on rele cap)
Carburettor needle valve sticking
Carburettor jets blocked (fuel contaminated)
Other fuel system fault (see Chapter 3)

Engine cuts out – other causes

Serious overheating
Major mechanical failure (eg camshaft drive)

Engine overheats

Ignition (no-charge) warning light illuminated

Slack or broken drivebelt – retension or renew (Chapter 2)

Brakes binding
Ignition timing incorrect or automatic advance malfunctioning
Mixture too weak

Low engine oil pressure

Gauge reads low or warning light illuminated with engine running
    Oil level low or incorrect grade
    Defective gauge or sender unit
    Wire to sender unit earthed
    Engine overheating
    Oil filter clogged or bypass valve defective
    Oil pressure relief valve defective
    Oil pick-up strainer clogged
    Oil pump worn or mountings loose
    Worn main or big-end bearings

Note: *Low oil pressure in a high-mileage engine at tickover is not necessarily a cause for concern. Sudden pressure loss at speed is far more significant. In any event, check the gauge or warning light sender before condemning the engine.*

Pre-ignition (pinking) on acceleration
    Incorrect grade of fuel
    Ignition timing incorrect
    Distributor faulty or worn
    Worn or maladjusted carburettor
    Excessive carbon build-up in engine

Whistling or wheezing noises
    Leaking carburettor or manifold gasket
    Blowing head gasket

Tapping or rattling
    Incorrect valve clearances
    Worn valve gear
    Worn timing chain or belt
    Broken piston ring (ticking noise)

Knocking or thumping
    Unintentional mechanical contact (eg fan blades)
    Worn drivebelt
    Peripheral component fault (eg dynamo/alternator)
    Worn big-end bearings (regular heavy knocking, perhaps less under load)
    Worn main bearings (rumbling and knocking, perhaps worsening under load)
    Piston slap (most noticeable when cold)

dures. However enthusiastic you may be about getting on with the job in hand, do take the time to ensure that your safety is not put at risk. A moment's lack of attention can result in an accident, as can failure to observe certain elementary precautions.

There will always be new ways of having accidents, and the following points do not pretend to be a comprehensive list of all dangers; they are intended rather to make you aware of the risks and to encourage a safety-conscious approach to all work you carry out on your vehicle.

Essential DOs and DON'Ts

DON'T rely on a single jack when working underneath the vehicle. Always use reliable additional means of support, such as axle stands, securely placed under a part of the vehicle that you know will not give way.

DON'T attempt to loosen or tighten high-torque nuts (e.g. wheel hub nuts) while the vehicle is on a jack; it may be pulled off.

DON'T start the engine without first ascertaining that the transmission is in neutral (or 'Park' where applicable) and the parking brake applied.

DON'T suddenly remove the filler cap from a hot cooling system – cover it with a cloth and release the pressure gradually first, or you may get scalded by escaping coolant.

DON'T attempt to drain oil until you are sure it has cooled sufficiently to avoid scalding you.

DON'T grasp any part of the engine, exhaust or catalytic converter without first ascertaining that it is sufficiently cool to avoid burning you.

DON'T allow brake fluid or antifreeze to contact vehicle paintwork.

DON'T syphon toxic liquids such as fuel, brake fluid or antifreeze by mouth, or allow them to remain on your skin.

DON'T inhale dust – it may be injurious to health (see *Asbestos* below).

DON'T allow any spilt oil or grease to remain on the floor – wipe it up straight away, before someone slips on it.

DON'T use ill-fitting spanners or other tools which may slip and cause injury.

DON'T attempt to lift a heavy component which may be beyond your capability – get assistance.

DON'T rush to finish a job, or take unverified short cuts.

DON'T allow children or animals in or around an unattended vehicle.

DO wear eye protection when using power tools such as drill, sander, bench grinder etc, and when working under the vehicle.

DO use a barrier cream on your hands prior to undertaking dirty jobs – it will protect your skin from infection as well as making the dirt easier to remove afterwards; but make sure your hands aren't left slippery. Note that long-term contact with used engine oil can be a health hazard.

DO keep loose clothing (cuffs, tie etc) and long hair well out of the way of moving mechanical parts.

DO remove rings, wristwatch etc, before working on the vehicle – especially the electrical system.

DO ensure that any lifting tackle used has a safe working load rating adequate for the job.

DO keep your work area tidy – it is only too easy to fall over articles left lying around.

DO get someone to check periodically that all is well, when working alone on the vehicle.

DO carry out work in a logical sequence and check that everything is correctly assembled and tightened afterwards.

DO remember that your vehicle's safety affects that of yourself and others. If in doubt on any point, get specialist advice.

IF, in spite of following these precautions, you are unfortunate enough to injure yourself, seek medical attention as soon as possible.

Asbestos

Certain friction, insulating, sealing, and other products – such as brake linings, brake bands, clutch linings, torque converters, gaskets, etc – contain asbestos. *Extreme care must be taken to avoid inhalation of dust from such products since it is hazardous to health*. If in doubt, assume that they *do* contain asbestos.

Remember at all times that petrol (gasoline) is highly flamm... Never smoke, or have any kind of naked flame around, when wo... on the vehicle. But the risk does not end there – a spark caused ... electrical short-circuit, by two metal surfaces contacting each oth... careless use of tools, or even by static electricity built up in your ... under certain conditions, can ignite petrol vapour, which in a con... space is highly explosive.

Always disconnect the battery earth (ground) terminal b... working on any part of the fuel or electrical system, and neve... spilling fuel on to a hot engine or exhaust.

It is recommended that a fire extinguisher of a type suitable fo... and electrical fires is kept handy in the garage or workplace at all t... Never try to extinguish a fuel or electrical fire with water.

Note: *Any reference to a 'torch' appearing in this manual sh... always be taken to mean a hand-held battery-operated electric lam... flashlight. It does NOT mean a welding/gas torch or blowlamp.*

Fumes

Certain fumes are highly toxic and can quickly cause unconsc... ness and even death if inhaled to any extent. Petrol (gasoline) va... comes into this category, as do the vapours from certain solvents ... as trichloroethylene. Any draining or pouring of such volatile ... should be done in a well ventilated area.

When using cleaning fluids and solvents, read the instruc... carefully. Never use materials from unmarked containers – they ... give off poisonous vapours.

Never run the engine of a motor vehicle in an enclosed space ... as a garage. Exhaust fumes contain carbon monoxide whi... extremely poisonous; if you need to run the engine, always do so i... open air or at least have the rear of the vehicle outside the workp...

If you are fortunate enough to have the use of an inspectio... never drain or pour petrol, and never run the engine, while the ve... is standing over it; the fumes, being heavier than air, will concentr... the pit with possibly lethal results.

The battery

Never cause a spark, or allow a naked light, near the veh... battery. It will normally be giving off a certain amount of hydroger... which is highly explosive.

Always disconnect the battery earth (ground) terminal b... working on the fuel or electrical systems.

If possible, loosen the filler plugs or cover when chargin... battery from an external source. Do not charge at an excessive ra... the battery may burst.

Take care when topping up and when carrying the battery. The ... electrolyte, even when diluted, is very corrosive and should n... allowed to contact the eyes or skin.

If you ever need to prepare electrolyte yourself, always add the ... slowly to the water, and never the other way round. Protect ag... splashes by wearing rubber gloves and goggles.

When jump starting a car using a booster battery, for negative ... (ground) vehicles, connect the jump leads in the following sequ... First connect one jump lead between the positive (+) terminals ... two batteries. Then connect the other jump lead first to the neg... (–) terminal of the booster battery, and then to a good ear... (ground) point on the vehicle to be started, at least 18 in (45 cm) ... the battery if possible. Ensure that hands and jump leads are cle... any moving parts, and that the two vehicles do not touch. Disco... the leads in the reverse order.

Mains electricity and electrical equipment

When using an electric power tool, inspection light etc, al... ensure that the appliance is correctly connected to its plug and ... where necessary, it is properly earthed (grounded). Do not use ... appliances in damp conditions and, again, beware of creating a ... or applying excessive heat in the vicinity of fuel or fuel vapour. ... ensure that the appliances meet the relevant national safety stand...

Ignition HT voltage

A severe electric shock can result from touching certain parts ... ignition system, such as the HT leads, when the engine is runni... being cranked, particularly if components are damp or the insulat... defective. Where an electronic ignition system is fitted, the HT vo... is much higher and could prove fatal.

Length (distance)

Inches (in)	X 25.4	= Millimetres (mm)	X 0.0394	= Inches (in)
Feet (ft)	X 0.305	= Metres (m)	X 3.281	= Feet (ft)
Miles	X 1.609	= Kilometres (km)	X 0.621	= Miles

Volume (capacity)

Cubic inches (cu in; in³)	X 16.387	= Cubic centimetres (cc; cm³)	X 0.061	= Cubic inches (cu in; in³)
Imperial pints (Imp pt)	X 0.568	= Litres (l)	X 1.76	= Imperial pints (Imp pt)
Imperial quarts (Imp qt)	X 1.137	= Litres (l)	X 0.88	= Imperial quarts (Imp qt)
Imperial quarts (Imp qt)	X 1.201	= US quarts (US qt)	X 0.833	= Imperial quarts (Imp qt)
US quarts (US qt)	X 0.946	= Litres (l)	X 1.057	= US quarts (US qt)
Imperial gallons (Imp gal)	X 4.546	= Litres (l)	X 0.22	= Imperial gallons (Imp gal)
Imperial gallons (Imp gal)	X 1.201	= US gallons (US gal)	X 0.833	= Imperial gallons (Imp gal)
US gallons (US gal)	X 3.785	= Litres (l)	X 0.264	= US gallons (US gal)

Mass (weight)

Ounces (oz)	X 28.35	= Grams (g)	X 0.035	= Ounces (oz)
Pounds (lb)	X 0.454	= Kilograms (kg)	X 2.205	= Pounds (lb)

Force

Ounces-force (ozf; oz)	X 0.278	= Newtons (N)	X 3.6	= Ounces-force (ozf; oz)
Pounds-force (lbf; lb)	X 4.448	= Newtons (N)	X 0.225	= Pounds-force (lbf; lb)
Newtons (N)	X 0.1	= Kilograms-force (kgf; kg)	X 9.81	= Newtons (N)

Pressure

Pounds-force per square inch (psi; lbf/in²; lb/in²)	X 0.070	= Kilograms-force per square centimetre (kgf/cm²; kg/cm²)	X 14.223	= Pounds-force per square inch (psi; lbf/in²; lb/in²)
Pounds-force per square inch (psi; lbf/in²; lb/in²)	X 0.068	= Atmospheres (atm)	X 14.696	= Pounds-force per square inch (psi; lbf/in²; lb/in²)
Pounds-force per square inch (psi; lbf/in²; lb/in²)	X 0.069	= Bars	X 14.5	= Pounds-force per square inch (psi; lbf/in²; lb/in²)
Pounds-force per square inch (psi; lbf/in²; lb/in²)	X 6.895	= Kilopascals (kPa)	X 0.145	= Pounds-force per square inch (psi; lbf/in²; lb/in²)
Kilopascals (kPa)	X 0.01	= Kilograms-force per square centimetre (kgf/cm²; kg/cm²)	X 98.1	= Kilopascals (kPa)
Millibar (mbar)	X 100	= Pascals (Pa)	X 0.01	= Millibar (mbar)
Millibar (mbar)	X 0.0145	= Pounds-force per square inch (psi; lbf/in²; lb/in²)	X 68.947	= Millibar (mbar)
Millibar (mbar)	X 0.75	= Millimetres of mercury (mmHg)	X 1.333	= Millibar (mbar)
Millibar (mbar)	X 0.401	= Inches of water (inH$_2$O)	X 2.491	= Millibar (mbar)
Millimetres of mercury (mmHg)	X 0.535	= Inches of water (inH$_2$O)	X 1.868	= Millimetres of mercury (mmHg)
Inches of water (inH$_2$O)	X 0.036	= Pounds-force per square inch (psi; lbf/in²; lb/in²)	X 27.68	= Inches of water (inH$_2$O)

Torque (moment of force)

Pounds-force inches (lbf in; lb in)	X 1.152	= Kilograms-force centimetre (kgf cm; kg cm)	X 0.868	= Pounds-force inches (lbf in; lb in)
Pounds-force inches (lbf in; lb in)	X 0.113	= Newton metres (Nm)	X 8.85	= Pounds-force inches (lbf in; lb in)
Pounds-force inches (lbf in; lb in)	X 0.083	= Pounds-force feet (lbf ft; lb ft)	X 12	= Pounds-force inches (lbf in; lb in)
Pounds-force feet (lbf ft; lb ft)	X 0.138	= Kilograms-force metres (kgf m; kg m)	X 7.233	= Pounds-force feet (lbf ft; lb ft)
Pounds-force feet (lbf ft; lb ft)	X 1.356	= Newton metres (Nm)	X 0.738	= Pounds-force feet (lbf ft; lb ft)
Newton metres (Nm)	X 0.102	= Kilograms-force metres (kgf m; kg m)	X 9.804	= Newton metres (Nm)

Power

Horsepower (hp)	X 745.7	= Watts (W)	X 0.0013	= Horsepower (hp)

Velocity (speed)

Miles per hour (miles/hr; mph)	X 1.609	= Kilometres per hour (km/hr; kph)	X 0.621	= Miles per hour (miles/hr; mph)

Fuel consumption*

Miles per gallon, Imperial (mpg)	X 0.354	= Kilometres per litre (km/l)	X 2.825	= Miles per gallon, Imperial (mpg)
Miles per gallon, US (mpg)	X 0.425	= Kilometres per litre (km/l)	X 2.352	= Miles per gallon, US (mpg)

Temperature

Degrees Fahrenheit = (°C x 1.8) + 32

Degrees Celsius (Degrees Centigrade; °C) = (°F - 32) x 0.56

*It is common practice to convert from miles per gallon (mpg) to litres/100 kilometres (l/100km), where mpg (Imperial) x l/100 km = 282 and mpg (US) x l/100 km = 235

FSC
www.fsc.org

MIX

Papier | Fördert
gute Waldnutzung

FSC® C083411

Zeitfracht Medien GmbH
Ferdinand-Jühlke-Straße 7
99095 Erfurt, Deutschland
produktsicherheit@kolibri360.de